Tourism on the Verge

Series Editors

Roman Egger, Innovation & Management in Tourism, Salzburg University of Applied Sciences, Urstein (Puch), Salzburg, Austria

Ulrike Gretzel, Annenberg School for Communication and Journalism, University of Southern California, Los Angeles, CA, USA

Tourism on the Verge aims to provide a holistic understanding of various phenomena that shape tourism and hospitality in profound and lasting ways, approaching research topics and practical issues from multiple perspectives. Each volume in the series will address transformations within a particular area, in order to advance both our theoretical understanding and practical applications. Books should be conceptual in nature and make highly relevant contributions to explaining these phenomena. Attention should also be drawn to cutting-edge methods, in order to stimulate new directions in tourism research. The series will publish works of the highest quality and which follow a logical structure, rather than merely presenting a collection of articles loosely related to a topic. Book editors will be asked to write a strong introductory chapter that offers a comprehensive overview of the selected topic areas / fields. Presenting a unique blend of scholarly research, the series will be an unparalleled reference source.

More information about this series at https://link.springer.com/bookseries/13605

Tindara Abbate • Fabrizio Cesaroni •
Augusto D'Amico
Editors

Tourism and Disability

An Economic and Managerial Perspective

Editors
Tindara Abbate (iD)
Department of Economics
University of Messina
Messina, Italy

Fabrizio Cesaroni (iD)
Department of Economics
University of Messina
Messina, Italy

Augusto D'Amico
Department of Economics
University of Messina
Messina, Italy

ISSN 2366-2611   ISSN 2366-262X   (electronic)
Tourism on the Verge
ISBN 978-3-030-93611-2   ISBN 978-3-030-93612-9   (eBook)
https://doi.org/10.1007/978-3-030-93612-9

© The Editor(s) (if applicable) and The Author(s), under exclusive license to Springer Nature Switzerland AG 2022
This work is subject to copyright. All rights are solely and exclusively licensed by the Publisher, whether the whole or part of the material is concerned, specifically the rights of translation, reprinting, reuse of illustrations, recitation, broadcasting, reproduction on microfilms or in any other physical way, and transmission or information storage and retrieval, electronic adaptation, computer software, or by similar or dissimilar methodology now known or hereafter developed.
The use of general descriptive names, registered names, trademarks, service marks, etc. in this publication does not imply, even in the absence of a specific statement, that such names are exempt from the relevant protective laws and regulations and therefore free for general use.
The publisher, the authors and the editors are safe to assume that the advice and information in this book are believed to be true and accurate at the date of publication. Neither the publisher nor the authors or the editors give a warranty, expressed or implied, with respect to the material contained herein or for any errors or omissions that may have been made. The publisher remains neutral with regard to jurisdictional claims in published maps and institutional affiliations.

This Springer imprint is published by the registered company Springer Nature Switzerland AG
The registered company address is: Gewerbestrasse 11, 6330 Cham, Switzerland

Acknowledgments

The authors of this book acknowledge the financial support provided by the Italian Ministry of Education, University and Research (MIUR), PON R&I 2014–2020 project "GOFORIT: L'esperienza prima della partenza" (D.D. MIUR 13/07/2017 n. 1735/Ric. "Avviso per la presentazione di progetti di Ricerca Industriale e Sviluppo Sperimentale nelle 12 aree di specializzazione individuate dal PNR 2015–2020").

Contents

Introduction 1
Tindara Abbate, Fabrizio Cesaroni, and Augusto D'Amico

Disabilities and Accessible Tourism: Recent Development and Future
Directions in Management Studies 5
Maria Cristina Cinici, Alba Marino, Luca Pareschi, and Daniela Baglieri

Part I   The Demand Side of Tourism for People with Disabilities

The Determinants of Length of Stay of Italian Senior Tourists 31
Maria Gabriella Campolo, Angelina De Pascale, Carlo Giannetto,
and Maurizio Lanfranchi

Tourism Flows in Italy: The Role of Local Public Policies Toward
Disability 51
Silvia D'Arrigo, Michele Limosani, Emanuele Millemaci, Fabio
Monteforte, and Dario Sciulli

Accessibility of Cultural Sites for Disabled People: Some Preliminary
Evidence from Sicily 73
Maria Daniela Giammanco, Lara Gitto, and Ferdinando Ofria

Part II   The Supply Side of Tourism for People with Disabilities:
A Context-Based Perspective

How to Improve Universal Accessibility of Smart Tourism Destinations:
The Case of Amsterdam City 89
Augusto D'Amico, Veronica Marozzo, and Valeria Schifilliti

Gender and Disabilities in the Tourism Industry 103
Carlo Vermiglio, Valeria Naciti, Guido Noto, and Luisa Pulejo

Social Farms in Support of Local and Accessible Tourism 115
Grazia Calabrò, Rosa Concetta Chirieleison, Carlo Giannetto,
and Maurizio Lanfranchi

**Part III   The Supply Side of Tourism for People with Disabilities:
A Tools-Related Perspective**

Tourism for All: From Customer to Destination after COVID-19 129
Carmen Bizzarri, Piera Buonincontri, and Roberto Micera

**Tourism for Disabled Travelers: Breaking Down Barriers
Through Network Interactions** 155
Patrizia Accordino, Raffaella Coppolino, and Elvira Tiziana La Rocca

**Eco-Innovation as a Tool to Enhance the Competitiveness of
"Tourism for All": The Italian Project "Turismabile"** 173
Giovanna Centorrino and Daniela Rupo

Conclusions 189
Tindara Abbate, Fabrizio Cesaroni, and Augusto D'Amico

Introduction

Tindara Abbate, Fabrizio Cesaroni, and Augusto D'Amico

This book deals with the topic of tourism and explores which conditions, policies, and actions should be promoted by various stakeholders to allow people with disabilities to fully enjoy a tourism experience. Despite the fact that it has been one of the industries that has suffered the most (and is still suffering) the negative effects of the worldwide economic downturn due to the Covid-19 pandemic, available economic data demonstrate that tourism is an area characterized by significant growth potential and might represent an important economic engine for many countries in the years to come. Moreover, tourism also presents a relevant social value as it expresses a primary need for exchange, socialization, culture, and leisure.

Among the various forms of tourism with promising economic and social expectations, both local and global, one segment that has attracted the attention of scholars, practitioners, and policy makers is today considered responsible tourism, whose basic principles are based on the valorization of the environment and of cultural heritage with particular attention paid to the more vulnerable sections of the population (Agovino et al., 2017). In fact, in Europe, there are approximately 50 million people with mobility disabilities and 130 million people with special needs. The elderly, who once traveled, are often facing temporary disabilities, with food intolerances, or other access needs resulting from various impairments, injuries, illness, or other particularly challenging conditions (Card et al., 2006; Daniels et al., 2005; Darcy, 2010; Israeli, 2002; Smith, 1987). A tourism offering that is designed and planned to meet the needs and requirements of such a broad and differentiated plethora of individuals should become accessible (Darcy & Buhalis, 2011) and universal (Darcy, 2006), oriented towards people suffering mobility, hearing, vision, and cognitive access problems, and therefore: "tourism for all" (Loi & Kong, 2017; UNWTO, 2015).

T. Abbate · F. Cesaroni (✉) · A. D'Amico
Department of Economics, University of Messina, Messina, Italy
e-mail: abbatet@unime.it; fabrizio.cesaroni@unime.it; damicoa@unime.it

© The Author(s), under exclusive license to Springer Nature Switzerland AG 2022
T. Abbate et al. (eds.), *Tourism and Disability*, Tourism on the Verge,
https://doi.org/10.1007/978-3-030-93612-9_1

The attention paid by the various actors of the tourism industry for accessible tourism designed for people with disabilities is reflected in the growing interest and concern expressed by policymakers towards this segment of the population. In fact, the rights of people with disabilities are now being mainstreamed into various European policies. We have come a long way since the adoption of the EU Disability Strategy 2010–2020, and good progress has been made in this respect (see, among others, the European Accessibility Act, the Directive on the accessibility of the websites and mobile applications of public sector bodies, the adoption of the first European ICT accessibility standard, the introduction of compulsory accessibility requirements in actions financed by the European Structural and Investment Funds Regulations (ESIF), the share of funding of research and development in ICT to support people with disabilities, such as research projects on web accessibility). The progress report of the implementation of the Strategy—published in 2017—highlighted that many improvements are still required in the field of accessibility, inclusion, and responsibility. At the European level, making tourism more accessible is not only a matter of social responsibility but is also a compelling business case for improving accessibility as it can boost the competitiveness of tourism in Europe. On the other hand, European Strategy fosters the use of the ICT to help people with disabilities, and the European research and innovation program (Horizon 2020) supports research and development of solutions for accessibility.

Thus, addressing the issue of accessible tourism focused on people with disabilities embraces different (social, cultural, economic, political) considerations. In turn, the main objective of this book is to explore the challenges and the opportunities linked to the development of a touristic proposal for people with disabilities by considering that this specific tourism market segment is undervalued both in numerical and economic terms (Agovino et al., 2017). The book seeks to examine which strategies, policies, actions, and initiatives—at both regional, national and international levels—can be designed and implemented to foster accessible tourism for people with disabilities by analyzing the different social, cultural, legal, information/interactive barriers that are important constraints to welfare, inclusion, integration, and promotion of civil rights, and that also bring problems to the detriment of tourists with disabilities. Additionally, the book aims at analyzing the characteristics and dynamics of that small section of the tourism industry more oriented to meet the specific travel requirements of people with disabilities and their preferences for travel services and facilities, differing from those of tourists without disabilities.

The book addresses both theoretical and practical viewpoints with a comprehensive and multidisciplinary approach, which is essential to tackle such a complex and multi-faceted problem where economic and managerial considerations meet social and cultural domains. In fact, the design of a proper tourism offer cannot overlook the total understanding of the explicit and latent needs of people with disabilities, expressed before and during the journey. Similarly, it must be recognized that tourism proposals are the complex result of the activity of various (private and public, for-profit and not-for-profit) actors that co-create value in a given and limited destination. Also, the presence of residents of a destination, who are not directly involved in the touristic offering but whose behavior and attitude may affect the

Introduction 3

shared culture that is experienced by a potential tourist with disability, cannot be overlooked and become an indirect and involuntary part of the tourism offer. To deal with all these elements, the book is divided into three main parts:

– The demand of tourism for people with disabilities
– The supply of tourism for people with disabilities—A context-based perspective
– The supply of tourism for people with disabilities—A tools-related perspective

Specifically, Part I is oriented towards the analysis of the demand of tourism for people with disabilities by investigating the various determinants of tourism flows for different categories of tourists. In this respect, the part explores the relationship between tourism flows and local welfare policies by suggesting useful insights for public policy makers in order to foster the social inclusion of people with disabilities. From the analyses depicted in the three chapters included in this part, it emerges that by pursuing their main social goal, such policies produce positive externalities for the benefits of the regional area and local community, both directly—through the growth of the overall tourism industry—and indirectly—through the increased demand of specialized services and facilities. In turn, policies and policy makers play a key role in this respect, as effectively designed policies may both directly increase the attraction of specific destinations for potential tourists with disabilities and, indirectly, stimulate local economic growth by leveraging the potential of the tourism industry.

With Part II, the book begins examining the supply side of tourism for people with disabilities by addressing, on the one hand, the contextual boundaries of the field of research. In particular, the topic of tourism for people with disabilities has been related to the concepts of: (1) Smart Tourism Destination, (2) gender equality, and (3) rural and social farms. The first contribution introduces the case of Amsterdam as a successful example of a smart tourism destination due to its various initiatives, activities, and services directed towards the specific requirements of people with disabilities. The second contribution looks at the social and cultural factors that cause gender discrimination and compares them with those related to disabilities by finding strong similarities between the two concepts and underlining the need for proper policy interventions for the development of impairments in the tourism context. Similarly, the comparison between the context of tourism for people with disabilities and that of rural and social tourism suggests that, in order to improve the social value of accessible tourism, a multi-dimensional approach should be adopted by including both actions directed at the reduction of structural barriers and ad-hoc services to create a system of relationships based on trust, shared knowledge, and reciprocity.

On the other hand, Part III includes three contributions focused on specific tools that could be used by the key actors to promote different forms of tourism for people with disabilities. Among these, the part specifically analyzes the case of online technological platforms that support people with disabilities to plan and remove barriers. Furthermore, the issue of which business models should be designed to promote the "tourism for all" approach is analyzed with the goal of underlining the benefits of potential destinations and their attractions. Finally, in the same way, the last chapter of Part III describes and discusses the potential benefits arising from a public, no-profit project developed by a consortium of public and private stakeholders oriented to improve the accessibility, sustainability, and competitiveness of specific local areas.

Given its multidisciplinary perspective, this book can be useful for both researchers and managers interested in studying and promoting the issue of tourism for people with disabilities under a "tourism for all" approach. Researchers can benefit from a variety of insights that may stimulate further qualitative and quantitative research focused on understanding the mechanisms of interaction between demand and supply of this market segment. Alternatively, managers may be inspired by the successful experiences and projects discussed in this book to design and implement effective business models and tools (i.e., online technological platforms) to meet the needs of people with disabilities by reducing the existing barriers that prevent them from fully exploiting the benefits of their tourism experiences.

References

Agovino, M., Casaccia, M., Garofalo, A., & Marchesano, K. (2017). Tourism and disability in Italy. Limits and opportunities. *Tourism Management Perspective, 23*, 58–67.

Card, J., Cole, S., & Humphrey, A. (2006). A comparison of the accessibility and attitudinal barriers model: Travel providers and travelers with physical disabilities. *Asia Pacific Journal of Tourism Research, 11*(2), 161–175.

Daniels, M. J., Drogin Rodgers, E. B., & Wiggins, B. P. (2005). "Travel Tales": An interpretive analysis of constraints and negotiations to pleasure travel as experienced by persons with physical disabilities. *Tourism Management, 26*, 919–930.

Darcy, S. (2006). *Setting a research agenda for accessible tourism*. Sustainable Tourism CRC.

Darcy, S. (2010). Inherent complexity: Disability, accessible tourism and accommodation information preferences. *Tourism Management, 31*(6), 816–826.

Darcy, S., & Buhalis, D. (2011). Introduction: From disabled tourists to accessible tourism. In D. Buhalis & S. Darcy (Eds.), *Accessible tourism: Concepts and issues* (pp. 1–20). Channel View.

Israeli, A. A. (2002). A preliminary investigation of the importance of site accessibility factors for disabled tourists. *Journal of Travel Research, 41*(1), 101–104.

Loi, K. I., & Kong, W. H. (2017). Tourism for all: Challenges and issues faced by people with vision impairment. *Tourism Planning & Development, 14*(2), 181–197.

Smith, R. W. (1987). Leisure of disable tourists. *Annals of Tourism Research, 14*(3), 376–389.

UNWTO. (2015). *Manual of accessible tourism for all: Public partnership and good practices*. World Tourism Organization (UNWTO) and Fundación ACS.

Disabilities and Accessible Tourism: Recent Development and Future Directions in Management Studies

Maria Cristina Cinici, Alba Marino, Luca Pareschi, and Daniela Baglieri

1 Introduction

Research into tourism and disability has gained increasing attention in academia and among policymakers and practitioners over the last two decades. Smith's (1987) work pioneered the field addressing the travel constraints experienced by persons with disabilities. Then, the research area evolved looking at (1) the characteristics of persons with disabilities who take part in the tourist experience and the economic potential of this market (Israeli, 2002; Poria et al., 2010) and (2) the legislation governing service provisions (Boyd Ohlin, 1993; Veitch & Shaw, 2010).

By emphasizing the socially constructed nature of this type of tourism, the field has now delved into the concept of accessible tourism. It now encompasses a broader range of access requirements (Darcy et al., 2020; Porto et al., 2019), more comprehensive than those classified as having a disability (Buhalis & Darcy, 2011). In so doing, the accessible tourism field has proved to be interdisciplinary, multidisciplinary, and transdisciplinary (Gillovic et al., 2018). Additionally, it has increasingly been considered that people with disabilities are not a homogenous grouping with segmentation needs. Each one must be regarded as considering the specific disability type (e.g., mobility, vision, hearing, cognitive, et cetera) and the level of an individual's support needs (Darcy & Pegg, 2011).

Authorship Contribution StatementMaria Cristina Cinici: Methodology, Software, Writing. Alba Marino: Conceptualization, Writing, Editing. Luca Pareschi: Methodology, Software, Writing. Daniela Baglieri: Supervision.

M. C. Cinici (✉) · A. Marino · D. Baglieri
Department of Economics, University of Messina, Messina, Italy
e-mail: mcinici@unime.it; alba.marino@unime.it; dbaglieri@unime.it

L. Pareschi
Department of Management and Law, University of Rome "Tor Vergata", Rome, Italy
e-mail: luca.pareschi@uniroma2.it

© The Author(s), under exclusive license to Springer Nature Switzerland AG 2022
T. Abbate et al. (eds.), *Tourism and Disability*, Tourism on the Verge,
https://doi.org/10.1007/978-3-030-93612-9_2

While the theme has received considerable attention in the literature, little retrospective work on the evolution of the accessible tourism research domain in management studies has been made. With the notable exception of Cunalata et al. (2021), which is published in Spanish, and Gillovic et al. (2018), which focuses exclusively on the language used in accessible tourism, there has been no literature review on this topic to the best of our knowledge.

To depict the development of accessible tourism literature and build on this result to adjust its scope and applications in management fields, we will concentrate on management studies and combine two methods: bibliometrics (Zupic & Čater, 2015) and topic modeling (Hannigan et al., 2019). It is widely recognized that mixed methods can better understand research phenomena and complex events than either approach alone (Edmondson & Mcmanus, 2007; Molina-Azorin, 2015; Turner et al., 2017). We shall apply both of them with dual intent. From one side, we aim at elaborating the results of one method with the findings from the other method; from the other side, we apply different techniques to different inquiry components. In more detail, we shall use bibliometrics to map the evolution of accessible tourism research. We shall apply topic modeling to uncover the latent themes characterizing the debate on accessible tourism and how the interest in those topics has evolved along the way.

The added value of this chapter is twofold. From a theoretical perspective, we depict the development of the accessible tourism literature and build on this outcome to adjust its scope and applications in the management fields. Specifically, we provide an in-depth analysis of accessible tourism literature evolution and shed new light on research avenues. From a methodological perspective, our chapter benefits from the application of two methods. The potential of applying these two methods to explore the progress of accessible tourism as a knowledge domain in the management fields has not been levied yet.

The chapter is structured as follows. Section 2 provides details on research methodology and design. Section 3 focuses on data analysis and findings. Section 4 calls for a future research agenda and concludes the chapter with final remarks.

2 Research Methodology and Empirical Design

To identify the most impactful studies on accessible tourism in the management fields, examine the research topics, and provide insights for future research in the domain, we combine two techniques that social scientists have increasingly used during the last decade, namely bibliometrics and topic modeling. While bibliometric analysis investigates the formal properties of knowledge domains by using mathematical and statistical methods (Godin, 2006), topic modeling (Blei et al., 2003) relates to the process of rendering constructs and conceptual relationships from textual data (Hannigan et al., 2019). Developed in recent years, thanks to the availability of numerous interdisciplinary bibliographic online databases (such as

Scopus, Web of Science, and Google Scholar), bibliometric methods have been used for providing quantitative analysis of written publications by investigating the distribution models of publications or identifying their impact within the scientific community (Ellegaard & Wallin, 2015). On the ground of mathematical and statistical techniques, it allows to review and update the debate on specific issues (e.g., Barnett et al., 2020; Di Stefano et al., 2010) and to quantify and compare scientific activities at various levels of aggregation (e.g., Podsakoff et al., 2008). In the same lineage, topic modeling uses statistical associations of words in a text to generate latent topic clusters of co-occurring words that jointly represent higher-order concepts (Ferri et al., 2018; Yau et al., 2014). Borrowed from computer science, it focuses on words that co-occur in documents, viewing documents as random mixtures of latent topics, where each topic is distributed among words (Blei et al., 2003).

Both techniques have been applied extensively to map the evolution of several areas of management research. Among the most cited study using bibliometrics, Ramos-Rodrìguez and Ruìz-Navarro (2004) identified the works that have had the most significant impact on strategic management research and analyzed the changes placed in the intellectual structure of this discipline. Zupic and Čater (2015) presented a workflow for conducting bibliometric studies with guidelines for researchers and performed a citation and co-citation analysis to map the intellectual structure of the Organizational Research Methods journal. Finally, Melin (2000) used co-authorship to research collaboration and investigated the reasons for and effects of cooperation for the individual scientist.

Concerning the use of topic modeling in management, Small et al. (2014) identified emergent topics in science and technology for consideration by decision-makers. Bao and Datta (2014) developed a variation of the latent Dirichlet allocation topic model and its learning algorithm for simultaneously discovering and quantifying risk types from textual risk disclosures. More recently, Kobayashi et al. (2018) described how text mining might add to contemporary organizational research, while Ferri et al. (2020) used topic modeling to describe the development of a field of knowledge. Specifically, it allows testing existing or new research questions with data that are likely to be rich, contextualized, and ecologically valid.

As far as this study is concerned, we gain from both methods and perform a procedure organized in three steps:

1. Firstly, we shall select our sample and provide its description through initial data statistics;
2. Secondly, we shall benefit from three bibliometrics techniques, namely co-authorship, keywords co-occurrence, and co-citation analyses, to dig deeper into the past evolution of the literature among the management fields as well as to identify the emerging research areas;
3. Thirdly and finally, we shall use topic modeling to unpack the publications' contents.

3 Data Analysis and Findings

3.1 Step 1: Sample Selection and Initial Data Statistics

We started our research by selecting the documents representing the accessible tourism literature in the management fields. We searched the areas of "hospitality leisure sport and tourism," "business," "management," and "economics" studies from 2010 to 2021 for English articles containing the topics "disab* AND touris*." We took articles from the Science Citation Index (SCI) and Social Science Citation Index (SSCI) databases from the Web of Science Core Collection on March 31st, 2021. The search strategy has produced 145 manuscripts that represent our final sample.

Figure 1 shows the publishing trend in the number of studies on accessible tourism from 2010 to 2021. Cumulative citations are also plotted. The 145 publications have been cited 2351 times, and the average citations per item have been 15.78. The h-index of the retrieved documents is 27.

As regards the publications, the sampled papers receiving the most significant number of citations are the following:

1. Uysal, M., Sirgy, M. J., Woo, E., and Kim, H. L.(2016). Quality of life (QOL) and wellbeing research in tourism. Tourism Management (242 citations; 40.33 average citations per year);
2. Darcy, S. (2010). Inherent complexity: Disability, accessible tourism and accommodation information preferences. Tourism Management (115 citations; 9.58 average citations per year);
3. McCabe, S., Joldersma, T., and Li, C. (2010). Understanding the benefits of social tourism: Linking participation to subjective wellbeing and quality of life. International Journal of Tourism Research (92 citations; 7.67 average citations per year);

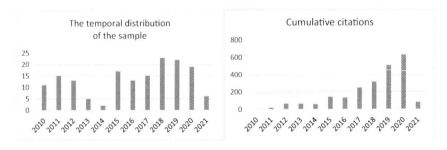

Fig. 1 The publishing trend of the accessible tourism literature

Disabilities and Accessible Tourism: Recent Development and Future... 9

Table 1 The most important sources of accessible tourism literature

Source title	No of papers (%)
Tourism Management	12 (8.27)
Accessible Tourism: Concepts and Issue (book series)	8 (5.55)
Annals of Tourism Research	8 (5.55)
Journal of Tourism Futures	8 (5.55)
International Journal of Contemporary Hospitality Management	7 (4.82)
International Journal of Hospitality Management	7 (4.82)
Journal of Sustainable Tourism	7 (4.82)
Current Issues in Tourism	6 (4.14)
Asia Pacific Journal of Tourism Research	5 (3.44)
Gran Tour	5 (3.44)
Journal of Travel Research	5 (3.44)

Source: our elaboration from ISI Web of Science

4. Small, J., Darcy, S., and Packer, T. (2012). The embodied tourist experiences of people with vision impairment: Management implications beyond the visual gaze. Tourism Management (75 citations; 7.5 average citations per year);
5. Morgan, N., Pritchard, A., and Sedgley, D. (2015). Social tourism and wellbeing in later life. Annals of Tourism Research (72 citations; 10.29 average citations per year).

Sixty-five sources have published the 161 publications of our sample. Table 1 lists the most important of them according to the number of papers on accessible tourism published so far. They account for more than 48% of the total publications.

Tourism Management, which is a journal with an impact factor of 7.437 and racked as a four-star in the 2018 Academic Journal Guide of the Chartered Association of Business Schools, hosts the most prolific debate on the topic, i.e. 12 out of 145 papers. It is followed by *Accessible Tourism: Concept and Issue (book series)*, *Annals of Tourism Research* (IF 5.98 and four-stars for ABS), and *Journal for Tourism Futures* (open-access journal). Each of them offers eight articles. Generally speaking, we can maintain that top-tier journals aiming at reaching the broadest audience have hosted the debate.

3.2 Step 2: Bibliometrics and Visualization of Similarities Among Publications

We used bibliometrics to filter the pool of documents collected in step 1 to more influential authors and publications. To do so, we used a software package. We decided on VOSviewer based on Van Eck and Waltman's (2014) VOS algorithm. The visualization of similarities (VOS) algorithm pictures connections between objects (i.e., co-occurrence and citations) that are located in such a way that the distance between any pair of them reflects their similarity as accurately as possible.

3.2.1 Co-authorship

We sifted through the authors to identify the most impactful by setting a threshold of a given number of published documents and citations per author. We put a cut-off value at 3 for printed documents and 20 for local citations as meaningful trade-offs for the author visualization. Of the 280 authors belonging to our sample, 23 meet the thresholds.

Table 2 lists the authors, their published documents, and local citations, i.e. the number of citations within the 145 publications of our dataset. Additionally, for each of the 23 authors, the software calculated the total strength of the co-authorship links with the other authors. A link is a connection or a relation between two items. Each link has a strength, represented by a positive numerical value where the higher the value, the stronger the link.

Items and links together constitute the co-authorships network. Figure 2 shows graphically the networks of relationships for authors as produced by VOSviewer. We left all the items in the network even though they were not connected. Authors having the same color are more likely to be co-authors of a given publication. Additionally, the bigger the label's size, the more often the author appears as co-author.

The map shows ten authors' clusters, but only three of them are connected. Specifically, they are as follows:

(a) The *red cluster* is composed of four authors. The most prolific is Simon Darcy (17 documents and a link strength of 10) of the University of Technology Sydney, AU. Tracey Dickson (University of Canberra, CA), Jennie Small (University of Technology Sydney, AU), and Laura Misener (Western University, CA) follow him, respectively, with three papers and a link strength of 4, 3, and 2. The research they have developed is mainly concerned with touristic experiences of people with disabilities, especially regarding their participation in sports events.

(b) The *purple cluster* is composed of two authors, namely Dimitrios Buhalis (Bournemouth University, UK) and Victoria Eichhorn (University of Surrey, UK). Their research focuses on tourism accessibility and people inclusion.

(c) The *orange cluster* is composed of two authors, namely Alison McIntosh (Auckland University of Technology, NZ) and Cheryl Cockburn-Wootten (University of Waikato, NZ). Their research is about the role of stakeholder engagement in achieving accessible tourism.

The remaining seven clusters of the map represent groups of authors that work separately from each other.

Table 2 The most influential authors of the sample

Author	Documents	Local citation	Total link strength	Author	Documents	Local citation	Total link strength
Darcy, S.	17	511	10	Small, J.	3	113	3
Poria, Y.	6	133	10	Misener, J.	3	58	2
Zhang, Y.	5	63	3	Eichhorn	3	46	1
Cole, S.	5	16	3	Eusebio	3	43	2
Morgan, N.	4	161	7	Dickson	3	38	4
Pritchard	4	161	7	Mcintosh	3	14	3
Reichel, A.	4	122	8	Naniopoulos	3	13	3
Buhalis, D.	4	116	2	Tsalis, P.	3	13	3
Sedgley, D.	4	97	6	Beal, J.	3	12	4
Pagan, R.	4	64	0	Shaw, G.	3	12	0
Kastenholz	4	54	2	Cockburn-Wootten, C.	3	11	3
Brandt, Y.	3	121	6				

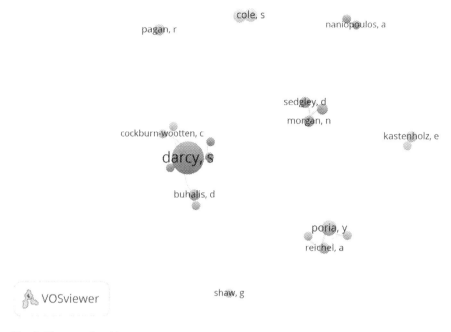

Fig. 2 The co-authorship map

3.2.2 Keywords Occurrence

A pool of 498 authors keywords was drawn from 145 publications. A threshold of 3 was chosen as the minimum number of occurrences of a keyword. Of the 498 authors' keywords, 19 meet this condition. Figure 3 visualizes the co-occurrence network of authors' keywords. The size of a circle indicates the number of publications that have the corresponding term in their keywords. Words that co-occur a lot tend to be located close to each other in the visualization.

The software has grouped the 19 keywords into six clusters. The clusters' size corresponds to five words only for the red-colored cluster. The other ones are composed of some words spanning from four to two. Table 3 provides details about the content for each of them.

The most occurred keyword is "disability" (46 occurrences) and is coupled with accommodation (3 occurrences). "Accessible tourism" (39 occurrences) is also a frequent keyword. It is used in connection with "disabled tourists" (5 occurrences) and "tourists with disabilities" (3 occurrences). Authors of ours sample give attention to social "constraints" (6 occurrences) that are treated contemporary to "barriers" (4 occurrences), "disabled people" (4 occurrences), and "obesity" (3 occurrences). Finally, issues related to "inclusive tourism" (6 occurrences) are observed with "social tourism" (6 occurrences) and "Spain" (4 occurrences).

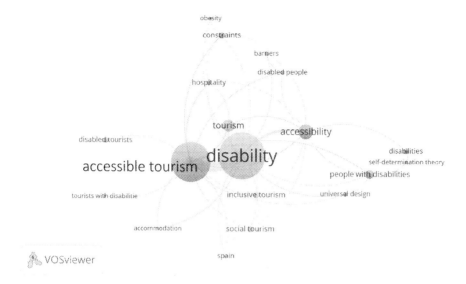

Fig. 3 The authors' keywords co-occurrence map

Table 3 Clusters of co-occurrence of keywords

Cluster	# keywords	Keywords and their occurrences
1	5	Accessibility (14), people with disabilities (8), disabilities (5), self-determination theory (3), universal design (4)
2	4	Constraints (6), barriers (4), disabled people (4), obesity (3)
3	3	Accessible tourism (39), disabled tourists (5), tourists with disabilities (3)
4	3	Inclusive tourism (6), social tourism (6), Spain (4)
5	2	Tourism (11), hospitality (5)
6	2	Disability (46), accommodation (3)

3.2.3 Co-citation Analysis

Finally, we applied the VOSviewer algorithm to the publications' network. It is broadly recognized that co-citation analysis provides a picture of a specific research field (Boyack & Klavans, 2010). Co-citation analysis employs the number of times papers are simultaneously cited to measure their similarity. If two documents are co-cited by a third one, this latter paper establishes a connection between the first two. The logic behind this method is that if others simultaneously and frequently cite two articles, they should be related to each other because they either focus on the same topic, employ the same theoretical framework, or respond to the same research question (Ferreira et al., 2016).

Thus, at this stage, our focus is on the cited references of the sample. We set the threshold at 15 local citations per publication to qualify for inclusion into a specific cluster. Of the 6031 cited references, 39 meet the threshold. They constitute the backbone of accessible tourism literature regarding topics and methodologies employed (Galvagno & Pisano, 2020). Table 4 lists the 20 most influential ones according to the citations they have received within the documents' sample.

The analysis resulted in the creation of three major clusters, as depicted in Fig. 4. Overall, the clusters show 726 links and a total link strength that account for 6194. Once we identified the clusters, we went through each cluster's content and further considerations, as shown in Table 5.

Cluster 1 (i.e., the red-colored one) is the largest one. It is located at the left of the picture and is composed of 17 documents published between 2004 and 2012. The most connected publications are Yau et al. (2014) (total link strength 703), Darcy (2010) (total link strength 609), and Buhalis and Darcy (2011) (total link strength 333). Scholars of this cluster focus mainly on the many practical and social obstacles that can inhibit the full participation of people with disabilities in tourism.

Cluster 2 (i.e., the green-colored one) is located on the right of the picture and comprises 12 documents published between 1987 and 2008. The most connected ones are Smith (1987) (total link strength 537), Daniels et al. (2005) (total link strength 509), and Ray and Ryder (2003) (total link strength 454). The main themes of this cluster relate to the marketing research area, and particularly, scholars mainly focus on the needs and experiences of disabled travelers.

Cluster 3 (i.e., the blue-colored one) is the least dense cluster in terms of the number of publications. It is located in the middle of the picture and is composed of ten items. The most connected ones are Burnett and Baker (2001) (total link strength 600), McKercher et al. (2003) (total link strength 564), and Shaw and Coles (2004) (total link strength 526). The main themes of this cluster concern the organization and management of the travel industry and destinations in facilitating the participation of disabled tourists.

3.3 Step 3: Topic Modeling and Textual Analysis of Publications

In step 3 of our research, we delved into the documents' content by adopting topic modeling techniques. To obtain a more homogenous sample of records, we consider 138 of the 145 documents of the original database. We ignored seven papers extracted from ISI that presented in English only the abstract.

Topic modeling analyzed publications and automatically identified words that co-occur in the same document more often than it would happen by chance. All the co-occurring words were placed in containers called "topics" (Mohr & Bogdanov, 2013). Next to this automatic stage, we were expected to understand the meaning of each topic inductively, according to the most critical words constituting each topic and to the most representative papers for each topic. In so doing, we obtained the following advantages: first, we dealt with a massive amount of text that was difficult

Disabilities and Accessible Tourism: Recent Development and Future. . .   15

Table 4 The backbone of the accessible tourism literature

Publications	Local citations
Yau, M. K. S., McKercher, B., and Packer, T. L. (2014). Traveling with a disability: More than an access issue.*Annals of Tourism Research*	68
Darcy, S. (2010). Inherent complexity: Disability, accessible tourism and accommodation information preferences. *Tourism Management*	55
Burnett, J. J., and Baker, H. B. (2001). Assessing the travel-related behaviors of the mobility-disabled consumer. *Journal of Travel Research*	54
McKercher, B., Packer, T., Yau, M. K., and Lam, P. (2003). Travel agents as facilitators or inhibitors of travel: perceptions of people with disabilities. *Tourism Management*	51
Shaw, G., and Coles, T. (2004). Disability, holiday making and the tourism industry in the UK: a preliminary survey. *Tourism Management*	50
Daniels, M. J., Rodgers, E. B. D., and Wiggins, B. P. (2005). "Travel Tales": an interpretive analysis of constraints and negotiations to pleasure travel as experienced by persons with physical disabilities. *Tourism Management*	47
Smith, S. L. (1987). Regional analysis of tourism resources. *Annals of Tourism Research*	47
Ray, N. M., and Ryder, M. E. (2003). "Ebilities" tourism: an exploratory discussion of the travel needs and motivations of the mobility-disabled. *Tourism Management*	41
Daruwalla, P., and Darcy, S. (2005). Personal and societal attitudes to disability. *Annals of Tourism Research*	39
Eichhorn, V., Miller, G., Michopoulou, E., and Buhalis, D. (2008). Enabling access to tourism through information schemes?. *Annals of Tourism Research*	33
Israeli, A. A. (2002). A preliminary investigation of the importance of site accessibility factors for disabled tourists. *Journal of Travel Research*	33
Darcy, S. (2002). Marginalised participation: Physical disability, high support needs and tourism. *Journal of Hospitality and Tourism Management*	32
Ozturk, Y., Yayli, A., and Yesiltas, M. (2008). Is the Turkish tourism industry ready for a disabled customer's market?: The views of hotel and travel agency managers. *Tourism Management*	30
Buhalis, D., and Darcy, S. (Eds.). (2011). *Accessible tourism: Concepts and Issues*	29
Darcy, S., and Dickson, T. J. (2009). A whole-of-life approach to tourism: The case for accessible tourism experiences. *Journal of Hospitality and Tourism Management*	29
Darcy, S. (1998). *Anxiety to access: Tourism patterns and experiences of New South Wales people with a physical disability*	28
Turco, D. M., Stumbo, N., and Garncarz, J. (1998). Tourism constraints for people with disabilities. *Parks and Recreation*	28
Darcy, S., and Pegg, S. (2011). Towards strategic intent: Perceptions of disability service provision amongst hotel accommodation managers. *International Journal of Hospitality Management*	24
Bi, Y., Card, J. A., and Cole, S. T. (2007). Accessibility and attitudinal barriers encountered by Chinese travellers with physical disabilities. International Journal of Tourism Research, 9(3), 205–216	22
Murray, M., and Sproats, J. (1990). The disabled traveller: Tourism and disability in Australia. *Journal of Tourism Studies*	22

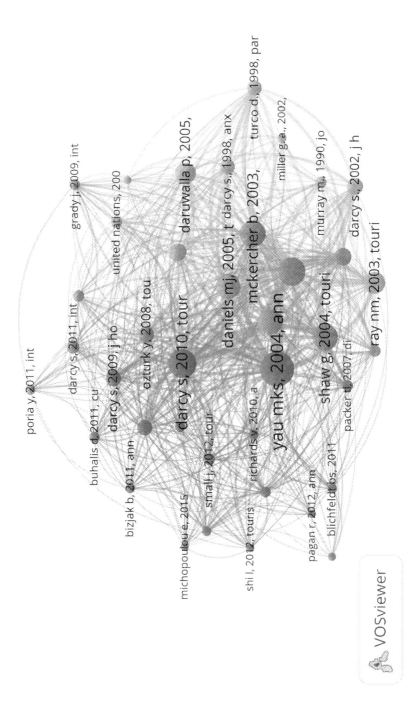

Fig. 4 The co-citation map

Disabilities and Accessible Tourism: Recent Development and Future... 17

Table 5 The co-citation clusters

Cluster	# publications	Most impactful publications	Main topics
1	17	Yau, M. K. S., McKercher, B., and Packer, T. L. (2014); Darcy, S. (2010); Buhalis, D., and Darcy, S. (Eds.). (2011)	People with disabilities, accessible tourism, and barriers
2	12	Smith, S. L. (1987); Daniels, M. J., Rodgers, E. B. D., and Wiggins, B. P. (2005); Ray, N. M., and Ryder, M. E. (2003)	Travel needs and experience
3	10	Burnett, J. J., and Baker, H. B. (2001); McKercher, B., Packer, T., Yau, M. K., and Lam, P. (2003); Shaw, G., and Coles, T. (2004)	Tourism industry, destination competitiveness, and facilitators

to analyze qualitatively; second, we actively contributed to the inductive phase by assigning meaning to topics; third, the technique recognized that words could have different meanings in different contexts; therefore, the same word appeared in other topics and contributed to constructing different meanings (DiMaggio et al., 2013).

To identify the main topics of the accessible tourism literature, we combined two software: MITAO (Heibi et al., 2019), a Python-based user-friendly interface developed at the University of Bologna, which relies on the NLTK and Gensim libraries, and Mallet (McCallum, 2002), a state-of-the-art software for performing Topic Modeling (Hannigan et al., 2019). In particular, we used MITAO for two tasks. Firstly, we used it to clean data and remove stop-words: following established procedures (Ferri et al., 2020), for each paper, we removed the authors' names and affiliations, the acknowledgments, and the reference lists to avoid "statistical noise." Secondly, we used MITAO for calculating the quality scores of different topic models. Specifically, we considered coherence, which is the most relevant score for evaluating the quality of a topic model (Cho et al., 2017). Nonetheless, perplexity requires splitting the corpus into two parts: training the model and testing it. In our case, as we need to inquire about the substantive content of papers, this procedure is not meaningful. Conversely, coherence depends on the pair-wise word similarity scores of the words in the same topic. It can be described as the semantic interpretability of the top terms used to describe discovered topics (O'Callaghan et al., 2015). The coherence score pointed out that, with our sample, the best model was the one containing seven topics. They jointly delineate the general scope of tourism for people with disabilities in management fields.

We then used Mallet for producing topic models. To complement quality score and inductive evaluation, as suggested by literature (DiMaggio et al., 2013), we elicited models composed of seven, eight, and nine topics. We analyzed those topics qualitatively and quantitatively, and we ended up confirming the selection of the seven topics model as the best one.

In the next part of this section, we describe each topic in detail and interpret them. In fulfilling this task, we relied on two main outputs of the algorithm: (a) the list of the 50 most occurred words for each topic that we report in Table 6; and (b) the

Table 6 The accessible tourism literature topics and the most occurred words

Improvement of tourism accessibility	Life satisfaction	Disability, accessibility, and barriers	Customer motivation and service attribute	Employees	Accessible tourism experience	Sports and events
Tourism	Tourism	Disabilities	Travel	Disabilities	Travel	Tourism
Accessibility	Disabilities	Disability	Service	Disability	Participants	Social
Information	Disabled	Disabled	Study	Employees	Experience	Disability
Accessible	Life	Accessible	Factor	Work	Tourism	Research
Destination	Satisfaction	Access	Attributes	Attitude	Experiences	Events
Tourist	Leisure	Accessibility	Value	Family	Study	Event
Countries	Trip	Darcy	Analysis	Attitudes	Social	Development
Destinations	Tourists	Accommodation	Satisfaction	Inclusive	Constraints	Community
Development	Activities	Physical	Importance	Hospitality	Research	Inclusive
Websites	Disability	Hotel	Results	Event	Studies	Inclusion
Euro	Holiday	Mobility	Motivation	Travelers with Mobility Impairments (TwMI)	Family	Group
Develop	Individuals	Market	Factors	Study	Children	Approach
Design	Group	Information	Passengers	Positive	Individuals	Participation
Services	Social	Barriers	Mobility	Negative	Leisure	Practices
World	Participation	Industry	Services	Special	Personal	Been
Visitors	Model	Impairments	Performance	Training	Help	Process
Public	Health	Service	Motivations	Caregivers	Activities	Opportunities
Cultural	Income	Tourism	Based	Employment	Impairment	Develop
Sites	Between	Wheelchair	Intention	Among	Families	Local
Competitiveness	Level	Facilities	Between	Statements	Because	Support
Data	Travel	Research	Travelers	Leadership	Participants	Framework
Market	Table	Guests	Among	Sustainability	Visual	Context
Area	Results	Staff	Customers	Research	Impaired	Deaf

Country	Significant	Hotels	Bus	Quality	Barriers	Between
Access	Respondents	Tourists	Customer	Industry	Group	Experience
Social	Variables	Services	Items	Model	Feel	Games
Content	Levels	Requirement	Help	Practices	Physical	Society
International	Age	Impairment	Table	Group	Tourist	Policy
Main	Data	Provide	Identified	Law	Obese	Stakeholders
Tourists	Survey	Design	Perceived	Goods	Been	Resources
Applications	Effects	Rooms	Challenges	Sample	Findings	Analysis
Areas	Sample	Study	Attribute	Annual	Vision	Focus
Index	Population	Impaired	Intrinsic	Business	Traveling	Economic
Application	Positive	Areas	Accessibility	Hotel	Like	Value
Technology	Relationship	Group	Flight	Conflict	Interviews	Festival
Between	Education	Environment	Level	Students	Researchers	Strategies
Group	Important	Level	Quality	Companies	Life	Create
Attractions	Wine	Adaptation	Theory	Resources	Home	Exam
Level	Effect	Room	Mean	Wilderness	Members	Understanding
Based	Higher	Issues	Significant	Behavior	Sense	Outcomes
Web	Household	Been	Levels	Studies	Difficulties	Planning
Specific	Mean	Lack	Relationship	Employee	Holidays	Practice
Online	Years	Exam	Data	Leadership	Hearing	Cultural
Important	Goal	Provided	Component	South	Flight	Communities
Network	Status	Because	Cluster	Cts	Holiday	Participants
Available	Study	Population	Air	Cognitive	Trip	Access
Natural	Research	Person	Challenge	Enrichment	Body	Knowledge
Monuments	Differences	Including	Reliability	Table	Person	Critical
Table	Constraints	Model	Scale	Job	Friends	Opportunity
Mobile	Variable	Customers	Percent	Evaluation	Back	City

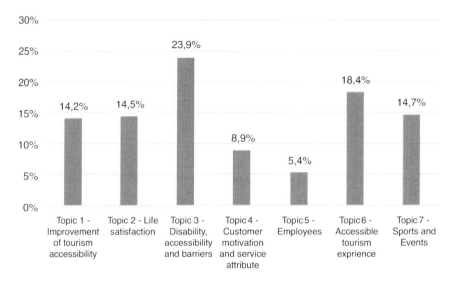

Fig. 5 The average use of accessible tourism literature topics

source per topic matrix, detailing the topic composition of each scientific paper. Additionally, in interpreting the topics, we considered the average use of topics found in the documents, as depicted in Fig. 5.

Topic 1—Improvement of Tourism Accessibility This topic is explicitly concerned with any interventions to improve the accessibility of touristic sites (e.g., Naniopoulos et al., 2015). Interventions proposed by scholars span from ecological design (Kisa Ovali, 2018) to social media (Dinis et al., 2020) and mobile applications (Ribeiro et al., 2018). Papers composed of this topic also reflect on feasible interventions appropriate for archeological sites and monuments (Naniopoulos & Tsalis, 2015).

Topic 2—Life Satisfaction This topic refers to the analyses of the contribution of holiday trips to the levels of life satisfaction of people with disabilities. Scholars provide broad evidence that tourism experiences and activities significantly affect tourists' overall life satisfaction and wellbeing (Pagán, 2015; Uysal et al., 2016).

Topic 3—Disability, Accessibility, and Barriers This is the most diffused topic in the sample. It examines the importance of several constraints as barriers to participation in tourism. Studies indicate that people with disabilities face physical, human, and financial obstacles (e.g., Wan, 2013). Researches draw evidence primarily from the hotel accommodation industry (e.g., Darcy & Pegg, 2011)

Topic 4—Customer Motivation and Service Attribute This topic focuses on the service performance and satisfaction of tourists with disabilities. Specifically, scholars discuss motivations for empowering people with disabilities' travel pursuits despite challenges (e.g., Zhang et al., 2019). They also provide managers in the tourism industry with strategic order of attribute implementations to maximize customer satisfaction (e.g., Zhang et al., 2019).

Topic 5—Employees This is the least questioned topic in the sample. It is concerned with the work and life experiences of employees with disabilities in the tourism and hospitality industry and the impact of disability-inclusive initiatives on such experiences (e.g., Luu, 2021). The potential effects of employing people with disabilities on safety, cost, efficiency, service quality, and management are investigated (e.g., Bengisu & Balta, 2011).

Topic 6—Accessible Tourism Experience This topic explores the experiences of people with disabilities to identify the difficulties they (or their caregiver) confront, reveal whether and how they overcome these difficulties, and learn how they manage the touristic experience. Disabilities scholars take into consideration are both physical and psychological and concern obesity (e.g., Poria & Beal, 2017), autism (e.g., Sedgley et al., 2017), epilepsy (e.g., McIntosh, 2020), and so on.

Topic 7—Sports and Events This topic draws attention to the extent to which events involving people with disabilities can influence broader community and society-level social change. Scholars' interest lies in understanding whether and how festivals or large-scale sporting events can contribute to develop more accessible infrastructure and positively influence attitudes towards persons with disabilities (e.g., Jamieson & Todd, 2020; e.g., Misener et al., 2015).

With the intent to assess the longitudinal use of the above-depicted topics, we attributed the documents to six temporal brackets. As expected, the scholars' debate on topic 3, i.e., disability, accessibility, and barriers, has been the most intense and has attracted the most significant contributions. Over time it has lost academic consent. Likewise, topic 2, i.e., life satisfaction, has also lost part of its attractiveness.

Conversely, topics 5, i.e., employees, and 7. i.e., sports and events, have increased their importance over time, and topic 7 represents the most debated in the last period under exam. The performance of topic 6, i.e., accessible tourism experience, is also good, registering a peak of interest in 2016–2019. It now appears pretty stable after a period of expansion, the popularity of both topics 1, i.e., improvements of tourism accessibility, and 4, i.e., customer motivation and service attributes (Fig. 6).

Finally, we drew attention to the use of the seven topics by the most cited papers. In so doing, we distinguished between the most cited per year (top 50%) and least cited per year (bottom 50%) documents and looked at the topics' distribution. We obtained that the most cited papers have concentrated mainly on topic 3, i.e., disability, accessibility, and barriers. They also sufficiently treated topics 2, i.e., life satisfaction, and 6, i.e., accessible tourism experience. In contrast, the least cited documents have focused essentially on topics 1, i.e., improvement of tourism accessibility, 3, i.e., disability, accessibility, and barriers, 6, i.e., accessible tourism experience, and 7, i.e., sports and events, while less considering the remainder of the topics (Fig. 7).

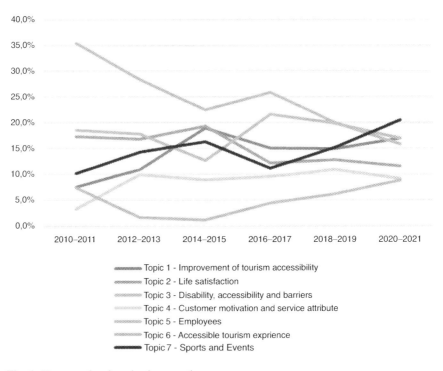

Fig. 6 The papers' topics adoption over time

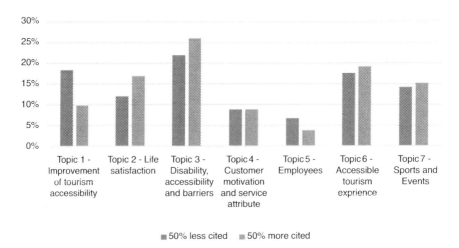

Fig. 7 The use of topics by the most cited paper

4 Conclusions

This chapter offers a first contribution in providing an original examination of the evolution of accessible tourism research in management studies. Specifically, it makes a theoretical contribution to the literature in the following directions.

First, our review finds that much has to be done despite the depicted evolution of this stream of research. Specifically, bibliometrics has highlighted that along with the two more consolidated research areas focusing on disabilities and people with disabilities experiences, a promising research area focusing on industry competitiveness and firm management is still emerging. Studies belonging to this area have paved the way to identify, measure, and systematize variables that determine the competitive position of tourism destinations and specific firms (Domínguez Vila et al., 2015; Porto et al., 2019).

Second, the findings of our review reveal the themes and latent topics upon which the management literature has evolved over the last 10 years. It is worth noting that the topic on employees and the topic on sports and events have constantly increased their importance and represent the most debated in the last period under exam.

Additionally, the present research makes a methodological contribution and suggests combining different approaches to reach the paper's goal. In so doing, our analysis adds to existing reviews on accessible tourism, such as by the recently authored by Gillovic et al. (2018), in terms of the number of sampled documents (145 vs. 83) and methods used to analyze them (bibliometrics and topic modeling vs. content analysis).

While the presented findings offer some theoretical and methodological contributions to the literature on accessible tourism, these findings are helpful to scholars who want to recognize potential new topics and gaps that may help raise further interesting questions and position their work in the literature.

First, a greater focus on regional and firm competitiveness will likely generate more mileage for future research in accessible tourism research. A fundamental challenge confronting regions and firms embedded in the traditional tourism industry is whether their traditional "competitive strategy" (standardization or differentiation of products and services) can be extended and adapted with minimal changes to accessible tourism. The conventional tourism "competitive strategy" is built on business models profiting from the top of the global economic pyramid. A focus on accessible tourism calls for more strategic attention and new business models built on how to profit from the global economic pyramid. In other words, simple adaptation and extension of the traditional approach may not be sufficient. While there is some convergence between people with and without disabilities, if the tourism industry only looks at these aspects of convergence, they may be trapped by its modest effort. Despite significant regional and country differences, accessible tourism may have enough common underlying logic to justify developing an alternative business model based on price-value trade-offs that are different from the traditional tourism industry. The accessible tourism strategy will help promote and advocate such research.

Second, to fulfill this research, management should bank on interdisciplinarity and cross-fertilization with other scientific disciplines, such as health, psychology, architecture, etc. Interdisciplinarity might be about creating something by thinking across boundaries and using methods and insights of several established disciplines. We advocate for multiple forms of interdisciplinarity. Building on Klein (1990), we propose to adopt both the synoptic (or conceptual) and the instrumental (pragmatic) view of interdisciplinarity. According to the synoptic view, different disciplines will likely converge into a coherent theory through methodological unification, like a jigsaw puzzle. According to the pragmatic view, interdisciplinarity will be used to tackle and solve specific problems. In this case, no cross-fertilization between disciplines will occur. It will bring practical and managerial benefits.

Besides making essential contributions to the extant research, the present study has some limitations derived from the methodological choice. The sample selection was based on keyword searches, which may have reduced the search scope. However, although increasing the number of keywords could have improved the sample's content, there is a flip side to the coin. It would have also added noise and made the selection progressively challenging to manage and analyze.

Overall, there is much cause for optimism about the future of accessible tourism in the management fields. We hope this review provides researchers with exciting new perspectives and ideas for their future work.

References

Bao, Y., & Datta, A. (2014). Simultaneously discovering and quantifying risk types from textual risk disclosures. *Management Science, 60*(6), 1371–1391.

Barnett, M. L., Henriques, I., & Husted, B. W. (2020). Beyond good intentions: Designing CSR initiatives for greater social impact. *Journal of Management, 46*(6), 937–964.

Bengisu, M., & Balta, S. (2011). Employment of the workforce with disabilities in the hospitality industry. *Journal of Sustainable Tourism, 19*(1), 35–57.

Bi, Y., Card, J. A., & Cole, S. T. (2007). Accessibility and attitudinal barriers encountered by Chinese travellers with physical disabilities. *International Journal of Tourism Research, 9*(3), 205–216.

Blei, D. M., Ng, A. Y., & Jordan, M. I. (2003). Latent Dirichlet allocation. *Journal of Machine Learning Research, 3*(4–5), 993–1022.

Boyack, K. W., & Klavans, R. (2010). Co-citation analysis, bibliographic coupling, and direct citation: Which citation approach represents the research front most accurately? *Journal of the American Society for Information Science and Technology, 61*(12), 2389–2404.

Boyd Ohlin, J. (1993). Creative approaches to the Americans with disabilities act. *The Cornell Hotel and Restaurant Administration Quarterly, 34*(5), 19–22.

Buhalis, D., & Darcy, S. (2011). *Accessible tourism: Concepts and issues.* Channell Views.

Burnett, J. J., & Baker, H. B. (2001). Assessing the travel-related behaviors of the mobility-disabled consumer. *Journal of Travel Research, 40*(1), 4–11.

Cho, Y. J., Fu, P. W., & Wu, C. C. (2017). Popular research topics in marketing journals, 1995–2014. *Journal of Interactive Marketing, 40,* 52–72.

Cunalata, T. G. M., Carrillo Rosero, D. A., & Ochoa Ávila, M. B. (2021). Turismo accesible: estudio bibliométrico (Accessible tourism: Bibliometric study). *Turismo y Sociedad, 28,* 115.

Daniels, M. J., Drogin Rodgers, E. B., & Wiggins, B. P. (2005). "Travel Tales": An interpretive analysis of constraints and negotiations to pleasure travel as experienced by persons with physical disabilities. *Tourism Management, 26*(6), 919–930.

Darcy, S. (1998). *Anxiety to access: Tourism patterns and experiences of NSW people with a physical disability*. Tourism New South Wales.

Darcy, S. (2002). Marginalised participation: Physical disability, high support needs and tourism. *Journal of Hospitality and Tourism Management, 9*(1), 61–72.

Darcy, S. (2010). Inherent complexity: Disability, accessible tourism and accommodation information preferences. *Tourism Management, 31*(6), 816–826.

Darcy, S., & Dickson, T. J. (2009). A whole-of-life approach to tourism: The case for accessible tourism experiences. *Journal of Hospitality and Tourism Management, 16*(1), 32–44.

Darcy, S., McKercher, B., & Schweinsberg, S. (2020). From tourism and disability to accessible tourism: A perspective article. *Tourism Review, 75*(1), 140–144.

Darcy, S., & Pegg, S. (2011). Towards strategic intent: Perceptions of disability service provision amongst hotel accommodation managers. *International Journal of Hospitality Management, 30*(2), 468–476.

Daruwalla, P., & Darcy, S. (2005). Personal and societal attitudes to disability. *Annals of Tourism Research, 32*(3), 549–570.

DiMaggio, P., Nag, M., & Blei, D. (2013). Exploiting affinities between topic modeling and the sociological perspective on culture: Application to newspaper coverage of U.S. government arts funding. *Poetics, 41*(6), 570–606.

Dinis, M. G., Eusébio, C., & Breda, Z. (2020). Assessing social media accessibility: The case of the Rock in Rio Lisboa music festival. *International Journal of Event and Festival Management, 11*(1), 26–46.

Di Stefano, G., Peteraf, M., & Verona, G. (2010). Dynamic capabilities deconstructed: A bibliographic investigation into the origins, development, and future directions of the research domain. *Industrial and Corporate Change, 19*(4), 1187–1204.

Domínguez Vila, T., Darcy, S., & Alén González, E. (2015). Competing for the disability tourism market—A comparative exploration of the factors of accessible tourism competitiveness in Spain and Australia. *Tourism Management, 47*, 261–272.

Edmondson, A. C., & Mcmanus, S. E. (2007). Methodological fit in management field research. *Academy of Management Review, 32*(4), 1155–1179.

Eichhorn, V., Miller, G., Michopoulou, E., & Buhalis, D. (2008). Enabling access to tourism through information schemes? *Annals of Tourism Research, 35*(1), 189–210.

Ellegaard, O., & Wallin, J. A. (2015). The bibliometric analysis of scholarly production: How great is the impact? *Scientometrics, 105*(3), 1809–1831.

Ferreira, J. J. M., Fernandes, C. I., & Ratten, V. (2016). A co-citation bibliometric analysis of strategic management research. *Scientometrics, 109*(1), 1–32.

Ferri, P., Lusiani, M., & Pareschi, L. (2018). Accounting for Accounting History: A topic modeling approach (1996–2015). *Accounting History, 23*(1–2), 173–205.

Ferri, P., Lusiani, M., & Pareschi, L. (2020). Shades of theory: A topic modelling of ways of theorizing in accounting history research. *Accounting History*. https://doi.org/10.1177/1032373220964271

Galvagno, M., & Pisano, V. (2020). Building the genealogy of family business internationalization: A bibliometric mixed-method approach. *Scientometrics*. https://doi.org/10.1007/s11192-020-03755-4

Gillovic, B., McIntosh, A., Darcy, S., & Cockburn-Wootten, C. (2018). Enabling the language of accessible tourism. *Journal of Sustainable Tourism, 26*(4), 615–630.

Godin, B. (2006). The linear model of innovation. *Science, Technology, and Human Values, 31*(6), 639–667.

Hannigan, T. R., Haan, R. F. J., Vakili, K., Tchalian, H., & Glaser, V. L. (2019). Topic modeling in management research: Rendering new theory from textual data. *Academy of Management Annals, 13*(2), 586–632.

Heibi, I., Peroni, S., Ferri, P., & Pareschi, L. (2019). catarsi/mitao: MITAO first release (Version v1.1-beta). *Zenodo.* https://doi.org/10.5281/zenodo.3258328.

Israeli, A. A. (2002). A preliminary investigation of the importance of site accessibility factors for disabled tourists. *Journal of Travel Research, 41*(1), 101–104.

Jamieson, K., & Todd, L. (2020). Negotiating privileged networks and exclusive mobilities: The case for a Deaf festival in Scotland's festival city. *Annals of Leisure Research,* 1–18.

Kisa Ovali, P. (2018). Improvements within the scope of ecological design: Dadia ecotourism area. *International Journal of Contemporary Economics and Administrative Sciences, 8*(2), 1–20.

Klein, J. T. (1990). *Interdisciplinarity: History, theory, and practice.* Wayne State Press.

Kobayashi, V. B., Mol, S. T., Berkers, H. A., Kismihók, G., & Den Hartog, D. N. (2018). Text mining in organizational research. *Organizational Research Methods, 21*(3), 733–765.

Luu, T. T. (2021). A tale of two countries: How do employees with disabilities respond to disability inclusive HR practices in tourism and hospitality industry? *Journal of Sustainable Tourism,* 1–31.

Melin, G. (2000). Pragmatism and self-organization: Research collaboration on the individual level. *Research Policy, 29*(1), 31–40.

McCabe, S., Joldersma, T., & Li, C. (2010). Understanding the benefits of social tourism: Linking participation to subjective well-being and quality of life. *International Journal of Tourism Research, 12*(6), 761–773.

McCallum, A. K. (2002). Mallet: A machine learning for language toolkit. http://mallet.cs. umass.edu.

McIntosh, A. J. (2020). The hidden side of travel: Epilepsy and tourism. *Annals of Tourism Research, 81,* 102856.

McKercher, B., Packer, T., Yau, M. K., & Lam, P. (2003). Travel agents as facilitators or inhibitors of travel: Perceptions of people with disabilities. *Tourism Management, 24*(4), 465–474.

Misener, L., McGillivray, D., McPherson, G., & Legg, D. (2015). Leveraging parasport events for sustainable community participation: The Glasgow 2014 Commonwealth Games. *Annals of Leisure Research, 18*(4), 450–469.

Mohr, J. W., & Bogdanov, P. (2013). Introduction-Topic models: What they are and why they matter. *Poetics, 41*(6), 545–569.

Molina-Azorin, J. F. (2015). Designing and performing a mixed methods research in strategic management. In *Research methods for strategic management.* 336. Routledge.

Morgan, N., Pritchard, A., & Sedgley, D. (2015). Social tourism and well-being in later life. *Annals of Tourism Research, 52,* 1–15.

Murray, M., & Sproats, J. (1990). The disabled traveller: Tourism and disability in Australia. *Journal of Tourism Studies, 1*(1), 9–14.

Naniopoulos, A., & Tsalis, P. (2015). A methodology for facing the accessibility of monuments developed and realised in Thessaloniki. *Greece. Journal of Tourism Futures, 1*(3), 240–253.

Naniopoulos, A., Tsalis, P., Papanikolaou, E., Kalliagra, A., & Kourmpeti, C. (2015). Accessibility improvement interventions realised in Byzantine monuments of Thessaloniki. *Greece. Journal of Tourism Futures, 1*(3), 254–268.

O'Callaghan, D., Greene, D., Carthy, J., & Cunningham, P. (2015). An analysis of the coherence of descriptors in topic modeling. *Expert Systems with Applications, 42*(13), 5645–5657.

Ozturk, Y., Yayli, A., & Yesiltas, M. (2008). Is the Turkish tourism industry ready for a disabled customer's market?. The views of hotel and travel agency managers. *Tourism Management, 29*(2), 382–389.

Pagán, R. (2015). The impact of holiday trips on life satisfaction and domains of life satisfaction. *Journal of Travel Research, 54*(3), 359–379.

Podsakoff, P. M., MacKenzie, S. B., Podsakoff, N. P., & Bachrach, D. G. (2008). Scholarly influence in the field of management: A bibliometric analysis of the determinants of University and author impact in the management literature in the past quarter century. *Journal of Management, 34*(4), 641–720.

Poria, Y., & Beal, J. (2017). An exploratory study about obese people's flight experience. *Journal of Travel Research, 56*(3), 370–380.

Poria, Y., Reichel, A., & Brandt, Y. (2010). The flight experiences of people with disabilities: An exploratory study. *Journal of Travel Research, 49*(2), 216–227.

Porto, N., Rucci Ana, C., Darcy, S., Garbero, N., & Almond, B. (2019). Critical elements in accessible tourism for destination competitiveness and comparison: Principal component analysis from Oceania and South America. *Tourism Management, 75,* 169–185.

Ramos-Rodríguez, A. R., & Ruíz-Navarro, J. (2004). Changes in the intellectual structure of strategic management research: A bibliometric study of the Strategic Management Journal, 1980–2000. *Strategic Management Journal, 25*(10), 981–1004.

Ray, N. M., & Ryder, M. E. (2003). "Ebilities" tourism: An exploratory discussion of the travel needs and motivations of the mobility-disabled. *Tourism Management, 24*(1), 57–72.

Ribeiro, F. R., Silva, A., Barbosa, F., Silva, A. P., & Metrôlho, J. C. (2018). Mobile applications for accessible tourism: Overview, challenges and a proposed platform. *Information Technology and Tourism, 19*(1–4), 29–59.

Sedgley, D., Pritchard, A., Morgan, N., & Hanna, P. (2017). Tourism and autism: Journeys of mixed emotions. *Annals of Tourism Research, 66,* 14–25.

Shaw, G., & Coles, T. (2004). Disability, holiday making and the tourism industry in the UK: A preliminary survey. *Tourism Management, 25*(3), 397–403.

Small, H., Boyack, K. W., & Klavans, R. (2014). Identifying emerging topics in science and technology. *Research Policy, 43*(8), 1450–1467.

Small, J., Darcy, S., & Packer, T. (2012). The embodied tourist experiences of people with vision impairment: Management implications beyond the visual gaze. *Tourism Management, 33*(4), 941–950.

Smith, S. L. J. (1987). Regional analysis of tourism resources. *Annals of Tourism Research, 14*(2), 254–273.

Turco, D., Stumbo, N., & Garncarz, J. (1998). Tourism constraints for people with disabilities. *Parks and Recreation, 33*(9), 78–83.

Turner, S. F., Cardinal, L. B., & Burton, R. M. (2017). Research design for mixed methods: A triangulation-based framework and roadmap. *Organizational Research Methods, 20*(2), 243–267.

Uysal, M., Sirgy, M. J., Woo, E., & Kim, H. L. (2016, April 1). Quality of life (QOL) and well-being research in tourism. *Tourism Management, 53*(C), 244–261. Elsevier.

Van Eck, N. J., & Waltman, L. (2014). Visualizing bibliometric networks. In Y. Ding, R. Rousseau, & D. Wolfram (Eds.), *Measuring scholarly impact* (pp. 285–320). Springer.

Veitch, C., & Shaw, G. (2010). Disability legislation and empowerment of tourists with disability: The UK case. In D. Buhalis & S. Darcy (Eds.), *Accessible tourism: Concepts and issues.* Channel View.

Wan, Y. K. P. (2013). Barriers for people with disabilities in visiting casinos. *International Journal of Contemporary Hospitality Management, 25*(5), 660–682.

Yau, C. K., Porter, A., Newman, N., & Suominen, A. (2014). Clustering scientific documents with topic modeling. *Scientometrics, 100*(3), 767–786.

Zhang, Y., Gao, J., Cole, S. T., & Ricci, P. (2019). Beyond accessibility: Empowering mobility-impaired customers with motivation differentiation. *International Journal of Contemporary Hospitality Management, 31*(9), 3503–3525.

Zupic, I., & Čater, T. (2015). Bibliometric methods in management and organization. *Organizational Research Methods, 18*(3), 429–472.

Part I
The Demand Side of Tourism for People with Disabilities

The Determinants of Length of Stay of Italian Senior Tourists

Maria Gabriella Campolo, Angelina De Pascale, Carlo Giannetto, and Maurizio Lanfranchi

1 Introduction

Following the growing global demographic aging, the interest related to the study of the existing link, or interconnection, between tourism and the active population aging increases (Otoo & Kim, 2018). The growing number of senior population leads to the consideration that, in the modern society, this segment should be considered as one of the most important ones for the tourism industry in the next decades (Alén et al., 2014; Oliveira et al., 2018). Since the early 1980s, several elements, among which better healthcare and social assistance and a greater understanding of the importance of free time for physical and mental healthcare, resulted in a longer life expectancy. Suffice it to think that among EU countries, Italy is characterized by one of the highest life expectancy, which is equal to 83.4 years, in 2018, respectively, 81.2 years for men and 85.6 for women, compared to the EU-28 average of 81 years (Eurostat, 2021). The evidence of the growing importance of wellbeing in the senior population is reflected in the welfare policies, in recognition of their contribution to the development, including economic progress, of the country, as well as in the distinct needs of today's "senior" segment. Some authors such as Losada et al. (2019), Thompson and Thompson (2009), Littrell et al. (2004) argue that the senior population has the potential to positively contribute to the growing national economic growth through their expenditure behavior, experience, and by integrating, in some cases, the workforce. In this regard, Lassen and Moreira (2014), Chand and Tung (2014), and Reece (2004) agree to establish that the senior

---

M. G. Campolo
Department of Economics, University of Messina, Messina, Italy
e-mail: mgcampolo@unime.it

A. De Pascale · C. Giannetto (✉) · M. Lanfranchi
Department of Economics, University of Messina, Messina, Italy
e-mail: adepascale@unime.it; giannettoc@unime.it; mlanfranchi@unime.it

© The Author(s), under exclusive license to Springer Nature Switzerland AG 2022
T. Abbate et al. (eds.), *Tourism and Disability*, Tourism on the Verge,
https://doi.org/10.1007/978-3-030-93612-9_3

population continues to hold a relatively large share of discretionary income although they allocate an appreciable part to tourism expenditure. This is also determined by the fact that investments concerning a house purchase have already been supported. An extremely high impact of home ownership among the oldest Italians is estimated (Cavapozzi & Zantomio, 2020; Lanfranchi et al., 2015), and their children are now independent.

The "baby boom" generation (namely the boomers, with reference to those who were born in the period from 1945 to 1955–1960, in Italy, between 1963 and 1965, that have attained or will attain the age of 65 between 2011 and 2031) highlights the importance of this phenomenon. Boomers are indicative since they were the first generation in the history of mankind to attain that age with a significant income and wealth, leading, as a consequence, to models of demand and consumption, which are different for many types of goods and services (Chand & Tung, 2014), including the tourist ones. Under this perspective, tourism and free time (Wang et al., 2005) may represent some of the main examples of this demographic tendency. According to Eurostat data (Eurostat, 2021), in Europe over 65, in 2019, made up almost 20% of the active population, and the highest share of seniors over the total population (22.8%) has been recognized in Italy (almost 14 million people); by 2050, the share of Italian travelers is set to expand further to reach a share of 20 million in Italy, equal to 3% of the population, compared to an EU average that, instead, will stop under 30% (WHO, 2020). According to Istat (Italian National Institute of Statistics) data (Istat, 2020), tourist expenditure (accommodation facilities and catering services) of Italian senior tourists can be estimated at around 5 billion euros per year and an additional 7 billion for recreational activities, shows, and culture must be added to this figure. Although many disciplines (i.e., social wellbeing and economy) have demonstrated a specific interest in investigating this market, the research in the tourist and leisure sector, in general, has not gone hand in hand (Otoo & Kim, 2018).

This paper contributes to bridging this gap, with the aim of analyzing the demand of senior tourism in Italy, providing comprehension of the senior segment in the home market, and of determining which factors influence their length of stay (LOS) (for tourist or leisure purposes), distinguishing between young seniors (55–64 years old, "young") and older seniors (65 years old and over, "senior"), even in the light of the benefits linked to concepts such as active aging and wellbeing, in the perspective of a post-pandemic scenario.

2 Post-Covid-19 Perspectives for the Senior Tourism Market

The Covid-19 pandemic has implied a series of restrictive measures concerning movements, as well as new and more stringent hygiene standards. This has consequently influenced the tourist market (Gössling et al., 2020). In many countries, we saw the implementation of measures consisting of obliged stays, national restrictions on the movements among regions, and the closure of the international borders (Škare et al., 2020). It is believed that the removal of such restrictions will be an integral part of tourism's recovery. First, the restart of tourism will occur at a national level, especially in the destinations where no other cases will be registered (Kreiner & Ram, 2020), and it will probably include campaigns for the promotion of domestic tourism to encourage people to travel at a regional level with the aim of stimulating the economy and of monitoring the contagion trends. It is estimated that the recovery will be uneven because markets will be aligned with different phases of tourism recovery (Hall et al., 2020). The emphasis on proximity tourism to reconnect to the family, business trips, nature tourism where it is possible to guarantee physical distancing will be initially at the center of a tourism revival. It follows that international voyages will be more complicated in terms of relaunch and, for most of the Countries, it will depend on the timing needed to spread the vaccine, as well as on the uncertainty and existence of market segments at risk, such as the one of senior tourism. This will entail evident changes in the trends and models of the post-Covid tourist demand. Post-Covid tourism, especially the senior ones, therefore, will be looking for safety, health, hygiene (Camilli, 2020) and will try to maximize their expenditure through more convenient and accessible bookings and customization of tourist services.

Senior travelers will be more inclined to travel independently or in small groups, avoiding visiting crowded tourist destinations and preferring lesser known places. Their travel options will be based on nature and culture while maintaining among their priorities destinations with suitable infrastructures and quality medical services (WTTC, 2020). As already mentioned, with a view to a progressive population aging with a growing available income, it becomes instrumental and prominent to implement suitable strategies to promote national senior tourism not only as a profitable segment from the point of view of tourist expenditure but also as an instrument to ensure safety, reliability, monitoring of the pandemic crisis and at the same time to satisfy the leisure and welfare reasons of the Italian senior population.

3   Definition of Senior Tourists

Although a definition based on age cannot be considered as a determining variable of the senior population's travel behavior (Boksberger & Laesser, 2009), in literature there is not an age standard univocally defined and used in the tourism sector, in general, to define the senior population. As well as the lack of a concrete definition and use of the age group, the terms used to address the senior population are often different in the literature on the topic. As regards age, several definitions linked to different age groups (50 and over, 55 and over, 60 and over 65 and over) are used. It appears that the age which is most frequently used and supported by literature is 55+ years old (González et al., 2017; Otoo et al., 2020; Otoo & Kim, 2020; Wang, Wu, et al., 2017). Others have also adopted 60 (Hung et al., 2016), above 60 (Carneiro et al., 2013; Eusébio et al., 2017), or above 65 (Kim et al., 2015), as the minimum age to define this population. In many works, the age group used varies among the different Countries and in relation to the population's retirement age.

This study defines two categories of senior tourists, using the classifications provided by da Hossain et al. (2003), which segment seniors into two subcategories:

- **Younger seniors** (55–64 years old) and
- **Older seniors** (65 and older)

4 Contributing Factors of Senior Tourists' LOS

LOS is one of the most interesting variables for any tourist destination, thanks to the positive relationship with tourism expenditure, and it also represents a key factor in the tourist's decisional process (Alén et al., 2014). LOS appears then to be linked by an interdependence relationship to many variables which explain the tourist experience (for example, the type of accommodation chosen, the destination, and so on) and by a subordinate relationship to a series of barriers and constraints represented by financial resources, by the availability of free time, by family needs (Dellaert et al., 1998). However, despite the importance given to this variable, few authors took interest in identifying their casual factors. In particular, in the literature, it is possible to identify four types of variables that determine LOS (socio-demographic, lifecycle, motivation, journey) (Alén et al., 2014).

4.1 Socio-demographic Variables

Many authors describe a positive relationship between age and LOS. According to Losada et al. (2019), senior tourists tend to prefer longer stays compared to the other types of tourists, precisely as a consequence of the fact that they generally have more free time (due to retirement) and a greater purchase power (also due to the children's abandonment of the household). As regards the gender variable, the studies on the topic are often discordant, even if Rodríguez et al. (2018) state that women tend to make longer trips compared to men, while Martínez-García and Raya (2008) do not find any relation. Even the educational level shows discordant aspects, and this is also confirmed by Santos et al. (2015), who claim the existence of a complex relationship between the educational level and LOS. Different authors, when analyzing the socio-demographic profile, claim that people with a higher educational level tend to prefer shorter stays compared to the less educated ones (Menezes et al., 2008; Salmasi et al., 2012). The effect of the country of origin depends essentially on the analyzed area, as suggested by Boto-García et al. (2018), as most of the literature is focused on LOS in a specific destination. Many authors include daily tourist expenses as an influent factor on LOS. In particular, according to Barros et al. (2008), LOS results to be positively correlated with the available income. This is consistent with the economic theory, since tourism is a normal good, LOS should increase as income increases. This aspect has also been taken up by Salmasi et al. (2012), who underlined how income positively influences LOS, while the price variable has a negative effect. Also, Alegre et al. (2011) find that the holiday's daily price has a negative effect on LOS. As a consequence, the greater is the expense, the lower is the LOS (Barros & Machado, 2010).

4.2 Variables Related to the Individual Life Cycle

Cooper et al. (1993) establish that both the propensity to travel and the type of tourist demand are correlated to the individual's lifecycle, taking into consideration the two essential constraints: time and available income. The differences among these several phases of lifecycle reflect the constraints imposed by age and/or by the household composition. Certainly, the latter are in turn influenced by other variables, the individual's working condition, the civil status (Grigolon et al., 2014). According to what discussed by Salmasi et al. (2012), married people tend to spend shorter stays compared to other categories (i.e., singles, widows).

4.3 Variables Related to Tourism Motivations

Many authors agree on the existence of a correlation between the reason of senior tourists' journey and LOS (Wang et al., 2008). Although the "holiday" reason is decisive in the journeys made by senior tourists, other reasons can be found in the visits to relatives and friends (Horneman et al., 2002; Hsu & Kang, 2009). This result is essentially due to the lack of costs linked to housing, which allows extending the permanence in the destination with the same available budget (Otoo & Kim, 2018). Many senior tourists perceive leisure travels to improve both physical and mental health. In this regard, the recent literature describes the emergence and the evolution of other forms of motivation. Hsu and Kang (2009) identify, among the main reasons, the need to travel to recover health and move away from daily stress and concerns. Borges Tiago et al. (2016) state that the main travel motivation of European boomers is the seaside holiday, followed by a visit to relatives and friends and to the contemplation of nature. Subordinate drivers are attributable to wellness, spa, and health treatments. This appears to be coherent to what established by Alén et al. (2014) and Ward (2014), who foresee, in the light of the demographic aging in Europe, that the tourism linked to health and wellbeing recovery will be among those with greater expansion. Also, according to Alén et al. (2015), Eusébio et al. (2015), Kim et al. (2003), and González et al. (2009), the purpose of the journey includes, beyond the holiday, the visit to relatives and friends, the possibility of improving and/or maintaining health (including medical, thermal, and wellness tourism). Hsu et al. (2007) explore the seniors' travel motivation through a model that distinguishes between external (social advancement, individual money, time, and healthiness) and internal conditions (ameliorating wellbeing, taking a break from daily routine, socialization, etc.). The improvement of mental and physical wellbeing represents, therefore, an important reason for senior tourists. With the increase of the available income, the seniors' standard of living has significantly improved, and after removing the family concerns, the senior population starts to think about how to improve their health, improve life expectancy, and feel active.

4.4 Variables Related to Travel Features

Destination Attributes Another group of factors that influence the explanation of LOS are the attributes of tourist destinations. From this point of view, in addition to prices (Alén et al., 2014), the variables linked to material and immaterial features such as climate seem to be relevant. According to Barros et al. (2010) and Barros and Machado (2010), tourists who give great importance to the natural environment, to the landscape, to the natural features present in the destination (Baloglu & Shoemaker, 2010; Boksberger & Laesser, 2009; Carneiro et al., 2013), and to climate show a greater propension to remain there longer. Nicolau and Más (2009) and Barros et al. (2010) conclude that the people who choose a destination for the climate have a greater LOS, because they can obtain a greater utility from the consumption of this attribute. Spasojević and Božić (2016) indicate as favorite tourist destinations among the potential senior tourists and mountain centers, including among the factors of choice costs, climate conditions, and the proximity to the destination and as a reason, relax, wellness, and uncontaminated nature. While Salmasi et al. (2012), by analyzing LOS in different destinations in Italy, find that the sea is the favorite destination for longer holidays and to increase one's wellbeing. Esichaikul (2012), by analyzing the reasons and the travel behavior of European tourists (aged over 55), has stated that natural attractions are one of the most important factors of senior tourism, so as to be attracted both by natural attractions and by the beauty of mountains and forests.

Type of Accommodation With regard to the types of accommodation preferred by senior tourists, Vigolo (2017) includes hotels, the houses of relatives and friends, second homes, and tourist apartments, among the housing choices of senior tourists. Bai et al. (1999) (mentioned in Alén et al., 2014) underline that around 54% of people aged over 65 and about 46% of people included in the 55–64 age group choose to stay at the home of friends and relatives. Alegre and Pou (2006) find that staying in a hotel would reduce LOS in the chosen destination and, as a consequence, the stays in the apartments (second homes, home of relatives and friends) contribute to extending LOS (Salmasi et al., 2012), probably because it is a free stay (Martínez-García & Raya, 2008). Nouza et al. (2015) show besides that LOS in second homes increases as people grow older.

Travel Arrangements (Solo Traveler or Group of Tourists) As the group dimensions grows, LOS decreases, probably due to economic restrictions (Alegre & Pou, 2006). Also, Boto-García et al. (2018) demonstrate that those who travel alone or with their partner show a greater propension to longer stays, compared to those who travel in groups.

Type of Trip (Package Holiday/Guided Tours/Self-Organized or Independent)
Holiday packages are the favorite mode of senior individuals compared to non-senior (Alén et al., 2014). However, if, on the one hand, holiday packages enable those who do not have enough time to organize their travel programs to rely on professionals, on the other hand, many boomers tend to bypass the travel agent ignoring tourist packages addressed to their age group since they do not want either to be labeled as "senior" or refer to and be limited to offers addressed to individuals who perceive being much older than them (Patterson & Pegg, 2009). Besides, according to Batra (2009), young seniors travel independently and prefer to plan the trip by themselves. This affects LOS because, according to Bai et al. (2001), those who travel autonomously usually stay longer compared to those who choose a tourist package. Besides, young seniors tend to organize their trips with shorter notice compared to seniors (Huh, 2006).

Distance and Destination The relationship between the tourist's destination of origin and the tourist destination is another key factor of the tourist demand since it influences the choices in terms of destination, activity, and interests (Bell and Leeworthy, 1990; Joo et al., 2017). Generally, the studies on the topic agree to establish that tourists coming from further destinations tend to show a propensity to stay there longer (Barros et al., 2010; Boto-García et al., 2018; Santos et al., 2015). Silberman (1985), in suggesting the existence of a positive relationship between distance and LOS, justifies this relationship with travel costs because travel costs are fixed and independent on the number of days spent in the destination, and longer stays would enable to distribute fixed costs on a longer period. A tourist will, therefore, be willing to make a longer trip if he can stay in the destination for a number of days sufficient to enable him to compensate the incurred LOS costs (Paul & Rimmawi, 1992).

Means of Transportation LOS variations can also be explained by the means of transport chosen. Generally, as stated by Wang, Fong, et al. (2017), air travel is associated with a longer stay. In the case of domestic tourism, the choice of this means can be linked to the presence of reasonable rates charged by low-cost companies (McKercher, 2008). Senior tourists who prefer to make several stops during the journey tend to use their own car (Zillinger, 2007). Public transport is the option most frequently chosen by senior tourists, compared to young seniors (Baloglu & Shoemaker, 2010).

5 Data

The sample is drawn from the "Trips and holidays," a focus included in the Households Budget Survey (provided by Istat) for the year 2019. The survey collects information on tourist flows of residents, and it provides a set of information on tourist trips, such as the duration and the characteristics of trips and of the destination, booking information, daily expenditure, the motives (if the trip was made for personal and business reasons).

In our study, we have only considered subjects that declared to stay at least 1 day on a trip in Italy and for reasons different from the business trip (holiday, wellness, religiosity, visit relatives and friends). Moreover, in accordance with the objective of our study, we only selected subjects aged 55 years or older.

In fact, our aim is to identify the differences in the determinant of the LOS in older tourists distinguishing between young older (55–64, identified as "young" for the sake of brevity) and senior older (65 and over, "senior"). The final sample is formed by 1129 subjects (581 in the first subsample and 581 in the second subsample). The general characteristics of the tourists were that they were female (52%), and 72% were married. The average year of schooling is equal to 12. The LOS (the dependent variable) is measured in the number of overnights. The average duration of the trip is equal to 5.7 days (S.D. 6.05), but it increases to 7 days for seniors (S.D. 7.25), while it decreases to 5 days (S.D. 4.41) for young people. Both groups prefer the summer season for the trip (39%). About the purpose of the trip, 62% are taken for holiday, 31% visiting relatives, 4% wellness, and 3% religiosity. The first destination, in general, is a sea place (30%), followed by the city (25%).

For a descriptive purpose, we report in Table 1 the characteristics of the complete sample (All) and divided by age (young older and senior older).

6 The Model

In our study, the dependent variable is the LOS, which represents the number of nights at the destination. Different econometric techniques were used to model the length of stay.

Alegre and Pou (2006), starting from the assumption that the duration of the vacation follows a binomial distribution, applied a discrete choice logit model to analyze the LOS on the Balearic Islands. A logit model was used by Nicolau and Más (2009) to analyze the LOS in Spain in a two-stage decision process. More sophisticated econometric methods were proposed starting from the study of Gokovali et al. (2007), who, analyzing the case of Turkey, were the first to use the duration models, also called "survival models." Following this study, Menezes et al. (2008) consider the LOS of tourists in Azores (Portugal) and analyze the survey data by means of a Cox proportional hazard model, while Martínez-Garcia and Raya (2008) consider the LOS of low-cost tourists in Spain (Costa Brava) using a

The Determinants of Length of Stay of Italian Senior Tourists

Table 1 Sample characteristics

	All (obs. 1129)		Young older (obs. 581; 51%)		Senior older (obs. 548; 49%)	
	Mean or %	Std. Dev.	Mean or %	Std. Dev.	Mean or %	Std. Dev.
Long trip	0.43		0.35		0.52	
Short trip	0.57		0.65		0.48	
Woman	0.52		0.55		0.49	
Education (years of schooling)	12.15	4.25	12.76	3.76	11.50	4.63
Worker	0.37		0.62		0.10	
Married	0.72		0.75		0.69	
Italian (born in Italy)	0.97		0.96		0.98	
N° member	1.83	0.71	1.93	0.80	1.72	0.57
Travel time						
Jan–Mar	0.15		0.15		0.14	
Apr–Jun	0.27		0.25		0.29	
Jul–Sep	0.39		0.38		0.40	
Oct–Dec	0.20		0.22		0.17	
Daily expenditure	80.87	68.32	86.28	70.49	75.14	65.53
Booking accommodation						
No reservation	0.59		0.56		0.63	
Direct reservation	0.21		0.20		0.21	
Agency reservation	0.20		0.24		0.16	
Booking transport						
No reservation	0.76		0.74		0.79	
Direct reservation	0.16		0.20		0.11	
Agency reservation	0.08		0.06		0.10	
Internet	0.28		0.37		0.18	
Transport						
Airplane	0.07		0.08		0.05	
Train	0.11		0.12		0.10	
Own vehicle	0.65		0.60		0.70	
Other	0.17		0.20		0.14	
Accommodation						
Hotel	0.39		0.41		0.37	
Extra-hotel	0.10		0.11		0.09	
Home	0.47		0.41		0.53	
Other	0.04		0.07		0.01	
Motives						
Holiday	0.62		0.64		0.60	
Visiting relatives	0.31		0.31		0.32	
Wellness	0.04		0.03		0.05	
Religious	0.02		0.02		0.03	
Destination						

(continued)

Table 1 (continued)

	All (obs. 1129)		Young older (obs. 581; 51%		Senior older (obs. 548; 49%)	
	Mean or %	Std. Dev.	Mean or %	Std. Dev.	Mean or %	Std. Dev.
City	0.25		0.30		0.20	
Sea	0.30		0.30		0.30	
Mountain	0.17		0.17		0.17	
Other	0.28		0.22		0.33	
Moving (from residential to destination)						
North-North	0.35		0.32		0.38	
North-Center	0.08		0.10		0.06	
North-South and Island	0.11		0.14		0.07	
Center-North	0.06		0.07		0.06	
Center-Center	0.12		0.09		0.14	
Center-South and Island	0.07		0.07		0.08	
South and Island-North	0.06		0.06		0.06	
South and Island-Center	0.05		0.06		0.05	
South and Island-South and Island	0.09		0.09		0.10	

Note: we report the Standard Deviation only for continuous values

log-logistics and Cox survival models. Barros et al. (2008), in order to analyze the LOS of Portuguese tourists in South America, compare different survival models. Barros and Machado (2010) use a sample selection survival model to estimate the determinants of the LOS for tourists in Portugal. Although more sophisticated techniques have been sought over time, recent studies (Thrane, 2012, 2016) have shown that the ordinary least squares (OLS) regression model produces qualitatively similar findings to much more complicated methods. Thrane (2012) has empirically shown that modeling the length of stay, the results produced by OLS regression and survival models were almost the same as those produced. Therefore, there is no reason to choose more complex models favoring moreover the principle of parsimony. Nevertheless, the common element that these studies have is the distributional form of the variable under study, which is truncated and strongly asymmetrical to the right. In fact, the error distribution in this context, by necessity, must be skewed to the right (Hosmer & Lemeshow, 1999). The characteristics and the nature of the dependent variable is highlighted in different studies that estimate the LOS fitting count models compared to ordinary least square models.

Also, if the Poisson distribution seems to be the natural choice, this distribution assumes that the mean and variance are the same. But, it may be that the data show an extra variation that is greater than the mean. This typical situation, related to the length of stay, is called overdispersion. As suggested by Grogger and Carson (1991), when there is overdispersion, the estimates from a truncated Poisson regression are inconsistent. The solution to this problem is to apply a negative binomial distribution that has one parameter more than the Poisson regression that adjusts the variance independently from the mean. We can conclude that estimate from a truncated, and negative binomial regression is more flexible in that regard than Poisson regression. Alén et al. (2014), to examine the factors that have an influence on seniors' LOS in Spain, apply a method based on the estimation of a count model based on the Negative Binomial distribution. In so doing, they solve two problems: the bias problem arising from the discrete character of the dependent variable; the inefficiency problems of the Multinomial Logit Model when analyzing the number of days a tourist spends on holiday. Truncated negative binomial models are estimated also by Brida et al. (2013) and Menezes and Moniz (2013). While Mortazavi and Cialani (2017) compare the results from two different modeling approaches: Zero-Truncated negative binomial and Ordinary least square. According to these studies, we apply the model based on the Negative Binomial distribution to the sample truncated at zero (ZTNB).

Explanatory variables used in the model provided demographic and socioeconomic information on the tourist such as gender (*Woman*), age (*Senior*), education level expressed in years of schooling (*Education*), if the tourist was born in Italy (*Italian*), a dummy variable that identifies if the subject is married (*Married*) and a dummy variable about the tourist's working status (*Worker*).

In order to explain the trip characteristics, we considered the number of other family members who attended the holiday ($N°$ *member*), the period/season in which the trip occurred (*Travel Time*), if the subject has made the reservation of the accommodation before departure (*Booking Accommodation*: 1 = no reservations as reference, 2 = direct reservation, 3 = booking through agency), a similar variable related to the means of transport (*Booking transport*: 1 = no reservations as reference, 2 = direct reservation, 3 = booking through agency), a dummy variable that assumes value one if the tourist has used the Internet for the booking of the transport and/or accommodation (*Internet*: 1 = yes, 2 = no), a categorical variable that identifies the means of transport (*Transport*: 1 = airplane, 2 = rail, 3 = own vehicle, 4 = boat, 5 = bus and others as Reference), and another one about the different types of accommodation (*Accommodation*: 1 = Hotel, Bed and Breakfast, residence for wellness and village as reference group, 2 = extra-hotel that includes apartment by rent, agritourism, 3 = home that includes stay at their holiday home or family/friends, 4 = other kind of accommodation). About the purpose of the trip (*Motives*), we distinguish between holiday, wellness, visiting relatives and friends, and religious reason. This last reason is our reference category. About the characteristics of the destination place where the tourist stayed, a categorical variable "*Destination*" was considered. This variable assumes value 1 if the destination is a city, 2 if it is a seaside, 3 if it is referred to a mountain place, and 4 for other types of destination (reference group that includes countryside, cruise, and other). Finally, we have considered the distance between the geographical area where the tourist lives, the residence, and the geographical area of the trip destination. Therefore, we have constructed a categorical variable (Movement: 1 = from North to North as reference, 2 = from North to Center, 3 = from North to South and Islands, 4 = from Center to North, 5 = from Center to center, 6 = from Center to South and Islands, 7 = from

South and islands to North, 8 = from South and islands to Center, 9 = from South and islands to South and islands).

7 Results

In our study, a zero-truncated negative binomial model (ZTNB) was used. Following prior studies (Mortazavi & Cialani, 2017; Thrane, 2016), we report the factor changes or incidence rates expressed in percentage. These can be interpreted as the factors by which the expected count for LOS changes for a unit change in the independent variables. Our model was estimated considering the full sample (Full), in which the age of the tourist was included as an independent variable and two subsamples (Young: age ranged between 55 and 64 years old; Senior: 65 and over).

In Table 2, we report the results.

The senior older tourist stays 26% longer than the young older. This difference can be related to the greater quantity of leisure time that the older tourist has compared to the younger. This result is consistent with the assumptions of Losada et al. (2019), who linked these findings both to the greater availability of free time (due to retirement) and to the greater purchasing power of senior tourists (because they no longer have to financially support their children). Furthermore, in our sample, only 10% of "senior" are employed. Consequently, if the tourist is a worker, the number of days spent on a trip decreases. In particular, for young older, this coefficient is statistically significant, and the factor change is equal to—12%. From the perspective of the educational level, the results show an alignment with the research conducted by Salmasi et al. (2012) and Menezes et al. (2008), which show that better-educated individuals tend to prefer shorter stays than less educated ones. With reference to marital status, the fact that married people do not show a high propensity for longer stays is in line with what was discussed by Salmasi et al. (2012).

Female tourists stay longer than males (on average 8%). This result appears to be in contrast with previous studies (i.e., Barros & Machado, 2010; Mortazavi & Cialani, 2017), but it is consistent with Rodríguez et al. (2018), who explains that men show a lower propensity to stay than women. If, in this study, it is not statistically significant.

According to Alegre and Pou (2006) and Boto-García et al. (2018), this study confirms that when the number of other family members who participated in the trip increases, the LOS decreases. Also, the daily expenditure has a negative effect on the LOS (50%). This result is confirmed with the statements made by Salmasi et al. (2012), Alegre et al. (2011), Lanfranchi et al. (2014), and Barros and Machado (2010).

As suggested by other studies, tourists prefer to travel during the summer months. In fact, tourists stay 77% longer during the summer period (93% if young and 57% if senior) and more or less 15% longer during the spring and autumn season, compared

The Determinants of Length of Stay of Italian Senior Tourists

Table 2 Estimation results: ZTNB. Dependent variable: Length of stay

Length of stay	All			Young			Senior		
	Coef	p	Factor change (%)	Coef	p	Factor change (%)	Coef	p	Factor change (%)
Senior—Age 65 and more (1 yes, 0 no)	0.23	***	26						
Woman (1 yes, 0 no)	0.08		8	0.09		9	0.08		8
Education (years of schooling)	0.00		0	0.01		1	−0.01		−1
Worker (1 yes, 0 no)	−0.08		−8	−0.13	*	−12	−0.02		−2
Married (1 yes, 0 no)	−0.05		−5	0.03		3	−0.13		−12
Italian (1 yes, 0 no)	0.23		26	0.07		7	0.28		32
N° family participant	−0.18	***	−16	−0.21	***	−19	−0.14	*	−13
Log daily expenditure	−0.71	***	−51	−0.68	***	−49	−0.73	***	−52
Travel time: ref. Jan–Mar									
Apr–Jun	0.14		15	0.27	*	31	0.04		4
Jul–Sep	0.57	***	77	0.66	***	93	0.45	***	57
Oct–Dec	0.13		14	0.06		6	0.2		22
Booking accommodation: ref. no reservation									
Direct reservation	0.58	***	79	0.44	***	55	0.76	***	114
Agency reservation	0.47	***	60	0.42	**	52	0.54	**	72
Booking transport: ref. no reservation									
Direct reservation	0.22	*	25	0.32	*	38	0.21		23
Agency reservation	0.35	**	42	0.4	*	49	0.41	*	51
Internet	−0.09		−9	−0.19	*	−17	0.02		2
Transport: ref. other									
Airplane	0.32	**	38	0.41	**	51	0.26		30
Train	−0.09		−9	−0.12		−11	−0.01		−1
Own vehicle	0.16		17	0.31	**	36	0.12		13
Accommodation (ref. hotel)									
Campsite	0.17		19	0.27		31	−0.08		−8
Extra-hotel	0.27	***	31	0.29	**	34	0.31	**	36
Home	−0.15		−14	−0.07		−7	−0.12		−11
Motivation (ref. religiosity)									

(continued)

Table 2 (continued)

Length of stay	All			Young			Senior		
	Coef	p	Factor change (%)	Coef	p	Factor change (%)	Coef	p	Factor change (%)
Holiday	0.25		28	0.15		16	0.21		23
Visiting relatives	0.39	*	48	0.19		21	0.44		55
Wellness	0.81	***	125	0.13		14	0.96	***	161
Destination (ref. other)									
City	−0.18	**	−16	−0.11		−10	−0.33	***	−28
Sea	0.54	***	72	0.44	***	55	0.7	***	101
Mountain	0.18	*	20	0.16		17	0.32	**	38
Moving (ref. North to North)									
North-Center	0.23	**	26	0.41	***	51	0.03		3
North-South and Island	0.58	***	79	0.49	***	63	0.72	***	105
Center-North	0.18		20	0.29	*	34	0.01		1
Center-Center	−0.42	***	−34	−0.5	***	−39	−0.36	***	−30
Center-South and Island	0.23	**	26	0.31	*	36	0.19		21
South and Island-North	0.35	***	42	0.53	***	70	0.25		28
South and Island-Center	0.28	*	32	0.14		15	0.37	*	45
South and Island-South and Island	−0.11		−10	−0.1		−10	−0.11		−10
Constant	3.14	***		3.09	***		3.38	***	
lnalpha	−1.58	***		−2.01	***		−1.59	***	
N	1129			581			548		

Note: $*p < .05$, $**p < .01$, $***p < .001$

to the reference group (winter season). In this perspective, these considerations are confirmed by the studies conducted by Baloglu and Shoemaker (2010), Boksberger and Laesser (2009), and Carneiro et al. (2013), according to which tourists who attribute great importance to the climate show a greater propensity to stay longer at the tourism destination. This increases in the group of young maybe because they are still part of the labor market and depend more on the vacation plan rather than a personal choice.

In line with what was established by Camilli (2020) regarding the preferences of post-Covid tourists, especially seniors, in this study, the LOS for tourists who book the structure where they will stay is, in general, longer than for those who do not make a reservation (79% if they book directly and 60% if they book through an agency). Moreover, these percentages are, in both cases, higher for the senior than for the young. This is also consistent with the assumptions made by Patterson and

Pegg (2009) and Bai et al. (2001), who indicate that often, independent travelers show a longer LOS than those who choose a tourist package.

Even in the case of booking the means of transport, we note that the duration of the trip increases when tourists make the booking (38% and 23% considering the direct reservation and 49% and 51% considering the agency reservation, for young and senior, respectively). Moreover, we can see that the trip durations for young senior tourists that use the Internet for booking accommodation or transport are 17% shorter than for those who do not use it.

In general, the LOS for tourists that travel by air or use their own car is longer than for those who travel by other types of means of transport, for example, bus, ferry boat, etc. (38% and 17%, respectively, when considering the full sample), as demonstrated by Wang, Fong, et al. (2017). While Zillinger (2007) associates the choice of their own car, as the mean of transportation, with those who prefer to make various stops during the journey. These percentages result higher for young than senior. Moreover, they are statistically significant only when considering the full sample and the subsample of younger. The reference accommodation mode is the hotel. As confirmed by the literature (i.e., Alegre & Pou, 2006; Martínez-García & Ray, 2008; Nouza et al., 2015; Salmasi et al., 2012) also in this research, most tourists stay in extra-hotel accommodation and compared to the reference accommodation mode they stay 31% longer (34% and 36%, related to young and senior, respectively). The coefficients for camping and home are not significant.

With respect to the trip of a religious nature (reference group), tourists stay, in general, 28% longer when traveling for a holiday motivation, but the coefficient is not significant also when we distinguish based on age. While it is significant when the motivation is related to the visit of relatives and friends (48%), but only for the full sample, as stated by Horneman et al. (2002) and Hsu and Kang (2009). Finally, a positive and significant coefficient is associated with the wellness trip, as demonstrated by several authors (e.g., Alén et al. 2015; Eusébio et al., 2015; Hsu & Kang, 2009), even if this result is not found in the group of young people. Regarding the characteristics of the destination, compared to the reference group (countryside, cruise, and other), the tourist stays 72% longer if the destination is a seaside (55% if young and 101% if senior), as demonstrated by Salmasi et al. (2012), and 20% longer if the destination is a mountain resort. This result partially confirms the evidence highlighted by Esichaikul (2012), who stated that natural attractions are one of the most important factors affecting the motivation of senior tourists and that they are interested both in holidays at the seaside and in the beauty of mountains. But in this last case, the coefficient is significant only for the second group with a higher percentage equal to 38%. Also, the coefficient relating to the "city" destination is significant only for this group, even if with a negative sign. In fact, the length to stay for seniors that travel to visit a city is 28% shorter than for the reference group.

Finally, we consider the distance between the residence and the destination. In this case, the reference group is formed by tourists that live in the North of Italy and for whom the destination place is always located in the North of Italy. When the subjects move within their own macro-area, the duration of the stay is reduced, while the further they move away from the place of residence, the more it increases. More evidence is found for movements from north to south in both subsamples. These findings are supported by the studies on distance and destination carried out by Barros et al. (2010), Boto-García et al. (2018), Santos et al. (2015), and Silberman (1985).

8 Conclusions

This paper had the objective of identifying the factors which influence the senior tourists' LOS in Italy by distinguishing between young seniors (55–64 years old, "young") and seniors (65 years and over, "senior"), in the light of the benefits linked to concepts such as active aging and wellbeing, even in the perspective of a post-Pandemic scenario. From what has been highlighted earlier, it emerges that many senior travelers have time to travel and are willing to spend a significant part of their savings in traveling. Italian seniors travel willingly, travel longer distances, and move away from longer (within national borders). The distance has a positive influence on tourism expenditure. As shown by Bianchi and Milberg (2016), travelers who cover longer distances generally show a greater propensity to spend on transports, food, shopping, entertainment compared to local visitors or to proximity tourists. This highlights that the Italian senior population represents a privileged market both for LOS and for the expenditure levels. Indeed, the picture that emerges is that of a senior tourist who spends his holidays in his own Country, who prefers to stay longer in distant places from their place of residence, who visits relatives and friends and prefers the contact with nature, and, in particular, relaxing among sun, seaside, and wellness, giving great importance to the climate aspect. In relation to the reasons and types of accommodations, visiting friends and relatives appears to be relevant, as well as the non-hotel sector. This enables to identify new perspectives of development for those companies operating in the tourist field to redesign goods and services "senior-tailored" for the firms providing health, residential, cultural, and recreational services, but also as a stimulus for small family businesses to compete on the market, and, in some cases, to exit the underground economy. In this regard, the tourist industry in the post-Covid and *aging society* era should try to intercept this target which prefers to plan their holiday also depending on the offered services and to identify new markets which enable him to travel safely and with the utmost comfort also in terms of movements and healthcare. Despite these implications, this research undergoes some limitations. Specifically, it focuses only on the determinants concerning the LOS in Italy of senior tourists, according to the available ISTAT data. Future research could be aimed at investigating the travel spending patterns of senior tourists in Italy, giving particular attention to Southern Italy and the Islands. Furthermore, it could be interesting to understand if the outcomes of this research can also be extended to other tourist segments even with different travel motivations.

References

Alegre, J., Mateo, S., & Pou, L. (2011). A latent class approach to tourists' length of stay. *Tourism Management, 32*(3), 555–563.

Alegre, J., & Pou, L. (2006). The length of stay in the demand for tourism. *Tourism Management, 27*(6), 1343–1355.

Alén, E., Losada, N., & de Carlos, P. (2015). Profiling the segments of senior tourists throughout motivation and travel characteristics. *Current Issues in Tourism, 20*(14), 1454–1469.

Alén, E., Nicolau, J. L., Losada, N., & Domínguez, T. (2014). Determinant factors of senior tourists' length of stay. *Annals of Tourism Research, 49*, 19–32.

Bai, B., Jang, S. S., Cai, L. A., & O'Leary, J. T. (2001). Determinants of travel mode choice of senior travelers to the United States. *Journal of Hospitality and Leisure Marketing, 8*(3-4), 147–168.

Bai, B., Smith, W., Cai, L. A., & O'Leary, J. (1999). Senior sensitive segments: Looking at travel behavior. In K. S. Chon (Ed.), *The practice of graduate research in hospitality and tourism*. The Haworth Hospitality Press.

Baloglu, S., & Shoemaker, S. (2010). Prediction of senior travelers' motorcoach use from demographic, psychological, and psychographic characteristics. *Journal of Travel Research, 40*, 12–18.

Barros, C. P., Correia, A., & Crouch, G. (2008). Determinants of the length of stay in Latin American tourism destinations. *Tourism Analysis, 13*(4), 329–340.

Barros, C. P., & Machado, L. P. (2010). The length of stay in tourism. *Annals of Tourism Research, 37*(3), 692–706.

Barros, C. P., Butler, R., & Correia, A. (2010). A length of stay of golf tourism: A survival analysis. *Tourism Management, 31*, 13–21. https://doi.org/10.1016/j.tourman.2009.02.010

Batra, A. (2009). Senior pleasure tourists: Examination of their demography, travel experience, and travel behavior upon visiting the Bangkok metropolis. *International Journal of Hospitality and Tourism Administration, 10*, 197–212.

Bell, F. W., & Leeworthy, V. R. (1990). Recreational demand by tourists for saltwater beach days. *Journal of Environmental Economics and Management, 18*(3), 189–205.

Bianchi, C., & Milberg, S. (2016). Investigating non-visitors' intentions to travel to a long-haul holiday destination. *Journal of Vacation Marketing, 23*(4), 339–354.

Boksberger, P. E., & Laesser, C. (2009). Segmentation of the senior travel market by the means of travel motivations. *Journal of Vacation Marketing, 15*(4), 311–322.

Borges Tiago, M. T. P. M., Couto, J. P. D. A., Tiago, F. G. B., & Dias Faria, S. M. C. (2016). Baby boomers turning grey: European profiles. *Tourism Management, 54*, 13–22.

Boto-García, D., Baños-Pino, J. F., & Álvarez, A. (2018). Determinants of tourists' length of stay: A Hurdle Count Data approach. *Journal of Travel Research, 42*, 357–371.

Brida, J. G., Meleddu, M., & Pulina, M. (2013). Factors influencing length of stay of cultural tourists. *Tourism Economics, 19*(6), 273–1292.

Camilli, M. (2020). The impact of COVID-19 on Italian tourism. Current scenario, opportunity and future tourism organizational strategies. Available at: https://www.researchgate.net/publica tion/341386975_Camilli_M_2020_The_impact_of_COVID-19_on_Italian_tourism_Current_ scenario_opportunity_and_future_tourism_organizational_strategies.

Carneiro, M. J., Eusébio, C., Kastenholz, E., & Alvelos, H. (2013). Motivations to participate in social tourism programmes: A segmentation analysis of the senior market. *Anatolia, 24*(3), 352–366.

Cavapozzi, D., & Zantomio, F. (2020). Senior tourism in Italy: The role of disability and socio-economic characteristics. *Population Ageing*. https://doi.org/10.1007/s12062-020-09286-3

Chand, M., & Tung, R. L. (2014). The aging of the world's population and its effects on global business. *Academy of Management Perspectives, 28*(4), 409–429.

Cooper, C., Fletcher, J., Gilbert, D., & Wanhill, S. (1993). *Tourism: Principles and practice*. Pitman.

Dellaert, B. G. C., Ettema, D. F., & Lindh, C. (1998). Multi-faceted tourist travel decisions: A constraint-based conceptual framework to describe tourists' sequential choices of travel components. *Tourism Management, 19*(4), 313–320.

Esichaikul, R. (2012). Travel motivations, behavior and requirements of European senior tourists to Thailand. *PASOS, Revista de Turismo y Patrimonio Cultural, 10*(2), 47–58.

Eurostat. (2021). Mortality and life expectancy statistics: Tables and figures. Available at: https://ec.europa.eu/eurostat/databrowser/view/demo_mlexpec/default/table?lang=en

Eusébio, C., Carneiro, M. J., Kastenholz, E., & Alvelos, H. (2015). Social tourism programmes for the senior market: A benefit segmentation analysis. *Journal of Tourism and Cultural Change, 15*(1), 59–79. https://doi.org/10.1080/14766825.2015.1117093

Eusébio, C., Carneiro, M. J., Kastenholz, E., & Alvelos, H. (2017). Social tourism programmes for the senior market: A benefit segmentation analysis. *Journal of Tourism and Cultural Change, 15*(1), 59–79. https://doi.org/10.1080/14766825.2015.1117093

Gokovali, U., Bahar, O., & Kozak, M. (2007). Determinants of length of stay: A practical use of survival analysis. *Tourism Management, 28*(3), 736–746.

González, A. M., Rodríguez, C., Miranda, M. R., & Cervantes, M. (2009). Cognitive age as a criterion explaining senior tourists' motivations. *International Journal of Culture, Tourism and Hospitality Research, 3*(2), 148–164.

González, E. A., Sánchez, N. L., & Vila, T. D. (2017). Activity of older tourists: Understanding their participation in social tourism programs. *Journal of Vacation Marketing, 23*(4), 295–306.

Gössling, S., Scott, D., & Hall, C. M. (2020). Pandemics, tourism, and global change: A rapid assessment of Covid-19. *Journal of Sustainable Tourism.* https://doi.org/10.1080/09669582.2020.1758708

Grigolon, A. B., Borgers, A. W. J., Kemperman, A. D. A. M., & Timmermans, H. J. P. (2014). Vacation length choice: A dynamic mixed multinomial logit model. *Tourism Management, 41*, 158–167.

Grogger, J. T., & Carson, R. T. (1991). Models for truncated counts. *Journal of Applied Econometrics, 6*(3), 225–238.

Hall, C. M., Scott, D., & Gössling, S. (2020). Pandemics, transformations and tourism: Be careful what you wish for. *Tourism Geographies,* 1–22. https://doi.org/10.1080/14616688.2020.1759131

Horneman, L., Carter, R. W., Wei, S., & Ruys, H. (2002). Profiling the senior traveler: An Australian perspective. *Journal of Travel Research, 41*(1), 23–37.

Hosmer, D. W., Jr., & Lemeshow, S. (1999). Applied survival analysis: Regression modelling of time to event data. *European Orthodontic Society,* 561–562.

Hossain, A., Bailey, G., & Lubulwa, M. (2003). Characteristics and travel patterns of older Australians: Impact of population ageing on tourism. In *International conference on population ageing and health: Modeling our future, Canberra, Australia.*

Hsu, C. H. C., Cai, L. A., & Wong, K. K. F. (2007). A model of senior tourism motivations—Anecdotes from Beijing and Shanghai. *Tourism Management, 28*(5), 1262–1273. https://doi.org/10.1016/j.tourman.2006.09.015

Hsu, C. H. C., & Kang, S. K. (2009). Chinese urban mature travelers' motivation and constraints by decision autonomy. *Journal of Travel and Tourism Marketing, 26*(7), 703–721. https://doi.org/10.1080/10548400903284537

Huh, C. (2006). *A study of changes in patterns of travel behavior over time: A cohort analysis approach.* PhD dissertation. Michigan State University.

Hung, K., Bai, X., & Lu, J. (2016). Understanding travel constraints among the elderly in Hong Kong: A comparative study of the elderly living in private and in public housing. *Journal of Travel and Tourism Marketing, 33*(7), 1051–1070.

ISTAT. (2020). Invecchiamento attivo e condizioni di vita degli anziani in Italia. Available at: https://www.istat.it/it/archivio/246504

Joo, D., Woosnam, K. M., Shafer, C. S., Scott, D., & An, S. (2017). Considering Tobler's first law of geography in a tourism context. *Tourism Management, 62*, 350–359.

Kim, H., Woo, E., & Uysal, M. (2015). Tourism experience and quality of life among elderly tourists. *Tourism Management, 46*, 465–476.

Kim, J., Wei, S., & Ruys, H. (2003). Segmenting the market of West Australian senior tourists using an artificial neural network. *Tourism Management, 24*(1), 25–34.

Kreiner, N. C., & Ram, Y. (2020). National tourism strategies during the Covid-19 pandemic. *Annals of Tourism Research.* https://doi.org/10.1016/j.annals.2020.103076

Lanfranchi, M., Giannetto, C., & De Pascale, A. (2014). Nature based tourism: Natural balance, impacts and management. *Quality - Access to Success, 15*(Suppl.1), 224–229.

Lanfranchi, M., Giannetto, C., & Pirnea, I. C. (2015). Rural tourism: Corporate social responsibility and sustainable tourism. *Quality - Access to Success, 16*(146), 83–88.

Lassen, A. J., & Moreira, T. (2014). Unmaking old age: Political and cognitive formats of active ageing. *Journal of Aging Studies, 30*, 33–46.

Littrell, M. A., Paige, R. C., & Song, K. (2004). Senior travellers: Tourism activities and shopping behaviours. *Journal of Vacation Marketing, 10*(4), 348–362.

Losada, N., Alén, E., Cotos-Yáñez, T. R., & Domínguez, T. (2019). Spatial heterogeneity in Spain for senior travel behavior. *Tourism Management, 70*, 444–452.

Martínez-García, E., & Raya, J. M. (2008). Length of stay for low-cost tourism. *Tourism Management, 29*(6), 1064–1075.

McKercher, B. (2008). The implicit effect of distance on tourist behavior: A comparison of short and long haul pleasure tourists to Hong Kong. *Journal of Travel and Tourism Marketing, 25*(3–4), 367–381.

Menezes, A. G., & Moniz, A. I. (2013). The determinants of length of stay in the Azores: A count model approach. *Revista Turismo and Desenvolvimento, 19*, 25–40.

Menezes, A. G., Moniz, A., & Vieira, J. C. (2008). The determinants of length of stay of tourists in the Azores. *Tourism Economics, 41*(1), 205–222.

Mortazavi, R., & Cialani, C. (2017). International tourists' length of overnight stay in Venice. *Tourism Economics, 23*(4), 882–889. https://doi.org/10.5367/te.2016.0556

Nicolau, J. L., & Más, F. J. (2009). Simultaneous analysis of whether and how long to go on holidays. *The Service Industries Journal, 29*(8), 1077–1092.

Nouza, M., Ólafsdóttir, R., & Sæþórsdóttir, A. D. (2015). Motives and behaviour of second home owners in Iceland reflected by place attachment. *Current Issues in Tourism, 21*(2), 225–242.

Oliveira, C., Brochado, A., & Correia, A. (2018). Seniors in international residential tourism: Looking for quality of life. *Anatolia, 29*(1), 11–23.

Otoo, F. E., & Kim, S. (Sam). (2018). Is there stability underneath health risk resilience in Hong Kong inbound tourism? *Asia Pacific Journal of Tourism Research, 23*(4), 344–358.

Otoo, F. E., & Kim, S. (2020). Analysis of studies on the travel motivations of senior tourists from 1980 to 2017: Progress and future directions. *Current Issues in Tourism, 23*(4), 393–417.

Otoo, F. E., Kim, S., & Choi, Y. (2020). Understanding senior tourists' preferences and characteristics based on their overseas travel motivation clusters. *Journal of Travel and Tourism Marketing, 37*(2), 246–257. https://doi.org/10.1080/10548408.2020.1740136

Patterson, I., & Pegg, S. (2009). Marketing the leisure experience to baby boomers and older tourists. *Journal of Hospitality Marketing and Management, 18*(2–3), 254–272.

Paul, B. K., & Rimmawi, H. S. (1992). Tourism in Saudi Arabia. *Annals of Tourism Research, 19*(3), 501–515.

Prayag, G. (2012). Senior travelers' motivations and future behavioral intentions: The case of NICE. *Journal of Travel and Tourism Marketing, 29*(7), 665–681.

Reece, W. S. (2004). Are senior leisure travelers different? *Journal of Travel Research, 43*(1), 11–18.

Rodríguez, X. A., Martínez-Roget, F., & González-Murias, P. (2018). Length of stay: Evidence from Santiago de Compostela. *Annals of Tourism Research, 68*, 9–19.

Salmasi, L., Celidoni, M., & Procidano, I. (2012). Length of stay: Price and income semi-elasticities at different destinations in Italy. *International Journal of Tourism Research, 14*(6), 515–530.

Santos, G. E. D. O., Ramos, V., & Rey-Maquieira, J. (2015). Length of stay at multiple destinations of tourism trips in Brazil. *Journal of Travel Research, 54*(6), 788–800.

Silberman, J. (1985). A demand function for length of stay: The evidence from Virginia Beach. *Journal of Travel Research, 23*(4), 16–23.

Škare, M., Soriano, D. R., & Porada-Rochoń, M. (2020). Impact of COVID-19 on the travel and tourism industry. *Technological Forecasting and Social Change.* https://doi.org/10.1016/j.techfore.2020.120469

Spasojević, B., & Božić, S. (2016). Senior tourist's preferences in the developing countries: Measuring perceptions of Serbian potential senior market. *European Journal of Tourism, Hospitality and Recreation, 7*(2), 74–83.

Thompson, N. J., & Thompson, K. E. (2009). Can marketing practice keep up with Europe's ageing population? *European Journal of Marketing, 43*(11/12), 1281–1288.

Thrane, C. (2012). Analyzing tourists' length of stay at destinations with survival models: A constructive critique based on a case study. *Tourism Management, 33*(1), 126–132.

Thrane, C. (2016). Modelling tourists' length of stay: A call for a 'back-to-basic' approach. *Tourism Economics, 22*(6), 1352–1366. https://doi.org/10.1016/j.tourman.2011.02.011

Vigolo, V. (2017). Hospitality and older tourists: A focus on accommodation choices. *Older Tourist Behavior and Marketing Tools*, 105–124.

Wang, L., Fong, D. K. C., Law, R., & Fang, B. (2017). Length of stay: Its determinants and outcomes. *Journal of Travel Research, 57*(4), 472–482.

Wang, W., Wu, W., Luo, J., & Lu, J. (2017). Information technology usage, motivation, and intention: A case of Chinese urban senior outbound travelers in the Yangtze River Delta region. *Asia Pacific Journal of Tourism Research, 22*(1), 99–115.

Wang, Y., Norman, W. C., & Mcguire, F. A. (2005). A comparative study of leisure constraints perceived by mature and young travelers. *Tourism Review International, 8*(3), 263–279.

Wang, Y., Zhang, Y., Xia, J., & Wang, Z. (2008). Segmenting the mature travel market by motivation. *International Journal of Data Analysis Techniques and Strategies, 1*(2), 193–209.

Ward, A. (2014). Segmenting the senior tourism market in Ireland based on travel motivations. *Journal of Vacation Marketing, 20*(3), 267–277.

World Health Organization. (2020). Global Health Observatory indicator views. Available at: https://www.who.int/data/gho/data/indicators.

WTTC (2020, September). To recovery and beyond: The future of travel and tourism in the wake of COVID-19. World Travel and Tourism Council. Available at: https://wttc.org/Research/Insights

Zillinger, M. (2007). Tourist routes: A time-geographical approach on German car-tourists in Sweden. *Tourism Geographies, 9*(1), 64–83.

Tourism Flows in Italy: The Role of Local Public Policies Toward Disability

Silvia D'Arrigo, Michele Limosani, Emanuele Millemaci, Fabio Monteforte, and Dario Sciulli

1 Introduction

According to estimates of the World Health Organization (WHO, 2020), about 15% of the global population live with some form of disability, and up to 4% face severe limitations in doing daily activities. The number of people with disabilities has increased over time (they were about 10% of the global population during the 1970s), also due to the aging process and the greater diffusion of chronic illness.

Disability has been associated for a long time with marginalization from many dimensions of individuals' life. During the last decades, however, the economic and social integration of people with disabilities has been promoted by governments and organizations through formal actions. A crucial role in the change of perspective about disability has been played by the innovative social model of disability, which widely replaced the medical model. The latter refers to disability as an individual problem directly connected to impairments (e.g., Ells, 2001). The social model, instead, focuses on removing social and environmental obstacles to enable full integration into society, as disability is primarily defined by barriers in society rather than impairments and differences (Aitchison, 2003).

Since the 1990s, in the light of the changed perception of disability, some Western countries have promoted innovative legislation aimed at supporting the integration of people with disabilities into their societies (e.g., Agovino et al., 2020). The Americans with Disabilities Act (ADA) was established by the US federal

---

S. D'Arrigo · M. Limosani · E. Millemaci · F. Monteforte (✉)
Department of Economics, University of Messina, Messina, Italy
e-mail: silvia.darrigo@unime.it; michele.limosani@unime.it; emillemaci@unime.it; fabio.monteforte@unime.it

D. Sciulli
Department of Economics, University of Chieti-Pescara, Chieti, Italy
e-mail: dario.sciulli@unich.it

© The Author(s), under exclusive license to Springer Nature Switzerland AG 2022
T. Abbate et al. (eds.), *Tourism and Disability*, Tourism on the Verge,
https://doi.org/10.1007/978-3-030-93612-9_4

government in 1990 to promote the integration of people with disabilities by ensuring access to facilities and non-discriminatory provision of services (Grady & Ohlin, 2009). In Italy, the Law n.104/92 defined different aspects aimed at the integration of people with disabilities and focused on various dimensions, including care, social integration, education, employment, elimination of barriers, public transport, housing, and the role of caregivers. Finally, the Disability Discrimination Act (DDA) was introduced in 1995 in the UK with similar aims and focused especially on employment, discrimination, education, and public transport. The novel approach finally resulted in a new definition of disability, the International Classification of Functioning, Disability and Health (ICF) promoted by the WHO in 2001.

The existing literature has emphasized that education and employment are key dimensions to be enforced to ensure the full integration of people with disabilities into societies (e.g., OECD, 2010). The integration process and life satisfaction of people, including those with disabilities, however, is crucially affected also by other aspects, such as the quality of leisure time (Addabbo et al., 2016), which includes the possibility of fully access tourism experiences. Kastenholz et al. (2015) stressed that tourism and leisure bring benefits for people with disabilities, improving personal development and quality of life, and contributing to social inclusion.

A growing body of literature (e.g., Agovino et al., 2017; Eichhorn et al., 2013; Minnaert et al., 2009) has stressed that tourism has a significant impact on the well-being of each individual, and the positive effects would be especially relevant for people with disabilities (Small et al., 2012). Social tourism has been recognized as a key factor to tackle social and economic inequality (e.g., McCabe, 2009; McCabe et al., 2010). The importance of guaranteeing accessible tourism has been recognized by the European Disability Strategy 2010–2020, which stressed that accessibility is a key element for full social inclusion.

Nevertheless, full access to tourism activities is still denied to people with disabilities, especially to those with severe disabilities (e.g., Pagán 2012), because of multiple factors attributable to economic, environmental, and informative barriers. For example, having scarce financial resources reduces the probability of being satisfied with the leisure time dimension (Addabbo et al., 2016; Eichhorn et al., 2013). Environmental barriers may include physical obstacles in transport services and accommodation facilities (e.g., Avis et al., 2005) and cultural problems because of discriminatory behaviors by people without disabilities (e.g., Bizjak et al. 2011). Staff accommodation skills and training are also important to improve the hospitality of people with disabilities (e.g., Darcy, 2010; Figueiredo et al., 2012; Grady & Ohlin, 2009). In this respect, gender differences are often observed as, for instance, comparing the air transportation staff, women are perceived as more prone to help people with disabilities than men (Chang & Chen, 2012). Finally, access to correct and comprehensive information is essential to reach people with disabilities and their families and allow them to program effective travels and vacations (Eichhorn et al., 2008; Huh & Singh, 2007).

From a supply-side perspective, the segment of people with disabilities represents an untapped and profitable niche market. Thus, removing the barriers and promoting accessible tourism would contribute to opening an important economic and business opportunity in the tourism industry, which, in turn, represents a key element for economic growth and job creation (e.g., Bizjak et al. 2011; Domínguez et al., 2013).

The role of the public sector in promoting tourism accessibility has been little explored. The scarce literature has emphasized the positive role of the public infrastructure facilities (e.g., Özogul & Baran, 2016) and the importance of accessible public transport (e.g., Folino, 1999). The Keroul experience in Quebec has stressed the important opportunities arising from the partnership among not-for-profit, public and private sectors (Darcy, 2006). The removal of physical and cultural barriers requires the contribution, and possibly the collaboration, of both public and private agents. Furthermore, it might have positive spillover effects: "An accessible environment, while particularly relevant for people with disabilities, has benefits for a broader range of people. For example, curb cuts (ramps) assist parents in pushing baby strollers. Information in plain language helps those with less education or speakers of a second language. Announcements of each stop on public transit may aid travelers unfamiliar with the route as well as those with visual impairments" (WHO, 2011, p. 169). More recently, Naniopoulos et al. (2016) highlighted the importance of the public sector to favor the accessibility of people with disabilities to public transport, open spaces, cultural sites, and so on. In this respect, they also stressed the need for having political representatives with disabilities among policymakers to promote innovative legislation to favor the inclusion of people with disabilities.

The promotion of tourism accessibility, indeed, may represent a win-win policy because it increases the quality of life of people with disabilities and their families, favors social integration, and, at the same time, boosts economic outcomes both at the local and national levels.

In this study, we seek to empirically determine how removing barriers has an impact on disabled tourism flows. In particular, to overcome data limitations on the barriers that a disabled tourist has to face, we check the broader question of whether the local sensibility and commitment toward the disabled needs and well-being can have an impact on the total tourism flows (recorded as overnight stays).

The choice of using an aggregated measure of tourism flows is not only due to data availability, but it is also more correct in our view as by recording only the disabled, we would underestimate their whole impact on tourism: indeed, a disabled in most cases does not travel alone, but with her own family or caregiver(s). Moreover, by employing overnight stays rather than the total number of tourists, we have a more accurate measure of the intensity of the tourism flow, and we avoid underestimating the overall impact of the disabled contribution to tourism, knowing that the average length of stay of disabled tourists and their families or caregivers is typically longer than that of the other tourists (e.g., UNWTO, 2015). As a measure of local commitment, we consider as the best available information the welfare expenditure toward the disabled, which in part can also benefit disabled tourists and is, in any case, a signal of the sensibility of local administrators and citizens toward the disabled needs and well-being.

We rely on a panel consisting of the 110 Italian provinces observed in the period between 2011 and 2018. We consider an added value relying on data at the provincial level, apart from the benefit of increasing the cross-section observations and allowing us to obtain better estimates, because, as a large share of the total welfare expenditures toward the disabled is provided by municipal and regional institutions, we observe in general large heterogeneity in terms of local policies and consequently benefits offered to the disabled.

The empirical exercise comprehends the use of a standard pooled-OLS method as well as fixed effects and individual time trends. Moreover, with the aim of removing other important sources of heterogeneity potentially responsible for omitted variable bias, the study investigates the role played by two of the determinants mostly suggested in the tourism flows literature, which are attractiveness and accessibility. Besides recognizing how the latter factor may play a key role in the disabled demand for tourism, we check for any potential multiplicative effect between the accessibility variables and expenditure for the disabled. To allow a better understanding of the relationships and to allow comparisons, the empirical analysis does not focus only on the disabled but also on other similar categories of individuals and specifically the elderly, which, it should be noticed, is the age group most populated by disabled.

This work has several merits. First, previous evidence on this subject is scarce and scanty. Second, to the best of our knowledge, this is the first attempt where data of the Italian provinces are employed, and in particular, data on the municipal welfare expenditure have never been used previously. Third, while most previous works focus on the effectiveness of private players initiatives in removing barriers and attracting disabled tourists, this study fills the gap investigating the role of local and national public players in providing specific attention to the disabled directly with welfare interventions or with more general interventions on the accessibility of cities and museums. Fourth, while most previous works use micro-level data from surveys, this study follows a macro approach. Notice that this macro approach can be considered complementary and more relevant to the effectiveness of public policy measures with respect to the one relying on data of origin-destination tourism flows.

The chapter is organized as follows: Sect. 2 describes the data; Sect. 3 specifies the empirical model; Sect. 4 discusses baseline results and shows additional results and checks for robustness. Finally, Sect. 5 draws some concluding remarks.

2 Data

2.1 Sources

We collected data at the subregional level over the period 2011–2018. More precisely, the unit of analysis is the territorial administrative divisions (provinces) of level 3 based on the NUTS 2016 classification released by Eurostat.[1] The NUTS classification (nomenclature of territorial units for statistics) is a hierarchical system used to subdivide the economic territory of the European Union (EU) member States into territorial units at different geographical levels. Following these criteria, the Italian administrative system comprises macro-regional geographical areas (NUTS level 1 or major socio-economic regions), regions (NUTS level 2 or basic regions for the application of regional policies), and provinces, each one consisting of a cluster of neighboring municipalities placed around its chief town (NUTS level 3 or small regions for specific diagnoses). Since provinces have homogeneous socio-economic and cultural characteristics, they constitute a suitable unit of analysis to examine the role of the attention paid by local public policies to the needs of more vulnerable people—especially the disabled and the elderly—in triggering tourist flows.

All data used in this study originate from the Italian National Institute of Statistics (ISTAT). Table 1 provides the definitions and sources of the main variables used in the econometric analysis, while Table 2 reports the descriptive statistics.

The dependent variable of the empirical model, *tourism_presences*, measures the presences (days) of native and foreign tourists in the province (reported in thousands) and is calculated as the number of nights spent at accommodation establishments.

Since public sector commitment and sensibility toward the disabled is treated as an unobserved, latent variable, we consider the expenditure in welfare policies managed by municipalities as a proxy for the capability of the territorial units to cover the needs for assistance and integration of frail people. Persons with disabilities—the main target group—are individuals with long-term physical, mental, intellectual, or sensory impairments hindering their usual daily activities, including personal care, mobility and locomotion, and communication, consistently with the definition provided by ISTAT (Multipurpose Survey on Health Conditions and Health Services) and international standards such as the United Nations Convention on the Rights of Persons with Disabilities (UN, 2006). In addition, since aging is a factor in the increasing incidence of chronic diseases, we also consider elderly recipients of social services—people aged 65 years or over. Therefore, the dataset includes local expenditures (euro) in welfare services for the target population, that is: (1) disabled people younger than 65 years old, living within the family (*expt_disabled*); (2) elderly residents (*expt_elderly*). Social services may consist of monetary payments but also specific policies of intervention for the target group, such as socio-educational support, social home care, and activities for social inclusion. Notice that disabled people aged 65 years and over are included in the category of elderly beneficiaries. Together with the aforementioned categories, we consider a more comprehensive measure of the local public expenditure programs providing cash assistance and in-kind benefits, i.e., the total local expenditure in social services

---

[1]Because of a large reorganization in the number and composition of its provinces (e.g., some municipalities passed to a different province), we do not consider Sardinia in the last 2 years of the time span under examination (2017 and 2018).

Table 1 Variables description

Variable	Description
tourism_presences	Presences of native and foreign tourists (days) in hotels and complementary businesses (reported in thousands)
expt_disabled	Social services and benefits of municipalities (euro) for the persons with disabilities over the target population. The target population is the disabled people less than 65 years of age living in the family, as measured by the Multipurpose Survey on Health Conditions and Health Services
expt_elderly	Social services and benefits of municipalities (euro) for the elderly persons over the target population. The target population is given by residents—with or without disabilities—aged 65 or over
expt_all	Social services and benefits of municipalities (euro) for all the categories of recipients over the target population. The categories include (1) number of members of the households with at least one minor; (2) persons with disabilities as described in *expt_disabled*; (3) persons with additions aged 15 years or over; (4) elderly people as described in *expt_elderly*; (5) immigrants and nomads; (6) residents aged 18–64 in poor economic conditions; (7) multipurpose beneficiaries. The target population is the sum of all target groups
school_services	Average (percentage) of the rates of availability of the following services: (1) infrastructures to eliminate architectural barriers (slip road ramp, lift, stairlift and/or lift platform, toilet/stairs/doors according to laws, accessible routes); (2) adapted computer stations
homecare_elderly	Elderly persons treated in socio-assistance home care over the total elderly population (65 years and over) (percentage)
population	Average resident population (reported in thousands)
density	Average resident population per unit of area (square kilometer)
museum	The number of state and non-state museums and similar institutes, including archeological sites and parks, monuments, monumental complexes, institutions organizing temporary exhibitions, and commercial galleries
dummy_airport	Dummy for the presence of an airport. The dummy includes only the airport stations with significant passenger traffics. Small islands airports having typically seasonal traffic flows—mainly concentrated during the summer—are excluded from the list
dummy_port	Dummy for the presence of a port
dummy_hsr	Dummy for the presence of high-speed rails

and benefits on the sum of target populations (*expt_all*) covering, in addition to the disabled and the elderly, other groups of vulnerable individuals and families.

We further examine alternative measures of the commitment and caring of local public services toward the disabled and the elderly. The indicator variable *school_services* denotes the availability of services for disabled pupils of state and non-state primary and lower secondary schools (in percentage points). It is worth noting that Italian laws forbid architectural barriers in school buildings that hinder the access and mobility of persons with disabilities. Besides, schools that are part of the national education system must provide technical equipment and educational services, such as adapted computer stations or a specialized support teacher assigned to the class of the disabled pupil, aimed at promoting her integration (Law n.104/

Tourism Flows in Italy: The Role of Local Public Policies Toward Disability 57

Table 2 Descriptive statistics

	Mean	St. dev.	Min.	Max.	N
tourism_presences	3632.176	5763.539	64.938	37,042.450	864
tourism_intensity	7.469	9.587	.278	62.818	864
expt_disabled	3444.054	2982.564	77	22,060	864
expt_elderly	106.353	131.669	5	1621	864
expt_all	115.560	71.053	6	597	864
school_services	60.501	6.516	41.102	77.743	864
homecare_elderly	1.325	.974	.100	5.800	762
population	554.357	605.773	57.252	4354.731	864
density	.265	.375	.031	2.649	864
museum	44.664	31.957	10	223	864
dummy_airport	.271	.445	0	1	864
dummy_port	.215	.411	0	1	864
dummy_hsr	.074	.262	0	1	864

Note: Variables *tourism_presences* and *population* are expressed in thousands of inhabitants

1992). The variable *school_services* is defined as the average percentage of the shares of available barriers-free infrastructures and adapted computer stations for disabled pupils who benefit from a learning support teacher. The variable *homecare_elderly* identifies the share of elderly people who benefited from social home care over the elderly population in percentage terms. In addition, for this variable, data are available for 1 year less (until 2017 rather than 2018).

The bottom part of Tables 1 and 2 lists the following set of additional variables: (1) demographic factors (average resident population, reported in thousands, and population density); (2) a proxy variable for the monumental, archeological, artistic, and natural heritage (sum of both state and non-state museums and similar institutes) considered as main sources of non-seasonal tourist attraction; (3) dummies for the presence of an airport station, a port, and high-speed rails as indicators of accessibility. With regard to the proxy variable (2), data collection was not conducted annually by ISTAT but in the years 2006, 2011, 2015, and 2017. Therefore, we imputed missing values by assuming that changes over time occur at a fixed geometric rate between two survey years and extending the geometric rate computed for the year between 2015 and 2017 to the last year of the timespan (2018).

2.2 Main Patterns

A visual representation of the spatial differences across Italian provinces in terms of the main variables of interest is provided in Fig. 1, where for ease of comparability we express variables as a share of the target population. Figure 1 is divided into two panels, where darker colors denote higher time averages of the variable under consideration. Panel (a) on the left depicts the number of tourists' overnight stays

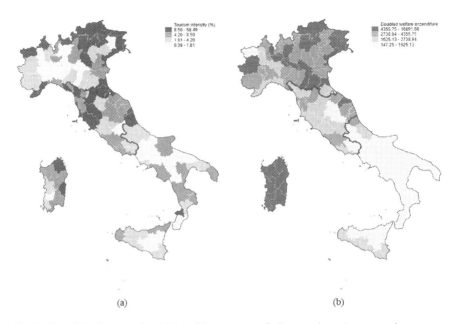

Fig. 1 Spatial distribution of variables of interest across Italian provinces (average values across the time span under consideration). *Note:* Panel (**a**) refers to the tourism intensity index, panel (**b**) depicts welfare expenditure toward people with disabilities. All expenditure figures are expressed in per-capita terms with respect to the eligible population

(tourism_intensity). Provinces in the North-East and those on the Alps display the highest tourism intensity, together with provinces in the Centre-North in Liguria, Tuscany, and Emilia-Romagna. Provinces in the Centre and the South record average and low values with two notable exceptions in Sardinia and one in Calabria. Panel (b) on the right provides figures for the local expenditure in welfare policies toward people with disabilities (*expt_disabled*). There is a remarkable divide between provinces in the North and the Centre, displaying the highest average values throughout the period under consideration, and the provinces in the South (again with the exception of Sardinia). The North-South divide in welfare expenditure is confirmed even if expanding the focus to figures for the elderly population and total local welfare expenditure, information provided in Fig. 4 in the Appendix.

Figure 2 reports the evolution over time of tourism intensity in Italian regions in the period 2011–2018, while Fig. 3 illustrates the 2011–2018 evolution of local welfare expenditure for people with disabilities. All information is reported at the regional level.

Focusing on Fig. 2, as already highlighted with the geographical representation of average values above, we uncover that tourism intensity shows some heterogeneities in levels among regions. The presence of native or foreign tourists for inhabitants in Trentino Alto Adige is almost 50 and in Aosta Valley is almost 30, while it is lower than 2 in Molise. In the analyzed period, there is no evidence of relevant changes in tourism intensity in absolute terms, while relative changes appear to be not

Tourism Flows in Italy: The Role of Local Public Policies Toward Disability

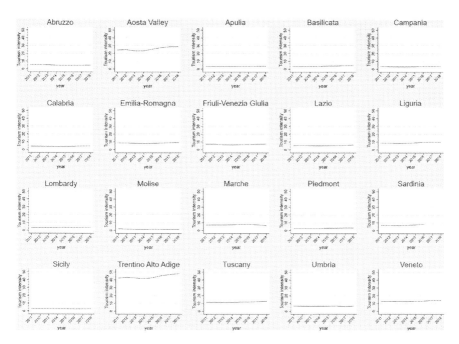

Fig. 2 Evolution of tourism intensity, 2011–2018

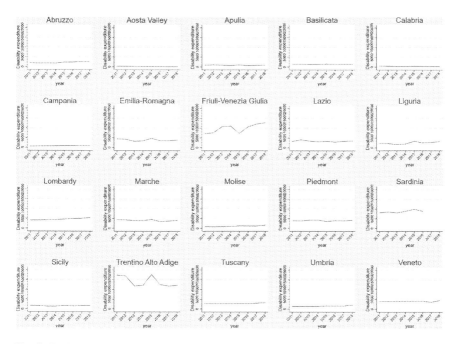

Fig. 3 Evolution of local welfare expenditure for disability per eligible inhabitant, 2011–2018

negligible in some regions. Considering the change between the first and last observed years, we note an increase in tourism intensity of about 35% in Basilicata and over 15% in Piedmont, Sardinia, and Aosta Valley. On the contrary, tourism intensity has lowered by more than 30% in Molise, by 15% in Abruzzo, and by almost 12% in the region Marche. Other regions show smaller changes, but for the majority of them, there was an increase in tourism intensity, suggesting a positive evolution, on average, of the presence of tourists in Italy in the 2011–2018 period. Quite interestingly, the regional disparities in tourism intensity have increased in the investigated period since the variance of the distribution of regional tourism intensity increased by about 35% between 2011 and 2018.

Figure 3 focuses on the evolution of local welfare expenditure for disability per eligible inhabitant. The absolute levels of expenditure display relevant differences among regions, ranging between about 100 euros per eligible inhabitant in Aosta Valley in 2018 and more than 12,000 euros per eligible inhabitant in Friuli-Venezia Giulia and Trentino Alto Adige in the same year. Looking at the evolution of the expenditure at the local level per eligible inhabitant, we note a quite relevant increase between 2011 and 2018 in relative terms. The greatest increases have taken place in Molise (about 95% more) and Campania (almost 80% more). Conversely, the greatest decrease in expenditure per inhabitant has been determined in Aosta Valley (about 67% less). On average, however, local welfare expenditure for disability per eligible inhabitant has increased in the majority of Italian regions. In addition, based on the mentioned evolution, we stress that territorial inequality in local welfare expenditure for disability per eligible inhabitant has decreased over time since the variance of the related distribution decreased by about 20%.

Finally, the relevant regional differences that emerged in the evolution of welfare expenditure for disability are somehow confirmed when looking at figures for the elderly population and total welfare expenditure (Figs. 5 and 6 in the Appendix).

3 Empirical Model

Referring to a kind of complementary approach with respect to that of considering the tourism flows between pairs of provinces, and therefore the estimation of the flows taking place between the various connections, this paper focuses on the total incoming tourism flow of a single province using its own aggregated variables as determinants. In doing so, we can better study the influence of public authorities' commitment to the needs and well-being of the disabled and the elderly while controlling for other macroeconomic variables affecting tourism. The econometric specification considered can be summarized as follows:

$$\text{tourism}_{i,t} = \alpha + \text{commitment}_{i,t} + X_{i,t}\gamma + \eta_t + \varepsilon_{i,t} \tag{1}$$

where X is a vector containing factors that, apart from allowing us to control for scale effects, help us to explain variability in the dependent variable. In particular, we focus on two main determinants of tourism flows, namely attractiveness, and accessibility. The equation ends with time dummies and an idiosyncratic error term.

As explained above, commitment is a latent unobserved variable. As our preferred choice, we rely on the municipal expenditure per disabled and elderly. While this measure is probably the most obvious and direct to signal the sensibility of a public authority toward the well-being of the disabled and the elderly, in the subsequent section, we will also consider other measures.

To estimate this equation, we consider two simple methods. As a baseline, we consider the pooled-OLS (POLS), with standard errors corrected for the likely correlation between observations of the same province in different years. Secondly, we consider a more flexible variation of the standard POLS by allowing for macro-area fixed effects and time trends (FETT). The need of adopting the FETT over the Italian macro-areas (North, Centre, and South) rather than over the regions is motivated by the fact that the latter option makes the number of independent variables increase above the number of province-clusters preventing us, as a consequence, from obtaining clustering-corrected standard errors. Furthermore, as seen in the previous section, the cross-sectional heterogeneity among the main variables of interest, in particular those pertaining to the welfare expenditure, displays a clear macro-regional pattern, with provinces in the North and the Centre recording significatively higher values of expenditure per eligible inhabitant than those in the South, though some variability, at a lower extent, is also found at the regional level.

We opt for the most straightforward linear specification over other common alternatives such as the log-linear and the log-log specifications because the distribution of the residuals obtained using this method already shows a bell-shaped curve.

4 Results

4.1 Main Results

Table 3 reports the main results from the estimation of the empirical model. While the dependent variable is always the number of nights spent in hotels and other accommodation (*tourism_presences*), the variable of interest is the expenditure for disabled over the number of disabled inhabitants (*expt_disabled*; col. I), expenditure for elderly over the number of elderly inhabitants (*expt_elderly*, col. II), total expenditure over the number of eligible inhabitants (*expt_all*, col. III).

All estimated equations include: (1) the sum of state and non-state museums as a measure of attractiveness; (2) dummies for the presence of an airport, high-speed rail, and port as measures of accessibility; (3) population and population density to control for scale and congestion effects; and, finally, (4) time dummies to control for common shocks. Columns IV to VI consider the same specifications of columns I–III with the only difference that the standard POLS estimator is in this case enriched with macro-area FETT. These additional controls allow to better account both for

Table 3 Impact of measures of commitment to the well-being of the disabled and the elderly on tourism

	(1)	(2)	(3)	(4)	(5)	(6)
expt_disabled	.4549**			.4219*		
	{0.208}			{0.227}		
expt_elderly		.4156***			.4042**	
		{0.145}			{0.156}	
expt_all			.7058**			.6507*
			{0.297}			{0.348}
population	.536***	.5991***	.6269***	.5977***	.6807***	.6734***
	{0.200}	{0.190}	{0.194}	{0.214}	{0.203}	{0.206}
density	−.06859	−.05859	−.08656	−.1176	−.1176	−.1269
	{0.095}	{0.078}	{0.093}	{0.102}	{0.086}	{0.100}
museum	.6351***	.4768**	.5039***	.4778*	.287	.3767
	{0.205}	{0.192}	{0.190}	{0.267}	{0.251}	{0.239}
dummy_airport	.09088	.09266	.08122	.1056	.1091	.0957
	{0.105}	{0.104}	{0.104}	{0.105}	{0.105}	{0.106}
dummy_port	.05211	.05541	.03584	.07357	.07886	.05539
	{0.080}	{0.076}	{0.080}	{0.086}	{0.082}	{0.089}
dummy_hsr	−.03383	−.03229	−.04301	−.02772	−.02609	−.03735
	{0.040}	{0.036}	{0.042}	{0.041}	{0.036}	{0.043}
N	864	864	864	864	864	864

Note: Elasticities implied by estimated parameter values evaluated at the mean of the independent variables. With all methods and specifications, time dummies are included and standard errors. reported in parenthesis, account for potential clustering of the same-province observations
*, and *** denote coefficients are significant at 10%, and 1%, respectively

(1) unobserved heterogeneity in fixed characteristics of the broader areas of the country and (2) asymmetric response to macroeconomic shocks. In the results tables, we report elasticities rather than the parameter values to make easier the interpretation of results in terms of their economic importance.

The main hypothesis in this paper, namely that the commitment of a local administration toward the needs and well-being of the disabled and the elderly may have beneficial effects on tourism, finds empirical support as the expenditure variables are all statistically significant. The effect on tourism appears economically important as the elasticity ranges between 0.40 and 0.70, depending on the recipient category and specification employed. In particular, increasing expenditure toward the disabled by 1 percentage point increases average provincial tourist flows by 0.45%. Moreover, we observe a larger elasticity in the case of expenditures benefiting the disabled (*expt_disabled*) rather than the elderly (*expt_elderly*). An even larger effect is observed when we focus on the broader welfare expenditure measure (*expt_all*). In this case, a 1% increase in welfare expenditure is associated with 0.71% more tourists in the province. This is not surprising as the category of the elderly is the one which is less likely to travel for tourism with respect to the others. Comparing results from the two methods employed, we find that the estimated coefficients are very similar and the most conservative estimate of the effect of a 1% increase in local public expenditure toward disability on tourist presences still accounts for 0.42%.

Tourism appears positively and statistically significantly associated with *museum*, in particular with the POLS, while it does not with the presence of airports, high-speed rails, and ports. We interpret the former result as jointly a confirmation that the measure can correctly capture the effect of attractiveness on tourism flows and, at the same time, the important role played by this factor in such a model, as suggested by the high value of the estimated elasticity. The somewhat surprising statistical insignificance of the accessibility variables does not allow us to clarify whether this hypothesis should be checked using more informative variables or whether the provincial differences observed in terms of accessibility are not large enough to affect tourism flows.

4.2 Additional Results and Robustness Checks

While the expenditure variables have undoubtedly merits, they also present some limitations. As explained in Sect. 2, *expt_disabled* is a measure of disability restricted to the population below the age of 65, leaving open the question of whether these results can be extended to older people with disabilities. Moreover, not distinguishing between the elderly with disability and the elderly without disability, the *expt_elderly* variable includes individuals with very heterogeneous needs. It is likely that a large share of the elderly does not receive any welfare benefit, causing the average expenditure to be significantly lower than that for the disabled. To overcome these problems, we identify alternative measures capturing the sensibility of a local administration toward the well-being of the disabled and the elderly. Table 4 reports results obtained after replacing the expenditure for the disabled variable with a synthetic score providing information on the diffusion and the degree of completeness of barrier-free schools (*school_services*), while the expenditure for the elderly was replaced by the percentage of elderly people receiving home care (*homecare_elderly*), both with POLS and the macro-area FETT. The results show that *school_services* is never statistically significant, while *homecare_elderly* appears to significantly affect tourism flows (although in one of the two specifications, the coefficient is significant only at a 10% confidence level). Moreover, the estimated elasticity is very similar to that previously obtained using the expenditure variable. The nonsignificant coefficient on *school_services* may originate from the fact that local administrations typically enjoy more degrees of freedom on local welfare measures, and therefore it may be considered a too noisy signal of local sensibility by the prospective tourists.

While accessibility by itself does not appear to play a crucial role in our data, we cannot exclude that it may play a multiplicative effect in combination with the commitment variables. To check for this hypothesis, we augment the specifications whose results are reported in Tables 3 and 4 with the interaction between the commitment measures and, in turn, each accessibility dummy. For the ease of brevity and simplicity, Table 5 only reports the elasticities of the interaction term and its clustering-corrected standard error obtained using both the POLS and the macro-area FETT. Moreover, the table omits the interaction terms with dummies for high-speed rail stations and ports because they never turned out to be statistically significant. On the contrary, the presence of an airport seems to play a multiplicative (positive) role on tourism flows together with both *expt_disabled* and *expt_elderly*, as well as with the *homecare_elderly* variable and weakly with *school_services*. The multiplicative effect appears larger for the disabled than for the elderly. In the case of *expt_all*, although the elasticity value is large, it is not significant because more imprecisely estimated. At a closer look, the significant effect of the interaction terms may not be very surprising, given the fact that the availability of facilities and personnel dedicated to people with disabilities is a specific requirement for the operativity of airports and airline companies, a requirement less stringent for trains and ships, the other two means of public transport considered.

Other variations related to the model—e.g., selection of the controls or definition of the variables—as well as to the data, provide similar results to those previously reported. More specifically, the alternative estimates included: (1) replacing the macro-area FETT with the regional FETT without standard errors corrected for clustering; (2) replacing the macro-area FETT with the regional fixed effects with standard errors corrected for clustering; (3) replacing the overnight stays with the per-capita overnight stays (*tourism_intensity*) as the dependent variable; (4) dropping all Sardinia observations to draw results from a balanced panel; (5) distinguishing between state and non-state museums and including in addition or substitution the number of recorded museum circuits.

Tourism Flows in Italy: The Role of Local Public Policies Toward Disability 65

Table 4 Impact of alternative measures of commitment to the well-being of the disabled and the elderly on tourism

	(1)	(2)	(3)	(4)
school_services	1.386		.1907	
	{0.985}		{0.924}	
homecare_elderly		.4498*		.5262**
		{0.236}		{0.243}
population	.3796*	.4339**	.4481*	.5814***
	{0.220}	{0.192}	{0.255}	{0.197}
density	.00782	.02139	−.05639	−.07116
	{0.083}	{0.080}	{0.096}	{0.084}
museum	.8435***	.7717***	.6762*	.4391
	{0.294}	{0.243}	{0.375}	{0.292}
dummy_airport	.1136	.1146	.1227	.1416
	{0.111}	{0.107}	{0.107}	{0.106}
dummy_port	.04533	.05583	.07279	.09381
	{0.084}	{0.080}	{0.088}	{0.084}
dummy_hsr	−.03862	−.03579	−.02948	−.02537
	{0.042}	{0.039}	{0.043}	{0.039}
N	864	762	864	762

Note: Elasticities implied by estimated parameter values evaluated at the mean of the independent variables. With all methods and specifications, time dummies are included and standard errors, reported in parenthesis, account for potential clustering of the same-province observations
*, **, and *** denote coefficients are significant at 10%, 5%, and 1%, respectively

Table 5 Impact of interactions between air-transport availability and welfare expenditure on tourism

	(1)	(2)
expt_disabled * airport	.2305*	.2321*
	{0.129}	{0.133}
expt_elderly * airport	.1743***	.1828***
	{0.042}	{0.037}
expt_all * airport	.277	.2913
	{0.179}	{0.184}
school_services * airport	1.009	1.130*
	{0.637}	{0.668}
homecare_elderly * airport	.3755***	.3558***
	{0.115}	{0.120}

Note: Selected elasticities implied by estimated parameter values evaluated at the mean of the independent variables. With all methods and specifications, time dummies are included and standard errors, reported in parenthesis, account for potential clustering of the same-province observations
*, and *** denote coefficients are significant at 10%, and 1%, respectively

5 Discussions and Conclusion

To the extent that the level and the quality of development and well-being in a society can be inferred by the way its weakest members are treated, removing barriers and enhancing accessibility at all levels for people with disabilities is undoubtedly an important policy goal toward a more inclusive and virtuous society. A salient aspect of the above is represented by the promotion of tourism flows of the disabled, developing an environment in which those individuals and their caregivers may interact easily (and possibly autonomously) as much as possible. This, in turn, almost certainly translates into increased economic growth opportunities both at the local and national levels. In this respect, the European Union is committed to increasing tourism accessibility through several actions aimed at increasing the travel opportunities for people with disabilities, promoting social inclusion, and improving the skills of staff in the tourism industry (e.g., the EU Regulation (EC) No. 1107/2006).

In this chapter, we provide preliminary evidence on the impact of local public authorities' increased sensibility toward the needs of people with disabilities and the elderly on tourism flows. Based on data for Italian provinces, we proxied policymakers' sensibility with the local welfare expenditure on services for the disabled and found a positive and significant effect on tourism. These findings are confirmed if we broaden the analysis to other weak members of the society, such as the elderly or the whole set of the eligible population of welfare policies. Moreover, the availability of air transport facilities seems to have a positive multiplicative effect.

The analysis in the present chapter, thus, confirms the beneficial effects of fostering participation and inclusion of people with disabilities across all aspects of living, including leisure time. Furthermore, those beneficial effects seem to extend beyond the disabled people per se, as the total level of tourism flows within the province is positively affected, providing an insight of positive spillover effects of the implementation and enforcement of policies addressed to the inclusion of the disabled for the society as a whole. However, the positive and significant effects on tourism are found with respect to variables pertaining to general inclusion policies, and we do not have data to investigate a single particular domain (such as public transport accessibility for the disabled). Indeed, the evidence points toward some degree of complementarity between a measure of public transport availability accessibility and the other policy measures. We interpret those results as a preliminary indication that greater sensitivity, attention, and commitment of an administration and a community, besides being certainly fair and advisable, can provide benefits in terms of an enhanced ability to attract tourists and therefore improving local economic prospects. Moreover, we do not interpret those results as an indication of simply increasing public expenditure on welfare tout court, rather as a sign that disability inherently affects all aspects of life and, since those aspects are all interconnected, the disabled will not be able to benefit fully from improvements in one domain if the others remain hardly accessible. Thus, effective public policy measures should be designed to acknowledge these complementarities, or, even better, the needs of people with disabilities should consistently permeate the standard general policymaking ("mainstreaming," WHO, 2011).

The effort undertaken in this chapter is just preliminary given the multiple facets that the relation between disability and tourism flows involve, not least because the analysis is constrained along several dimensions. First and foremost, there is a data availability issue: more detailed policy implications could be inferred if only more data on policymaking in this particular sector had been available. The need for more detailed monitoring of disability, and a correspondingly good-quality data collection, was already recognized at the utmost international level by the WHO as one of the explicit objectives of its Global Disability Action Plan 2014–2021 (WHO, 2015) and has received a first response at international level with the Model Disability Survey, developed in 2016. However, the need for more detailed and disaggregated data at the subnational level is still remarkable.

Related to what just stated is the limit concerning transport accessibility proxies. In this work, we captured only the availability of different means of transport in general, with no direct link to the disability domain. Furthermore, we have to acknowledge that people with disabilities may primarily travel using private means of transport (in particular for short transfers). Moreover, our dummies do not provide any information on the level of disabled-friendly infrastructure available for the different means of public transport.

One of the present study's main contributions is its focus on the public policy aspect of the relationship between disability and tourism. However, it is undisputed that the enhancement of tourism flows of people with disabilities implies a complementary commitment of all agents in the market, both in the public and the private sector. Disabled people need to find appropriate solutions to their specific needs in terms of public transport as well as other public sector spheres (barrier-free environments in tourism attractions, public information, and communication), but those must be complementary to corresponding satisfying solutions in the private sector facilities they may employ (accommodations, restaurants, private information, and communication). More in general, a successful and fulfilling tourism experience for people with disabilities should entail the removal (or at least the reduction) of all social and environmental barriers. We leave the comprehensive evaluation of the impact of those aspects taken together to future research.

Acknowledgments The usual disclaimer applies. All authors contributed equally to each section of the manuscript.

Appendix (Figs. 4, 5, and 6)

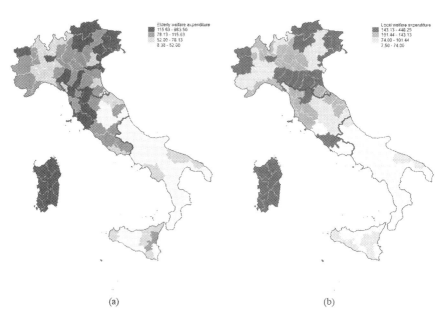

Fig. 4 Spatial distribution of variables of interest across Italian provinces (average values across the time span under consideration). *Note:* Panel (**a**) refers to welfare expenditure toward the elderly population, panel (**b**) depicts total local welfare expenditure. All expenditure figures are expressed in per-capita terms with respect to the eligible population

Tourism Flows in Italy: The Role of Local Public Policies Toward Disability 69

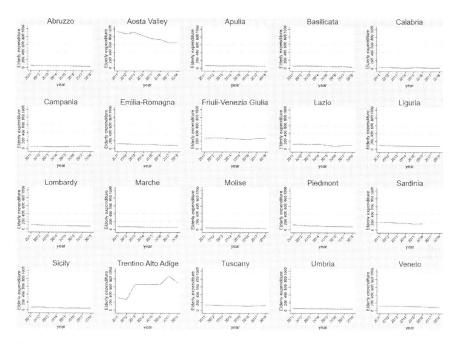

Fig. 5 Evolution of local welfare expenditure for the elderly per eligible inhabitant, 2011–2018. *Note*: Local per-capita expenditure (euro per eligible inhabitant) in welfare services for elderly residents by Region over time. For comments, see main text

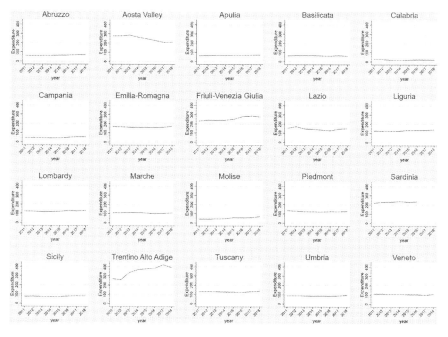

Fig. 6 Evolution of local welfare expenditure per eligible inhabitant, 2011–2018. *Note*: Total local per-capita expenditure (euro per eligible inhabitant) in social services by Region over time. For comments, see main text

References

Addabbo, T., Sarti, E., & Sciulli, D. (2016). Disability and life satisfaction in Italy. *Applied Research in Quality of Life, 11*, 925–954.

Agovino, M., Casaccia, M., Garofalo, A., & Marchesano, K. (2017). Tourism and disability in Italy. Limits and opportunities. *Tourism Management Perspective, 23*, 58–67.

Agovino, M., Parodi, G., & Sciulli, D. (2020). *Aspetti socioeconomici della disabilità: lavoro, reddito e politiche.* Giappichelli Editore.

Aitchison, C. (2003). From leisure and disability to disability leisure: Developing data, definitions and discourses. *Disability & Society, 18*(7), 955–969.

Avis, A. H., Card, J. A., & Cole, S. (2005). Accessibility and attitudinal barriers encountered by travelers with physical disabilities. *Tourism Review International, 8*(3), 239–248.

Bizjak, B., Knežević, M., & Cvetrežnik, S. (2011). Attitude change towards guests with disabilities. Reflections from tourism students. *Annals of Tourism Research, 38*(3), 842–857.

Chang, Y. C., & Chen, C. F. (2012). Meeting the needs of disabled air passengers: Factors that facilitate help from airlines and airports. *Tourism Management, 33*, 529–536.

Darcy, S. (2006). *Setting a research agenda for accessible tourism.* University of Queensland: Sustainable Tourism, CRC.

Darcy, S. (2010). Inherent complexity: Disability, accessible tourism and accommodation information preferences. *Tourism Management, 31*(6), 816–826.

Domínguez, T., Fraiz, J. A., & Alén, E. (2013). Economic profitability of accessible tourism for the tourism sector in Spain. *Tourism Economics, 19*(6), 1385–1399.

Eichhorn, V., Miller, G., Michopoulou, E., & Buhalis, D. (2008). Enabling access to tourism through information schemes? *Annals of Tourism Research, 35*(1), 189–210.

Eichhorn, V., Miller, G., & Tribe, J. (2013). Tourism: A site of resistance strategies of individuals with a disability. *Annals of Tourism Research, 43*, 578–600.

Ells, C. (2001). Lessons about autonomy from the experience of disability. *Social Theory & Practice, 27*(4), 599–615.

Figueiredo, E., Eusébio, C., & Kastenholz, E. (2012). How *diverse* are tourists with disabilities? A pilot study on accessible leisure tourism experiences in Portugal. *International Journal of Tourism Research, 14*(6), 531–550.

Folino, B. (1999). *Taxis and people with a disability: Issues for government and industry.* Disability Council of NSW.

Grady, J., & Ohlin, J. B. (2009). Equal access to hospitality services for guests with mobility impairments under the Americans with Disabilities Act: Implications for the hospitality industry. *International Journal of Hospital Management, 28*(1), 161–169.

Huh, C., & Singh, A. J. (2007). Families travelling with a disabled member: Analysing the potential of an emerging niche market segment. *Tourism and Hospitality Research, 7*(3/4), 212–229.

Kastenholz, E., Eusébio, C., & Figueiredo, E. (2015). Contributions of tourism to social inclusion of persons with disability. *Disabil Soc, 30*(8), 1259–1281.

McCabe, S. (2009). Who needs a holiday? Evaluating social tourism. *Annals of Tourism Research, 36*(4), 667–688.

McCabe, S., Joldersma, T., & Li, C. (2010). Understanding the benefits of social tourism: Linking participation to subjective well-being and quality of life. *International Journal of Tourism Research, 12*, 761–773.

Minnaert, L., Maitland, R., & Miller, G. (2009). Tourism and social policy. The value of social tourism. *Annals of Tourism Research, 36*(2), 316–334.

Naniopoulos, A., Tsalis, P., & Nalmpantis, D. (2016). An effort to develop accessible tourism in Greece and Turkey: The MEDRA project approach. *Journal of Tourism Future, 2*(1), 56–70.

OECD. (2010). *Employment outlook: Moving beyond the jobs crisis.* OECD.

Özogul, G., & Baran, G. G. (2016). Accessible tourism: The golden key in the future for the specialized travel agencies. *Journal of Tourism Future, 2*(1), 79–87.

Pagán, R. (2012). Time allocation in tourism for people with disabilities. *Annals of Tourism Research, 39*(3), 1514–1537.

Small, J., Darcy, S., & Packer, T. (2012). The embodied tourist experiences of people with vision impairment: Management implications beyond the visual gaze. *Tourism Management, 33,* 941–950.

UN. (2006). *Convention on the rights of persons with disabilities.* United Nations.

UNWTO. (2015). *Manual of accessible tourism for all: Public partnership and good practices.* World Tourism Organization (UNWTO) and Fundación ACS.

WHO. (2001). *International classification of functioning, disability and health.* World Health Organization.

WHO. (2011). *World report on disability.* World Health Organization.

WHO. (2015). *WHO global disability action plan 2014-2021. Better health for all people with disability.* World Health Organization.

WHO (2020). *Disability and health.* https://www.who.int/news-room/fact-sheets/detail/disability-and-health. Accessed 15 Apr 2021.

Accessibility of Cultural Sites for Disabled People: Some Preliminary Evidence from Sicily

Maria Daniela Giammanco, Lara Gitto, and Ferdinando Ofria

1 Introduction

In the past years, the EU Disability Strategy 2010–2020, developed within the Employment, Social Affairs & Inclusion DG initiatives, aims at realizing a barrier-free Europe in order to empower people with disabilities to participate fully in society.

The attention to disability had been reflected in other interventions in national legislation.

In the UK, two laws have provided a definition of disability: the Equality Act 2010[1] and, before, the Disability Discrimination Act 1995.[2] According to them, a person has a disability if several conditions coexist. First of all, there has to be a physical or mental impairment. Secondly, such impairment must have a substantial and long-term adverse effect on the person's ability to carry out normal day-to-day activities.

This definition may cover both fluctuating and permanent conditions, such as rheumatoid arthritis, chronic fatigue syndrome-myalgic encephalitis (CFS-ME) (Pheby et al., 2021), HIV, cancer (Linebaugh, 2021), neurological or progressive

---

[1] https://www.gov.uk/

[2] https://www.legislation.gov.uk/ukpga/1995/50/contents

M. D. Giammanco
Department of Political and Social Sciences, University of Catania, Catania, Italy
e-mail: maria.giammanco@unict.it

L. Gitto
Department of Economics, University of Messina, Messina, Italy
e-mail: Lara.Gitto@unime.it

F. Ofria (✉)
Department of Economics, University of Messina, Messina, Italy
e-mail: ofriaf@unime.it

© The Author(s), under exclusive license to Springer Nature Switzerland AG 2022
T. Abbate et al. (eds.), *Tourism and Disability*, Tourism on the Verge,
https://doi.org/10.1007/978-3-030-93612-9_5

conditions as epilepsy, multiple sclerosis, even if the person is not currently experiencing any adverse effects (Gitto, 2017), muscular dystrophy, and forms of dementia. A range of conditions are treated as a disability as long they have a substantial and long-term impact on the ability to carry out normal day-to-day activities. Therefore, causes of disability may include sensory impairments, such as those affecting sight or hearing (Loi & Kong, 2017); organ-specific conditions, including respiratory conditions such as asthma; cardiovascular diseases, including heart disease (Laurence, 2021); developmental conditions, such as autism (Proulx, 2020) and hyperactivity disorder; and even mental health conditions such as anxiety, phobias, depression,[3] and schizophrenia.[4]

The guidance produced by the above-mentioned sources cannot provide an exhaustive list of conditions that qualify as impairments, as some disabilities could be caused by substance addiction or other dependencies.[5]

According to the World Health Organization (WHO), 6–10% of the population of Europe experience disability: this means that approximately 135 million individuals suffer from physical and/or mental impairment with adverse and long-term impacts on their lives. Due to population aging and the upsurge of non-communicable diseases, sometimes caused by injuries, this number is set to increase in the future[6] (Brenna & Gitto, 2016; Verropoulou & Tsimbos, 2017).

Eurostat Data, referring to 2014 (last update), show that the shares of people declaring to have some physical and sensory functional limitations are 36.6% of the total Italian population (36.7% of the total population of the EU-28); 57.6% of the 65–74 years old population (same percentage in EU-28) and 83.3% of adults aged 75 years or more (79.2% in Europe).[7] Though the figures relating to the whole EU-28 are similar, in 2014, Italy had the highest percentages of people suffering from walking impairments in all age groups.

The preamble of the Convention on the Rights of Persons with Disabilities (United Nations, New York, 13 December 2006,[8] acknowledges the relevance of

---

[3] Depression is considered a psychiatric disability under the American Disabilities Act (ADA). It is a significant mood disorder that may interfere with daily activities, including the ability to work.

[4] Someone who is no longer disabled, but who met the requirements of the definition in the past, may still be covered (for example, someone who is in remission from a chronic condition).

[5] See: *Should Drug Addiction be Considered a Disability?* https://www.hr-dp.org/contents/205.

[6] https://www.euro.who.int/en/health-topics/Life-stages/disability-and-rehabilitation/areas-of-work/disability. Last accessed: 22 January 2021

[7] https://appsso.eurostat.ec.europa.eu/nui/submitViewTableAction.do, last accessed 21 January 2021. It also emerges from Eurostat data that in 2014 10.2% of the Italian adult population (aged 15 years or more) had some sort of severe physical and sensory functional limitations: 2.0% suffered from visual impairments; 4,1% from hearing impairment; 7.2% from walking impairment. These percentages increase but not dramatically, if only 65–74 years old people are considered: 14.6% had some severe impairment; 2.2% a visual impairment; 5.4% a hearing impairment; 9.7% a walking impairment. The increase is considerable if only people aged 75 or over are taken into account: 44.9% had some severe impairment; 8.8% a visual impairment; 18.9% a hearing impairment; 36.6% a walking impairment.

[8] https://www.un.org/disabilities/documents/convention/convoptprot-e.pdf

an accessible social, economic, and cultural setting in order to empower disabled people to thoroughly experience their unalienable rights and primary liberties. Article 30 of the Convention, "*Participation in cultural life, recreation, leisure and sport*," states that:

> 1. States Parties recognize the right of persons with disabilities to take part on an equal basis with others in cultural life and shall take all appropriate measures to ensure that persons with disabilities: . . . Enjoy access to places for cultural performances or services, such as theatres, museums, cinemas, libraries and tourism services, and, as far as possible, enjoy access to monuments and sites of national cultural importance.
>
> 5. With a view to enabling persons with disabilities to participate on an equal basis with others in recreational, leisure and sporting activities, States Parties shall take appropriate measures:(c) To ensure that persons with disabilities have access to sporting, recreational and tourism venues.

Tourism is envisaged as one of the means to achieve the full development of all individuals, whether in full health or suffering from disabilities, and the United Nations call States Parties to action to develop accessible tourism. Given the high and growing numbers of disabled people all over the world, this suggests that the attention to accessible tourism—which must be driven by the quest to guarantee basic human rights to all—is also relevant for the profit-oriented tourism sector. The healthy development of the tourism industry requires consideration of all the stakeholders involved.

While much academic attention has been given to major tourist markets and other principal stakeholder groups, such as businesses and general tourists, tourism/hospitality studies on the people with disabilities market are relatively more uncoordinated and fragmented (Loi & Kong, 2017).

This literature suggests that the information required to enable different categories of disabled persons to access and use tourism facilities will vary greatly depending not only on the type of disability but also on the way this information is designed and managed (Ray & Ryder, 2003; WHO, 2016; Williams et al., 2006).

When a tourist with a disability chooses her/his travel options and the place to visit, she/he has a limited set of choices, significantly smaller than the choice set available to non-disabled people. As far as accessibility is concerned, she/he does not address the classic trade-off characterized by an increase in the amount of an asset in view of reducing another one to remain on the same indifference curve. This is because, in the case of disability, accessibility cannot be compensated with another options asset. For example, a disabled tourist will not be able to visit cultural institutions if such sites are not made accessible (e.g., by providing devoted parking spaces; specific routes with no ramps or stairs; audio descriptions) or if they require personal assistance to be visited (unless this assistance is provided on-site). Moreover, she/he must also have relevant information concerning accessibility.

For this reason, the need for competent operators for each type of disability underpins the functioning of this tourism market segment (Burns et al., 2009; Figueiredo et al., 2012).

As far as accessibility for a wheelchair user is concerned, it is self-evident that the absence of wheelchair-accessible routes is the major barrier preventing a disabled visitor from enjoying tourist venues. It is less evident, but no less important, that one of the major obstacles to accessibility is the lack of information, defined in the literature as "information barrier" (Eichhorn et al., 2008) or "interactive barrier" (Smith, 1987). The information allows the disabled to define her/his choice set to operate a fully informed choice. It is, therefore, essential to provide reliable and timely data on the accessibility conditions at the destination (Darcy, 1998; Shi et al., 2012).

In Sicily, there is a lack of detailed information concerning the accessibility to tourist/cultural sites; this can be explained by the absence of a Regional Plan devoted to disability. Yet, a detailed data collection concerning accessibility is a necessary, prior requirement to corrective and ameliorative actions.[9]

The aim of our study is to use the scanty information drawn from surveys carried out yearly by the *Assessorato Regionale per i beni culturali e ambientali*—the local authority for the promotion and maintenance of cultural goods to shed some light on the correlation between physical and informational accessibility in 78 Sicilian cultural sites and the demand of disabled people for accessing such sites.

As a rough proxy for the demand of people with disabilities, we suggest using the ratio of free tickets on the total tickets issued by each specific tourist site. We are well aware that this is a coarse criterion, as free tickets are granted to people under 18, and since we are using annual data (the only ones available), we are not able to adjust for seasonality.

Nevertheless, a positive correlation between free tickets and physical and information accessibility would suggest a sensitivity to a barrier-free environment in the demand of disabled people as this would allow them to fully or partially enjoy the venue.

We believe that this analysis will offer a blurred, but not distorted, image of the phenomenon, and we also believe that such a picture is better than having no image at all.

The contribution is organized as follows: the next section will describe the normative context within which the issue of accessibility can be framed, mentioning both international, national, and local legislation. Then, the dataset built for the present analysis and the resulting evidence will be described. Insights for deepening the analysis, with a view to encouraging the draft of policy guidelines on the accessibility to cultural institutions, will conclude the present work.

---

[9] In spite of the great potential of Sicily, efforts still have to be done to fulfil the assistance needs of disabled tourists—through appropriate care or dedicated touristic structures (see: Lo Bue et al., 2020).

2 The Institutional Setting. The "State of the Art" Looking at the Current Situation

The United Nations Convention on the Rights of Persons with Disabilities (UNCRPD), which entered into force in the EU in 2010, is the first human rights convention ratified by the EU.[10]

This Convention adopts a broad categorization of *disabled subjects*, reaffirming that all persons with every type of disability must fully enjoy human rights and fundamental freedoms. It clarifies how all categories of rights apply to persons with disabilities and identifies intervention areas where ameliorative actions must be taken to allow persons with disabilities to effectively exercise their rights. It also identifies areas where such rights have been so openly violated that an assertive, protective action is called for.

The European disability strategy 2010–2020 builds upon the UNCRPD and supports all Member States in its implementation. It also complements the EU's strategy for smart, sustainable, and inclusive growth (so Called "Europe 2020") and the European Charter of Fundamental Rights, stemming from the Lisbon Treaty.[11]

The European disability strategy 2010–2020 describes a set of objectives and actions for the implementation of the disability policy in Europe. It focuses on eight priority areas, including the following: *Accessibility*—ensuring that people with disabilities have access to goods, services, and assistive devices; *Participation*—ensuring that people with disabilities can exercise all their fundamental rights as European citizens; *Equality*—ensuring that policies promoting equality are implemented (both at EU and national level); *External action*—promoting the rights of people with disabilities at an international level. The European disability strategy has led to various initiatives: the *European Accessibility Act*,[12] which sets accessibility requirements for products and services and the Regulations on the Rights of Passengers with reduced mobility; the EU disability card[13] project, which makes it easier for people with disabilities to travel across these Member States. The latter has been piloted in 8 Member States: Belgium, Cyprus, Estonia, Finland, Italy,[14] Malta, Romania, and Slovenia.

The European Accessibility Act[15] aims at improving the functioning of the internal market for accessible products and services by removing barriers created by differing rules among Member States. Persons with disabilities and elderly people will benefit from: (a) more accessible products and services in the market; (b) more

---

[10] https://ec.europa.eu/social/main.jsp?catId=89 & furtherNews=yes & newsId=9894 & langId=en.

[11] https://eur-lex.europa.eu/legal-content/EN/TXT/?uri=LEGISSUM%3Aem0047.

[12] https://eur-lex.europa.eu/legal-content/EN/TXT/?uri=COM:2015:0615:FIN.

[13] https://ec.europa.eu/social/main.jsp?catId=1139 & langId=en.

[14] See: http://www.disabilitycard.it/files/sintesi-dati.pdf

[15] https://eur-lex.europa.eu/legal-content/EN/TXT/?uri=CELEX%3A32019L0882.

competitive prices; (c) fewer barriers when accessing transport, education, and an open labor market; (d) more jobs available where accessibility expertise is needed.

The European Accessibility Act covers products and services of major importance for persons with disabilities, which are not equally accessible across the EU countries. They are products and services related to air, bus, rail, and waterborne passenger transport.

The EU disability card helps people with disabilities to travel more easily between EU countries; with this aim, the EU is developing a voluntary system of mutual recognition of disability status and some associated benefits based on the EU disability card.

Currently, there is no mutual recognition of a disability status between the EU Member States. This causes problems for people with disabilities, as their national disability cards might not be recognized in the other Member States. The EU disability card ensures equal access to benefits across borders for people with disabilities, mainly in the fields of culture, leisure, sport, and transport. The card is mutually recognized between EU countries participating in the system on a voluntary basis. The pilot use of the card was launched in February 2016 in a group of eight EU countries: Belgium, Cyprus, Estonia, Finland, Italy,[16] Malta, Romania, and Slovenia. The card does not change national eligibility criteria or rules. Member States retain their discretion to decide who is eligible to receive the Card based on their national definition of disability and to determine the issuing procedure.

In Italy, the first important step in the creation of accessible environments was taken with Law No. 13/89 and Ministerial Decree 236/86, whose objective was the removal or overcoming of architectural barriers in buildings.

Another step was to support disabled tourists financially by providing preferential treatment in the form of free admission or reduced entrance fee (D.M. 23/12/2014).[17]

Recently, Law No. 145/2018 (Budget Law, 2019) established the EU disability card. This law, ratifying the UNCRPD, also establishes a Fund for the accessibility and mobility of people with disabilities at the Italian Ministry of Infrastructure and Transport. In 2019 a budget of 5 million euros was destined for interventions aimed at the technological innovation of structures, markings, and signs for the mobility of people with disabilities. Significant measures in favor of the mobility of disabled persons can be found in Law No. 178/20 (Budget Law, 2021).[18]

The Sicilian Region, endowed with Special Statute, has ratified the UNCRPD with Law No. 10/2019, but it has not yet formulated an organic law on disability.[19]

---

[16] See: http://www.disabilitycard.it/files/sintesi-dati.pdf

[17] In Italy, admission to public museums, monuments, galleries, and archeological areas is free for all people under the age of 18 belonging to the European Union. Admission is also free for disabled people and their accompanying person (a family member or a certified care-giver, member of social or health assistance services).

[18] http://www.anffas.net/dld/files/MISURE%20DELLA%20LEGGE%20DI%20BILANCIO% 202021%20DI%20INTERESSE%20PER%20LE%20PERSONE%20CON%20DISABILITA%20 LORO%20FAMILIARI%20E%20ASSOCIAZIONI.pdf

[19] https://www.superando.it/2020/10/09/ma-esiste-in-sicilia-una-programmazione-sulla-disabilita/

Hence, the development of a wide range of projects aimed at creating and/or strengthening accessible tourism supply in Sicily is still underway.

Not only would these projects promote equity by allowing disabled people to enjoy culture at a national and European level, but they would also make the Sicilian cultural heritage available to a group of stakeholders too often neglected. This would generate a positive impact on the regional economy, especially in those areas that are better equipped from the tourist-cultural point of view (Gitto, 2021).

3 Accessibility of Cultural Sites: Some Preliminary Evidence from Sicily

Among the Italian regions enjoying significant tourist flows, Sicily stands out for some peculiarities: first of all, the exceptional concentration of historical and archeological sites, probably the largest in the Mediterranean. As noted in previous studies (Musumeci, 2000) and in various regulatory projects, in Sicilian urban centers, there are as many as 800 sites of historical relevance and 12,000 of architectural interest; Sicily also boasts 256 museums, 334 municipal historical archives, and around 1700 libraries.

Whether disabled people can enjoy such a bountiful treasure of tourist sites depends on their *physical* accessibility. Certain types of cultural/tourist sites might be considered more or less accessible per se. For example, an archeological site might be more difficult to visit than a museum. Nevertheless, we believe the *availability of information* on *accessibility*, i.e., an indication of whether there is a barrier-free environment, to be a major attractor for people with some physical impairment. For this reason, we investigate the pairwise correlations between a proxy for the demand for tourist sites of disabled people and the *physical* characteristic of the tourist site, the presence of a dedicated website, the availability of information on the web, information concerning parking availability, other kinds of information useful for disabled tourists, respectively.

Data employed in the analysis have been collected by the Department for Cultural and Environmental Heritage of the *Assessorato ai Beni Culturali ed Ambientali, Dipartimento dei Beni culturali e dell'Identità siciliana*. Observed include archeological areas, archeological museums, ethno-anthropological museums, and monuments.[20]

The dataset of the Department for Cultural and Environmental Heritage collects information on 78 attractions, observed in 2017. The cultural sites considered are irregularly distributed in the nine Sicilian provinces—in alphabetical order: Agrigento (AG), Caltanissetta (CL), Catania (CT), Enna (EN), Messina (ME), Palermo (PA), Ragusa (RG), Siracusa (SR), Trapani (TP).

---

[20] http://www.regione.sicilia.it/beniculturali/dirbenicult/database/dipartimento_2/siti_list.asp

The variables included in the dataset are associated with the year (the number of paying visitors, the number of visitors with a free ticket, and the total number of visitors, which also includes visitors from other destinations or with a "combined ticket," i.e., a ticket that allows visiting more than one attraction) and the type of cultural institution.

With regard to the latter variable and in spite of the classification adopted by the Regional Department, the observed units were grouped into the following: (1) archeological areas, (2) museums and galleries, (3) churches, castles, and mansions.

This grouping determines the type of fruition that can be enjoyed (Richards, 2002): for example, an archeological area will require a greater physical effort for a visit. This implies that safety measures must be observed, and guided itineraries must be designed for the visitors with disabilities, for the elderly, or the young (children or students on a school trip, for example).

An archeological area will attract visitors who are more interested in living an outdoor experience and getting to know the place to contextualize the attraction visited (a temple, a theater, a necropolis, for example, which are all attractions whose relevance in the urban environment and in ancient society can be grasped by visiting the site).

The opposite can be observed in the other two types of cultural institutions. To fully benefit from a visit to a museum or a mansion, it is preferable to have previously acquired some knowledge on the works of art displayed and/or on the history of the territory (Marty, 2007; Soren, 2009).

In this case, the greatest effort has to come from the management of the destination, which must facilitate the fruition of the attraction for all categories of visitors through information, guided tours, and the on-site presence of staff likely to provide information (Avena, 2019).

Other—qualitative—variables included in the dataset are associated with the information that can be obtained on each attraction. "Devoted website" is a dummy variable that assumes value $= 1$ if the cultural institution has its own website (Kravchyna & Hastings, 2002) and $= 0$ otherwise; "Information through institutional web-sites" is a dichotomous variable with values 0/1, depending on whether or not tourist information is obtainable. Such information is related to opening hours, accessibility for visitors with disabilities, location of the attraction, photos, etc. and can be mainly obtained from institutional websites (Regional Department for Cultural Heritage, *Pro Loco*, province website, municipalities, etc.); "Parking" indicates the information relating to the presence of on-site parking spaces; "Disabled services" indicates whether information on facilities and services that are provided for travelers with disabilities (for example, accompanied tours, information panels in braille language, audio guides, etc.) can be obtained through an online search.

4 Results

Table 1 shows the relevant variables sorted by province. The data presented are quite alarming and call for an immediate intervention aimed at creating a *culture of accessible information* among the management.

Looking at the total data, it emerges that only 21 out of 78 cultural sites have a devoted website, while information can be retrieved through the internet by vising institutional sites and other tourism sites. In fact, there are 49 occurrences of the dummy variable "Information through institutional websites." It is worth noticing that in the provinces of Catania and Messina, which have no devoted websites, the relevance of the institutional websites is paramount. The information concerning parking accessibility is available for 19 sites only, and other general information relevant for disabled people is present on the web for 16 cultural sites only.

Table 2 presents pairwise correlations among variables of the dataset.

From the correlations presented, it emerges that:

– There is no statistically significant relationship between the proxy or the demand of disabled people for visits to tourist sites (DD) and any of the three types of cultural institution.
– In contrast, a positive and statistically significant correlation can be observed between DD and the existence of a website devoted to the cultural site.
– No statistically significant correlation emerges between DD and general information concerning the cultural institution available from the web, usually through institutional websites.
– There is a positive statistically significant correlation between DD and the availability of parking information on the website or on the web.
– There is also a positive statistically significant correlation between DD and the presence, on the devoted website or on the web, of useful information on the site accessibility.

These results suggest that, for disabled people planning a visit to a cultural attraction, the relevance of specific pieces of information concerning a barrier-free environment is of major importance.

Our results are in line with the relevant literature: the information that must be made available to enable different categories of visitors to access and use tourism facilities may depend on the way such information is planned and managed (see among others, Eichhorn & Buhalis, 2010; WHO, 2016; Williams et al., 2006).

Disabled tourists do not judge certain cultural sites more accessible than others a priori. They are interested in acquiring knowledge on the facilities available in order to plan an accessible and enjoyable trip.

In addition to the correlations presented in Table 2, it is worth mentioning the high positive correlation (0.7473* is the value of the correlation that has been estimated, although not reported in the table) between the availability of information on parking and other information concerning services for disabled people, extracted from either the attraction's dedicated website or institutional websites.

Table 1 Frequencies of the relevant variables sorted by province

| Province | Frequencies | | | | | | |
	Archeological sites	Museums	Castles/historical mansions	Devoted websites	Information through institutional websites	Parking	Other information
AG	4	2	1	5	2	2	2
CL	0	4	0	1	1	1	1
CT	3	3	1	0	7	1	1
EN	2	3	0	1	5	1	1
ME	5	3	3	0	10	2	2
PA	4	7	9	5	15	5	5
RG	2	2	1	1	1	0	0
SR	3	3	5	3	4	3	3
TP	3	3	2	5	4	4	1
Total	**26**	**30**	**22**	**21**	**49**	**19**	**16**

Accessibility of Cultural Sites for Disabled People: Some Preliminary... 83

Table 2 Pairwise correlations

	Proxy of the demand of the disabled people for visits of touristic sites
Archeological site	0.1287
Museum	−0.1087
Castle/historical mansion	−0.0164
Devoted website	0.2942*
Information from institutional websites	0.0496
Information on parking availability	0.2359*
Information on services for disabled people availability	0.2459*

* statistical significance at 5%

This suggests that the managers of these tourist attractions who are sensitive to a specific aspect of the information disclosed, or the agents who introduce information on tourist sites on the web, either institutionally or on a voluntary basis, are likely to be sensitive to all its aspects.

Therefore, there is a need for awareness campaigns aimed at tourist managers (Presenza & Formato, 2018), who might undervalue the power of communication via the web and, especially, via a devoted website (Lončarić et al. (2013).

5 Conclusions

The present study has provided some reflections on the dimensions to consider in order to facilitate visit planning to tourist sites and cultural institutions among disabled people and has attempted to perform an empirical analysis by using, as a proxy for their demand, the ratio number of visitors with free ticket/total number of visitors. We are aware that the analysis is at a preliminary stage as some statistically significant correlations may be spurious, and we acknowledge the need to carry out further analysis in order to address them.

Data employed relate to the year 2017 and have been collected by the *Assessorato ai Beni Culturali ed Ambientali, Dipartimento dei Beni culturali e dell'Identità siciliana*, i.e., the regional authority for tourism and cultural heritage in Sicily. Qualitative variables looking at the characteristics of the sites considered that could be appealing for disabled visitors have been included in a correlation analysis investigating the relevance of these very general characteristics in determining a higher ratio of free tickets issued.

Results confirm the relevance of information accessibility and concur with the existing literature on the importance of providing reliable and timely data on the accessibility conditions at the destination (Darcy, 1998; Shi et al., 2012).

They also endorse the role of information retrieved through the web and suggest that actions can and must be taken not only by the managers of the tourist sites and by the institutions (local authorities) but by patients themselves.

Patient associations (e.g., AISM, *Associazione Italiana Sclerosi Multipla*, for patients with multiple sclerosis) can play an active role in finding information for travelers, organizing tours and excursions, checking transport availability, etc.).[21]

Overall, the major obstacle that disabled people face in the field of tourism is lack of information, defined in the literature as "information barrier" (Eichhorn et al., 2008) or "interactive barrier" (Smith, 1987).

The conclusions reached by the present contribution confirm the aspects mentioned by an expert travel blogger with disabilities, Simona Anedda, in a brief interview.[22]

When asked "*which factors will a disabled traveler who wants to leave for a holiday have to take into account?*" (for example, accessibility of places, guided tours, on-site assistance, etc.), Simona stressed how it is necessary to be well informed about accessibility, and first of all, about means of transport (airplanes, trains, buses, etc.). Regarding tours and excursions on-site, Simona emphasizes how local tourist offices play a fundamental role for people with disabilities even when they are experienced travelers like herself.

Accessibility is crucial in choosing if and where to go on vacation, and lack of it can become a deterrent for the disabled willing to travel. It is even more relevant than the opportunity to benefit from a reduced/free admission ticket for an accompanying person, which is the proxy adopted in this analysis. Still, a discounted/free ticket represents an interesting incentive because it encourages the disabled person to discover places and cultures that, otherwise, would not have been explored. Most importantly, it is matched with a priority over the queue at the entrance of the site, contributing to guarantee real accessibility to the places.

Simona's words are of great value and suggest a path to follow in designing further developments of the analysis: listen to the travelers, whether they are disabled or not.

In this perspective, it could be advisable to perform a survey on travelers' motivations, aimed at getting qualitative information and knowing more about aspects to improve.

The survey was administered to all the usual visitors of a destination to highlight differences in their requests and type of fruition compared to those of people with special needs.

---

[21] AISM has conducted training projects on accessible tourism, such as WAT, Woman Accessibility Tourism, in collaboration with Costa Cruises. This was a theoretical and practical training directed at women with multiple sclerosis who traveled on board of a cruise ship in Mediterranean, to test the accessibility of the ship and trace routes for excursions in the various cities where the ship was headed.

AISM does not provide direct information on prices, destinations, means of transport, etc., but it manages dedicated facilities for travelers with disabilities.

[22] We thank Simona Anedda, who has provided details about her personal experience as traveler with special needs. See her website: http://www.inviaggioconsimona.org/.

Accessibility of Cultural Sites for Disabled People: Some Preliminary... 85

Acknowledgments In this work by Maria Daniela Giammanco, Lara Gitto and Ferdinando Ofria the names appear in alphabetical order, the contribution of the authors is to be considered equivalent.

References

Avena, G. (2019). Studio sul profilo dei visitatori dei siti archeologici di Reggio Calabria e di Locri Epizefiri. *Humanities, 8*(2), 1–22.

Brenna, E., & Gitto, L. (2016). *Financing elderly care in Italy and Europe. Is there a common vision?* (DISCE - Working Papers del Dipartimento di Economia e Finanza def047). Università Cattolica del Sacro Cuore, Dipartimenti e Istituti di Scienze Economiche (DISCE). http://dipartimenti.unicatt.it/economia-finanza-def047.pdf

Budget Law. (2019). Italian Law, no. 145/2018. https://www.gazzettaufficiale.it/eli/gu/2018/12/31/302/so/62/sg/pdf

Budget Law. (2021) Italian Law, no. 178/20. https://www.gazzettaufficiale.it/eli/id/2020/12/30/20G00202/sg

Burns, N., Paterson, K., & Watson, N. (2009). An inclusive outdoors? Disabled people's experiences of countryside leisure services. *Leisure Studies, 28*(4), 403–417.

Darcy, S. (1998). *Anxiety to access: Tourism patterns and experiences of New South Wales people with a physical disability.* Tourism New South Wales.

Eichhorn, V., & Buhalis, D. (2010). Accessibility a key objective for the tourism industry. In D. Buhalis & S. Darcy (Eds.), *Accessible tourism: Concepts and issues* (pp. 44–46). Channel View.

Eichhorn, V., Miller, G., Michopoulou, E., & Buhalis, D. (2008). Enabling access to tourism through information schemes? *Annals of Tourism Research, 35*(1), 189–210.

European Commission. (2010, November 15). European disability strategy 2010-2020: A renewed commitment to a barrier-free Europe. https://ec.europa.eu/eip/ageing/standards/general/general-documents/european-disability-strategy-2010-2020_en#:~:text=Participation%20%3A%20ensure%20that%20people%20with,of%20quality%20community%2Dbased%20services.

European Commission. (2019). The European Accessibility Act. https://eur-lex.europa.eu/legal-content/IT/TXT/PDF/?uri=CELEX:32019L0882&from=EN

Figueiredo, E., Eusébio, C., & Kastenholz, E. (2012). How diverse are tourists with disabilities? A pilot study on accessible leisure tourism experiences in Portugal. *International Journal of Tourism Research, 14*(6), 531–550.

Gitto, L. (2017). Living with multiple sclerosis in Europe: Pharmacological Treatments, cost of illness, and health-related quality of life across countries. In I. S. Zagon & P. J. McLaughlin (Eds.), *Multiple sclerosis: Perspectives in treatment and pathogenesis.* Codon.

Gitto, L. (2021). L'offerta di beni culturali in Sicilia: analisi econometrica dei flussi turistici negli anni 1999 e 2000, 2021a. MPRA Paper no. 105309. https://mpra.ub.uni-muenchen.de/105309. https://doi.org/10.13140/RG.2.2.27796.12165.

Kravchyna, V., & Hastings, S. K. (2002). Informational value of museum web sites. *First Monday, 7*(2), 1–16.

Laurence, B. K. (2021). Disability determination for heart problems & cardiovascular disease. https://www.alllaw.com/articles/nolo/disability/determination-heart-problems.html.

Linebaugh, M. (2021). Social security disability process for cancer patients. Available at: https://www.nolo.com/legal-encyclopedia/social-security-disability-process-cancer-patients.html#:~:text=Qualifying%20for%20Social%20Security%20disability,to%20show%20either%20that%201).

Lo Bue, S., Arnone, R., & Parenti, I. (2020). Health and wellness tourism in Sicily: Development and enhancement. *European Journal of Public Health, 30*(5), 165–982.

Loi, K. I., & Kong, W. H. (2017). Tourism for all: Challenges and issues faced by people with vision impairment. *Tourism Planning & Development, 14*(2), 181–197.

Lončarić, D., Bašan, L., & Marković, M. G. (2013). Importance of DMO websites in tourist destination selection. In *23rd CROMAR Congress: Marketing in a dynamic åEnvironment–Academic and practical insights* (pp. 373–386).

Marty, P. F. (2007). Museum websites and museum visitors: Before and after the museum visit. *Museum management and curatorship, 22*(4), 337–360.

Musumeci, M. (2000). *Innovazione tecnologica e beni culturali. Uno studio sulla situazione della Sicilia (No. 200008).* Centre for North South Economic Research, University of Cagliari and Sassari.

Pheby, D. F., Araja, D., Berkis, U., Brenna, E., Cullinan, J., de Korwin, J. D., Gitto, L., Hughes, D., Hunter, R., Trepel, D., & Wang-Steverding, X. (2021). A literature review of GP knowledge and understanding of ME/CFS: A report from the Socioeconomic Working Group of the European Network on ME/CFS (EUROMENE). *Medicina, 57*(1), 7.

Presenza, A., & Formato, R. (Eds.). (2018). *Management della destinazione turistica. Attori, strategie e indicatori di performance.* Franco Angeli.

Proulx, A. (2020). Is autism a disability. https://www.therecoveryvillage.com/mental-health/autism/faq/is-autism-a-disability/

Ray, N. M., & Ryder, M. E. (2003). "Ebilities" tourism: An exploratory discussion of the travel needs and motivations of the mobility-disabled. *Tourism Management, 24*(1), 57–72.

Richards, G. (2002). Tourism attraction systems: Exploring cultural behavior. *Annals of Tourism Research, 29*(4), 1048–1064.

Shi, L., Cole, S., & Chancellor, H. C. (2012). Understanding leisure travel motivations of travelers with acquired mobility impairments. *Tourism Management, 33*(1), 228–231.

Sicilian Region. (2019). Law no. 10/2019. http://www.gurs.regione.sicilia.it/Gazzette/g19-30o/g19-30o.pdf

Smith, R. W. (1987). Leisure of disable tourists: Barriers to participation. *Annals of tourism Research, 14*(3), 376–389.

Soren, B. J. (2009). Museum experiences that change visitors. *Museum Management and Curatorship, 24*(3), 233–251.

United Nations. (2006, December 13). *Convention on the rights of persons with disabilities.*

Verropoulou, G., & Tsimbos, C. (2017). Disability trends among older adults in ten European countries over 2004-2013, using various indicators and Survey of Health, Ageing and Retirement in Europe (SHARE) data. *Ageing and Society, 37*(10), 2152.

WHO (World Health Organization). (2016). *Global Health Observatory (GHO) data. World Health Statistics 2016: Monitoring health for the SDGs.* Retrieved from http://www.who.int/gho/publications/world_health_statistics/2016/Annex_B/en/.

Williams, R., Rattray, R., & Grimes, A. (2006). Meeting the on-line needs of disabled tourists: An assessment of UK-based hotel websites. *International Journal of Tourism Research, 8*(1), 59–73.

Part II
The Supply Side of Tourism for People with Disabilities: A Context-Based Perspective

How to Improve Universal Accessibility of Smart Tourism Destinations: The Case of Amsterdam City

Augusto D'Amico, Veronica Marozzo, and Valeria Schifilliti

1 Introduction

Smart Tourism Destinations (STDs), by using advanced technologies, platforms, and infrastructures, help tourists anticipate their needs, make decisions, and improve their touristic experience (Boes et al., 2015; Wang et al., 2013). Indeed, different devices can support the creation and facilitation of a real-time tourism experience and, consequently, improve the effectiveness of tourism resource management throughout the destination (Buhalis & Amaranggana, 2013). The result is the personalization of touristic products and services (Buhalis & Amaranggana, 2013) by fitting them to tourists' preferences to offer real-time activities and/or services that are important or interesting to them (Batet et al., 2012). In the perspective of People with Disabilities (PwDs), thus, this appears more relevant as STDs could be able to guarantee, as far as possible, totally independent use of available facilities and services by all customers by analyzing a large amount of dynamic and hetero-geneous data (e.g., from different sources) to improve their tourist experiences (Gretzel et al., 2015).

Research on tourism and disability has received increasing scholarly attention over the last decades. From a political perspective, governments have addressed their strategies and marketing activities for tourism accessibility. Among others, the European Commission approved in March 2021 the new Strategy for the rights of persons with disabilities 2021–2030 with the aim of a "barrier-free Europe" for the empowerment of People with Disabilities so they can use their rights to be actively involved in society and economy. However, although the improvements of the past years, PwDs have to deal with significant barriers and an increasing probability of poverty and social exclusion (European Commission, 2021). Therefore, considering

---

A. D'Amico · V. Marozzo (✉) · V. Schifilliti
Department of Economics, University of Messina, Messina, Italy
e-mail: augusto.damico@unime.it; veronica.marozzo@unime.it; valeria.schifilliti@unime.it

© The Author(s), under exclusive license to Springer Nature Switzerland AG 2022
T. Abbate et al. (eds.), *Tourism and Disability*, Tourism on the Verge,
https://doi.org/10.1007/978-3-030-93612-9_6

these risks, the European Union aims at supporting Member States to promote their national policies and plans to embody the Convention on the Rights of Persons with Disabilities (CRPD) and the EU regulation in line with the 2030 Agenda for Sustainable Development of the United Nations.[1]

In the Global Disability Action Plan, the World Health Organization (WHO) estimated that more than one million people live with a disability, almost 15% of the global citizens and 93 million are children with a limited or serious disability. Additionally, more than 190 million people encounter significant functioning difficulties, and this number will constantly increase due to the aging population and the growth of chronic health conditions internationally (WHO, 2015). Around 135 million people live with a disability at the European level, hence almost ten people out of 100.

The latest publication of UNWTO on the world tourism scenario shows that 1.5 billion arrivals in the world were registered in 2019, with Europe as a leading destination with 51% of visitors of the global market. However, people with disabilities comprise a relevant, undervalued part of the tourism market from a numerical and economic point of view. When different grades of disability are analyzed, the incidence of longstanding limitations rises with age and the gender health gap (Eurostat, 2020). Furthermore, women with disabilities were more than the number of males in 2019, and 7.3% of individuals between 16 and 24 years old have (low or severe) longstanding limitations, a percentage that increased to 72.1% for people of 85 and over.

People with disabilities cannot be considered a homogeneous group since these individuals should be considered depending on the type of disability and the degree of individual's requirements (Darcy, 2010; Natalia et al., 2019; WHO, 2015). Generally, people with disabilities are not favored to benefit from tourism activities due to the existence of physical, environmental, economic and social, and/or other barriers characterizing a destination (Bizjak et al., 2011; Eichhorn et al., 2008).

Over the last years, academics underlined the importance of accessibility as a way to improve the competitiveness of the tourism destinations (Domínguez et al., 2015; Figueiredo et al., 2012; Natalia et al., 2019; UNWTO, 2020) and only recently Smart Tourism Destinations has become an evolving field of research. By considering that STDs allow data and information collection thanks to the use of sophisticated ICT to help tourists improve the touristic experience (Boes et al., 2015; Wang et al., 2013), stakeholders may use this information to both recognize problems and customize possible solutions to address those problems (Buhalis & Amaranggana, 2015). Furthermore, promptly exchanging information led to the creation of Big Data that may be examined to uncover people's needs, and Smart Tourism Destinations may use this data to provide precise services customized to visitors' preferences at the right moment (Buhalis & Amaranggana, 2015). Indeed, different devices can support the creation and facilitation of a real-time tourism experience and, consequently, improve the effectiveness of tourism resource management throughout the

---

[1] The 2030 Agenda for Sustainable Development. Retrieved from https://sdgs.un.org/2030agenda

destination (Buhalis & Amaranggana, 2013). The smartness of a destination contemplates offering costumed services to tourists by considering not only the access of instantaneous information of customers' data but also real-time opinion on the service and dynamic platforms that allow data exchanging among several stakeholders to support the integration of services. Besides, through historical data, visitors' preferences can be predicted in order to develop specific services or dynamic recommender systems (Buhalis & Amaranggana, 2015).

The existing literature, thus, has provided complex, fragmented and mixed results in this field by showing that research on tourism and disability has mainly focused on travelers with disabilities, encompassing topics such as travel barriers/constraints (McKercher et al., 2003), benefits derived from tourism participation (Kim & Lehto, 2013), and travel needs/motivations (Ray & Ryder, 2003). Therefore, intending to fill this gap, the chapter aims to identify areas of convergence between smart tourism destinations and disabilities and suggest opportunities for future research by collecting evidence regarding how STDs apply the smartness concept to meet the specific requirements of people with disabilities. Specifically, the smart tourism and disabilities have been matched in this study with the aim to present: (1) a review of the main contributions in the intersection of these two research areas, trying to unravel their possible linkage; (2) a collection of evidence of STDs oriented to satisfy the segment of people with disabilities; (3) a contribution to moving forward in this area through cross-fertilization between theory and practice, with some suggestions for further research in a still underexplored field of study. To achieve these mentioned objectives, this study collects evidence concerning initiatives, actions, and solutions that Amsterdam has developed and implemented to serve this segment better. Scholars can use this study to understand the state of the art in STDs and disabilities, while practitioners can find an instrument for developing strategies.

The chapter is structured as follows. We represent the theoretical background by describing both the STDs approach and the people with disability framework in the tourism sector in Sect. 2. Section 3 describes the Amsterdam case as an exemplary smart tourism destination. Finally, Sect. 4 provides some conclusions and suggestions for future research.

2 Theoretical Background

Smart Tourism Destination (STD) refers to a strategic way of developing tourism destinations by using dynamic platforms interconnecting with several stakeholders through ICT that enable promptly exchanging information on tourism activity (Buhalis & Amaranggana, 2015; Gretzel et al., 2015). The recent growing body of publications on the topic confirms the interest of scholars covering several aspects of STD. The result of a detailed analysis on the comprehensive database Elsevier's Scopus shows that research on this topic emerged in 2013, with a total amount of 97 documents published until 2021 (see Fig. 1). However, several authors affirmed

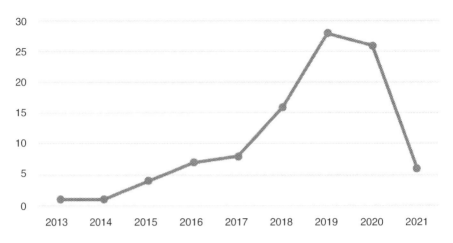

Fig. 1 Total number of STD publications by year. Source: Elsevier's Scopus

that, despite the increasing research on the phenomenon, work on smart tourism is insufficient and did not entirely examine how smartness is applied to destinations (Femenia Serra & Perea Medina, 2016; Gretzel et al., 2015).

As stated by previous researchers, the development of Smart Cities led to the notion of Smart Tourism Destinations (Buhalis & Amaranggana, 2013). According to Lamsfus and Alzua-Sorzabal (2013), the idea of Smart Destinations emerged from the Smart City concept that incorporates smart city facilities with precise services for visitors. However, the two concepts cannot be considered the same (Tran et al., 2017). In order to explain the concept of smart cities, academics have tried to select the critical aspects of these innovative cities. In defining smart cities, Caragliu et al. (2009) considered three characteristics that improve the city sustainable financial progress and a better quality of life: (1) investment in human capital with its essential role in the city actions that lead the smartness; (2) development of high-tech organizations that comprise the entire city; (3) information circulation around the city, which is crucial for augmenting the city functions and increasing the quality of life.

Several studies analyzed STDs by defining the main characteristics and dynamics. According to Buonincontri and Micera (2016), *"Bringing smartness into tourism destinations requires the use of a technological platform on which information on local resources, tourists, their actions, and their consumption habits, can be integrated and made available to several stakeholders"* (p. 286). Hence, the adoption of technology in tourism destinations positively impacts tourists' experience and the competitiveness of the touristic destinations (Buhalis & Amaranggana, 2013). As stated by Zhang et al. (2012) and Wang et al. (2013), three technological components are essential for the smartness of a destination: cloud computing services, internet of things (IoT), end-user systems. These elements require an active contribution of stakeholders who are actively involved in the platform adoption, with tourism service providers working together to co-create their touristic experience

(Buhalis & Amaranggana, 2013). In their study on the co-creation of stakeholders' involvement in smart tourism destinations in Europe, Buonincontri and Micera (2016) analyzed how the use of these three technological components may increase the tourism experience as effective instruments that tourists can utilize by contributing to the rise of the competitiveness of a destination. While examining the tourists' co-creation experience in Venice and Salzburg applying smart technologies, they found that using ICT components increases the co-creation strategy of a destination. Likewise, according to Tussyadiah and Fesenmaier (2009), the role of technology supports tourism experience by developing crucial practical information. Nevertheless, as Lamsfus and Alzua-Sorzabal (2013) stated, the smartness of a destination should focus both on tourists' and residents' needs. Their paper enlightened how ICT allows tourists to receive tailored information at any time and place and how technological devices provide information regarding tourists to destinations and stakeholders using cloud tools to give a better tourism experience.

Hence, despite some scholars being more focused on applying technology for STDs, Boes et al. (2015) gave more emphasis to social factors, particularly human and social capital, innovation, and leadership. According to the authors, Smart Tourism Destinations can be defined as places where the use of technological tools, on one side, improves organizations in terms of wealth, profit, and benefits, and, on the other side, the systems used to analyze tourists demand and supply facilitate their value co-creation, preference, and experience.

For Buhalis and Amaranggana (2015), Smart Tourism Destinations should allow tourists to interact through technological platforms for exchanging immediate information that generates Big Data. The correct use of these data may reveal tourist tendencies so that stakeholders can be instantly aware, and information can be used to improve tourism experiences "*by offering right services that suit users' preference at the right time*" (Buhalis & Amaranggana, 2015, p. 378). According to these authors, tourism governments should guarantee open access to the information flows from new applications without unhelpful extra costs to recognize problems and personalize possible solutions.

Thanks to the availability of a massive number of tourists' data, Buhalis and Amaranggana (2015) highlighted the "personalization" perspective in collecting every tourist preference to offer what they want at the exact moment. Personalization has the good advantage of improving the tourist comfort level both emotionally and physically, although travelers have their favorite tendencies and necessities (Michopoulou & Buhalis, 2013). Besides, Big Data helps to profile tourists' needs in order to assist the customer by showing only useful information for the decision-making process while providing better services (Buhalis & Amaranggana, 2015).

Therefore, destinations should activate a bottom-up process based on the development of elaborate technologies and processes customized to the local needs (Neirotti et al., 2014). However, STD involves several structural and managerial activities that allow simplification of the sharing information process, development of mutual strategies, and the promotion of the destination by individuals. Furthermore, Destination Management Organizations (DMOs) may take advantage of Smart City facilities and deliver different services to those offered to local people while collecting other information and needs to fulfill their managerial obligations (Lamsfus & Alzua-Sorzabal, 2013).

With the accessibility of a massive amount of data, destinations are likely to offer tailored services depending on the different types of tourists to meet their expectations and improve their tourism experience afterward (Buhalis & Amaranggana, 2015). Sharing instant information is an essential aspect of the hospitality sector in order to solve problems while tourists are still in the location promptly. Therefore, the continuous collaboration between guests and tourism organizations is ideal for offering innovative products that best meet tourists' preferences (Schaffers et al., 2011). In the same context, Lee et al. (2017), in their study on happiness and the role of smart tourism technology, built a model to illustrate how smart technology affects tourists' experience through the direct impact of ICT on their satisfaction.

One of the tourism sector characteristics is the interaction of many stakeholders that they have several interests and needs; thus, the smartness of a destination appears to be essential with people with disabilities. Since, in the tourism sector, there is increasing attention to people with disabilities, technological platforms may simplify the connection with ultimate users thanks to various services that support tourism experiences. Despite the definition of disability varies depending on the context, medical, functional, and social aspects are the most considered, thus even though for some people disability is believed to be a disease, promoters of the social model consider People with Disability (PwD) as ordinary individuals living with an exceptional condition (Lehto et al., 2018). Several researchers broadly accept the social model considering disability as a social paradigm and physical barriers as minor barriers compared to discrimination (Shaw & Coles, 2004; Thiara et al., 2012). To some extent, the Convention on the Rights of Persons with Disabilities (CRPD) describes PwD as individuals with long-term physical, mental, intellectual, or sensory impairments that may not actively participate in society due to several barriers; while people with access needs as those with short-term disability, older population, expecting women and families with small children (Darcy & Dickson, 2009; Dickson et al., 2017).

Within the tourism context, people with disabilities are not favored to benefit from tourism activities due to physical, environmental, economic and social, and/or other barriers characterizing a destination (Bizjak et al., 2011; Eichhorn et al., 2008). Many studies analyzed the problems experienced by people with disabilities and the accessibility of tourism accommodation (Bi et al., 2007; Daniels et al., 2005; Darcy, 2010; Darcy & Dickson, 2009; Natalia et al., 2019). As Darcy (2010) stated, the most critical problems are related to the documentation of accessible accommodation information. In his study on the complex level information required for People with Disability in Australia to make a well-informed choice on their accommodation requirements, the author found a well-organized response after presenting information for accessible rooms depending on the complete and openly defined conditions of the accommodation. In addition, Natalia et al. (2019) analyzed accessible tourism for Australia, New Zealand, Argentina, and Brazil creating the Tourism Accessibility Index (TAI) in order to measure, through some key variables, the tourism accessibility of the four countries with different tourism background. In this study,

Amsterdam has been considered one of the leading tourism destinations at the European level by analyzing accessible tourism for people with disabilities.

However, scholars have identified several barriers that represent, for people living with disabilities, difficulties engaging in tourism. These barriers include cultural, economic, physical, and informational barriers, such as architectural barriers or a not insufficient level of information provided. In the case of cultural barriers, governments of several countries encouraged various awareness campaigns and legal limitations recognized in accessibility policies to provide information on applying their needs in different environments (Agovino et al., 2017). Economic barriers have been widely studied from a social tourism perspective as essential factors in attaining social and economic equality (McCabe, 2009; Michopoulou et al., 2015; Minnaert et al., 2009). In the tourism sector, the main problems are the lack of information (so-called information barriers) (Eichhorn et al., 2008) which, together with inadequacy by the tourism stakeholders, produce accessibility problems to tourists with disabilities (Agovino et al., 2017). Thus, these barriers are one of the numerous reasons why the rate of participation and quality of tourism experience are minor compared to the average population (Buhalis & Darcy, 2010; McKercher & Darcy, 2018).

Consequently, McKercher and Darcy (2018) identified several barriers that affect the participation in tourism of people with disabilities. According to the authors, constraints can be categorized into three groups of intrapersonal barriers related to psychological factors such as religion, health, and attitudes, interpersonal barriers that include travel company and social communication, while structural barriers focus on costs, family duties, and an inadequate level of opportunity (Crawford et al., 1991; McKercher & Darcy, 2018). Concerning interpersonal barriers, Lehto et al. (2018) examined the tourism experience of people with disabilities and their caregivers in the Chinese context measuring their tourism experience and providing an understanding of their shared tourism adventure.

However, other studies analyzed additional aspects of disability in the tourism sector. In particular, Domínguez et al. (2015) examined the competitiveness of the disability tourism market in Spain and Australia, suggesting that an accessible tourism market depends on the specific regulations and planning of the destination, while Kim and Lehto (2013) identified motivational aspects of families traveling with disabled children showing that physical capability of children with a disability seems to be the primary reason for the family.

Agovino et al. (2017) stated that information barriers include problems of access to some channels such as internet pages not suitable for the diverse types of disabilities or the lack of accessible information of the places to visit that a Smart Tourism Destination may cover. Therefore, Smart Tourism Destinations may provide measures that enable this type of customers a better travel experience as soon as services are accessible to tourists with disabilities, representing an opportunity for comprehensive social integration (Figueiredo et al., 2012).

3   Amsterdam: The Exemplary Case of Smart Tourism Destination

The present work focused the attention on one of the leading Smart Tourism Destinations in Europe, that is Amsterdam. With around 860,000 citizens, Amsterdam falls within the large cities' category, and its success in the smart cities' arena makes it an ideal sample to study. To confirm its success and its international positioning as a smart city, there are plenty of awards that Amsterdam has received during the last years (Mora & Bolici, 2015), such as the European Parliament award, which has included the Netherlands' capital among the six most successful smart cities in Europe (Manville et al., 2014). Therefore, Amsterdam is considered an example of a "democratic bottom-up Smart City project" (Papa et al., 2013, p. 6) and was selected as a successful case regarding the development of user-oriented projects. Additionally, in the last times, Amsterdam has devoted much attention to aspects relating to inclusiveness, becoming a smart tourist destination capable of satisfying the needs of people with disabilities that, due to the existence of the various type of destination' barriers (e.g., physical, environmental, economic and social) are often not favored to benefit from tourism activities (e.g., Eichhorn et al., 2008).

In Amsterdam, indeed, there is a lot of accessibility for disabled people, starting from Airport until the hotels. Geographically speaking, many of the bridges in Amsterdam are a little hilly. However, the city's landscape is fairly level by all accounts, and this makes getting around relatively easy for a wide range of people with mobility issues. Moreover, accessibility is taken seriously in the Netherlands, especially in the tourism industry. Furthermore, since Amsterdam is the number one tourist destination in the country, they take it seriously here too. The level of transparency is high. The majority of the attractions in Amsterdam (and in the country) are accessible to wheelchair users and provide accommodations to people with other access needs and disabilities. Furthermore, most importantly, all necessary information is available online.

3.1   The Service for People with Disabilities

Previous research has treated disability as a single-dimensional construct (e.g., Boxall et al., 2018). Several studies in this area found little differentiation between the dimensions of access, except for an important limited exception (e.g., Murray & Sproats, 1990; Woodside & Etzel, 1980). According to Darcy (2010), disability is a multi-dimensional construct, with each dimension having its own access requirements that are significantly different from each other. Indeed, most disability statistics today recognize the multi-dimensional construct that consists of: (1) mobility, (2) hearing, (3) vision, (4) cognitive/learning, (5) mental health, and (6) sensitivities and long-term health conditions (Disability Discrimination Act (DDA), 1992).

Understanding the multi-dimensionality of the construct is focal to help people with disabilities most efficiently and effectively possible by providing the correct access requirements such as ramps, tactile ground surface indicators, or wayfinding signage. With this logic, an individual with multiple dimensions of access problems will necessitate multiple levels of access provision. For example, an individual with cerebral palsy may have a communication dimension (e.g., through an associated speech impairment) by needing a communication board and, at the same time, may have a mobility dimension by needing the use of a wheelchair. Therefore, this person needs an accessible physical environment and assistive technologies, and social policy inclusions.

To do this, Amsterdam has organized a series of activities and services that make it an exemplary case of STD by starting from the first contact with the tourist. The tourists that arrive in Amsterdam by plane land at one of the best airports in the world for accessibility (i.e., Schiphol). Specifically, Schiphol Airport offers numerous accessibility features for disabled travelers, such as services for deaf/hard of hearing, blind/visually impaired, and people with wheelchairs, highlighting the city's considerable attention in offering services covering different dimensions of the disability's concept right from landing. For getting from Schiphol to Amsterdam, people with disabilities can choose between two alternatives: taxi or public transportation. About the latter, tourists can use all modes in the country with only one travel card valid for both international trains and local transportation. The system is simple to understand and follow, thanks to maps and the app. Moreover, tactile pavement can be found almost anywhere. Concerning the taxi service, booking a wheelchair-accessible taxi in advance is needed (both to and from the airport and throughout the area) to ensure the respect of the plane time. Public transport from Schiphol Airport is easily accessible from the airport's main lobby area; trains arrive and depart from the platform area immediately below this, and buses depart from just outside the building too. Taking the train from Schiphol into the city is relatively straightforward, and the trip takes less than 20 min.

The tourists that arrive in Amsterdam by train will most likely arrive at the main train station, that is Amsterdam Central, fully accessible to wheelchair users (e.g., lifts and escalators at every track). The station has other services available for people with other disabilities (e.g., a tactile map). At most stations, lifts or ramps make it possible for wheelchair users to reach the platforms. The stations are also furnished with guidelines to ticket machines, tickets shop, and the check-in/out points or the gates. Travelers with a hearing impairment can use the audio connection in the ticket shops or at the information desks.

Concerning the public transport in Amsterdam, the system consists of subways, trams, and buses that are well connected. All underground and overground stations in Amsterdam are wheelchair accessible. Also, trams and buses are wheelchair accessible, but there are a few things to consider. All vehicles are technically wheelchair accessible, but not all stops are. Specifically, some tram stops are raised and narrow. Additionally, certain older vehicle models require manual assistance (e.g., ramp to be lowered). On all public transportation, stops are announced both visibly and audibly. At stations, some boards announce when the next vehicle is arriving. There are buttons blind or visually impaired people can push to hear this information.

The Netherlands is known as a country made for cycling as well as in Amsterdam. There are many places to rent bikes in the city, including at least one that offers adapted bikes for disabled customers by offering an accessible cycling service. Moreover, tourists with disabilities can avail of a guide of five wheelchair-accessible routes in Amsterdam concerning the city's major tourist areas.

In Amsterdam, there are numerous hotels, many of which have people with disabilities accessible rooms and services. For example, accessible features include accessible elevators, accessible meeting rooms, bathroom and bedroom's doors at least 32 in. wide, braille elevator, digital alarm clock available with sound and strobe light, emergency call button on the phone, roll-in shower, strobe alarms, vibrating fire alarm, visual alarm for hearing impaired (also in hallways). By providing these different services able to meet the needs of people with disabilities, Amsterdam has confirmed itself as an STD very attentive to the multi-dimensional concept of disability. In line with the personalization concept of Buhalis and Amaranggana (2015), service providers in Amsterdam are adapting their facilities to meet PwD needs by collecting important information that is used to provide the right offer at the right moment.

Amsterdam has some of the best cultural and entertainment attractions globally, and most of them have a diverse array of accessibility offerings (for example, Anne Frank House, Van Gogh Museum, Amsterdam Museum, and Heineken Experience). All exhibits in the museums are wheelchair accessible, with all floors accessible by lift. In some of them, wheelchairs and rollators are available to borrow by making a reservation. Scooters are allowed most of the time (not everywhere), but they can be at the discretion of security during hectic times. There are wheelchair-accessible toilets noted on the floor plans. The information is also available for people with other (non-physical) disabilities. There are also audio guides for blind or visually impaired visitors, and the written versions of the audio tour are available for the Deaf or Hard of Hearing. The museums offer hearing loops and guided tours in international sign language. There is a specific section on their website with more information for people who are Deaf or Hard of Hearing. There is also a specific section for visitors with sensory sensitivity. Furthermore, with the use of ICT, service providers are offering more personalized services and generating more satisfactory experiences. Thus, it is quite evident that, also in this context, the Amsterdam city manages to be accessible for different dimensions of the concept of disability, confirming itself as an exemplary case of accessible STD.

Among other activities and attractions offered by the Netherlands' capital, tourists with mobility disabilities can book a wheelchair-accessible Canal cruise (e.g., the Jordaan and Amsterdam Islands canal cruise that is a "75 minutes" cruise through the unique UNESCO Heritage listed Golden Age canals of Amsterdam), by reserving the time slots available for wheelchair users. In the Canal cruises' cases, Amsterdam city needs to improve its accessibility by making the services available also for tourists with different disabilities than the mobility one. Finally, it is possible to book tours specifically designed for wheelchair users and people who are blind or

Table 1 Accessible services for people with mobility, vision, and hearing disabilities

	Mobility	Vision	Hearing
Airport	Yes	Yes	Yes
Transport	Yes	Yes	–
Hotels	Yes	Yes	Yes
Museums	Yes	Yes	Yes
Canal cruises	Yes	–	–
City tour	Yes	Yes	–

Source: Authors' elaboration

visually impaired, such as the "Historical wheelchair accessible walking tour through Amsterdam," a 3 hours' tour with the possibility to visit the Amsterdam canals, the Old Church, the Royal Palace, Begijnhof, t' Spui, the Hidden book market, and De Waag.

The services offered by Amsterdam to people with disabilities are remarkable (see Table 1) and still growing, making the capital of the Netherlands an example to be taken to improve accessibility so that all tourists can enjoy the tourist experience in the same way.

4 Conclusion

The present work aims at recognizing points of convergence between Smart Tourism Destinations (STDs) and disabilities by collecting evidence on how the smartness of a destination may improve the tourism experiences of people with disabilities (PwDs). Specifically, a cross-fertilization approach between theory and practice was adopted to better understand the under-investigated concepts. The combination of research-based theory and practitioner-oriented approach creates the kind of cross-fertilization needed to advance both the knowledge and application of smartness in a tourism destination with a particular focus on the interests of PwDs. This study's analysis was developed by applying the informative framework of the Amsterdam case study, revealing that the city uses a series of activities and services that offers numerous accessibility features for disabled travelers. An important aspect of Smart Tourism Destinations is the offering of tailored services to visitors by considering different dimensions, in particular, the access to instantaneous information with the aim of collecting tourists' data and feedback on offered service. Likewise, a dynamic platform helps several stakeholders in the data exchange to encourage service integration and promptly predict visitors' preferences using historical data. Therefore, applying the smartness concept to a destination seems essential to possibly increase the tourism experience. In the perspective of People with Disabilities, thus, this appears more appropriate as STDs may guarantee, to the greatest extent, completely independent use of available facilities and services by all customers by examining a large amount of dynamic and heterogeneous data (e.g., from different sources) to enhance their tourist experiences (Gretzel et al., 2015).

In the case of Amsterdam, the city has taken into consideration several aspects related to inclusiveness, becoming a smart tourist destination able at satisfying the requirements of people with disabilities that, due to the presence of a variety of destination' barriers (e.g., physical, environmental, economic, and social) are usually not encouraged to engage into tourism activities (e.g., Eichhorn et al., 2008). This study may be considered a starting point to better understand the role of smart technologies in the experience of tourists with disabilities. Scholars can use this study to understand the state of the art in STDs and disabilities, while practitioners can find an instrument for developing strategies.

Acknowledgments Authors are listed in alphabetical order and they have equally contributed to the study.

References

Agovino, M., Casaccia, M., Garofalo, A., & Marchesano, K. (2017). Tourism and disability in Italy. Limits and opportunities. *Tourism Management Perspectives, 23*, 58–67.

Batet, M., Moreno, A., Sánchez, D., Isern, D., & Valls, A. (2012). Turist@: Agent-based personalised recommendation of tourist activities. *Expert Systems with Applications, 39*(8), 7319–7329.

Bi, Y., Card, J. A., & Cole, S. T. (2007). Accessibility and attitudinal barriers encountered by Chinese travellers with physical disabilities. *International Journal of Tourism Research, 9*(3), 205–216.

Bizjak, B., Knežević, M., & Cvetrežnik, S. (2011). Attitude change towards guests with disabilities: Reflections from tourism students. *Annals of Tourism Research, 38*(3), 842–857.

Boes, K., Buhalis, D., & Inversini, A. (2015). Conceptualising smart tourism destination dimensions. In I. Tussyadiah & A. Inversini (Eds.), *Information and communication technologies in tourism 2015* (pp. 391–403). Springer.

Boxall, K., Nyanjom, J., & Slaven, J. (2018). Disability, hospitality and the new sharing economy. *International Journal of Contemporary Hospitality Management, 30*(1), 539–556.

Buhalis, D., & Amaranggana, A. (2013). Smart tourism destinations. In *Information and communication technologies in tourism 2014* (pp. 553–564). Springer.

Buhalis, D., & Amaranggana, A. (2015). Smart tourism destinations enhancing tourism experience through personalisation of services. In *Information and communication technologies in tourism 2015* (pp. 377–389). Springer.

Buhalis, D., & Darcy, S. (Eds.). (2010). *Accessible tourism: Concepts and issues*. Channel View.

Buonincontri, P., & Micera, R. (2016). The experience co-creation in smart tourism destinations: A multiple case analysis of European destinations. *Information Technology & Tourism, 16*(3), 285–315.

Caragliu, A., Del Bo, C., & Nijkamp, P. (2009). Smart cities in Europe. *Journal of Urban Technology, 18*, 65–82.

Convention on the Rights of Persons with Disabilities (CRPD) | United Nations Enable. (n.d.). Retrieved April 9, 2021, from https://www.un.org/development/desa/disabilities/convention-on-the-rights-of-persons-with-disabilities.html

Crawford, D. W., Jackson, E. L., & Godbey, G. (1991). A hierarchical model of leisure constraints. *Leisure Sciences, 13*(4), 309–320.

Daniels, M. J., Drogin Rodgers, E. B., & Wiggins, B. P. (2005). "Travel Tales": An interpretive analysis of constraints and negotiations to pleasure travel as experienced by persons with physical disabilities. *Tourism Management, 26*(6), 919–930.

Darcy, S. (2010). Inherent complexity: Disability, accessible tourism and accommodation information preferences. *Tourism Management, 31*(6), 816–826.

Darcy, S., & Dickson, T. J. (2009). A whole-of-life approach to tourism: The case for accessible tourism experiences. *Journal of Hospitality and Tourism Management, 16*(1), 32–44.

Dickson, T. J., Misener, L., & Darcy, S. (2017). Enhancing destination competitiveness through disability sport event legacies: Developing an interdisciplinary typology. *International Journal of Contemporary Hospitality Management, 29*(3), 924–946.

Domínguez, T., Darcy, S., & Al, E. (2015). Competing for the disability tourism market - a comparative exploration of the factors of accessible tourism competitiveness in Spain and Australia. *Tourism Management, 47*(1), 261–272.

Eichhorn, V., Miller, G., Michopoulou, E., & Buhalis, D. (2008). Enabling access to tourism through information schemes? *Annals of Tourism Research, 35*(1), 189–210.

European Commission. (2021). Union of equality: Strategy for the rights of persons with disabilities 2021-2030 - Employment, Social Affairs and Inclusion. Retrieved April 11, 2021, from https://ec.europa.eu/social/main.jsp?catId=1484andlangId=en

Eurostat. (2020). Functional and activity limitations statistics. *Statistics Explained*. Online Publications, (October), 1–18. Retrieved from https://ec.europa.eu/eurostat/statistics-explained/index.php/Functional_and_activity_limitations_statistics

Femenia Serra, F., & Perea Medina, M. J. (2016). Analysis of three Spanish potential smart tourism destinations. In *En 6th international conference on tourism: New challenges and boundaries in tourism: Policies, innovations and strategies (Nápoles, Italia).* Del (vol. 29).

Figueiredo, E., Eusébio, C., & Kastenholz, E. (2012). How diverse are tourists with disabilities? A pilot study on accessible leisure tourism experiences in Portugal. *International Journal of Tourism Research, 14*(6), 531–550.

Gretzel, U., Koo, C., Sigala, M., & Xiang, Z. (2015). Special issue on smart tourism: Convergence of information technologies, experiences, and theories. *Electronic Markets, 25*(3), 175–177.

Kim, S., & Lehto, X. Y. (2013). Travel by families with children possessing disabilities: Motives and activities. *Tourism Management, 37*, 3–24.

Lamsfus, C., & Alzua-Sorzabal, A. (2013). Theoretical framework for a tourism internet of things: Smart destinations. *TourGUNE Journal of Tourism and Human Mobility, 2*, 15–21.

Lee, J., Lee, H., Chung, N., & Koo, C. (2017). An integrative model of the pursuit of happiness and the role of smart tourism technology: A case of international tourists in Seoul. In *Information and communication technologies in tourism 2017* (pp. 173–186). Springer.

Lehto, X., Luo, W., Miao, L., & Ghiselli, R. F. (2018). Shared tourism experience of individuals with disabilities and their caregivers. *Journal of Destination Marketing and Management, 8*(April), 85–193.

Manville, C., Cochrane, G., Cave, J., Millard, J., Pederson, J. K., Thaarup, R. K., & Kotterink, B. (2014). *Mapping smart cities in the EU*. European Parliament. Directorate-General for Internal Policies. Policy Department: Economic and Scientific Policy A.

McCabe, S. (2009). Who needs a holiday? Evaluating social tourism. *Annals of Tourism Research, 36*(4), 667–688.

McKercher, B., & Darcy, S. (2018). Re-conceptualizing barriers to travel by people with disabilities. *Tourism Management Perspectives, 26*(January), 59–66.

McKercher, B., Packer, T., Yau, M. K., & Lam, P. (2003). Travel agents as facilitators or inhibitors of travel: Perceptions of people with disabilities. *Tourism Management, 24*(4), 465–474.

Michopoulou, E., & Buhalis, D. (2013). Information provision for challenging markets: The case of the accessibility requiring market in the context of tourism. *Information and Management, 50*, 229–239.

Michopoulou, E., Darcy, S., Ambrose, I., & Buhalis, D. (2015). Accessible tourism futures: The world we dream to live in and the opportunities we hope to have. *Journal of Tourism Futures, 1*(3), 179–188.

Minnaert, L., Maitland, R., & Miller, G. (2009). Tourism and social policy. The value of social tourism. *Annals of Tourism Research, 36*(2), 316–334.

Mora, L., & Bolici, R. (2015). How to become a smart city: Learning from Amsterdam. In *International conference on smart and sustainable planning for cities and regions* (pp. 251–266). Springer.

Murray, M., & Sproats, J. (1990). The disabled traveller: Tourism and disability in Australia. *Journal of tourism studies, 1*(1), 9–14.

Natalia, P., Ana, R., Simon, D., Noelia, G., & Barbara, A. (2019). Critical elements in accessible tourism for destination competitiveness and comparison: Principal component analysis from Oceania and South America. *Tourism Management, 75*(May), 169–185.

Neirotti, P., De Marco, A., Cagliano, A. C., Mangano, G., & Scorrano, F. (2014). Current trends in smart city initiatives: Some stylised facts. *Cities, 38*, 25–36.

Papa, R., Gargiulo, C., & Galderisi, A. (2013). Towards an urban planners' perspective on Smart City. *TeMA Journal of Land Use, Mobility and Environment, 6*(01), 5–17.

Ray, N. M., & Ryder, M. E. (2003). "Ebilities" tourism: An exploratory discussion of the travel needs and motivations of the mobility-disabled. *Tourism Management, 24*(1), 57–72.

Schaffers, H., Komninos, N., Pallot, M., Trousse, B., Nilsson, M., & Oliveira, A. (2011). Smart cities and the future internet: Towards cooperation frameworks for open innovation. In *The future internet assembly* (pp. 431–446). Springer.

Shaw, G., & Coles, T. (2004). Disability, holiday making and the tourism industry in the UK: A preliminary survey. *Tourism Management, 25*(3), 397–403.

Thiara, R. K., Bashall, R., & Harwin, N. (2012). *Disabled women and domestic violence: Responding to the experiences of survivors.* Jessica Kingsley.

Tran, H. M., Huertas, A., & Moreno, A. (2017). (SA)[6]: A new framework for the analysis of smart tourism destinations. A comparative case study of two Spanish destinations. In *Seminario Internacional Destinos Turísticos* (pp. 190–214).

Tussyadiah, I. P., & Fesenmaier, D. R. (2009). Mediating tourist experiences. access to places via shared videos. *Annals of Tourism Research, 36*(1), 24–40.

UNWTO. (2020). International tourism growth continues to outpace the global economy | UNWTO. Retrieved April 11, 2021, from https://www.unwto.org/international-tourism-growth-continues-to-outpace-the-economy

Wang, D., Li, X., & Li, Y. (2013). China's "smart tourism destination" initiative: A taste of the service-dominant logic. *Journal of Destination Marketing and Management, 2*(2), 59–61.

Woodside, A. G., & Etzel, M. J. (1980). Impact of physical and mental handicaps on vacation travel behavior. *Journal of Travel Research, 18*(3), 9–11.

World Health Organization-WHO. (2015). *WHO global disability action plan 2014-2021. Better health for all people with disability* (pp. 1–32). World Health Organization.

Zhang, L.-Y., Li, N., & Min, L. (2012). On the basic concept of smarter tourism and its theoretical system. *Tourism Tribune, 27*, 66–73.

Gender and Disabilities in the Tourism Industry

Carlo Vermiglio, Valeria Naciti, Guido Noto, and Luisa Pulejo

1 Introduction

In the last decade, international organizations and scholars have highlighted the importance of focusing on the role of women in sustainable development (Langer et al., 2015; Lohani & Aburaida, 2017; Naciti et al., 2021). The Organization for Economic Cooperation and Development (OECD, 2008) observed that the female share of human capital is undervalued and underutilized worldwide.

Although notable steps have been taken on the road to women's rights, full gender equality today is still an objective to be achieved. More recently, Gender equality was addressed in Goal 5 of the 2030 Agenda for Sustainable Development Goals (SDGs) (United Nations, 2015) entitled "Achieve gender equality and empower all women and girls."

In this context, gender inequality is addressed as one of the biggest obstacles to sustainable development, economic growth, and poverty reduction.

However, in a society where people with disabilities are often treated "neutrally," it is difficult to achieve full gender equality. In fact, among disabled people, there is no inclination to reflect on the various aspects of life in terms of gender; it is as if disability exceeds and covers all other characteristics of the person. Therefore, it can be understood that gender equality—as the most significant indicator of the overcoming of discrimination affecting persons with disabilities—is far from being achieved and that the general situation of multi-discrimination suffered by disabled people is showing itself in all its criticality.

From a sectoral view, there is a wide consensus around the role played by the tourism industry in the achievement of several UN Sustainable Development Goals.

C. Vermiglio (✉) · V. Naciti · G. Noto · L. Pulejo
Department of Economics, University of Messina, Messina, Italy
e-mail: cvermiglio@unime.it; vnaciti@unime.it; gnoto@unime.it; pulejol@unime.it

© The Author(s), under exclusive license to Springer Nature Switzerland AG 2022
T. Abbate et al. (eds.), *Tourism and Disability*, Tourism on the Verge,
https://doi.org/10.1007/978-3-030-93612-9_7

Among others, tourism entrepreneurship is fundamental for gender equality targets (SDG 5).

The United Nations World Tourism Organization (UNWTO) includes the tourism and hospitality industry among the largest socio-economic sectors in the world, with an estimated impact of around 10% of the world's gross domestic product (GDP).

Nevertheless, scholars noted that tourism has always been a site for and a contributor to social inequality (Morgan & Pritchard, 1999; Walton, 2005; Cole & Morgan, 2010). For instance, Carvalho et al. (2019) stated that the "tourism sector still seems to be reinforcing gender inequalities rather than challenging them." These inequalities exist both in the perspective of workers (Cole & Morgan, 2010)—since the tourism industry often creates seasonal and low-skilled employment—and tourists—tourists may be discriminated against based on the income level and other characteristics.

The European Institute for Gender Equality (EIGE) observed that while the contribution to economic and social development is widely acknowledged in the literature, little attention has been paid to the relation between tourism and gender diversity over the years.

More in detail, people with disabilities are among the gender categories which have been substantially overlooked and whose voices have been underrepresented and marginalized over time in the tourism debate (Gilovich & McIntosh, 2020).

Starting from this assumption, this chapter analyzes gender equality in the context of sustainable development goals and with a specific focus on the tourism and hospitality industry.

The method used assumes a theoretically critical approach, and through the consideration of the immense literature on the different items considered, it is based on a conceptual analysis of themes of gender and disability in the tourism industry. A critical approach to these problems and concepts can help us effectively understand how tourist companies meet external requests and offer adequate services to the multiple discrimination to which people with disabilities are subject.

Among people with disabilities. The perception of discrimination linked to gender is quite widespread, as well as that linked to disability; what is less usual is to find women with disabilities (or, more generally, disabled people) than in reflecting on these issues also consider the intersection between these two variables. Many people with disabilities (including women) have the same attitude regarding gender issues that many non-disabled people have regarding disability issues: they think it is a question of sensitivity and politically correct, and not of rights. The multiple discrimination (Taddei, 2020) to which women with disabilities are subject can be grasped only by considering both gender and disability simultaneously.

This conceptual path helps researchers and businesses themselves to understand the relationship between gender and disability. Only by understanding its underlying meaning will it be possible to make it one is own and pursue it correctly truly.

2 Theoretical Background

2.1 The Multidimensional Diversity

The difficulties that arise from having a disability are well known to those who experience this condition firsthand and to those who, for various reasons, deal with it: physical, perceptual, and communication barriers, absence or lack of assistance services, prejudices, and stereotypes related to disability, difficulty in exercising the right to study and work in conditions of equality, less access to services, etc. (Malaguti, 2011). Moreover, it appears that women with disabilities are not equally conscious of the challenges that gender affiliation poses to all women, including those with disabilities. This happens because disability has the potential to overshadow all other aspects of a person's personality, and many women with disabilities claim that they are discriminated against more as disabled people than as women. Multiple discrimination, in this context, is a situation in which several grounds of diversity interact in such a way that they become inseparable. It can be clearly understood that the tendency to consider the different characteristics of the same person separately prevents us from understanding that the intertwining of the variable of disability with that of gender may cause an exponential effect in inequalities, i.e. multiple discrimination that makes women with disabilities more disadvantaged compared to other women, and to disabled men. The multiplier effect is not limited to circumscribed situations; it has important repercussions in most areas of the life of girls and women with disabilities: study, work, opportunities, economics, health (Casebolt, 2020), interpersonal relationships, and participation in social life.

2.2 An Overview of the Literature

Over the last decades, gender mainstreaming (GM) has attracted a great deal of attention among several economic actors (Daly, 2005; Mukhopadhyay, 2016; Addabbo et al., 2018, Calabrese et al., 2021, Galletta et al., 2021). The European Institute for Gender Equality (EIGE) defines GM as a strategy that "involves the integration of a gender perspective into the preparation, design, implementation, monitoring, and evaluation of policies, regulatory measures, and spending programs, with a view to promoting equality between women and men, and combating discrimination."

The increased awareness of gender activities has put more pressure on both private and public organizations to communicate information regarding such activities and respond to several requirements imposed by stakeholders (Miotto et al., 2019).

Also, in the tourism industry, the topic of gender has gained attention over the last decades (Kinnaird & Hall, 1996; Burrell et al., 1997).

The following graphs show a significant increase in the number of articles that framed the issue of gender equality in the tourism and hospitality industry and within social sciences, business, management, and accounting studies. The trends have been observed at the beginning of 2021 through the Scopus database (Fig. 1).

Figueroa et al. (2015) provide a critical accounting of the sub-field of tourism gender research, pointing out three main research topics: *gendered tourists,* which refers to "gendered consumption and consumer behavior in tourism experience"; the *gendered impact* of tourism in host communities, entrepreneurial opportunities and development of local cultural fabric (Figueroa-Domecq et al., 2020); *gendered labor,* concerning female empowerment in the labor force (Ferguson, 2011; Ferguson & Alarcón, 2015; Bakas et al., 2018; Hutchings et al., 2020; Dashper, 2020), salary gap (Iverson, 2000; Skalpe, 2007; Thrane, 2008; Mūnoz-Bullón, 2009), sexual harassment (Pritchard, 2014). In this regard, UNWTO (2020) stated that tourism could empower women, particularly through the provision of direct jobs and income generation in tourism and hospitality-related enterprises (Fig. 2).

According to Figueroa et al. (2015), tourism inquiry has been surprisingly gender-blind and reluctant to engage gender-aware frameworks in comparison to cognate disciplines and subject fields. Je et al. (2020) proposed a systematic literature review to assess potential implementation gaps between theory and practice in gender-oriented policies so far developed by tourism organizations. In this regard, Carvalho et al. (2019) noted that both research and industry devoted less attention to organizational culture, interaction with colleagues, and individual identities. Furthermore, Mooney (2020) noted that gender theory has evolved to fill this gap, shifting away from the static "category of the individual" associated with earlier feminist studies (Broadbridge & Simpson, 2011) to the processes that create and reinforce the organization.

Scholars have explored the interconnections between gender equality and sustainable development goals with a specific focus on the tourism industry (Ferguson, 2011; Lee-Gosselin, 2013; Alarcón & Cole, 2019; Rinaldi & Salerno, 2020), highlighting how women and other disadvantaged groups (i.e., people with disabilities, LGBT communities, etc..) greatly benefit from employment and entrepreneurial opportunities in this sector.

The issue of gender has been framed under the lens of "diversity management," where the differences of the population in terms of gender, culture, ethnicity, age, sexuality, and physical ability have been problematized by scholars with various approaches.

As noted by Thanem (2008), although the majority of diversity management research has focused on the diverse aspects of gender, race, and culture, a small body of literature has investigated issues of disability in organizations (Thanem, 2008; Woodhams & Corby, 2007; Yang & Konrad, 2011).

Kato (2019) stated that "the gender equality discourse has the power to open up possibilities for non-divisive thinking and tourism has a role in fulfilling in the advancement of knowledge production."

Like gender debate, whose diverse treatment essentially arises from social construction (Ridgeway, 1991; Lorber, 1994; Löw, 2006), *disability* is a social construct

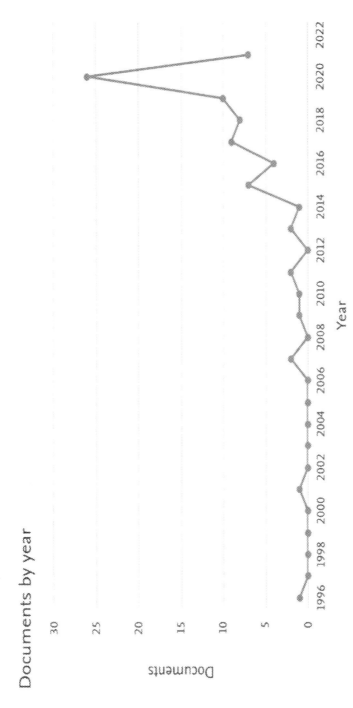

Fig. 1 Number of documents per year focused on gender and the tourism sector. Source: Scopus

Documents by subject area

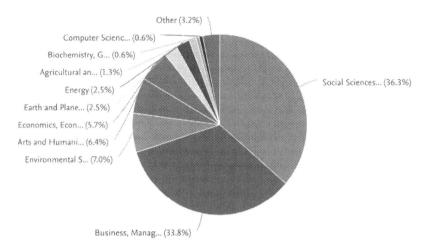

Fig. 2 Distribution of studies on gender and tourism per field of study. Source: Scopus

and can only exist within a social environment which devalues difference (Woodhams & Danieli, 2000).

Scholars framed disabilities in the tourism and hospitality industry emphasizing aspects related to the workforce of people with disabilities (Bengisu & Balta, 2011; Jasper & Waldhart, 2013), travel experience, and consumer behaviors (Burnett & Baker, 2001; Daniels et al., 2005; Darcy & Dickson, 2009), marketing practices (Cloquet et al., 2018), accessibility (Yau et al., 2004; Darcy et al., 2010).

The World Health Organization (WHO, 2012) reported that over 15% of the world population lives with some form of disability, and this percentage will tend to increase in the med-long term, leading to a shift from 1 billion people who suffer various forms of disability today, to 1.2 billion by 2050 (Vila et al. 2020).

More recently, aging has become a matter of relevance as it determines an increase in the population with disabilities which demands, among others, tourism and hospitality services.

These data ask for greater attention by policymakers, scholars, and media to tackle the remaining gaps of gender inequalities in the tourism industry.

Social sciences, and more specifically, business management and accounting, are the main fields wherein the topic has been framed over the last decade—namely from 2011 to 2020. Figures 3 and 4 clearly depict the trends observed at the beginning of 2021 through the Scopus database.

Ferreira et al. (2020) noted that facilitating the access of people with disabilities to tourism should be considered a prerequisite for the sustainability of tourism itself. Similarly, Gilovich and McIntosh (2020) observed that disability, especially the perspectives and experiences of people with disabilities, cannot be neglected when addressing the Sustainable Development Goals in tourism.

Fig. 3 Number of documents per year focused on disability and the tourism sector. Source: Scopus

Documents by subject area

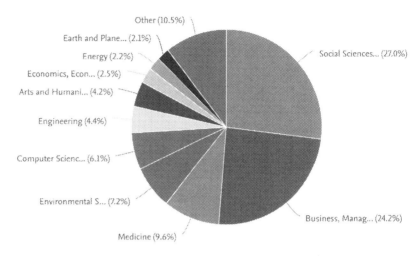

Fig. 4 Distribution of studies on disability and tourism per field of study. Source: Scopus

Both academics and practitioners believe that tourism can empower women and people with disabilities in multiple ways (i.e., through the provision of jobs and income-generating opportunities in small- and larger-scale tourism and hospitality-related enterprises).

Although the 2030 Agenda for Sustainable Development frames tourism within Goal 8 (decent work) and Goal 12 (responsible consumption and production), several reasons suggest broadening the vision starting to address the importance of tourism and hospitality industry to achieve different targets.

3 Discussion and Conclusion

This study tried to build a critical link between gender equality and disability in the tourism industry. Being a woman with disabilities means being subjected to double discrimination. This means confronting all the barriers that already limit or prevent people with disabilities from participating fully in social life and enjoying their rights and fundamental freedoms. The combination of these two conditions of exclusion also causes a multiplier effect on inequalities, making them more discriminated against than other women and, obviously, compared to other men with disabilities.

The lack of specific data and statistics elaborated by public bodies on discrimination affecting women and girls with disabilities also makes it impossible to analyze their participation in social life and thus the recognition of equal opportunities in all sectors of life, hindering them, in fact, the adoption of dedicated political measures and actions.

Despite little attention so far, framing disability within the gender debate can offer alternative ways to understand the relationship between the development of gender and tourism and provide inspiration for creative and progressive ways to take advantage of tourism to meet people with disabilities (Ferguson, 2011).

In this context, tourism can be a social power due to the ability to promote contact between peoples, which are increasingly needed to understand each other and work harmoniously in a world where space, resources, and options decrease quickly (Higgins-Desbiolles, 2006). Therefore, a critical approach to these issues and concepts can effectively help us to understand:

1. How tourism companies are responding to demand of the need of people with disabilities and to the challenges of sustainable development; and
2. What new practical approach tourism companies could adopt to achieve gender equality (i.e., UN SDGs).

From the literature analysis, it emerges that over the years, the interest in accessible tourism issues has grown significantly, both for the potential development of a strategic economic sector and for the recognized ability of tourism and leisure activities to promote social inclusion of people with disabilities. In the face of academics' increased interest, the number of initiatives dedicated to tourists with specific needs has also grown significantly (Dickson et al., 2017; Rubio Escuderos et al., 2021).

However, the main problem that seems to limit the potential in this field is the lack of managerial tools available to managers for measuring the phenomenon and being accountable for the results achieved in terms of organizational well-being. Managers in the tourism industry need to be aware of gaps in gender, disability, and other sources of diversity. This information is key to inform future strategies aimed at addressing sustainable development as defined by SDGs.

This study brings to light both practical and theoretical implications: change of perspective could be decisive both in academia and in the tourism and hospitality industry. Indeed, the topic of gender and disabilities in general and its application to the tourism industry would be of great interest to academics, industry players, private investors/entrepreneurs looking to expand their business, and policymakers.

First, through research and in-depth study, scholars can properly emphasize the importance of the "multi-diversity" aspect for the actual achievement of gender equality. Furthermore, scholars might be interested in exploring this topic from multiple viewpoints, such as CSR impact, consumer behavior, stakeholder management, and value chain management.

Second, like all the other players in our society, tourism companies are called upon to respond to the problems committed to the multi-discriminatory aspect and make their own contribution by creating value and increasing collective well-being. To do that, strategy and accounting practices such as plans and budgets including different diversity dimensions (such as gender and disability) could be pivotal to pave the way toward improved organizational well-being. When assessing market structure, competitive performance, and differentiating characteristics of their value proposition, firms operating in the sector may find it helpful to address managerial trade-offs.

Finally, policymakers may be aided in determining whether to promote the development of impairments in tourism and, if so, to what amount and with what types of measures.

References

Addabbo, T., Klatzer, E., Schlager, C., Villa, P., & De Villota, P. (2018). Challenges of austerity and retrenchment of gender equality. In A. O'Hagan & E. Klatzer (Eds.), *Gender Budgeting in Europe* (pp. 57–85). Palgrave Macmillan.

Alarcón, D. M., & Cole, S. (2019). No sustainability for tourism without gender equality. *Journal of Sustainable Tourism, 27*(7), 903–919.

Bakas, F. E., Costa, C., Breda, Z., & Durão, M. (2018). A critical approach to the gender wage gap in tourism labor. *Tourism Culture & Communication, 18*(1), 35–49.

Bengisu, M., & Balta, S. (2011). Employment of the workforce with disabilities in the hospitality industry. *Journal of Sustainable Tourism, 19*(1), 35–57.

Broadbridge, A., & Simpson, R. (2011). 25 years on: Reflecting on the past and looking to the future in gender and management research. *British Journal of Management, 22*(3), 470–483.

Burnett, J. J., & Baker, H. B. (2001). Assessing the travel-related behaviors of the mobility-disabled consumer. *Journal of Travel Research, 40*(1), 4–11.

Burrell, J., Manfredi, S., Rollin, H., Price, L., & Stead, L. (1997). Equal opportunities for women employees in the hospitality industry: A comparison between France, Italy, Spain and the UK. *International Journal of Hospitality Management, 16*(2), 161–179.

Calabrese, A., Fede, M. C., Naciti, V., & Rappazzo, N. (2021). Female careers in Italian universities: The role of gender budgeting to achieve equality between women and men. *Zeszyty Naukowe Uniwersytetu Ekonomicznego w Krakowie/Cracow Review of Economics and Management, 5*(989), 31–47.

Carvalho, I., & C., Costa, and A. Torres. (2019). Gender awareness and women managers in tourism: Perceptions of inequality and what could be done. In E. T. Pereira & P. Paoloni (Eds.), *Handbook of research on women in management and the global labor market* (pp. 218–238). IGI Global.

Casebolt, M. T. (2020). Barriers to reproductive health services for women with disability in low-and middle-income countries: A review of the literature. *Sexual & Reproductive Healthcare, 24*, 100485.

Cloquet, I., Palomino, M., Shaw, G., Stephen, G., & Taylor, T. (2018). Disability, social inclusion and the marketing of tourist attractions. *Journal of Sustainable Tourism, 26*(2), 221–237.

Cole, S., & Morgan, N. (2010). *Tourism and inequality: Problems and prospects*. CABI.

Daly, M. (2005). Gender mainstreaming in theory and practice. *Social Politics: International Studies in Gender, State & Society, 12*(3), 433–450.

Daniels, M. J., Rodgers, E. D. B., & Wiggins, B. P. (2005). "Travel Tales": An interpretive analysis of constraints and negotiations to pleasure travel as experienced by persons with physical disabilities. *Tourism Management, 26*(6), 919–930.

Darcy, S., Cameron, B., & Pegg, S. (2010). Accessible tourism and sustainability: A discussion and case study. *Journal of Sustainable Tourism, 18*(4), 515–537.

Darcy, S., & Dickson, T. J. (2009). A whole-of-life approach to tourism: The case for accessible tourism experiences. *Journal of Hospitality and Tourism Management, 16*(1), 32–44.

Dashper, K. (2020). Holidays with my horse: Human-horse relationships and multispecies tourism experiences. *Tourism Management Perspectives, 34*, 100678.

Dickson, T. J., Misener, L., & Darcy, S. (2017). Enhancing destination competitiveness through disability sport event legacies: Developing an interdisciplinary typology. *International Journal of Contemporary Hospitality Management, 29*(3), 924–946.

Ferguson, L. (2011). Promoting gender equality and empowering women? Tourism and the third millennium development goal. *Current Issues in Tourism, 14*(3), 235–249.

Ferreira, A. F., Akasaka, Y., de Oliveira Pinheiro, M. G., & Chang, S. K. (2020). Information as the first attribute of accessibility: A method for assessing the information provided by urban rail systems to tourists with reduced mobility. *Sustainability, 12*(23), 10185.

Ferguson, L., & Alarcon, D. M. (2015). Gender and sustainable tourism: Reflections on theory and practice. *Journal of Sustainable Tourism, 23*(3), 401–416.

Figueroa-Domecq, C., Pritchard, A., Segovia-Pérez, M., Morgan, N., & Villacé-Molinero, T. (2015). Tourism gender research: A critical accounting. *Annals of Tourism Research, 52*, 87–103.

Figueroa-Domecq, C., de Jong, A., & Williams, A. M. (2020). Gender, tourism & entrepreneurship: A critical review. *Annals of Tourism Research, 84*, 102980.

Galletta, S., Mazzù, S., Naciti, V., & Vermiglio, C. (2021). Gender diversity and sustainability performance in the banking industry. In *Corporate Social Responsibility and Environmental Management*, 1–14.

Gilovich, B., & McIntosh, A. (2020). Accessibility and inclusive tourism development: Current state and future agenda. *Sustainability, 12*(22), 9722.

Higgins-Desbiolles, F. (2006). More than an "industry": The forgotten power of tourism as a social force. *Tourism Management, 27*(6), 1192–1208.

Hutchings, K., Moyle, C. L., Chai, A., Garofano, N., & Moore, S. (2020). Segregation of women in tourism employment in the APEC region. *Tourism Management Perspectives, 34*, 100655.

Iverson, K. (2000). The paradox of the contented female manager: An empirical investigation of gender differences in pay expectation in the hospitality industry. *Hospital Management, 19*(1), 22–51.

Jasper, C. R., & Waldhart, P. (2013). Employer attitudes on hiring employees with disabilities in the leisure and hospitality industry. *International Journal of Contemporary Hospitality Management, 25*(4), 577–594.

Je, J. S., Khoo, C., & Yang, E. C. L. (2020). Gender issues in tourism organisations: Insights from a two-phased pragmatic systematic literature review. *Journal of Sustainable Tourism*, 1–24.

Kato, K. (2019). Gender and sustainability–exploring ways of knowing–an ecohumanities perspective. *Journal of Sustainable Tourism, 27*(7), 939–956.

Kinnaird, V., & Hall, D. (1996). Understanding tourism processes: A gender-aware framework. *Tourism Management, 17*(2), 95–102.

Langer, A., Meleis, A., Knaul, F. M., Atun, R., Aran, M., Arreola-Ornelas, H., . . . Frenk, J. (2015). Women and health: The key for sustainable development. *The Lancet, 386*(9999), 1165–1210.

Lee-Gosselin, H., Briere, S., & Ann, H. (2013). Resistances to gender mainstreaming in organizations: Toward a new approach. *Gender in Management: An International Journal, 28*(8), 468–485.

Lohani, M., & Aburaida, L. (2017). Women empowerment: A key to sustainable development. *The Social ION, 6*(2), 26–29.

Lorber, J. (1994). "Night to his day": The social construction of gender. *Paradoxes of gender, 1*, 1–8.

Löw, M. (2006). The social construction of space and gender. *European Journal of Women's Studies, 13*(2), 119–133.

Malaguti, E. (2011). Donne e uomini con disabilità. Studi di genere, disability studies e nuovi intrecci contemporanei. Ricerche di Pedagogia e Didattica. *Journal of Theories and Research in Education, 6*(1), 1–13.

Miotto, G., López, M. P., & Rodríguez, J. R. (2019). Gender equality and UN sustainable development goals: Priorities and correlations in the top business schools' communication and legitimation strategies. *Sustainability, 11*(2), 302.

Mooney, S. K. (2020). Gender research in hospitality and tourism management: Time to change the guard. *International Journal of Contemporary Hospitality Management, 32.*

Morgan, N., & Pritchard, A. (1999). *Power and politics at the seaside: The development of Devon's resorts in the twentieth century.* University of Exeter Press.

Muñoz-Bullón, F. (2009). The gap between male and female pay in the Spanish tourism industry. *Tourism Management, 30*(5), 638–649.

Mukhopadhyay, M. (2016). Mainstreaming gender or "streaming" gender away: Feminists marooned in the development business. In W. Harcourt (Ed.), *The Palgrave handbook of gender and development* (pp. 77–91). Palgrave Macmillan.

Naciti, V., Cesaroni, F., & Pulejo, L. (2021). Corporate governance and sustainability: A review of the existing literature. *Journal of Management and Governance.* https://doi.org/10.1007/s10997-020-09554-6

Organisation for Economic Co-operation and Development. (2008). *OECD Factbook 2008.* OECD Publishing.

Pritchard, A. (2014). *Gender and feminist perspectives in tourism research* (pp. 314–324). The Wiley Blackwell companion to tourism.

Ridgeway, C. (1991). The social construction of status value: Gender and other nominal characteristics. *Social Forces, 70*(2), 367–386.

Rinaldi, A., & Salerno, I. (2020). The tourism gender gap and its potential impact on the development of the emerging countries. *Quality & Quantity, 54*(5), 1465–1477.

Rubio-Escuderos, L., García-Andreu, H., Michopoulou, E., & Buhalis, D. (2021). *Perspectives on experiences of tourists with disabilities: Implications for their daily lives and for the tourist industry* (pp. 1–15). Tourism Recreation Research.

Skalpe, O. (2007). The CEO gender pay gap in the tourism industry—Evidence from Norway. *Tourism Management, 28*(3), 845–853.

Taddei, A. (2020). *Come fenici: donne con disabilità e vie per l'emancipazione.* Franco Angeli.

Thanem, T. (2008). Embodying disability in diversity management research. *Diversity Management Research, 27*(2), 581–586.

Thrane, C. (2008). Earnings differentiation in the tourism industry: Gender, human capital and socio-demographic effects. *Tourism Management, 29*(3), 514–524.

United Nations. (2015). Transforming our world: The 2030 agenda for sustainable development. Outcome document for the UN summit to adopt the Post-2015 development agenda: Draft for adoption, New York

United Nations World Tourism Organization. (2021). *International tourism highlights* (2020th ed.). UNWTO. https://doi.org/10.18111/9789284422456

Vila, T. D., González, E. A., & Darcy, S. (2020). Accessibility of tourism websites: The level of countries' commitment. *Universal Access in the Information Society, 19*(2), 331–346.

Walton, J. K. (Ed.). (2005). *Histories of tourism: Representation, identity and conflict.* Channel View Publications.

Woodhams, C., & Danieli, A. (2000). Disability and diversity–a difference too far? *Personnel Review, 29*(3), 402–416.

Woodhams, C., & Corby, S. (2007). Then and now: Disability legislation and employers' practices in the UK. *British Journal of Industrial Relations, 45*(3), 556–580.

World Health Organization-WHO: A66/12. (2012). Disability. Report by the secretariat. Published 11 March 2012, including EB132/10.

Yang, Y., & Konrad, A. M. (2011). Understanding diversity management practices: Implications of institutional theory and resource-based theory. *Group & Organization Management, 36*(1), 6–38.

Yau, M. K. S., McKercher, B., & Packer, T. L. (2004). Traveling with a disability: More than an access issue. *Annals of Tourism Research, 31*(4), 946–960.

Social Farms in Support of Local and Accessible Tourism

Grazia Calabrò, Rosa Concetta Chirieleison, Carlo Giannetto, and Maurizio Lanfranchi

1 Introduction: Social Tourism

In the last decade, different forms of tourism were born, also including "social tourism." Different meanings are attributed to the expression "social tourism," and these entail different interpretations which are linked to an ethical approach, in some cases related to marketing. This form of tourism is organized by public and private bodies in order to spread and enhance the territory's resources. A first and basic definition that can be attributed to social tourism is the one proposed in 2006 by the International Bureau of Social Tourism, which defines it as access to travel and leisure opportunities for all. Academic literature has long highlighted the ethical and economic importance of social tourism for companies, territories, and tourists. Indeed, it seeks to carry out a cultural change aiming at thinking and designing the spaces and services of tourist structures in order to make them accessible to everyone without any distinction. All of this characterizes a more inclusive and evolved social model (Kastenholz et al., 2015). Therefore, alongside green tourism, there is the vital need for an inclusive tourism that is able to overcome social, cultural, gender, and age barriers, with the ultimate aim of guaranteeing to each individual the right to travel. In this context, it is fundamental to involve local communities in the promotion of their own territory as a place for receiving social tourists. In order to protect the territory, it is necessary to create sustainable and responsible tourist pathways involving local communities (Altinay et al., 2016). Only then can the tourist make use of the services, but at the same time, he can be an actor and become a true and proper "community animator." One of the objectives of social tourism is to allow access to travel to the weakest social categories and to groups of disadvantaged

---

G. Calabrò · R. C. Chirieleison · C. Giannetto (✉) · M. Lanfranchi
Department of Economics, University of Messina, Messina, Italy
e-mail: grazia.calabro@unime.it; rchirieleison@unime.it; giannettoc@unime.it; mlanfranchi@unime.it

© The Author(s), under exclusive license to Springer Nature Switzerland AG 2022
T. Abbate et al. (eds.), *Tourism and Disability*, Tourism on the Verge,
https://doi.org/10.1007/978-3-030-93612-9_8

individuals for economic, physical, or cultural reasons (such as less fortunate people, disabled, families with children, elderly, etc.). The concept of social tourism is therefore linked to that of accessible tourism; the common goal is that of making each tourist feel like an active protagonist of his holiday (Scheyvens & Biddulph, 2018). The offer of accessible hospitality is an indicator of efficiency, professionality, and quality of the service itself, classifying the structure that manages to do so as highly competitive (Brodeala, 2020). There are certainly different competitive benefits that this type of hospitality can bring to tourist structures, but, *in primis*, they could provide a valid contribution to face the problem of the depersonalization of demand as well as an opportunity in terms of differentiation of supply (Domínguez et al., 2013). This conceptual study shows how accessible tourism is positioned within rural tourism. The aim is to better understand cultural, social, financial, and environmental implications resulting from accessible tourism. The practical and theoretical contribution of this study can be summarized in two terms: improvement and realization of universal accessibility. In our opinion, these terms should encourage innovation in the private and public activities of tourism businesses.

2 An Overview of Accessible Tourism

According to the World Tourism Organization (WTO), accessible tourism is the form of tourism that is attentive to the needs of everyone and presents a very high-quality offer. In this definition, the concept of need is very wide and includes, for example, the necessities of children, the elderly, people with disabilities, those who suffer from allergies, difficulties related to food, etc. These requirements should prompt tourist companies to create hospitality aimed at reception, dialogue, and technical knowledge. According to this definition of disability, the WTO estimates 38 million potential tourists in Europe and 3.5 million tourists in Italy. To these figures, the multiplying factor estimated at 2.8 million companions must be added. The development and realization of accessible tourism have the primary objective of creating a network of means, information, accommodation, and restaurants that can prove to be accessible to all types of tourists who represent the demand. Creating accessible tourism means offering autonomy to travel, ensuring the connection between different services, and the reliability of the information on structures and itineraries. According to this version, every tourist must have the possibility of independently assessing the level of compliance of the structure to their needs. According to Darcy et al. (2010), accessible tourism is composed of a complex of structures and services made available to people with disabilities or special needs so that they can enjoy the possibility of traveling, staying, and taking part in events without encountering problems or difficulties, in full autonomy, but also in safety and comfort. According to Caldas et al. (2021), the accessibility of places does not have to determine the holiday, but the tourist should choose a destination or a tourist structure because he or she likes it and not because it is the only accessible one. In

2020, the European Commission Enterprise and Industry indicated that accessible tourism, as well as representing a social responsibility, is an economic tool for competitiveness for tourist businesses. The difficulties of undertaking a journey for people with disabilities are represented not only by the holiday experience but often also by all that consists in the organization before departure and in retrieving information on the place that one decides to visit (Matausch et al., 2009). Indeed, most people with special needs often do not choose the destination for their holidays because it is the one they wish to visit, but their choice depends on the lack of information regarding the places, the receptive structures, the transports, the services available, etc. According to Altinay et al. (2016), in the field of accessible tourism, precisely for the lack of objective findings and clear and credible information sources, word of mouth becomes the most efficient communication tool. According to Brodeala (2020), depending on the need and disability, tourists with particular requirements need different information, and for this reason, it is important to create tourist structures accessible to all needs. According to De La Fuente-Robles et al. (2020), it is necessary to qualify and train the "human capital" which operates within the tourist structure and which can understand and meet any need expressed by the tourist. Finally, according to Gillovic and McIntosh (2020), in the context of reception and of accessible tourism, first of all, some stereotypes linked to the concept of disability should be broken down. Indeed, when a relationship with a disabled tourist is established, the principles must be the same as those established with all the other tourists (Eusébio et al., 2021; Takeda & Card, 2002).

3 Accessible Tourism: The Quality of Accommodation and of Hotel and Non-Hotel Hospitality

Talking about accessible tourism implies the need to reorganize the sector with the objective of ensuring that the innovations introduced in terms of organization and management, aimed at making it more inclusive, have general positive impacts on all types of users. Indeed, what tourism often lacks, to be truly accessible, is not so much the attention given to the organizational aspects, but rather the limited capacity for coordination and synergies among the actors involved in various ways (Buhalisa & Michopouloub, 2011).

Very frequently, there is the will to create specific and sectoral forms of tourism rather than rethinking the touristic offering in order to make it as inclusive as possible or to focus on some aspects while losing sight of others which are essential to be able to speak about tourist experience. Many of the barriers to accessible tourism identified by Cassia et al. (2021) are represented by elements that, if carefully managed, would not only lead to an improvement in the quality and accessibility of the tourist service but would have positive effects also on the general context and on people's quality of life. As a consequence, it is up to the tourism entrepreneur to seize the opportunity deriving from breaking down these barriers also to orientate tourism toward sustainability and conformity to the goals of the 2030 Agenda. According to Cassia et al. (2021), three types of limits result from the analysis of the literature on accessible tourism:

1. The studies have mainly focused on the most structural and infrastructural aspects rather than an assessment of the tourist experience.
2. Attention has almost always been paid to single initiatives and not on an integrated and global organization.
3. The role of technology is limited almost exclusively to the accessibility of information and little on the opportunities that can derive from it in terms of tourist fruition and experience.

It follows that coordination, cooperation, clear identification of roles and responsibilities, and efficient communication represent the strengths to be able to efficiently speak about accessible and inclusive tourism. To this end, paying attention to quality in the organization of tourist service represents an indispensable condition in order to improve the touristic offering and the wide possibility of fruition by many numerous categories of subjects, especially where, as in the case of rural areas, it is necessary to create numerous conditions that may represent a driving force for the sector (Burnett & Baker, 2001; Leal et al., 2020).

Moreover, in order to ensure the quality, accessibility, and the inclusiveness of touristic offer, a predominant role is played by the context in which the supply is developed, given that the possibility to fully and satisfactorily enjoy the tourist experience is also strongly dependent on the ways of managing and socially integrating disabled people in everyday life and not only in their role of tourists. (Domínguez Vila et al., 2019).

Indeed, there is no doubt that the territorial context has a determining influence both on the organization and on the quality perception of the touristic offer; as a consequence, the context becomes an integral part of the tourist experience (Calabrò & Vieri, 2016). Hence there is a need, when speaking of accessible tourism, to deviate from exclusive attention toward organizational measures that can be undertaken with the aim of enabling and improving physical accessibility to tourism and to focus more on the relational dynamics between tourists, reference context, and sector operators (Leal et al., 2020). It follows that when considering the need to organize the tourist sector in order to expand the supply and make it more inclusive, it must be ensured that the key elements which characterize the quality of touristic offer are organized among themselves, especially in such a way as to be positively perceived by tourists (Calabrò & Vieri, 2014). Indeed, it is by now well known that the quality path develops through a systemic approach whose elements, closely interlinked, influence each other to the point that a bad quality perception of one of the elements of the system will inevitably have negative effects on the quality perception of the whole system. There are numerous elements that can influence quality perception. These can depend on the phase preceding the fruition of the tourist service and are implied in the fact that tourism is an experience good; as a consequence, great attention must also be paid to the search phrase, which must be as easy and efficient as possible.

Some studies have highlighted the role of common information and navigational tools for the search phase (Altinay et al., 2016), which, despite having an important role, especially with regard to accessible tourism, sometimes did not prove they were up to it (Domínguez Vila et al., 2018).

But also, the virtual relational aspect acquires a significant role since this relational dynamic represents the prelude to a real dynamic that turns into a judgment. Therefore, the relational dynamic is one of the key points in the quality management within the service. It is no coincidence that the interaction moment is defined as a "moment of truth," that is, the moment in which waiting turns into judgment (Joo & Cho, 2012). It goes without saying that much of the attention that must be devoted to the organization of an accessible and quality tourist service must be paid to the staff training, in terms of competence but, above all, in terms of attitude. In the complex dynamic of the service, characterized by peculiar elements that make absolutely necessary careful strategic planning, it is not possible to entrust the success of the result to the operators' sensitivity, but it is necessary to be able to develop such a level of awareness that the operator's attitude may be perceived by customers in a positive way and, as a consequence, the judgment measured on the received service may be such as to ensure the possibility of business survival in the long term. Training must be adaptable and flexible since, at any moment, the tourist sector operator must be able to operate in such a way as to ensure the maximum customer satisfaction, without revealing emotions or feelings that, to some extent, may even offend her and therefore turn the organizational investment made to improve the service quality into a negative perception. As a matter of fact, competitiveness among the different forms of touristic offers is ensured not only by "what" is offered to the tourist, but especially by "how" it is offered and, within the service, by "who" plays the main role in developing the moment of truth. Some studies (Di Nardo et al., 2014) have highlighted that some demographic variables, such as age or gender, can influence the attitude toward the relationship, in general, with disabled people. This would concern, in particular, women and the youngest or oldest age group (Parasuram, 2006). This could represent a potential strength for the development of accessible tourism in rural areas, where women, youngsters, and elders have an important role in the organization of the touristic offer. Indeed, there are plenty of experiences that have shown how the creation of relational synergy between the people from rural areas and those tourists with specific needs has given life to a mutual exchange of positive experiences (Giraud et al., 2020). As a consequence, the structurally advanced rural areas already have by themselves some features, such as a good degree of integration between the different economic activities present on the territory and a closer relationship between the different actors and the territorial context, such as to configure a more human-centered socio-economic system, predisposing to promote inclusion through better accessibility (Cassia et al., 2021).

4 Rural Tourism and Accessibility

Over the past few years, there has been an evolution in the tourist's behavior and preferences since we have passed from a form of mass tourism toward a personalized type of tourism based on sustainable holidays (Darcy & Pegg, 2011). Rurality can represent a great engine of development for a territory since, through a suitable rural development policy, it is possible not only to safeguard the environmental and landscape heritage but also to curb the process of economic-structural crisis. The reference parameters to identify rural areas are the population density, the demographic impact, and the related old-age index, the employment rate, and the degree of intensity of the agricultural activity. Indicators measuring the degree of rural intensity are the total agricultural area (TAA), the utilized agricultural area (UAA), the average company UAA, and the businesses with activities connected to agriculture and food industry. A development of the rural world that can be considered as modern aims not only at increasing economic indicators such as the gross domestic product (GDP), since the well-being of the community is also measured based on the acquisition of higher levels of quality of life (Bianchi et al., 2020; Michopoulou et al., 2009). Traditional monetary indicators, such as income and wealth, are indeed incomplete and partial measures, not suited to measure a person's life quality. The development of a rural area must provide for the activation of a series of sustainable and endogenous production activities; therefore, the role fulfilled by agriculture becomes central. Agriculture is able to integrate itself with other production activities in the territory providing services and generating a relevant income from the economic and social point of view. Modern agriculture has an environmental function and can have a tourist function. It, therefore, adjusts its production function to the need of the environmental one, recognizing its priority role. The centrality of agriculture enables to identify a local rural development system. The farm had once the only function of providing the urban environment with products intended to satisfy the primary need for nutrition (Lanfranchi & Giannetto, 2015). Today, instead, the agricultural entrepreneur also guarantees the quality of products, environmental sustainability, territorial development, and rural tourism.

Rural tourism offers the opportunity to escape from the city and detach oneself from the stressful urban rhythms, also combining with the desire for curiosity and for a return to nature. This includes different forms of tourism directly linked to the resources of rural territory, namely all those forms of tourism in which the rural culture is the most important element (Lanfranchi et al., 2014). The resources of rurality consist of agriculture with its typical products, of eno-gastronomic and folkloristic traditions, of the protected green areas, of handicraft, and of the cultural and artistic heritage present in the little centers of rural areas. This type of sustainable tourism linked to agricultural activity and to the rediscovery of tradition and local cultures is undoubtedly one of the priorities that the land development policy should pursue in order to revitalize the economy of rural areas. The relevant role covered by the typical Italian agri-food heritage is supported by the fact that the presence of typical agriculture interrelated with the territory attracts important touristic flows, which give life to different types of alternative and environmentally friendly tourism. Indeed, the importance of exploiting synergies between agriculture, territory, and tourism is highlighted by some contingent elements, which show how this link may represent a real opportunity for the future development of the local economy. This form of tourism in the years has recorded an increase in demand which has favored the appearance of a tourist offer diversified at the local level.

Rural tourism performs many functions, such as creating a supplementary income and new professional figures, promoting disadvantaged territories and enhancing the related infrastructures, creating exchanges and synergies between the rural and the urban environment, and multiplying investments. Among the main goals of rural tourism, we can find that of encouraging the re-balance between the ecological, socioeconomic, and cultural system, improving the level income of agricultural entrepreneurs, and creating diversified and accessible tourism. This form of rural tourism is influenced by a series of actions and initiatives that must be implemented by the local government through a suitable and efficient policy of socioeconomic and environmental planning of rural territory, in order to safeguard the natural and cultural resources and to adjust the infrastructural system to the changeable and growing needs of the local population. Rural tourism also aims at satisfying the growing interest toward the natural, cultural, and local heritage, creating a relationship of cohesion and social exchange. The tourists who are attracted by this form of tourism usually look for a new and different lifestyle which may take them away from urban life and help them rediscover contact with nature. The activity of rural tourism enhances food, sport, nature, and health. The main segments are cultural tourism, ecotourism, slow tourism, adventure tourism, eno-gastronomic tourism, folklore tourism, tourism of popular traditions, sports tourism, and agritourism. The latter represents the exemplary model of multifunctionality in agriculture. Multifunctionality must be seen as a resource for the individual citizen since it includes many functions that can be expressed in as many activities that go alongside the traditional ones of the primary sector (Caldas et al., 2021). In specific terms, we refer to activities ranging from agritourism, for example, educational farms, to zero-kilometer sales, to the exploitation of alternative energies, to the valorization of social tourism, and, not least, to social-therapeutic farms. As stated above, with the term multifunctionality, the terms agriculture, social tourism, and rural tourism are linked together. With this tourist form, the concept of accessible tourism, in which agricultural enterprises provide a series of services to disabled people, is implemented. These services improve the life quality of the most disadvantaged people, considering the weakest social groups and those who risk marginalization.

Realizing a project on accessible tourism, regardless of the limits and territorial features, implies a great effort since it is necessary to approach a transversal social, engineering, and architectural study related to the techniques which have accessibility and disability as their object. It is not sufficient to send a tourist package that exalts only natural attractions and the heritage of the territory or the excellence in the comfort of hotels or restaurants, but it is essential to highlight the concept of integration and of applied accessibility. Therefore, by accessibility, we do not only mean the elimination of architectural barriers, but it is a much more complex concept, a wide and variegated process (Jurado Almonte, 2014). The participation of people with disabilities (PWD) in rural tourism has only recently received growing academic interest. Inclusion has to be examined from a legislative, marketing, and communication point of view. From this latter point of view, the images and representations of tourists with disabilities must be highlighted as images of users included in society, and in particular within a family context. However, it is pointed out that communication for PWD rarely caters to the whole family members, making the tourist's experience difficult in the pre-journey phase. These results indicate a weak implementation of the concept of inclusiveness (Cloquet et al., 2018). For this reason, it is pointed out that accessible tourism in rural areas should provide the ease of use and enjoyment, for all people, of the different tourist experiences. Giving tourists with disabilities a fair chance of accessing and participating in recreational and tourist activities helps create a positive sentiment which is consequently extended to their relatives and friends (Wan 2015).

According to Buhalisa and Michopouloub (2011), accessible tourism market is not homogenous but includes different subsegments which have different needs and requirements. According to this study, every tourist is unique in his capacities and preferences, and this is more evident in the rural tourism market. The main requirements of these segments focus on three interconnected elements, which are (1) the accessible environment, (2) the information on accessibility, and (3) the information accessible online. Information and communications technologies (ICT) can facilitate the fruition of tourist destinations and address more easily the particular needs of this market segment. The customization of the tourist package enables the users themselves to specify their own needs. Through the use of ICT, users are able to declare their own needs and their habits and to accurately formulate their own needs and requests. Therefore, destinations can offer products and services adapted to the specific needs of each traveler and favor the participation corresponding to the social model of disability (Sica et al., 2021). Although the provisions adopted to meet the needs of tourists with disabilities have increased, still today, especially for rural tourism, there are many problems (discriminatory barriers and practices) that make traveling difficult for tourists with disabilities. Besides, still today, it should be noted that there are a limited number of actors involved in ensuring the ease of accessibility to tourists with disabilities (Bianchi et al., 2020). The results of different studies reveal that often, in rural areas, there are deficient pedestrian paths, with relevant problems of accessibility in the different tourist routes. It is specified that innovative measures to improve accessibility are necessary. These measures may represent an instrument for the development of new tourist packages in the context of rural areas to strengthen the competitiveness of the tourist destination (Santana-Santana et al., 2020).

Besides, the analysis of the literature shows that there is a strong lack of cooperation among the actors present in the rural tourist sector to create an accessible tourist development (Vinogradova et al., 2015). The results show that the stakeholder should adopt an organic, circulatory, and collaborative relationship to realize inclusive tourism in an innovative way. To this end, four innovative interrelated themes are considered: control and coordination, communication, clearness of roles and responsibilities, cooperation and integration (Nyanjom et al., 2018). Finally, the results of various studies have found that accessible tourism represents a critical dimension consisting of a series of interdependent commercial agreements extending beyond the business sphere. Therefore, it is necessary to improve the experiences of accessible destinations by all tour operators in order to adequately satisfy the accessible tourism market (Darcy et al., 2010).

5 Conclusions

The process of social and cultural awareness raising for PWD has led to a change in the concept of destinations resulting from the need to make the territory accessible to everyone. Therefore, accessibility is configured as one of the most important features on which the touristic offer has to focus, since it enables to meet demand and offers the possibility of satisfying all the needs of PWD. As we have explained in this work, the target of tourists with disabilities represents a very large market share that the whole tourist sector must be able to adequately intercept and satisfy, in order to ensure from the economic point of view a significant contribution in terms of turnover. Accessible tourism, therefore, as well as affirming the social and ethical value of a population, represents a promising business leverage that could bring a considerable increase to the revenues of the whole tourist sector. As highlighted in this study, PWD tends to travel always in company, thus ensuring a multiplier effect on the numbers. The possibility of discovering new realities, of coming into contact with new cultures, of tasting a typical product, or of visiting a city of art, must not be an exclusive privilege of the people considered as non-disabled, but a pleasure that connects everyone, which is why it becomes necessary to design and develop tourist resorts in such a way as to be able to welcome any kind of person with specific needs. Therefore, the objective that the management of the employees in the accessible tourism sector proposes is to concretize a network of structures and activities which may enable everyone to be able to decide where to spend their free time or their holiday based on personal wishes and choices, not having to contemplate at first sight the accessibility of a destination with respect to another one.

When disability is concerned, it is normally thought that the only solution to provide is the elimination of architectural barriers, not considering the further problems that affect the physically weakest individuals. The fact that this category can also include some types of disabilities with other kinds of difficulties, such as the subjects with allergies or food intolerances, the elderly, or the families with children, is frequently overlooked. In this regard, we highlight the importance of the social value of accessible tourism, meant as wellness not only for PWD but as wellness for society as a whole. Certainly, as regards the receptive structures, creating a completely accessible place is highly expensive both for the design of new structures and the adjustment of already existing buildings to the proposed standards. This problem emerges in particular for those tourist facilities present in rural areas which have greater difficulties in fully adapting to the standards. For them, the process appears to be longer both for economic and structural problems. Despite this, through the agricultural sector and the agricultural entrepreneur's multifunctionality, it is possible to develop interesting agricultural and social tourism activities. These activities offer a different way to develop rural areas since they manage to bring out all the potentials and opportunities of a local community, which is based not only on food production but on the realization of ad hoc services for the tourist in order to create a system of relationship based on trust, knowledge, and reciprocity. Through agriculture and social tourism, agricultural enterprises can ensure a series of services both to tourists with disabilities and to the whole rural community. We aim to extend our future research by increasing the debate on accessible tourism and by improving the use and integration of accessible tourism tools in order to allow tourism economic actors involved to improve the accessibility of the tourism offer and make it more competitive in terms of quality of service.

References

Altinay, Z., Saner, T., Bahçelerli, N. M., & Altinay, F. (2016). The role of social media tools: Accessible tourism for disabled citizens. *Educational Technology and Society, 19*(1), 89–99.

Bianchi, P., Cappelletti, G. M., Mafrolla, E., Sica, E., & Sisto, R. (2020). Accessible tourism in natural park areas: A social network analysis to discard barriers and provide information for people with disabilities. *Sustainability, 12*(23), 9915.

Brodeala, L. C. (2020). Online recommender system for accessible tourism destinations. In *RecSys 2020 - 14th ACM Conference on Recommender Systems*, 787–791.

Buhalisa, D., & Michopouloub, E. (2011). Information-enabled tourism destination marketing: Addressing the accessibility market. *Current Issues in Tourism, 14*(2), 145–168.

Burnett, J. J., & Baker, H. B. (2001). Assessing the travel-related behaviors of the mobility-disabled consumer. *Journal of Travel Research, 40*, 4–11.

Calabrò, G., & Vieri, S. (2014). The environmental certification of tourism: A tool to enhance the unicity of a territory. *Quality - Access to Success, 15*(1), 44–54.

Calabrò, G., & Vieri, S. (2016). The food and wine tourism: A resource for a new local development model. *Amfiteatru economic, 18*(Special Issue 10), 989–998.

Caldas, I., Sousa, B., Sampaio, H., Vareiro, L., & Machado, H. (2021). Accessible tourism: Stakeholders perspective in the City of Braga, smart innovation. *Systems and Technologies, 208*, 341–352.

Cassia, F., Castellani, P., Rossato, C., & Baccarani, C. (2021). Finding a way towards high-quality, accessible tourism: The role of digital ecosystems. *The TQM Journal, 33*(1), 205–221.

Cloquet, I., Palomino, M., Shaw, G., Stephen, G., & Taylor, T. (2018). Disability, social inclusion and the marketing of tourist attractions. *Journal of Sustainable Tourism, 26*(2), 221–237.

Darcy, S., Cameron, B., & Pegg, S. (2010). Accessible tourism and sustainability: A discussion and case study. *Journal of Sustainable Tourism, 18*(4), 515–537.

Darcy, S., & Pegg, S. (2011). Towards strategic intent: Perceptions of disability service provision amongst hotel accommodation managers. *International Journal of Hospitality Management, 30*(2), 468–476.

De La Fuente-Robles, Y. M., Muñoz-De-Dios, M. D., Mudarra-Fernández, A. B., & Ricoy-Cano, A. J. (2020). Understanding stakeholder attitudes, needs and trends in accessible tourism: A systematic review of qualitative studies. *Sustainability, 12*(24), 1–23.

Di Nardo, M., Kudlacek, M., Tafuri, D., & Sklenarikova, J. (2014). Attitudes of preservice physical educators toward individuals with disabilities at university Parthenope of Napoli. *Acta Gymnica, 44*(4), 211–221.

Domínguez, T., Fraiz, J. A., & Alén, E. (2013). Economic profitability of accessible tourism for the tourism sector in Spain. *Tourism Economics, 19*(6), 1385–1399.

Domínguez Vila, T., Alén González, E., & Darcy, S. (2018). Website accessibility in the tourism industry: An analysis of official national tourism organization websites around the world. *Disability and Rehabilitation, 40*(24), 2895–2906.

Domínguez Vila, T., Alén González, E., & Darcy, S. (2019). Accessible tourism online resources: A northern European perspective Scandinavian. *Journal of Hospitality and Tourism, 19*(2), 140–156.

Eusébio, C., Teixeira, L., Moura, A., Kastenholz, E., & Carneiro, M. J. (2021). The relevance of internet as an information source on the accessible tourism market, smart innovation. *Systems and Technologies, 208*, 120–132.

Gillovic, B., & McIntosh, A. (2020). Accessibility and inclusive tourism development: Current state and future agenda. *Sustainability, 12*(22), 1–15.

Giraud, T., Di Loreto, I., & Tixier, M. (2020). The making of accessibility to rural place for blind people: The relational design of an interactive map. In *DIS 2020 – Proceedings of the 2020 ACM Designing Interactive Systems Conference*, Eindhoven, Netherlands; 6 July 2020 through 10 July 2020.

Joo, N., & Cho, K. (2012). Study on the utilization of restaurant services by the disabled and their demand for better access in Korea. *Asia Pacific Journal of Tourism Research, 17*(3), 338–353.

Jurado Almonte, J. M. (2014). The accessible tourism in Andalusia and Portugal. *Cuadernos de Turismo, 33*, 121–150.

Kastenholz, E., Eusébio, C., & Figueiredo, E. (2015). Contributions of tourism to social inclusion of persons with disability. *Disability and Society, 30*(8), 1259–1281.

Lanfranchi, M., & Giannetto, C. (2015). A case study on the role of farmers' markets in the process of shortening the food chain and the possible economic benefits for consumers. *Quality - Access to Success, 16*(144), 94–98.

Lanfranchi, M., Giannetto, C., & De Pascale, A. (2014). A consideration of the factors influencing tourism development in relation to biodiversity conservation. *WSEAS Transactions on Business and Economics, 11*(1), 508–513.

Leal, N., Eusebio, C., & da Rosa, M. J. (2020). Attitudes towards people with disabilities: A systematic literature review. *Revista Brasileira de Educacao, 26*(4), 689–710.

Matausch, K., Miesenberger, K., Pühretmair, F., Strasser, A., Lassnig, M., & Markus, M. (2009). Promoting "design for all" in the (e-)tourism industry: An approach towards inclusion. *Assistive Technology Research Series, 25*, 533–537.

Michopoulou, E., Darcy, S., Ambrose, I., & Buhalis, D. (2009). Accessible tourism futures: The world we dream to live in and the opportunities we hope to have. *Journal of Tourism Futures, 1*(3), 179–188.

Nyanjom, J., Boxall, K., & Slaven, J. (2018). Towards inclusive tourism? Stakeholder collaboration in the development of accessible tourism. *Tourism Geographies, 20*(4), 675–697.

Parasuram, K. (2006). Variables that affect teachers' attitudes towards disability and inclusive education in Mumbai, India. *Disability and Society, 21*(3), 231–242.

Santana-Santana, S. B., Peña-Alonso, C., & Pérez-Chacón Espino, E. (2020). Assessing physical accessibility conditions to tourist attractions. The case of Maspalomas Costa Canaria urban area (Gran Canaria, Spain). *Applied Geography, 125*, 102327.

Scheyvens, R., & Biddulph, R. (2018). Inclusive toorism development. *Tourism Geographies, 20*(4), 589–609.

Sica, E., Sisto, R., Bianchi, P., & Cappelletti, G. (2021). Inclusivity and responsible tourism: Designing a trademark for a national park area. *Sustainability, 13*(1), 1–11.

Takeda, K., & Card, J. A. (2002). U.S. tour operators and travel agencies: Barriers encountered when providing package tours to people who have difficulty walking. *Journal of Travel and Tourism Marketing, 12*(1), 47–61.

Vinogradova, M. V., Larionova, A. A., Suslova, I. A., Povorina, E. V., & Korsunova, N. M. (2015). Development of social tourism: Organizational, institutional, and financial aspects. *Regional and Sectoral Economic Studies, 15*(2), 123–136.

Wan, Y. K. P. (2015). Equal access to integrated resort amenities for people with disabilities. *International Journal of Hospitality and Tourism Administration, 16*(3), 251–252.

Part III
The Supply Side of Tourism for People with Disabilities: A Tools-Related Perspective

Tourism for All: From Customer to Destination after COVID-19

Carmen Bizzarri, Piera Buonincontri, and Roberto Micera

1 Introduction

Globalization has allowed the mobility of people from one end of the planet to the other, stimulating all people to use their free time to travel. Over time, the diversity of people involved in tourism and, above all, their needs have become clear.

At the same time, the attention of tourists has focused on accessible tourism, a peculiar tourism aimed at making accessible to all the resources of a destination, with specific attention to the weakest population targets (Darcy & Buhalis, 2010; Darcy & Dickson, 2009; Darcy et al., 2010; Michopoulou et al., 2015).

In 1989, the Declaration on Human Rights and Disability (Stein, 2017; Degener, 2016) asked governments to implement policies to enable people with disabilities to engage in tourism and to include them in the tourism experiences. These two diverse tourism needs led to the birth of "tourism for all," aimed at helping all people to travel, despite his or her own abilities and needs.

The "tourism for all" paradigm aims at standardizing these diversifications to ensure the quality of services and the well-being required by the tourists, but it also aims at making the experiences of tourists unique, trying to put the person at the center.

C. Bizzarri
Università Europea di Roma, Rome, Italy
e-mail: carmen.bizzarri@unier.it

P. Buonincontri
Istituto di Studi sul Mediterraneo (ISMed), Consiglio Nazionale delle Ricerche (CNR), Rome, Italy
e-mail: piera.buonincontri@ismed.cnr.it

R. Micera (✉)
University of Basilicata, Potenza, Italy
e-mail: roberto.micera@unibas.it

© The Author(s), under exclusive license to Springer Nature Switzerland AG 2022
T. Abbate et al. (eds.), *Tourism and Disability*, Tourism on the Verge,
https://doi.org/10.1007/978-3-030-93612-9_9

At the international level, the rights of people with disabilities are fully integrated with the strategic planning tools, but in Italy there are still many improvements to be made, particularly in the areas of accessibility and inclusion.

The chapter's aim is to analyze how existing business models in tourism can be adapted to the "tourism for all" paradigm, thanks to which all people can benefit from the destination and its attractions.

The chapter is structured into five sections.

After the introduction section, the theoretical background is rooted in the literature on tourists with access needs and on the definition of factors that characterize a destination that applies the "tourism for all" paradigm.

The first part shows how both the number of tourists with these needs and the spread of these tourists around the world are growing. The second part focuses on how destinations should be equipped to welcome these tourists so that those elements of quality and safety useful in the choice of destination are communicated.

The fourth section is of empirical nature and illustrates the case study of Bibione, in the Veneto region (Italy), to explore how the tourism for all is slowly spreading in Italy. Bibione, in fact, represents a destination for all, putting into practice the new humanism and successfully changing the operational tools of hospitality.

Finally, the conclusions describe the theoretical and practical implications of the work, as well as the limits of the research and possible future developments.

2   Tourists with Access Needs: Features and Numbers

The importance of accessibility has started to be universally recognized in the tourism sector in the last three decades. The concept of accessible tourism is inclusive of all people with access needs and has developed as a process able to embrace a large portion of tourists focusing on three important values: independence, equity, and dignity. Accessible tourism, in fact, can be defined as a process of enabling people with access requirements to function independently and with equity and dignity through the delivery of universal tourism products, services, and environments (Darcy, 2006, p. 4). It refers not only to people with disabilities but to all people with different access needs (not always visible), which can be caused by impairment, illness, injury, age, stature, foreign language proficiency, or culture. Any person, who faces some difficulties in accessing, using, or enjoying tourism services and facilities fully, comfortably, safely, and independently, will prioritize accessible places (WTO, 2016): persons who have permanently or temporarily peculiar access requirements as a result of an accident or injury, persons with motor, hearing, vision, or speech impairments, cognitive impairments, long-term health problems (e.g., respiratory and circulatory conditions or invisible disabilities), elderly people with age-related impairments such as restricted mobility, ability to receive and process information, spatial and temporal orientation, difficulty in hearing, seeing, speaking, etc., pregnant women, parents with children, persons with allergies, asthma, and other chronic diseases, persons with injuries, people with foreigners, people carrying heavy luggage, or carers of persons with disabilities. In this sense, the definition of accessible tourism is overlapped with those of "tourism for all" and is inclusive of the mobility, vision, hearing, and cognitive dimensions of access. It is aimed at providing tourism experiences that anybody can enjoy regardless of their abilities, age, height, race, gender, sexual orientation, beliefs, ideology, or cultural background (Polat & Hermans, 2016). Consequently, accessible tourism for all embraces all the segments of tourists who prefer accessing tourism experiences more easily, in autonomy, comfort, and safety (Libro Bianco sul Turismo per Tutti in Italia, 2013).

The main innovation in the concept of accessible tourism is the focus shift from the tourism offers to the tourists: the person is at the center of attention, with his or her needs, decisions, acts, and behavior.

Consumer behavior is the study of the actions directly involved in obtaining, consuming, and disposing of products and services, including the decision processes that precede and follow these actions (Engel et al., 1995). A number of different approaches have been adopted in the study of consumer behavior. Collodi et al. (2005) identify two different epistemological perspectives.

The first perspective is the positivist one, which focuses on the study of the individual's motivational system (consumer learning process, perceived risk, and behavior system). This perspective encompasses the behaviorist and cognitivist approaches. The behaviorist approach focuses on the prediction and control of consumer behavior, considering only the environmental stimuli external to the individual. This approach recognizes the presence of cognitive aspects within the decision-making sphere of the individual but does not consider them since they are too difficult to identify (Bifulco & Ilario, 2007). On the contrary, in the cognitivist approach, studies focus on the individual and on his or her decision-making processes before, during, and after the purchase of a product. According to this approach, behavior is the result of an interaction between the consumer's mental processes and external stimuli. Cognitivist studies, therefore, analyze the way in which individuals acquire information from the external and how they use it to direct their behaviors toward the achievement of their predetermined goals (Dalli & Romani, 2003; cited by Bifulco & Ilario, 2007).

The second epistemological proposal is the interpretivist one, which includes emerging approaches that give more attention to emotions and senses rather than to cognitive aspects (Collodi et al., 2005; Solomon, 2002). There are four main approaches related to the interpretivist perspective. The first approach is the social one, which considers the consumer within a social and relational context, kept alive through the purchase and consumption of products and services. The products and services, therefore, are chosen not only for their ability to satisfy individual needs but also to promote the identification of the individual in a social context. The second approach is the existential one, which considers products and services as a means through which consumers form and transmit their identity to others. The third approach is the post-modern approach, which gives importance to the ability of goods and services to create and strengthen relationships between individuals. The purchase of certain products, in fact, allows the consumer to become part of groups with a well-defined system of values that are shared by those who belong to it. Finally, the fourth is the experiential approach, which shifts the focus of study from the act of purchase and from the cognitive aspects to the concept of consumer experience and to the emotional aspects. The products and services that consumers buy are valued for the experience they are able to provide and not only for their functional value.

In the last decade, the stronger competitiveness among destinations and the increasing role of tourists as co-creators of their own tourist experiences has determined greater attention to tourist behavior (Cohen et al., 2014). Despite the fact that studies on the topic are still at an early stage and are often a replication of general theories and models adapted to the tourism sector, Cohen et al. (2014) have analyzed 126 papers published in the three top-tier tourism journals (*Annals of Tourism Research*, *Tourism Management*, and *Journal of Travel Research*), with the aim of identifying the main aspects of this concept. The study reveals that tourist behavior is a complex process, influenced by factors external and internal to the individual, composed of rational, affective, and emotive aspects, and by a mix of decisions developed along different places and moments.

In the behavior of modern tourists, what has acquired more importance is a perspective of visits aimed at satisfying not only cognitive needs but at involving the tourists at cognitive, emotive, and sensorial levels. Tourists do not only want to observe the tourist attractions, but they want to live the destination and enjoy the emotions and experiences that can live through them (Sharma & Sharma, 2011, Stancioiu, 2004). According to Dioiu et al. (2012), modern tourists are also interested in the atmosphere of the places, the sensations they can experience, the immersion in the local culture, the involvement of all the senses, the development of new abilities and competences, the active participation in activities related to the traditions, and identity of the places. These new aspects of the tourist behavior imply the identification of new targets, which cannot be identified on the basis of the traditional sociodemographic variables and that are based on different experiential needs. Families with children, for example, are in search of a peculiar tourism experience: generally, children influence all the tourism activities, are more oriented to share their experiences, want to communicate with the other family members, and need simple and appealing information and explanations. This target is growing in number and in interest since the children represent the potential future visitors of a destination. Another important target is represented by the seniors, who have more free time that is, however, still little used for tourism. The main obstacles to tourism activities for the senior target are represented by poor information and limited mobility. The elderly often travel through associations or volunteer groups; the main incentives for traveling are discounts, free access to resources, and the availability of services to support the visits.

Another growing target is made up of people with temporary or permanent disabilities (motor or sensory impairments). These are people with specific needs, very different from each other, which depend on individual conditions, age, or specific moments in life. Factors inhibiting the tourism activities are the absence of information on the accessibility at the destination and its attractions in the pre-visit phase, the presence of architectural barriers, and the absence of specific services to support the different disabilities.

In order to satisfy these targets, it is essential to consider all the characteristics, needs, and expectations of different typologies of tourists, with their temporary or permanent requirements, with the aim of creating unique experiences and allowing tourism for all.

The increasing interest in accessible tourism and on the needs of all the targets of tourists is related to both cultural and economic impacts. As regards the cultural aspects, accessible tourism is strictly related to the concept of sustainability and inclusion, and it reflects the ethical assumption according to which "Everyone— regardless of whether they have any disabilities—should be able to travel to the country, within the country and to whatever place, attraction or event they should wish to visit" (Nordiska Handikappolitiska Rådet, 2002, p. 17). In economic terms, tourism for all is an important market opportunity since it is able to positively act on the revenue of tourism firms, on employment, and on the competitiveness of destinations. The economic impact of tourism for all is also related to the important weight that tourists with accessible needs are acquiring in these last few years, both at the national and international level.

According to the World Health Organization, there are over 1 billion permanently disabled people in the world (15% of the world population)—this proportion rises to around 40% of the world population when including other categories of people who may temporarily need accessible services. In the tourism sector, it is a very important target since it is estimated that almost 70% of persons in the target group needing accessible tourism services have both the economic and physical resources to travel (Van Horn, 2002). Many tourists with access needs, in fact, have a stable income, leisure time, technological skills, and demand accessible services in order to travel without difficulty (Bizzarri, 2019). In Europe, there are more than 150 million people with access needs, and about 800 million trips per year within the EU are made by people with access needs (European Commission, 2014). These data show that accessible tourism cannot be considered a market niche since it is a growing target that currently represents 17% of the European population and will represent 31.8% of the market in 2050, comprising both people with disabilities, elderly with more than 65 of age, and families with children (UNWTO, 2016). It is a growing target also taking into account that the percentage of people over age 60, which in 2000 was 11%, will be 18.5% of the world population in 2050 (data by the World Health Organization, cited in Bizzarri, 2019). The target of seniors will represent two billion people and two billion opportunities for the tourism sector.[1] At the European level, the number of seniors by 2025 will represent 35% of the total EU population. Target covering tourism for all is not only an interesting target in terms of numbers, but also in terms of revenues: data show that the average expenditure of tourists with disabilities is in excess of 800 euros, compared with just over 600 euros for tourists without disabilities (UNWTO, 2016). It means that considering 268 million potential

---

[1] http://www.who.int/ageing/en. Accessed on July second, 2021.

Table 1 Peculiarities of tourism for all

Elements	Description
Main targets	Families with children Disabled people traveling with caregivers Seniors traveling in groups
Specific needs	Sharing of the experience with the group Sharing the experience with others (inclusion) Support in accessibility, impacting on security, sense of independence, and comfort Simple and appealing information Supporting tools to the visit Discounts
Opportunities	More free time Small groups traveling together Access to information in the pre-visit phase (no last-minute tourists) Travels also in the low seasons Preferences to domestic destinations Attitude to become loyal tourists
Involvement of tourists	Cognitive, emotive, physical, and sensorial
Objectives	To live the local culture, knowing more about the traditions and identity of the place Immersion in the local culture, interacting with local communities Development of new abilities and knowledge

Source: Our elaboration

European tourists that need accessible tourist services, the incomes related to this target are €214 billion.

Furthermore, senior citizens, disabled people, and families with children can also often travel in low seasons, enjoying the fact that these periods are less busy, and travelers can often have greater accessibility to services. This allows the destinations to be less linked to the traditional months dedicated to the vacancies and to develop specific offers for these targets. It is also important to take into account that tourists with access needs favor domestic destinations and are loyal tourists. Another interesting aspect is that people with disabilities often do not travel alone but need a carer to face a trip. The number of tourists involved in accessible tourism is, therefore, more than those of the target. On average, every disabled tourist brings one companion who visits the destination with him or her, and tourists with access needs are able to strongly influence decisions where the family or group will go for a holiday or where a business meeting will take place.

Following the recent literature on tourist behavior and on accessible tourism, Table 1 summarizes the main elements that a destination should take into account in the development of a business model aimed at satisfying all typologies of tourists according to the purpose of tourism for all.

The overall tourism offering, composed of products, services, and experiences provided to tourists, should be reorganized in order to consider the growth of these targets and with the aim of satisfying the specific needs of these new tourists. The crisis of the tourism industry as a consequence of the COVID-19 pandemic could be considered an interesting opportunity to strongly insert accessible tourism in the national recovery plans and to support the destinations in developing strategies more oriented to tourism for all. According to data on March 2021 by the UNWTO Travel Restrictions Report (2021), one in three destinations worldwide is completely closed to international tourism due to the emergence of new variants of the COVID-19 virus. Almost 40 destinations have been closed for at least 40 weeks and, at the same time, 34% of worldwide destinations are now partially closed to international tourists. It is a great opportunity for destinations that refer to tourism for all, since tourists with access needs are more oriented to spend the holidays in their country of origin, enhancing the domestic destinations.

A study conducted on 700 members of a community of travelers with access needs[2] reveals that 90% of interviewers were worried by COVID-19 as a serious and real danger for their health, and only 14% were willing to travel. 46% of respondents indicated that they would not travel until a COVID-19 vaccine was available. This is an important opportunity for accessible destinations, taking into account that more fragile persons and their caregivers are the first to access vaccines, becoming the firsts to overcome the main barrier from fully enjoying tourism experiences.

3 Destination for All: New Strategies for Post-Covid Tourism

Destinations that decide to devote their efforts to the development of tourism for all can be defined as "destinations for all." They are the result of a very strictly collaborative process between supply and demand. Collaboration among tourists and locals is an opportunity for the development of an ever-closer network, able to satisfy all possible needs (Buhalis & Darcy, 2011). The immersion in the local culture interacting with local communities, as shown in Table 1, is also strictly appreciated by the tourists. This collaboration is one of the main aims of the local population, in order to fully satisfy the tourists, for living a good experience included in the local life. This experience is really the added value for appreciating the local cultural heritage, as required by the Universal Declaration of Human Rights (UN, 1989).

To satisfy the specific needs of all tourists, the "destinations for all" have been designed well through the universal design, with strategies that support the use of distinctive resources that focus on enhancing the independence of both movements and decisions also for tourists with problems related to mobility, vision, hearing, and cognitive dimensions, experiencing with equity and human dignity the use of services.

---

[2] https://wheelchairtravel.org. Accessed on July 2, 2021.

To ensure that tourists experience a sense of independence by feeling at the same time a sense of security and comfort, destinations for all aim to their involvement in the constant improvement of services. In the post-COVID era, this involvement aimed at improving the tourism services is very important because the tourists with fragilities more than the others have to pay close attention to all the aspects of hygiene and sanitation for living a good experience and they have to respect and follow all the local rules in order to limit the infection. In this pandemic period, both the tourists and the local community have to organize and manage with responsibility their behavior to respect the social distances to limit the development of the pandemic.

Beyond this specific period, it is useful to highlight that people with disabilities play a decisive role in the development of the destination. Their proactive collaboration is not only useful to develop tourism services but also to verify if these are able to satisfy diversified needs. When tourists with special needs collaborate in the development of tourism services at a destination for all, they can also develop new abilities and knowledge in an independent but safe context. It allows them to be involved in cognitive, emotive, physical, and sensorial levels.

Other people are more likely to participate in the entertainment activities provided in the tourism experience. So, all people—residents, tourists, person with or without disabilities—live a good experience and are expected to support each other and stay well together, because it depends on how one welcomes the support offered by the residents or third parties (Shaw & Agarwal, 2012).

The collaboration between the local community and people achieves the desired results when all areas in the destination are accessible:

- Physical/environmental accessibility of tourist attractions
- Accessibility of information/communication and reservations areas
- Accessibility in transport or mobility way
- Economic accessibility
- Psychosocial accessibility

These types of accessibility should be included in a value chain (tourist supply chain for all) that determines the success of the destination and allows all users to be able to have a service that facilitates their tourist experience, adding value to services and goods (Coccia, 2013).

When a destination focuses on accessibility, in fact, every movement of the tourist is simplified.

In the post-COVID era, a destination scheduled each movement and each activity and all information systems to limit the infection. The right communication of social distance is the first phase to live in wellness and serenity. This communication will take place on the website and on the booking stage and will be very easy in all languages for all persons with fragilities. This statement is also very important during the visit and the stay, so that all persons respect the rules to achieve wellness and an atmosphere of serenity.

Building this type of offering means offering a high level of service quality, in which security becomes an essential element and a priority to the development itself.

It is a matter of connecting all the businesses involved in the tourism service so that each service is linked to the other and the continuous improvements that can be produced, also thanks to the experience, cascade throughout the chain and in turn for the entire destination (Darcy, 2010).

A prerequisite for communicating this activity is the certification of accessibility. This documentation could be undertaken only when all due procedures have been activated that can detect and give certainty of the quality achieved, also in terms of safety and security.

Accessibility cannot disregard safety and prevention, especially when we are talking about tourism for all: if the destination facilitates access and the use of resources, natural and otherwise, it is essential that every service is carried out in safe conditions, also given the number of possible users. To achieve this result, it is necessary to prevent any kind of problem and to have the right conditions to solve them.

In this direction, the design for all method must be planned and implemented using the prevention of any type of risk for it to be effectively successful. In fact, every service designed for all, in addition to being functional and pleasant, necessarily creates well-being in the person. If safety and prevention are undisputed criteria of the accessibility process (Borlini & Memo, 2009), it is also necessary to create a human fabric and a social conscience on the part of the local community aimed at eliminating all the social, psychological, and human barriers that hinder the realization of tourism for all. At this moment, after the pandemic era, the design for all is implemented in the whole supply chain to distance and take in sanitation for all services (Fig. 1). In the post-COVID situation, the medical centers and services can be reached and accessible to all and in smart time.

To achieve this result, it is fundamental to focus on the tourist as a human being, that is, as a person capable, with her or his characteristics and dignity, of being authentically inserted into the social context, with mutual respect for rules and social norms. In this process, accessibility must also be combined with quality in every part of the touristic offer so that the service is evaluated as a whole, providing the destination with tools to activate a network capable of involving all the companies involved so that the service requested is adapted to the needs of the users.

Table 2 highlights all the necessary features for a destination to be inclusive for all, especially those with disabilities, across the board in strategic sectors for tourism. Implementing accessibility, quality, and safety, as well as taking measures that can protect both the destination and the tourist from unfortunate incidents, means putting tourism development on a solid foundation.

The increase in tourist flows does not imply a decrease in the quality levels of the services offered if the set of tourist product features have the capacity to satisfy the explicit and implicit needs of the tourist.

Achieving the required level of quality means using resources sustainably and spreading positive impacts over the long term. It should be stressed that all resources must be readily adaptable and flexible to the needs of tourists, making it useful to carefully monitor all aspects and possible uses of the tourist before a tourist is welcomed. Table 2, therefore, should be considered a useful guide to the success

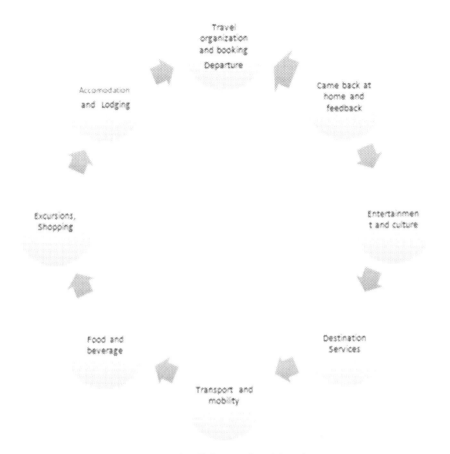

Fig. 1 Value chain in the destination for all. Source: Our elaboration

of the tourism experience, remembering that each destination adapts its resources to the different needs and types of practiced tourism.

If such interventions are desirable for territories offering tourism products for the first time, it could be even more stimulating to reconvert and relaunch a traditional destination with new types of tourists, precisely those with special needs: in this case, however, the territory needs new planning and programming models to respond to the new tourism demand.

In these destinations, since the touristic offering has already been tested and verified, accessibility determines an expansion and improvement of the functioning of the existing structures: to adapt the existing one to the new tourist needs and to evaluate its sustainability, many verifications will have to be carried out, inside and outside the infrastructures, evaluating their load capacity, efficiency, and functionality, and making sure that they respond to the different needs of the new tourists.

Table 2 Resources and criteria for accessible destination

Resources	Accessibility	Prevention	Quality	Safety
Ecosystem, natural resources	To facilitate direct contact with natural resources Adopting infrastructure that allows activities to be carried out for all and in a sustainable manner	Checking possible allergens and declare them, informing tourists in advance. Risk knowledge, including natural ones, and of possible escape routes	Use technologies whose effects and impacts are well known and ultimately certified, implementing the European principle of prevention. Sustainable waste management: Sorted and recycled	Route tracking and alerting devices for law enforcement and each individual user Risk knowledge and use of renewable energy with quality certification
Information, communication, booking	Communication tools for all types of disabilities, reservations for all attractions facilitated by pervasive digitization at destination level	During the booking phase, have clear and easily recognizable attractions. Having communication designed for every type of disability so that from this first phase every detail of the visit can be planned	Building standard communication templates, in multiple languages and easily recognizable	Verification and monitoring of published destination news
Mobility and infrastructure	Have barrier-free transportation modes and infrastructure (including public toilette and hospitals)	Activate, from the moment of the reservation, a service (h 24) of answer to the diversified requirements (customer care)	Communicate transport timetables and modes of use in the various public and private facilities so that everyone can be informed, through language and communication appropriate to different abilities	Transportation tracking online services, possibly with customized areas for customers Use and sharing of electric cars with related focus on accessible refueling
Economic	Provide adequate infrastructure for everyone in shopping centers and individual stores Activate shopping tourism with social prices	Communicate and inform about local craftsmanship and facilities in the destination for people with disabilities Dedicated services to help in the choice of local purchases	Activate a network, local and supranational that can certify local production	The use of appropriate technology and established brands in collaboration with local networks to secure stores

(continued)

Table 2 (continued)

Resources	Accessibility	Prevention	Quality	Safety
Psychological-social	Facilitate the meeting between tourists and through the associations present in the destination that will have the function of facilitator and mediation	Identifying non-profit associations, recognized as a gathering point, in places that are easily accessible and barrier-free, especially in small towns in the center of the city	Recognized associations for these purposes may have a mark issued by local authorities	Safety in these cases was derived from social control by public safety agencies and from the number of incidents and articles in newspapers that came out during the year

Source: Bizzarri (2019)

Such a process, which is clearly not suddenly, could lead to changes in land use resulting in a decision by households, businesses, and investors to locate in new ways, triggering a new development cycle and an increase in the land and building costs (Cass et al., 2005).

To avoid overcrowding, the implementation of accessibility could be achieved through new programming models carefully evaluated by the local community in co-production and co-creation of services.

The construction of tourism for all in a destination that is already touristy should be planned, following the principle of the value chain: service quality derives from the organization of the various underlying and communicating processes.

A person with difficulties that books a hotel, or a tourist amenity suited to his or her needs but remains inside of it, could not feel enlivened or fulfilled by the vacation since he or she is excluded and marginalized from the social and environmental destination context.

A tourist with a different ability should be considered as any other person: if other tourists are free to move and independent in their choices, so should the disabled person.

The tourism destination program should be organized in advance, with modular and flexible systems to meet the needs of all tourists: involving in the planning phase the residents that know very well these needs of tourists. These residents are different stakeholders that represent or take part in the association of particular needs, the representation of tourist supply, and the public or private management of the destination (Golledge, 1993).

It is, therefore, necessary to activate the co-production service with the associations and constantly verify that the service process functions as a value chain with all the businesses that, directly and indirectly, are in contact with the tourist. This touristic offer could achieve that competitive advantage useful to the destination to renew the offer and to enable new technologies and innovations, thus reactivating the production of services.

To provide a service quality that can be recognized as such to generate security and sustainability at the international level. For this reason, it is preferred to use the method of universal design coined by architect Ronald Mace in 1985, who, suffering from polio, was forced to use a wheelchair and a respirator.

The architect has thus laid the groundwork for designing any asset in such a way that the user—and not only people with disabilities—is put at the center of the project. The required solution is adaptable to people with disabilities, with low costs compared to existing technologies, and simplifies the conditions of use, making spaces and information accessible.

These operational bases have been spread to design not only every good but also services, and particularly in tourism the social role of the designer, having to combine the needs of the destination with those of the person, has increased. The designer will have to make sure that every intervention on the destination respects the seven principles of universal design:

1. Equitable use, the good/service must be useful and marketable for people with different abilities.
2. Flexibility in use, the good/service adapts to a wide range of individual preferences and abilities.
3. Simple and intuitive use, the use of the good/service must be easy to understand, regardless of the user's experience, knowledge, language skills, or current level of concentration.
4. Perceptible information, the good/service must communicate the necessary information to the user, regardless of the conditions of the environment or the sensory abilities of the user, offering a differentiation between the main and detailed information, even if it may be redundant.
5. Tolerance for error, the good/service must minimize risks and negative, unintended consequences or actions.
6. Low physical effort, the asset/service must be able to be used efficiently and comfortably with a minimum of fatigue.
7. Size and space for approach and use, the good/service has an appropriate size and space for reaching, handling, and use regardless of body size, posture, and mobility.

Street signs, signage, and directions of various kinds, as well as accessible and intuitive websites, should conform to universal design to give information regardless of the individual's capabilities (Lettieri, 2013).

This methodology applied in tourism avoids various types of problems for the tourist both in the booking phase and in the practice phase of tourism.

Using the technique of universal design, the tourist can overcome some limitations that can, however, make the experience negative. If the information is not clear and immediately accessible, the tourist can disorientate and will have difficulty in using transportation and in moving around the destination itself (Schiefelbusch et al., 2007).

Therefore, every activity should be designed with the universal design methodology both online and offline, i.e., during the vacation, if the destination wants to welcome all tourists.

The application of universal design extends its benefits in all sectors of the economy and in daily life to all those who are in the destination either for work or for vacation. For this reason, both the World Health Organization and the European Union are encouraging the application of universal design and are spreading it, especially in view of the increase in the number of elderly people living in developed countries. In addition to improving lifestyles, the implementation of universal design in the various sectors of the tourism industry contributes to the definition of global quality criteria. According to tourism for all paradigm and universal design, it is needed to change the business model, achieving co-production of tourism services (Bizzarri, 2015) in which the persons with fragilities, together with the residents and tourism enterprises, develop flexible and adaptive tourism services. The beneficiaries of this tourist supply are all, so residents and tourists collaborate and eradicate every form of conflict (Zmyslony et al., 2020). All tourist expenses become a local value added, and this economic model is sustainable not only for social and economic tools but also for environmental impact because the use of universal design involves innovation and technologies, minimizing the use of natural resources.

Moreover, the implemented measures become beneficial not only for tourists but also for the local population as they improve mobility, information, communication, and location. So, in another way, if residents consider the tourist a temporary resident, tourists are not considered in a different way, but all are a part of the territory and use facilities and commodities for the benefit of all, minimizing the negative impacts of this use of resources.

4 Research Method: Case Analysis of Bibione Destination

For the empirical part of this chapter, it was decided to use the case study method in order to accurately understand how a destination can become a "destination for all" by approaching its specific peculiarities, uniqueness, and complexity.

In this phase of the research, the analysis was carried out exclusively through the use of secondary data, trying to triangulate data extracted from the official website, information coming from strategic planning documents, and data extrapolated from the consultation of general documentary archives (press reviews, etc.).

Realizing an inclusive destination, as it has been written, is a very complex process since it requires the involvement not only of tourism businesses and public institutions but, above all, of the community.

The case study selected is that of Bibione, a tourism destination located in the Municipality of San Michele al Tagliamento in Veneto (Italy), a peninsula bordered to the east by the mouth of the Tagliamento River, to the south by the Adriatic Sea, to the west by the inland valley system, called Baseleghe harbor, to the north-west by the channel called Litoranea Veneta, and, finally, connected to the hinterland by the bank of the Tagliamento River. Its surface is 28.41 km^2 and includes, besides the built-up area, the beach, one of the most extended in Italy (10.4 km of coast), the valleys, and the pinewoods that, together with the system of the mouth of the river Tagliamento, represent the area of greatest beauty and environmental interest of the surrounding territory.

The town is developed mainly along the coast and can be divided into three main locations (Bibione Spiaggia, Lido del Sole, and Bibione Pineda) for the different characteristics of urban and landscape.

Bibione is a destination known for the wide and long beach of fine and soft sand, for the suggestive landscapes, the lagoon, the green pinewoods, and the valleys, with typical flora and fauna.

It is a fit destination for leisure tourism: from the bathing to the sporting one, passing for slow tourism, in which the level of the reception is highly qualified. Before the pandemic, it recorded about six million visitors per year.

The decision to analyze this case was made because Bibione was the first Italian tourist destination to invest in accessible tourism, having undertaken the path provided by the "Destination4all" project.

This path identifies, through a specific brand, "Tourist Destinations that care about the Hospitality of tourists with accessibility needs using International standards and working methodologies." A path for the improvement of tourist destinations that want the welfare of its citizens with accessibility needs, improve visibility in the international market, and promote accessible tourism at all levels laying the groundwork to bring cities closer to the UN 2030 Goals on Inclusive Cities.

The project, therefore, envisaged a series of interventions that concerned the local tourism chain in the direction of full accessibility of the tourist destination as a whole—a project that has already created positive contamination on the Veneto territory, laying the groundwork for the realization of the longest accessible and inclusive coastline in Italy.

For this reason, the project "Bibione Destinazione Ospitalità Accessibile" won the Village for all Award 2019 and 2020, a prestigious national recognition, which for the first time rewarded the accessibility of a tourist destination as a whole and not a single segment, thus confirming the value of the initiative launched this year by the Venetian seaside resort, which aims to become, in time, the first totally accessible Italian destination.

The working process for the same nature of inclusion can never be said to be finished but in continuous improvement. Despite this continuous progress to update the conditions of accessibility and inclusion, Bibione is certainly a very interesting case study for the quality of services provided. At the base, in fact, of the construction of the inclusive destination, there are some shared values between those who managed the process and the local authorities, such as that of valuing the needs of the individual person and offering services as much as possible built on the person.

The first step of this process was to identify a mission and a vision as much as possible shared between the stakeholders of the territory.

For this reason, the purpose of the project was to make *Bibione the first Italian seaside resort all disability-friendly,* and this *would be translated in terms of performance to increase the number of visitors to the Venetian resort of 10% in 5 years.*

The strategic subject of this process of transformation of the destination was the *Consorzio di Promozione Turistica Bibione Live* (Bibione Live Tourist Promotion Consortium), which, with the intention of obtaining the Village for All brand, made its own the algorithm developed by Roberto Vitali and Silvia Bonoli, founder of Village for all V4A®.

A roadmap was created, based on four main items: inform, train, communicate, promote. As shown in the following figures (Figs. 2, 3, 4, and 5), from each item is possible to develop several specific trajectories.

In relation to services, the key service is identifiable in the presence of a disability manager to whom each guest can turn to request a transfer or assistance service directly at the hotel and provide an orthopedic bed, lift, anti-decubitus mattress, stair lift, scooter, shower chair, wheelchair, lift, and also health personnel specifically trained to provide maximum care and attention to the person.

Considering that seaside tourism is the leading product of the area, the first interventions concerned the beaches. In fact, inclusive beaches have been provided, that is, without barriers for people with motor disabilities, also building wide walkways and equipping them with devices to bring people with motor problems into the sea. The beach office also provides a video interpreting service in sign language to orient and show the services offered to people with hearing impairment and deafness.

"On the Bibione beach, tourists have Service Islands, structure, accessible also to tourists with disabilities, that are equipped with first aid points, ticket offices, information offices, cabins, showers, toilets, nursery for mothers and bars and restaurants for breakfast, snacks and lunches to be tasted by the sea."

Since 2014, Bibione has been certified with the European Environmental Certification EMAS, synonymous with concrete eco-sustainable tourism, being the sand a natural ecosystem derived from the Friulian Dolomites and transported downstream by the course of the river Tagliamento. For this reason, it is possible to consider that the sands of Bibione are 100% local and, without artificial contributions from others in total harmony with the natural environment and biodiversity, an authentic "DOC Sand," protected as the other precious elements that make up the ecosystem of the resort.

In addition to environmental quality, inclusion allows for the service implementation that by their very nature are of high quality, precisely because they are tailored to the individual.

Among the most appreciated services, there is the opportunity to take advantage of some types of care that force many people not to travel because of the daily need to go to health facilities. Bibione, in fact, can provide to its tourists not only the first aid tools, the medical guard and pediatrician services, but it has also a center for hemodialysis, open from May 1st to September 30th, with two shifts. There are also other easily bookable services, such as animation and entertainment for children, but there is also the opportunity to practice many water sports without barriers, such as diving and snorkeling lessons also for children.

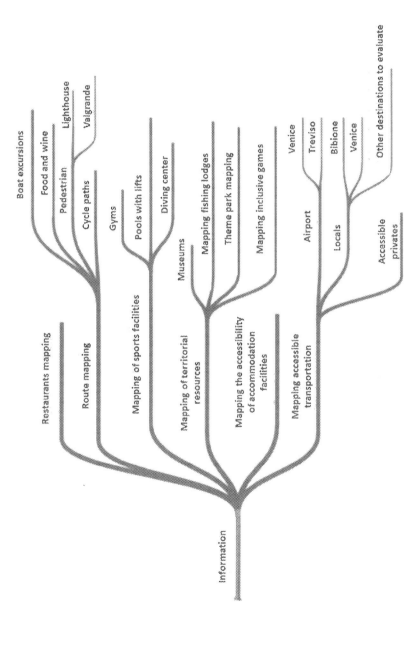

Fig. 2 Information RoadMap. Source: Vitali R., Destinazione Bibione Ospitalità Accessibile, BTO 2019

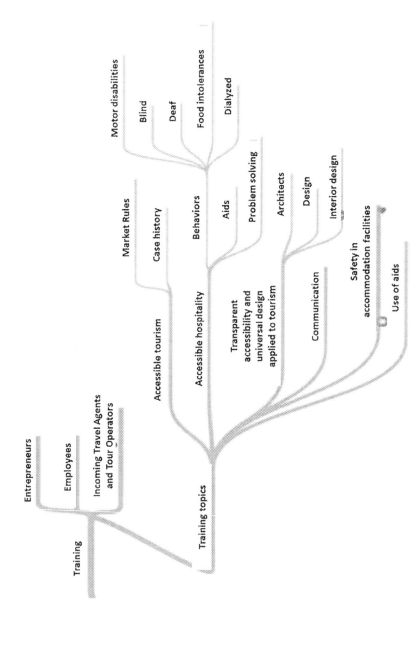

Fig. 3 Training Roadmap. Source: Vitali R., Destinazione Bibione Ospitalità Accessibile, BTO 2019

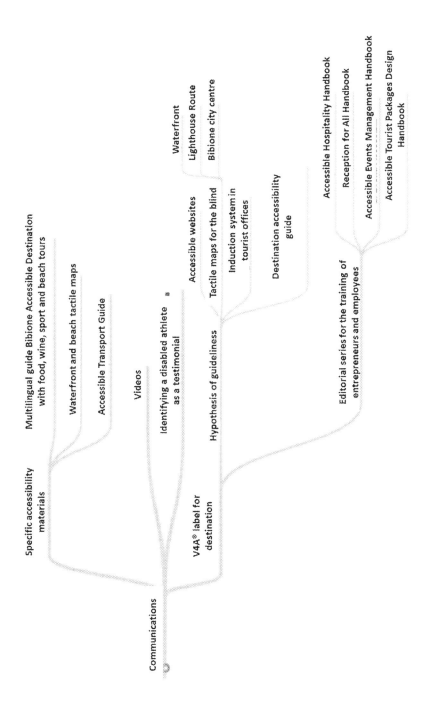

Fig. 4 Communication RoadMap. Source: Vitali R., Destinazione Bibione Ospitalità Accessibile, BTO 2019

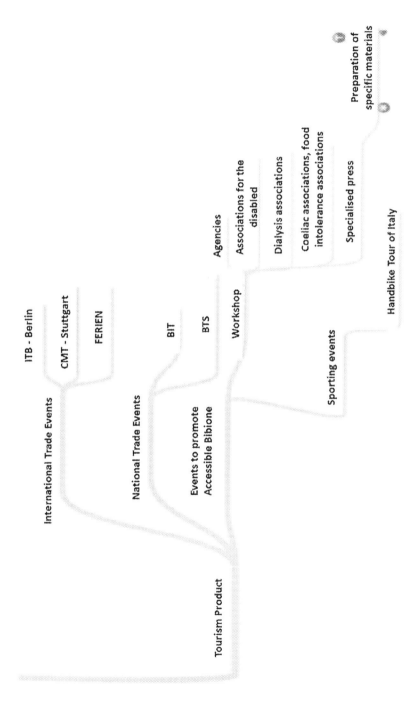

Fig. 5 Promotion RoadMap. Source: Vitali R., Destinazione Bibione Ospitalità Accessibile, BTO 2019

In Bibione, accessibility and inclusion have also been extended to other types of accommodation and wellness, such as the spa. In addition to being easily accessible, the spa includes an area entirely dedicated to physiotherapy and rehabilitation, equipped with cutting-edge technologies and a highly qualified team, as well as facilities and infrastructure without barriers that also allow, for example, those in wheelchairs to dive into the thermal waters: swimming pools and spa are equipped with mobile lifts, adjustable beds, and the latest generation of machines, adjustable for every need. The access chain is not activated only when you enter the spa, but from the moment you arrive at the entrance, and in fact, the parking lot has parking spaces reserved for holders of CUDE mark and services and aids to reach the spa. The very large structure is divided into four buildings, all accessible without obstacles and equipped with large elevators that serve the different floors. The bar, like all restaurants and hotels, as well as many bathing establishments offers sweet and savory dishes for celiac and intolerant people.

Bibione has not only its beach, but also a logoon, which extends for many kilometers, and it is possible to cross it, on foot or a bicycle with the baby carriages thanks to a bike path to which many services, including the possibility to rent bicycles for people with disabilities, are connected.

The lagoon, very famous for its biodiversity and natural beauty, can be visited thanks to a pier for public use for inland navigation. You can also admire the naturalistic oasis that remained intact with a path that winds through the fossil dunes on the sea and the banks of the river, covered by spontaneous vegetation, and some examples of local fauna such as birds, lizards, and rare tortoises. With the integration between sea and inland areas, thanks to the use of integrated routes, the territory is enhanced and, in particular, the rural, cultural, artistic, natural, and architectural values. But what makes the difference is always the experience and how you live the experience.

The following table summarizes the results that emerged from the empirical research (Table 3).

5 Conclusions

This chapter focuses on the theme of tourism for all, with a specific emphasis on trends and peculiarities of tourists with special needs and the provision of infrastructure and useful services to the tourism system to make the "destination for all."

In this context, the chapter intends to be part of the scientific debate on "tourism for all" because the COVID-19 pandemic has increased the needs of accessibility of destinations. These new requirements are very important to orientating the decision of the recovery plans.

Many destinations are activating a series of completely new and technologically advanced tourism services, providing benefits to all tourists, laying the foundations for increasingly innovative and immersive experiences.

Table 3 Bibione: an application of criteria for accessible destination

Resources	Accessibility	Prevention	Quality	Safety
Ecosystem, natural resources	Massive presence of infrastructure that facilitates direct contact with natural resources and allows activities to be carried out for all and in a sustainable manner In particular: • Accessible beach • Accessible lighthouse • Accessible paths • Spa of Bibione. • Inclusive diving • Water without barriers	Destination and service maps show hazards and their escape routes	Waste management represents one of the most important challenges in terms of environmental protection and sustainable development ASVO and the municipalities of Caorle and San Michele al Tagliamento aim to increase the percentage of recycling collection and to reduce the conferment of waste in the dry non-recyclable	Great attention to energy saving and the use of alternative energies
Information, communication, booking	As underlined in Fig. 3, there are specific materials for each type of disability (i.e., guide Bibione Destinazione Accessibile) and reservations for all attractions are facilitated by the use of new technologies	The communication tools implemented in Bibione allow to plan the visit experience in detail	It will be developed a guidelines document that can provide standard templates for communication	Constant monitoring of information disseminated via the web
Mobility and infrastructure	Thanks to the presence of companies specialized in inclusive mobility, access to services and infrastructure is guaranteed in an impartial and easy way The destination also has barrier-free infrastructure	It is active a service of customer care 24hsu24h	The diffusion of transport timetables and modes of use provide communication systems appropriate to different disabilities	Transportations are traceable online In many accommodations (villages) the use of electric cars and e-bikes is provided

(continued)

Table 3 (continued)

Resources	Accessibility	Prevention	Quality	Safety
Economic	Businesses are accessible to all	There are services activated to support vulnerable people in the purchase of typical local products	One of the goals of the V4A label is precisely to create a network of accessible destinations	Businesses use the V4A label
Psychological-social	There will be workshops with the associations of fragile subjects and the operators of the territory to facilitate the knowledge of the experience of visiting Bibione	There are a lot of associations that serve as a gathering place for frail individuals	The associations that provide educators and social workers use Bibione.EU brand	An action of social control by the organs of public security is foreseen

Source: Our elaboration

The case analysis of Bibione shows what can be the benefits and the opportunities of tourism for all for a destination. The case study highlights how this path of transformation of the supply system has been undertaken, focusing on the mission and vision of the development plan but also on the strategic and operational tools.

This project, thanks to its pervasiveness, is a model to be followed to transform tourist destinations into tourist destinations for all and highlights the positive impacts on the entire tourism of the Veneto region. For this reason, Bibione could have a high level of replicability in many other Italian and European destinations without losing the elements and resources that characterize individual territories.

This case study, moreover, could highlight several implications for policymakers and destination managers to implement in a destination the rule for accessibility and realize the guidelines to make usable for all the resources of local attractiveness.

It provides useful information for decision-makers to identify policies and initiatives that can enable the sustainable development of the destination, initiating paths in which the rights of all tourists are protected, without any constraints or barriers.

However, it should be emphasized that this research on these topics is still in the exploratory stage, so it should be considered as a starting point in the formation of a stream of research dedicated to tourism for all.

For this reason, several limitations can be highlighted. The most important is certainly the highly informative character of this contribution, which can only be achieved for the data that are not specific and are taken from websites, official documents, and general documents. It follows that the research will necessarily have to be further deepened through interviews with key informants and stakeholders of the destination Bibione. In addition, new studies could also look at the analysis of a larger number of cases.

Further research can be conducted to investigate how the co-construction of a destination for all can act on its attractiveness and thus whether and how tourists are influenced by choice of making the destination strongly accessible. A longitudinal analysis could be realized to understand the main changes in the different steps to the destination becoming a destination for all so as to support the stakeholders and destination manager in the management of tourism for all.

References

Bifulco, F., & Ilario, A. (2007). Il consumatore culturale experience-driven: evidenze di fruizione del sistema museale napoletano. Convegno annuale Società Italiana Marketing. *Marketing dei talenti*, Roma.

Bizzarri, C. (2015). *La co-produzione nelle aree marine protette per una gestione sostenibile* (pp. 10–13). GEOTEMA. ISSN: 1126–7798.

Bizzarri, C. (2019). *Geografia E Turismo Inclusivo*. Ifpress.

Borlini, B., & Memo, F. (2009). *Ripensare L'accessibilità Urbana*, Cittalia.

Buhalis, D., & Darcy, S. (2011). *Accessible tourism: Concepts and issues*. Channel View Publications.

Cass, N., Shove, E., & Urry, J. (2005). Social exclusion, mobility and access. *The Sociological Review, 53*(3), 539–555. https://doi.org/10.1111/j.1467-954X.2005.00565.x

Coccia, F. (2013). Le Motivazioni Del Libro Bianco. In *Accessibile è Meglio. Primo Libro Bianco Sul Turismo Per Tutti, a cura di Comitato Per La Promozione e Il Sostegno Del Turismo Accessibile*. Presidenza Del Consiglio Dei Ministri.

Cohen, S. A., Prayag, G., & Moital, M. (2014). Consumer behaviour in tourism: Concepts, influences and opportunities. *Current Issues in Tourism, 17*(10), 872–909. https://doi.org/10.1080/13683500.2013.850064

Collodi, D., Crisci, F., & Moretti, A. (2005). Consumer behavior nei prodotti artistici: una prospettiva di ricerca. IV Convegno Le tendenze del marketing in Europa, Ecole Superieure de Commerce de Paris.

Dalli, D., & Romani, S. (2003). *Il comportamento del consumatore: Teoria e applicazioni di marketing*. Franco Angeli.

Darcy, S. (2006). *Setting a research agenda for accessible tourism*. Sustainable Tourism CRC.

Darcy, S. (2010). Inherent complexity: Disability, accessible tourism and accommodation information preferences. *Tourism Management, 31*(6), 816–826. https://doi.org/10.1016/j.tourman.2009.08.010

Darcy, S., & Buhalis, D. (2010). Introduction: From disabled tourists to accessible tourism. In D. Buhalis & S. Darcy (Eds.), *Accessible tourism* (pp. 1–20). Channel View Publications. https://doi.org/10.21832/9781845411626-004

Darcy, S., Cameron, B., & Pegg, S. (2010). Accessible tourism and sustainability: A discussion and case study. *Journal of Sustainable Tourism, 18*(4), 515–537. https://doi.org/10.1080/09669581003690668

Darcy, S., & Dickson, T. J. (2009). A whole-of-life approach to tourism: The case for accessible tourism experiences. *Journal of Hospitality and Tourism Management, 16*(1), 32–44. https://doi.org/10.1375/jhtm.16.1.32

Degener, T. (2016). A human rights model of disability. In P. Blanck & E. Flynn (Eds.), *Routledge handbook of disability law and human rights* (pp. 47–66). Routledge. https://doi.org/10.4324/9781315612881

Engel, J. F., Blackwell, R. D., & Miniard, R. W. (1995). *Consumer behavior*. Dryden Press.

European Commission. (2014). *Economic impact and travel patterns of accessible travel in Europe* – Final report.

Golledge, R. G. (1993). Geography and the disabled: A survey with special reference to vision impaired and blind populations. *Transactions of the Institute of British Geographers, 18*(1), 63–85. https://doi.org/10.2307/623069

Lettieri, T. (2013). Geografia e Disability Studies: spazio, accessibilità e diritti umani. *Italian Journal of Disability Studies, 1*, 133–150.

Michopoulou, E., Darcy, S., Ambrose, I., & Buhalis, D. (2015). Accessible tourism futures: The world we dream to live in and the opportunities we hope to have. *Journal of Tourism Futures, 1*(3), 179–188. https://doi.org/10.1108/JTF-08-2015-0043

Nordiska Handikappolitiska Rådet. (2002). *Aktuellt i norden turism för alla*. Vällingby.

Polat, N., & Hermans, E. (2016). A model proposed for sustainable accessible tourism (SAT). *Tékhne, 14*(2), 125–133. https://doi.org/10.1016/j.tekhne.2016.11.002

Presidenza del Consiglio dei Ministri. (2013). Accessibile è meglio. Primo libro bianco sul turismo per tutti in Italia.

Schiefelbusch, M., Jain, A., Schäfer, T., & Müller, D. (2007). Transport and tourism: Roadmap to integrated planning developing and assessing integrated travel chains. *Journal of Transport Geography, 15*(2), 94–103. https://doi.org/10.1016/j.jtrangeo.2006.12.009

Sharma, R., & Sharma, V. (2011). Experiential marketing: A contemporary marketing mix. *International Journal of Management and Strategy, 2*(3), 1–10.

Shaw, G., & Agarwal, S. (2012). Disability, representation and access to tourism. In S. McCabe, L. M. Scott, & A. Diekmann (Eds.), *Social tourism in Europe: Theory and practice* (pp. 145–161). Channel View Pubblication.

Solomon, M. R. (2002). *Consumer behavior: Buying, having, being* (5th ed.). Prentice Hall.

Stancioiu, A. F. (2004). *Strategii de marketing în turism*. Economică.

Stein, M. A. (2017). Disability human rights. In R. West (Ed.), *Nussbaum and law* (pp. 3–49). Routledge.

UN. (1989). Convenzione delle nazioni unite sui diritti delle persone con disabilità (Uncrpd). Retrieved from http://www.Un.Org/Disabilities/Convention/Conventionfull.Shtml

UNWTO. (2016). unwto tourism highlights: 2016 edition. Retrieved from http://www.e-unwto.org/doi/pdf/10.18111/9789284418145.

Van Horn, L. (2002). Travellers with disabilities: market size and trends. available at: http://ncpedp.org/access/isu-travel.htm.

World Tourism Organization. (2016). *Accessible tourism for all: An opportunity within our reach*. UNWTO.

Zmyslony, P., Kowalczyk-Anioł, J., & Dembinska, M. (2020). Deconstructing the overtourism-related social conflicts. *Sustainability, 12*, 1695.

Tourism for Disabled Travelers: Breaking Down Barriers Through Network Interactions

Patrizia Accordino, Raffaella Coppolino, and Elvira Tiziana La Rocca

1 Introduction

The importance of accessible tourism dates back to the United Nations Declaration on the Rights of Disabled Persons in 1975. Later in 1991, the General Assembly of the WTO highlighted the issue of tourist services availability, considering the need for ensuring the development of barrier-free access at the global level (Michopoulou et al., 2015). During the years, due to a rich debate, the concept of accessible tourism has moved from a dimension limited to disabilities with access requirements, including mobility, vision, hearing, and cognitive aspects, to a more complex one also involving gender, race, ability, or sexual diversity and every kind of inequality (Darcy & Buhalis, 2011). Furthermore, it has become clear that disability and tourism match with sustainability. Therefore, benefits deriving from tourism accessibility could enhance the quality of life for people with disabilities (Darcy et al., 2010).

However, only over the last few decades, the market for tourists with disabilities or reduced mobility or those with access needs has emerged and has currently increased, showing a considerable impact on economic performance. The previous effect, perhaps, coincides with the initiative of the United World Tourism Organization, which, in 2016, dedicated the year to World Tourism Day, a campaign on the theme "Tourism for all—Promoting universal accessibility," and started to pay particular attention to it. In addition to this, the European Union—especially through European Accessible Tourism Organizations, like the European Network for

---

P. Accordino (✉)
Department of Political and Juridical Sciences, University of Messina, Messina, Italy
e-mail: paccordino@unime.it

R. Coppolino · E. T. La Rocca
Department of Economics, University of Messina, Messina, Italy
e-mail: rcoppolino@unime.it; tlarocca@unime.it

© The Author(s), under exclusive license to Springer Nature Switzerland AG 2022
T. Abbate et al. (eds.), *Tourism and Disability*, Tourism on the Verge,
https://doi.org/10.1007/978-3-030-93612-9_10

Accessible Tourism (Enat) and the European Disability Forum (EDF), hardly working together to achieve the related objective—has also carried on a European disability strategy started in 2010 and enforced in 2019, based on several Actions and Directives to enhance accessibility in connection with tourism policy.

Although facilitating travel for people with disabilities or various access needs is now considered a human right, and also a considerable opportunity to help personal development through the removals of barriers and the assurance of full and effective participation in social life (Della Fina et al., 2017), in many countries, a framework developing all the related products and the variety of access requirements have not yet been implemented, and it is not on the agenda of governments. Only forward-thinking operators and policymakers have clearly realized the need for an approach providing inclusive social policies and improving access conditions while creating job opportunities and enhancing the related economic system (Scheyvens & Biddulph, 2018).

Nevertheless, considerable limits cannot be denied. Firstly, the lack of knowledge and coordination and the difficulties in sharing information among the various operators in the field. Despite the fact that a great part of accessible tourism development is linked with accommodation facilities, inclusive infrastructure, and transport accessibility (Buhalis & Michopoulou, 2011), disabled tourists need to rely on the support of digital platforms and websites offering services, practical guidelines, news, and information which can be easily used when planning a trip or during it (Rodriguez Moreno, 2017). Moreover, platforms could play a relevant role in improving tourist experiences, influencing their tastes, and impacting their loyalty and satisfaction. Consequently, they can also impact the economic side of the medal (Azis et al., 2020; Cassia et al., 2020).

Therefore, the European Commission has proposed projects related to the creation and implementation of digital accessible tourism facilities available to people with special needs by improving regulations and stimulating stakeholders to promote best practices, as in the case of Pantou (Della Fina et al., 2017), directly supporting the development of platforms and websites.

In this context, the chapter aims to fill the research gap, investigating the subject of how online platforms can remove barriers for disabled tourists and people with access needs. In line with the objective, the chapter is structured as follows. Section 2 presents a review of the existing literature. Section 3 presents a desk analysis on the way digital platforms contribute to removing barriers for disabled tourists. Therefore, it describes the method, research setting, data collection, and findings. Finally, Sect. 4 presents conclusions, implications, and future research.

2 From Disabled Tourist to Accessible Tourism: A Literature Review

Until almost the end of the last century, the accessibility of tourist sites for the disabled was a theme concerning most of all the "civic right to holiday traveling" (Wilken, 1992) of disabled persons. With time and the awareness that, in addition to being a medical problem, disability entails the rise of social as well as physical obstacles, even the leisure sector has started to seek a way to remove all access and fruition barriers for disabled people. In particular, several studies focused on tourism for people with disabilities in order to guarantee their "civic right to holidaying" (Wilken, 1997).

To understand the interest of the scholars in the field, a literature review (Tranfield et al., 2003) was carried out, starting from the question: "How is the topic dealt with in the literature?", considering the publications indexed in the database SCOPUS and having as last reference period March 23, 2021.

The search string used to identify the publications relating to our theme was [TITLE-ABS-KEY (touris*) AND TITLE-ABS-KEY (disab*)]. The terms are asterisked, and the Boolean "AND" format was chosen rather than the entire string in quotes as the goal was to identify publications, in any research area, that in the indicative parts of the content include the focus of our analysis, i.e., both tourism (and therefore tourists) and disability (and also mere references to disabled people). In this first step, 558 documents were identified and 325 secondary documents, i.e., those indicated in the lists of references but not indexed on Scopus.

Analyzed results highlight a growing interest in this topic over the past 20 years. Especially in the last three years, we find several types of research with funding sponsors such as the European Regional Development Fund (9 from 2018 to 2021), Fundação para a Ciência e a Tecnologia (9 in 2019 and 2020), and the European Commission (5 from 2013 to 2020). This interest seems to be aimed at bridging the incongruity, also highlighted by Domínguez Vila et al. (2018, 2019, 2020). Indeed, the incomplete accessibility of the official tourism websites of countries, despite having a stronger background in legislation on accessible tourism, can hardly fulfill their duty to guarantee their effective participation as stated in the Convention on the Rights of Persons with Disabilities (CRPD).

To answer our question, it is important to identify those contributions that aim at identifying and removing access barriers and, therefore, living leisure experiences. For this reason, a screening was carried out by introducing a new keyword to be searched for within the document: barrier*. Then, it has been added as indicative of a propensity to understand the methods and/or difficulties of access and barriers to be removed.

No screening has been carried out regarding the research areas, as disabled tourism is one of those topics that are enriched by interdisciplinarity and the contributions of studies deriving from different areas often fertilizing the scientific landscape. Not even a screening based on the type of documents was carried out, as each contribution helps the formation of the scientific landscape.

The results of this second step highlighted 234 documents with 24 secondary documents. Bibliographic data for author(s), titles, abstracts, and keywords articles were exported in CSV format and were preprocessed to make sure that all records were valid; then the co-word analysis using VOSviewer software (van Eck et al., 2010) was applied to identify the co-occurrence pattern of the words and achieve the relationships among the keywords used by the authors of the scientific documents highlighted (van Eck & Waltman, 2017).

The results of the co-occurrence analysis of all the keywords used by the authors of published articles in the field showed that there are 1277 keywords with the occurrence, of which 65 meet the threshold of a minimum of 5 occurrences. The most frequent words are "disability" (98), "accessible tourism" (74), "tourism" (62), "accessibility" (54), "people with disabilities" (26), and "tourist destination" (18), and, in fact, they are those that have a greater total link strength; those with a lower occurrence are on the threshold of 5.

Figure 1 presents the scientific panorama highlighted by the relationships among the keywords related to the studies carried out in the different research areas. The whole landscape is divided into 5 clusters composed of closely related keywords. Table 1 shows the division of keywords into clusters. The largest cluster is the red one, made up of 20 items. The smaller is cluster number 5 that consists of two keywords.

The cohesion of the network is based on the proximity of the keywords to each other. The size of nodes indicates the frequency of occurrence. The distance between 2 nodes indicates the relatedness of the nodes: the shorter the distance, the larger the number of co-occurrences.

The central area is identifiable within the most frequent keywords, and there is the keyword "human right" that looks peripheral but is linked with at least one keyword from each cluster. This allows us to underline how attention to human rights is not just a keyword linked to all clusters but highlights how accessibility is a right that concerns all human beings and is not an exception for a few (Darcy et al., 2020; ENAT, 2007).

The spatial proximity among the keywords in the clusters identifies a high cohesion of the network. Although clusters are well defined, all the keywords characterizing them and the links among them highlight an incremental enrichment of studies on tourism for the disabled by disciplines belonging to different scientific areas. This evident cross-fertilization has probably allowed us to move from a perspective of analysis focused on the tourist disability to another one focused on the accessibility of the tourist system and its inclusiveness (Darcy et al., 2020; Darcy & Buhalis, 2011). This is most evident in Fig. 2.

In the overlay visualization, it is possible to highlight the evolution, over the years, of studies related to disabled tourism, which are increasingly focused on accessibility not only physical but, increasingly, informative, and tend to foster inclusion by facilitating immediate use, through web applications.

In this context, several studies were conducted on the accessibility of websites and the use of mobile applications (Ribeiro et al., 2018; Domínguez Vila et al., 2018, 2019, 2020; Fernández-Díaz et al., 2021).

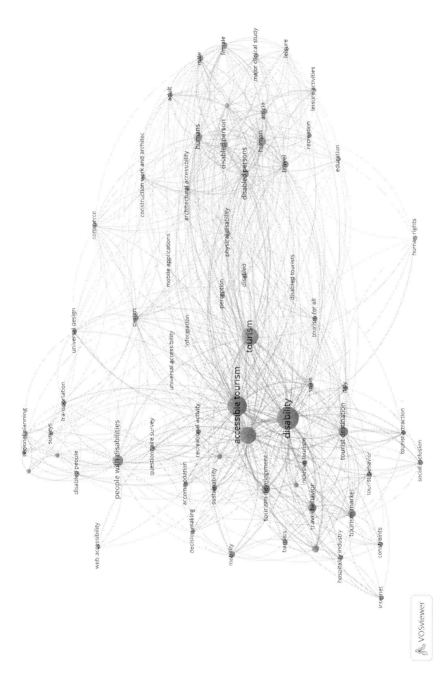

Fig. 1 VOSViewer network visualization (items:65; minimum frequency:5; weight: occurrence)

Table 1 Division of keywords into clusters

Cluster 1 (26 items)	Cluster 2 (20 items)	Cluster 3 (13 items)	Cluster 4 (4 items)	Cluster 5 (2 items)
Accessibility	Adult	Commerce	Disabled tourists	Human rights
Accessible tourism	Architectural accessibility	Design	Information	Tourism
Accommodation	Article	Disabled people	Mobile application	
Barriers	Construction work and architecture	Environmental protection	Universal accessibility	
Constraints	Controlled study	People with disabilities		
Decision making	Disabled	Questionnaire survey		
Disability	Disabled person	Regional planning		
Hospitality industry	Disabled persons	Surveys		
Inclusive tourism	Education	Transportation		
Internet	Female	Universal design		
Italy	Human	Web accessibility		
Mobility	Humans	Wheelchair users		
Recreational activity	Leisure	Wheelchairs		
Social inclusion	Leisure activities			
Spain	Major clinical study			
Sustainability	Male			
Sustainable tourism	Perception			
Tourism development	Physical disability			
Tourism for all	Recreation			
Tourism management	Travel			
Tourism market				
Tourist attraction				
Tourist behavior				
Tourist destination				
Tourist with disabilities				
Travel behavior				

Source: our elaboration

Tourism for Disabled Travelers: Breaking Down Barriers Through Network...   161

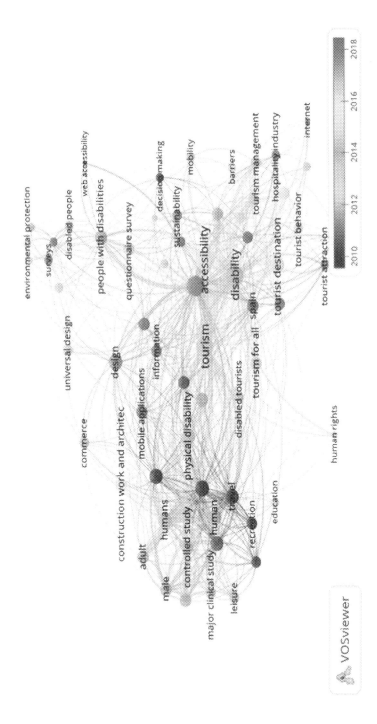

Fig. 2 VOSViewer overlay visualization (items:65; weights: links; scores: time since publication)

Another consideration is that until the early 2000s, the attention was focused on physical problems, as highlighted by the keywords "disabled person" and "travel" "architectural accessibility." Many studies have been carried out by using "questionnaire survey" to understand the perceptions of service users (see also Tavakoli & Mura, 2018; Michopoulou & Buhalis, 2011), up to the most recent contributions, where the theme of accessible tourism is mostly social as shown by the terms "universal accessibility," "web accessibility," "sustainability," and "social inclusion" (see also Darcy et al., 2020).

This attention to web accessibility and the need for interactive tools that act as "facilitators" for the disabled tourist pushes us to further skim the sample searching for the word "platform*." According to Tavakoli and Mura (2018), platforms producing interactions between tourists and suppliers and their development are based on the feedback received from their customers. Then, accessibility leads toward personalization of services by a "digital service that facilitates interactions between two or more distinct but interdependent sets of users (whether firms or individuals) who interact through the service via the Internet," i.e., the online platforms (OECD, 2019). The result of this further screening was 22 articles with 121 keywords. Being focused on the analysis of recent studies, it has been chosen to indicate 2 as a minimum number of occurrences of a keyword, and 18 keywords have been identified that meet the threshold, as shown in Fig. 3.

The overlay visualization highlights the progressive focus of the studies toward personalization and collaboration. The evolution of studies on accessible tourism platforms seems to start from highlighting the need for a communication network to facilitate access for disabled tourists (Wu & Cheng, 2008), moving toward the birth of collaborative platforms for travel operators, and arriving at the proposals of mobile technology platforms where all stakeholders interact to remove barriers and guarantee the access to tourism experiences through collaborative platforms (Darcy et al., 2020; Ribeiro et al., 2018). The platform, in fact, by interaction among interlocutors allows better customization of the offer and the sharing of information among operators and facilitates the construction of an interactive interface that allows the user to grasp the best possible offer concerning their specific needs.

Starting from these considerations, the further step of our analysis focuses on the ability of digital platforms to involve several stakeholders working together to break down barriers for disabled tourists.

3 Digital Platforms and Their Contribution to Remove Barriers

This section analyzes the results of qualitative analysis. Through the snowball sampling technique (Biernacki & Waldorf, 1984; Handcock & Gile, 2011; Heckathorn, 2011), a group of digital platforms is selected. The first step was to identify the sample by entering the string "accessible tourism platform" (with and

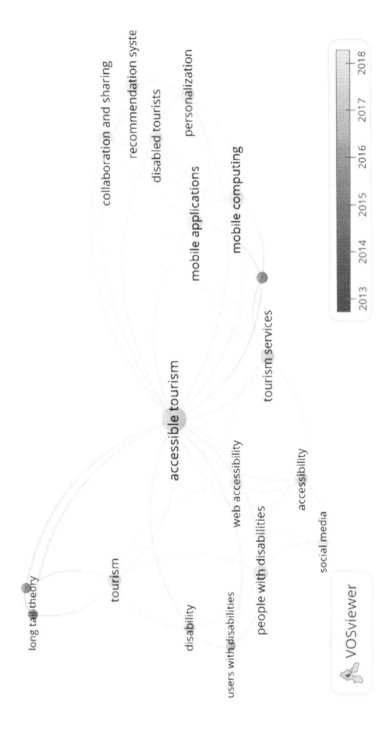

Fig. 3 VOSViewer Overlay visualization (items:22; weights: links; scores: time since publication)

Table 2 Digital platforms sample

Platform	URL	Platform	URL
Accessible Madrid	https://www.accessiblemadrid.com/en	Kimap	https://kimap.it/
AT platform	https://accessibletravelplatform.com	N.O. barrier	http://www.nobarrier-project.eu/en/
Bed and care	https://www.bedandcare.it/	Native hotels	https://www.nativehotels.org/
Bookingbility	https://it.bookingbility.com/	Rome and Italy	https://www.romeanditaly.com/accessible/
ENAT—Pantou	https://www.accessibletourism.org/ https://pantou.org/	Travaxy	https://www.travaxy.com/
ExtraMilers	https://www.extramilers.eu/en	Tur4all	https://www.tur4all.com/
Globe4all	https://globe4all.net/en/posts/all/greece-launches-accessible-tourism-platform	Turismabile	https://www.turismabile.it/
Handysuperabile	https://www.handysuperabile.org	Viaggi senza barriere	https://www.viaggisenzabarriere.it/
HereWeGo	https://www.f6s.com/herewego	Villagefor all	https://www.villageforall.net/it/
Isto	https://isto.international/	Wheeltheworld	https://gowheeltheworld.com/

Source: our elaboration

without quotes) on the Google search engine. The platforms identifiable in the first five search pages were considered. In each of them, the connections with other operators and other portals useful for our analysis were investigated, and some referred to the regional sites (which, however, dedicate only a few pages or few news on the topic, referring to third sector associations or portals already identified) and others to the ENAT site (the European Network for Accessible Tourism) to which reference was made both by analyzing the *Pantou* platform and by searching the "projects and good practices" page for references for accessible tourism portal projects.

Thirteen pages containing 147 projects were monitored. Some concerning the training of operators in the sector, or the certification of good practices adopted in breaking down barriers; others involved the creation of web pages or portals. These sites were analyzed, and the simple web pages, portals that were still under construction or in maintenance, and those that, over the years, seemed to have changed the primary target audience, or had been closed, or no longer updated for at least five years, were eliminated from the sample.

The results of the analysis led to the identification of a sample of 20 accessible tourism platforms (Table 2).

An exploratory analysis was carried out to analyze the sample (Stebbins, 2008; Mason et al., 2010). What was observed during each data collection session was recorded and then verified by each researcher. From the comparison of the data and their processing, some common properties have been identified, leading to the analysis of four key moments in which the platforms seem to clearly show their contribution to the removal of barriers for the disabled: the mission, i.e., the essential goal that justifies the existence of platforms, the offered services, the way they gather and update information, and their network.

3.1 The Mission

The accessible tourism digital platforms here investigated are mainly dedicated to developing a barrier-free context for people who, because of their physical or sensorial disabilities, do not have the possibility of using conventional websites and promoting accessible travel experiences all over the world, in some specific countries or regions. In this field, the mission of ENAT, European Network for Accessible Tourism, is "...to make European tourism destinations, products and services accessible to all travelers and to promote accessible tourism around the world." ENAT's digital platform *Pantou* is specifically developed to meet the need for a reliable and comprehensive international guide to all kinds of accessible tourism services, helping to make tourism everywhere "Accessible for all." For other platforms such as *Globe4all,* the mission is to cover all aspects of barrier-free travel allowing them to find interesting and convenient leisure at their destination.

Furthermore, in other cases, the mission is also to ensure that people with disabilities can enjoy tourism and leisure activities in a normalized environment with human assistance and contributes to improve participants' health and encourage self-sufficiency and social interaction. Some interesting mission examples for encouraging touristic activities and raising awareness of people with disabilities as active people who search to live their life fully are *Gowheeltheworld* and *TUR4all.* The former is concerned with guaranteeing everyone the opportunity to travel but also inspiring with their experiences by overcoming those prejudices that hinder the processes of social integration. *TUR4all* wants to empower tourists with accessibility needs to share information about their accessible destinations and experiences and to give others the confidence to travel. It wishes to raise awareness among tourist destinations and establishments about the advantages of accessibility for the development and growth of their businesses. *ExtraMilers'* mission is to promote the artistic and cultural development of small communities by supporting and promoting accessible tourism of Greek destinations, as well as to incite a movement of change for improving services based on accessibility standards for people with disabilities.

For other platforms, the mission is to create added value for both travelers and travel agents in the disability travel environment. This is the case of *ISTO* that promotes accessible and responsible tourism, bringing together stakeholders from the tourism sectors from all over the world.

3.2 The Offered Services

The examined digital platforms can be divided into three categories based on "services offered": services for people with disabilities, services for tourism operators, and services as intermediaries.

The first services category arises from the consideration that most existing online booking sites do not have the tools or knowledge to provide services to travelers with various disabilities; the possibilities are very few and often do not satisfy travelers' special needs. For disabled persons, it is not obvious to book a flight ticket or a hotel room online, renting an accessible car, and most sites do not even have the option, and where there are services, they do not cover a whole holiday and require the traveler to spend a lot of time on phones calls, e-mails, and online searches. Nowadays, travelers with disabilities must call or send an e-mail to the service providers explaining their specific needs. This makes it difficult to book a trip due to physical challenges and additional restrictions. Sometimes much information on blogs and websites is outdated so that a traveler with a disability may arrive on-site and discover that it is not accessible. Some platforms, like *Pantou*, cover the entire tourism and travel value chain around the world; others, like *HereWeGo* and *Gowheeltheworld*, offer accessible travel and tour experiences, allowing "stakeholders" to book a local host that will show travel destination. In Spain, *Accessible Madrid* offers accessible services and products for travelers with disabilities or limited mobility. The key success factor of *Bookingbility* is facilitating the online booking for people with disabilities, making clear the real accessibility of the rooms. Another noteworthy example is *Travaxy*, the world's travel and booking platform that enables people with disabilities and senior citizens to plan and book accessible trips. *Viaggi senza barriere* offers several tourist packages and wheelchair-accessible excursions and allows people with reduced mobility to choose their holiday by using specific filters, by price, by location, by room type. Very interesting is *TUR4all*, a collaborative platform (app and website) where everyone can provide feedback about tourism establishments, resources, and services based on accessibility for all so that it gives information about physical, visual, hearing, and cognitive accessibility as well as other types of travelers' needs. Village for all provides tourist information to meet the needs of visually impaired, blind, hard of hearing, deaf people, those with motor disabilities for various reasons, and those with cognitive and/or behavioral disabilities. *KimapCity*, developed by the startup *Kinoa*, shows the accessibility of urban routes, public transport stops, and points of interest for citizens with physical disabilities.

As regards the second services category, many digital platforms offer services for tourism operators. *TUR4all* also offers training services and accessibility consultancy for tourism operators. Thanks to its partners, it can run courses and seminars on accessibility and customer care for people with different specific needs in the tourism sector. Furthermore, it runs workshops to create inclusive tourism experiences and products. Providing advice and services on accessibility in different fields: construction, town planning, transport, education, etc., *ISTO* offers training and research services for professionals in the sector and tourism providers. Thanks to key partners, members of *ISTO*, it aims to inspire professionals in the sector with good practices from different countries and structures. *Turismabile* provides information and services for tourism operators and host structures operating in a specific Italian region (Piemonte—Italy). *BedandCare* platform, with its team, made up of professionals in the health and the tourism sector, offers services for tourism operators and equipment in the host structures and provides rental assistance services for the disabled (bringing to the hotel: beds, lifters, commode chairs, scooters, beach chairs, manual and motorized wheelchairs) and accessible transfers (tourist buses with platforms, rental of accessible vehicles with or without driver). In addition to this, the Disability Manager is a new specific service designed by *BedandCare* and *V4All* for supporting tourism operators in assisting people with disabilities, successfully helping most tourism operators to respond to the needs of disabled customers.

The third category is formed by some platforms operating as intermediaries and joining the demand side in the disability travel field and the touristic offer (accommodation and tours). Searching for reliable tours and trustworthy travel agents can be very difficult. The amount of work that goes into preparation, researching, discussing options, and checking to find a suitable tour and travel agent is intense. To make this search process easier, Accessible Travel Platform (ATP) creates a bridge and a direct connection between disabled travelers and travel agents specializing in accessibility. ATP is designed for improving both the destination and the journey, offering a wide variety of tours for wheelchair users, tourists with reduced mobility, vision impaired, hearing impaired, and speech impaired and accepting just tour operators who can provide clear and transparent information about offered tours and to which clients they can serve. *Handy superabile* works as intermediaries among seekers and travel agencies and proposes support, experience, and knowledge to public organizations and companies wishing to improve accessibility and/or design and create places accessible to all. It offers promotion services for operators and searches for ad hoc facilities for the disabled. In addition to this, it promotes awareness campaigns and sporting and cultural initiatives to help disabled people to overcome their isolation and become as autonomous as possible.

3.3   *The Way they Gather and Update Information*

Pantou directory provides a wide variety of reliable information on tourism services offered by suppliers listed in it, including accommodation, transport, tours, venues and attractions, equipment rental and sales, personal assistance—making tourism inclusive and accessible for people who have a disability or other specific accessibility requirements. To be listed with *Pantou*, tourism suppliers must indicate the offered services and the target. *ISTO* has several types of partners, such as national governments, regional and local authorities, e.g., communities, state-owned companies, private companies, associations, and social tourism cooperatives whose activities are based on the values and goals of a social and sustainable economy. *Globe4all* helps with excursions for accessible tourism, and all information is checked and updated. Getting to the site, the user chooses the kind of travel and the level of accessibility on the journey. Following this, all the content is constructed. There is also a section focused on the editorial work, including the preparation of articles and news about the development of accessible tourism in the world, a description of the accessibility of various infrastructure facilities for tourists with special needs—transport, hotels, and attractions. The editorial block publishes reviews, life hackings, useful tips, and experience. In *TUR4all*, a solution for tourists, public administrations, and private sector companies alike, there is a specific protocol, updated periodically, designed for tourism establishments and routes, in collaboration with PREDIF (the Spanish Representative Platform for People with Physical Disabilities, a Spanish state-approved nonprofit organization) and with many relevant Spanish institutions (CEAPAT—social entities in Spain that represent people with disabilities, ONCE—represents people with learning or development difficulties, the Spanish Confederation of Families of the Deaf, the Spanish National Confederation for the Deaf) and different professionals from the tourism sector. Using this protocol, *TUR4all* has analyzed thousands of Spanish tourism establishments and resources. Those with the best accessibility conditions have been published in several inclusive tourism guides about different resources: accommodation, restaurants, museums and cultural venues, natural spaces, leisure, and recreational facilities, accessible greenways, accessible wine routes, and lastly, the Accessibility Guide for All for the Way of Saint James. To facilitate access to all the information through new technologies, PREDIF has developed, with Fundación Vodafone España, the *TUR4all*, "Accessible Tourism for all" mobile app, which contains the tourism resources published in the guides and which are continually updated. Tourism establishments and resources reviewed by accessibility experts and published in the *TUR4all* App are awarded *TUR4all* Accessible Tourism insignia.

3.4 The Network

The main network identified is ENAT, which works with the global community of decision-makers, tourism authorities, large and small businesses, non-governmental organizations, educational institutions, professionals, and individuals by helping them to reach their goals and providing networking opportunities. At the same time, ENAT values the network diversity of experience and expertise, sharing good practices for learning and growing as a global community. Together with *Pantou*, the platform enables suppliers and destinations to find new partners and build networks of accessible services for the benefit of visitors, local businesses, and communities.

Other relevant network examples are the following. *HereWeGo* has a global network of local hosts so that a tourist with disability has more options when choosing a travel destination. *Viaggi senza barriere* has a network of hotels, flights, car rentals selected for disabled wheelchair-accessible excursions in Europe, the Caribbean, the USA, the Middle East, the Indian Ocean, and African countries. *Travaxy* partners can change the way travelers with disabilities and senior travelers plan and book a holiday tailored for their needs, and they can lease accessibility items in Amsterdam, London, New York, Tel Aviv, Berlin, or Barcelona. *Handy superabile* collaborates with public institutions and private entities, and it has carried out dozens of high-end projects with social value for improving life quality and mobility for people with motor and sensory disabilities. Among its partners, it also collaborates with the Group of integrated tourism *Alpitour* World, for the "Special Guest" project, and with the international certification body Bureau Veritas for the "Veritable" project. *Bed*and*Care* coordinates a network of specialized suppliers who operate daily in the area in assisting people with disabilities and the elderly who are not self-sufficient. Thanks to the participation in the PON Business and Competitiveness 2014–2020, *Bed*and*Care* works on the creation of a Global Distribution System (GDS) for supporting local tourism systems.

Analyzing these platforms, two main criticalities are highlighted: the first concerns the importance of complementarity and collaboration between system actors, especially in terms of bridging the gap in inclusiveness; the second one regards the involvement of countries in facilitating the removal of access barriers. Concerning the last point, it has been noted how often there has been a strong desire to affirm the values of the inclusion of the social rights of disabled tourists, and, at the same time, most of the institutional websites show evident shortcomings.

However, the European Union Commission has set aside several actions to increase accessibility in tourism. Therefore, Member States are implementing national and regional laws and programs mainly linked to public funding or developed in partnership with private resources.

All of them provide benefits and tax incentives for improving infrastructure, technology, services, plant engineering, and equipment. Furthermore, platforms operating as innovative startups could enjoy huge advantages.

Nowadays, a large and growing number of people and businesses use digital platforms to sell goods or provide services. Nevertheless, income earned is often hidden in the attempt to avoid taxes, above all when digital platforms operate in several states.

Subsequently, after the OECD issued the Action 1 of the BEPS Project 15 (OECD, 2015) and the European Commission (EU COM, 2018) released a proposal on a uniform definition of "Digital Permanent Establishment," many Member States have introduced a tax on revenues from digital services. In addition to this, the Directive on Administrative Cooperation n. 7 (DAC 7) applying from January 1, 2023, obliges digital platform operators to report the income earned by sellers on their platforms and EU countries to automatically exchange this information allowing tax authorities to value the related tax obligations.

4 Conclusions and Implications

This chapter analyzes to what extent online platforms are able to remove barriers for disabled tourists and people with access needs. Two main steps lead to the drafting of this chapter. In the beginning, a specific literature review on tourism for the disabled was developed to highlight the scientific landscape of research and to understand its evolution. The analysis was increasingly focused on studies on collaboration through digital platforms aimed at removing access barriers for disabled tourists and to verify the state of the art in this field. Then, the second step is a field analysis. Considerations and issues that emerged in the previous first step were used as input for designing the second qualitative phase based on an exploratory analysis aimed at identifying main platforms dedicated to accessible tourism.

Digital platforms identified and analyzed here present different peculiarities related to (a) their mission, (b) the services offered for disabled tourists, for operators, as intermediaries, (c) collected and updated public, private, user-partner information, and (d) networking.

In general, this study highlights that, thanks to the network synergies, collaborations in digital platforms allow planning a complete tourism experience for people with access needs.

Some interesting implications are provided. From a theoretical point of view, this study outlines current achievements and the main trends of the literature and highlights the progressive focus on network collaboration. The research evolution on accessible tourism platforms starts from the concept of platform as a communication network for travel operators and move toward technological platforms where all stakeholders interact to remove barriers.

From a practical point of view, this chapter provides implications both for firms and for policymakers. Firstly, it gives a mapping of different digital platforms for accessible tourism, their peculiarities, and the variety of services offered. Furthermore, this work contributes to deepening the debate on the relevance of complementarity and collaboration among tourism stakeholders, especially in terms of bridging the gap in inclusiveness. To facilitate accessibility barriers, there is strong potential in building a network that includes countries, governments, municipalities, social partners, cooperatives, or any not-for-profit association. Policymakers need an approach providing inclusive social policies and improving access conditions while creating jobs opportunities and enhancing the related economic system.

Finally, making an overview of the environment and legislation affecting accessible tourism, this study gives some tips regarding benefits and tax incentives for improving infrastructures, technology, services, plant engineering, and equipment.

References

Azis, N., Amin, M., Chan, S., & Aprilia, C. (2020). How smart tourism technologies affect tourist destination loyalty. *Journal of Hospitality and Tourism Technology, 11*(4), 603–625.

Biernacki, P., & Waldorf, D. (1984). Snowball sampling: Problems and techniques of chain referral sampling. *Sociological Methods and Research, 10*(2), 603–625. https://doi.org/10.1177/004912418101000205

Buhalis, D., & Michopoulou, E. (2011). Information-enabled tourism destination marketing: Addressing the accessibility market. *Current Issues in Tourism, 14*(2), 145–168. https://doi.org/10.1080/13683501003653361

Cassia, F., Castellani, P., Rossato, C., & Baccarani, C. (2020). Finding a way towards high-quality, accessible tourism: The role of digital ecosystems. *The TQM Journal, 33*(1), 205–221.

Darcy, S., & Buhalis, D. (2011). Introduction: From disabled tourists to accessible tourism. In D. Buhalis & S. Darcy (Eds.), *Accessible tourism: Concepts and issues* (pp. 1–20). Channel View Publications.

Darcy, S., Cameron, B., & Pegg, S. (2010). Accessible tourism and sustainability: A discussion and case study. *Journal of Sustainable Tourism, 18*(4), 515–537. https://doi.org/10.1080/09669581003690668

Darcy, S., McKercher, B., & Schweinsberg, S. (2020). From tourism and disability to accessible tourism: A perspective article. *Tourism Review, 75*(1), 140–144.

Della Fina, V., Cera, R., & Palmisano, G. (Eds.). (2017). *The United Nations convention on the rights of persons with disabilities: A commentary*. Springer.

Domínguez Vila, T., Alén González, E., & Darcy, S. (2018). Website accessibility in the tourism industry: An analysis of official national tourism organization websites around the world. *Disability and Rehabilitation, 40*(24), 2895–2906. https://doi.org/10.1080/09638288.2017.1362709

Domínguez Vila, T., Alén González, E., & Darcy, S. (2019). Accessible tourism online resources: A northern European perspective. *Scandinavian Journal of Hospitality and Tourism, 19*(2), 140–156.

Domínguez Vila, T., Alén González, E., & Darcy, S. (2020). Accessibility of tourism websites: The level of countries' commitment. *Universal Access in the Information Society, 19*(2), 331–346. https://doi.org/10.1007/s10209-019-00643-4

ENAT. (2007). *Rights for tourists with disabilities in the European Union framework*, December 2007. https://www.accessibletourism.org/resources/enat_study_1_rights_final_en.pdf

EU COM. (2018). *Proposal for a COUNCIL DIRECTIVE laying down rules relating to the corporate taxation of a significant digital presence*. Brussels, 21.3.2018, 147 final 2018/0072 (CNS). Retrieved from https://ec.europa.eu/taxation_customs/business/company-tax/fair-taxation-digital-economy_en

Fernández-Díaz, E., Correia, M. B., & Matos, N. D. (2021). Portuguese and Spanish DMOs' accessibility apps and websites. *Journal of Theoretical and Applied Electronic Commerce Research, 16*, 874–899.

Handcock, M. S., & Gile, K. J. (2011). Comment: On the concept of snowball sampling. *Sociological Methodology, 41*(1), 367–371.

Heckathorn, D. D. (2011). Comment: Snowball versus respondent-driven sampling. *Sociological Methodology, 41*(1), 355–366. https://doi.org/10.1111/j.1467-9531.2011.01244.x

Mason, P., Augustyn, M., & Seakhoa-King, A. (2010). Exploratory study in tourism: Designing an initial, qualitative phase of sequenced, mixed methods research. *International Journal of Tourism Research, 12*(5), 432–448.

Michopoulou, E., & Buhalis, D. (2011). Stakeholder analysis of accessible tourism. In D. Buhalis & S. Darcy (Eds.), *Accessible tourism: Concepts and issues* (pp. 260–273). Channel View Publications.

Michopoulou, E., Darcy, S., Ambrose, I., & Buhalis, D. (2015). Accessible tourism futures: The world we dream to live in and the opportunities we hope to have. *Journal of Tourism Futures, 1*(3), 179–188.

OECD. (2015). *Addressing the tax challenges of the digital economy, action 1–2015 final report,* OECD/G20 Base Erosion and Profit Shifting Project, OECD Publishing, Paris. Retrieved from https://doi.org/10.1787/9789264241046-en.

OECD. (2019). What is an "online platform"? In *An introduction to online platforms and their role in the digital transformation.* OECD Publishing. https://doi.org/10.1787/19e6a0f0-en

Ribeiro, F. R., Silva, A., Barbosa, F., Silva, A. P., & Metrôlho, J. C. (2018). Mobile applications for accessible tourism: Overview, challenges and a proposed platform. *Information Technology and Tourism, 19*(1), 29–59.

Rodriguez Moreno, D. C. (2017). Tecnologìas de informaciòn y comunicaciòn para el turismo inclusivo. *Revista Facultad de Ciencias Econòmicas, 26*(1), 125–146. https://doi.org/10.18359/rfce.3142

Scheyvens, R., & Biddulph, R. (2018). Inclusive tourism development. *Tourism Geographies, 20*(4), 589–609. https://doi.org/10.1080/14616688.2017.1381985

Stebbins, R. A. (2008). Exploratory data analysis. In L. M. Given (Ed.), *The sage encyclopedia of qualitative research methods* (Vol. 1, pp. 325–326). Sage Publications.

Tavakoli, R., & Mura, P. (2018). Netnography in tourism–beyond web 2.0. *Annals of Tourism Research, 73*(C), 190–192.

Tranfield, D., Denyer, D., & Smart, P. (2003). Towards a methodology for developing evidence-informed management knowledge by means of systematic review. *British Journal of Management, 14*(3), 207–222.

van Eck, N. J., & Waltman, L. (2017). Citation-based clustering of publications using CitNetExplorer and VOSviewer. *Scientometrics, 111*(2), 1053–1070.

van Eck, N. J., Waltman, L., Dekker, R., & van den Berg, J. (2010). A comparison of two techniques for bibliometric mapping: Multidimensional scaling and VOS. *Journal of the American Society for Information Science and Technology, 61*(12), 2405–2416.

Wilken, U. (1992). Disability, vacation and travel--goals of a humane travel culture. *Die Rehabilitation, 31*(2), 104–106.

Wilken, U. (1997). Tourism and disability-advances in travel and holiday mainstreaming. *Occupational Health and Industrial Medicine, 37*(4), 204.

Wu, Y. C. J., & Cheng, M. J. (2008). Accessible tourism for the disabled: Long tail theory. *Emerging technologies and information Systems for the Knowledge Society.* In M. D. Lytras, J. M. Carroll, E. Damiani, & R. D. Tennyson (Eds.), *WSKS lecture notes in computer science, 5288.* Springer. https://doi.org/10.1007/978-3-540-87781-3_61

Eco-Innovation as a Tool to Enhance the Competitiveness of "Tourism for All": The Italian Project "Turismabile"

Giovanna Centorrino and Daniela Rupo

1 Introduction

The world population is aging with a consequent increase of people with disabilities (Pulsiri et al., 2019). As a result, there is a growing interest in the issue of disability from numerous points of view. Both national and international legislative and social and economic interventions reflect important developments. These factors have to be taken into consideration when approaching the different measurements and definitions of disabilities. The new approach to disability was developed and endorsed by the International Classification of Functioning, Disability, and Health (ICF), at the 54th World Health Assembly in May 2001, and with a resolution on "disability, including prevention, management and rehabilitation" (www.who.int) at the 58th World Health Assembly in May 2005. Accordingly, the World Health Organization (WHO) now increasingly recognizes the need to reduce the burden associated with health conditions concerning the matter of disabilities (Stucki and Gerold 2005). As a result, the WHO framework for measuring disability classifies health by considering functioning as related not only to interaction with the health condition of a person (e.g., disorder or disease) but also to personal and environmental factors. Among the key functions, measures related to participation and involvement in life situations are envisaged (Cobigo et al., 2012). Therefore, any restriction to taking part in activities is seen as a problem to be considered in the individual experience, as functioning and health are contemplated in association with personal and environmental factors (Stucki and Gerold 2005). The notion of social participation also includes the possibility of freely enjoying places (museums, libraries, theaters), goods and services, and being able to live cultural, artistic, and physical-sporting experiences that generate well-being. In addition, the removal of any barriers that prevent full

G. Centorrino (✉) · D. Rupo
Department of Economics, University of Messina, Messina, Italy
e-mail: gcentorrino@unime.it; drupo@unime.it

© The Author(s), under exclusive license to Springer Nature Switzerland AG 2022
T. Abbate et al. (eds.), *Tourism and Disability*, Tourism on the Verge,
https://doi.org/10.1007/978-3-030-93612-9_11

citizenship, formation of social capital, and complete and rewarding social participation has taken on a new impetus (Cass et al., 2005). In this approach, participation in various forms of tourism and leisure activities guarantees disabled people an improvement in personal development and quality of life by contributing to social inclusion.

It is well known that tourism is an important social need that has a positive effect on people, and accessible tourism is about making it easy for everyone to enjoy touristic experiences by removing barriers and considering a set of devices and facilities aimed to enable accessibility through innovative information technology (IT). Accessibility indicates how easy it is for everybody to approach, enter, and use structures, outdoor spaces, and other facilities, autonomously, without the need for special arrangements (Westcott, 2004).

Accordingly, accessibility should also be understood as those principles and techniques to be observed when designing, constructing, maintaining, and updating websites and mobile applications to make them more accessible to users, in particular persons with disabilities (Directive (EU) 2016/2102). Providing information on accessibility and improving access benefits a wide range of people who want to travel, but who may find it difficult. Moreover, useful information allows disabled people to determine whether a service or destination is accessible to them in its current condition, while increasing the market potential for the tourism sector (Westcott, 2004).

The planning and use of current technology involving computers and web browsers are being designed more and more to be of aid to those with many kinds of disabilities, demonstrating that the challenge of web accessibility (Carter & Markel, 2001) for every user is considered of great importance. This is the case of the implementation of assistive technologies (AT) that enable people with disabilities to access information or control their environment and guarantee an improvement both in their personal development and quality of life by contributing to social inclusion. For example, in the use of interface, which as is well known can be complex and certainly not always easy to use, especially by those with disabilities, obstacles should not be encountered right from the first phase of seeking tourist information on a tourist website. Small tricks that go beyond the commonly accepted standards can make the difference, moving toward an idea of tourism characterized by acceptance and accessibility criteria aimed at everyone. Thus, under the umbrella of the accessibility principle, it is worth considering how much IT could significantly improve the quality of life also for people with disabilities by increasing their independence and participation in the community and social world.

Current innovation includes a new vision of the word "accessibility" as a term addressed not only to people with disabilities but to everyone and aims at improving overall accessibility. Thus, people with disabilities need not be considered as a specific touristic category belonging to a niche of customers that must be protected. On the contrary, as long as a complete barrier-free environment exists and specialized personnel is provided, people with disabilities can experience the same joy from pleasure travel as the average tourist, including the elderly, young children, and pregnant women (Wu and Cheng, 2008).

In the current context, growing attention is given to tourism characterized as "responsible," pivoted on the principles related to the enhancement of the environment and cultural heritage, with particular attention to the weaker sections of the population. To guide countries concerning the rights of persons with disabilities, the adoption of the 2030 Agenda (Transforming our World: the 2030 Agenda for Sustainable Development) was a landmark achievement, foreseeing a shared global vision toward sustainable development for all (tourism for all), including persons with disabilities by encouraging them to become active members in society. The agenda aims to leave no one behind and moves together to the future: its success also involves the application of digital technologies for people with disabilities.

The 2030 Agenda is guided by the purposes and principles of the Charter of the United Nations and grounded, inter alia, in the Universal Declaration of Human Rights and international human rights treaties. The 2030 Agenda is therefore linked to the Convention on the Rights of Persons with Disabilities (CRPD), and its implementation by, for, and with persons with disabilities increasingly incorporates the disability perspective in all aspects of its realization, monitoring, and evaluation. It provides a powerful framework to guide local communities, countries, and the international community toward the achievement of disability-inclusive development (Disability and Development Report, 2018).

Notwithstanding the evidence of the growing debate on the social, economic, and environmental situation and despite both public and numerous private interventions aimed to create accessible tourism for people with disabilities, tourism is still today far from accessible to many of those suffering from disabilities (Kastenholz et al., 2015) due to the existence of physical, environmental, economic and social, and/or other barriers. Empirical studies show that disabled persons continue to have a lower possibility of accessing touristic activities than non-disabled people.

For these reasons, this chapter intends to offer a contribution to the study of touristic opportunities for people with disabilities, shedding some light on an Italian nonprofit project called *Turismabile* that, since 2007, has been engaged in several activities aimed to improve Piedmont tourist accessibility and promoting Piedmont (a region in the north-west of Italy with Turin as the capital town) as a touristic destination for all. *Turismabile* was the first project in Italy to consider accessible tourism in a new way: not just as a hotel without architectural barriers but a whole territory that considers usability by everyone, such as the quality of the offers and places.

The chapter is structured as follows. Section 2 introduces a theoretical framework on tourism and disabilities. Section 3 outlines the methods and research data. Section 4 illustrates the empirical case of *Turismabile*, as an emblematic Italian example of an innovative project related to "tourism for all." Sect. 5 presents the discussion. Section 6 sums up the main insights and conclusive remarks.

2 Theoretical Framework

In recent years, tourism for people with disabilities has generated a growing interest from the point of view of both (a) accessibility (Kastenholz et al., 2015), i.e., the absence of architectural, cultural, and sensorial barriers, and the indispensable conditions to allow the use of tourist heritage, and (b) a more social approach, as a dimension regarding the belief that disability is a social construct characterized by different social behavior over time, being influenced by the human, sociocultural, economic, technological, physical, political, and legal environment in which it operates.

Today, the social dimension highlights how society has to remove all socially constructed constraints, to reduce any difficulties related to the tourist experience (Agenda, 2030). It is therefore essential to grant access to tourist experiences to all citizens regardless of their personal, social-economic, and other conditions that could limit such experiences (Fig. 1).

Central to accomplishing this path is the awareness that also people with disabilities have to be provided with specific instruments that can allow them to easily enjoy infrastructure and services (Eichhorn et al., 2008).

Among the instruments aimed at information dissemination and accessibility, online tools are the most commonly used by organizations since they enable a more direct and immediate presentation of corporate statements and sustainability initiatives (Siano et al., 2016). According to Wu et al. (2014, p. 2083) in the touristic field, "the Internet is a tool that can transcend culture, graphically and informatively promoting specific travel companies and places of interest around the world. With its rising accessibility, the Internet has become an important resource for travel and tourism information and a marketing medium with a very efficient cost structure." These characteristics are to be considered as the main assumptions when trying to

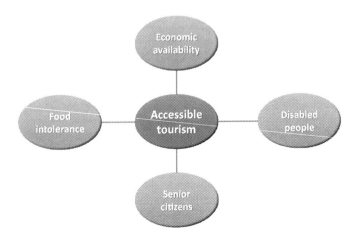

Fig. 1 Accessible tourism. Source: own elaboration

Table 1 Persons categorized by severity of limitations in activities usually carried out

People categorized by the degree of severity of limitations	Absolute values in thousands	Percentage values
Severe limitations	3150	5.2
Minor limitations	9838	16.4
Without limitations	44,016	73.2
Not indicated	3115	5.2
Total	60,120	100.0

Source: (own elaboration from http://dati.disabilitaincifre.it/dawinciMD.jsp)

answer needs that are essential for tourism for disabled people by providing equal opportunities (Ramesh Babu et al., 2014).

In Italy, in 2019, people with total disabilities numbered 3,150,000 (5.2% of the population) and 9,838,000 with minor disabilities (16.4% of the population) (Table 1).

The elderly population is the most affected: almost 1.5 million over 75 (22% of the elderly population) are disabled, and one million are women.

The "geography of disability" shows the Italian islands with the highest level, with a prevalence of 6.5%, against 4.5% in the north-west of the country.

Lombardy and Trentino Alto Adige, on the other hand, are the regions with the lowest prevalence: 4.1% and 3.8%, respectively.

Twenty-nine percent of people with disabilities live alone, 27.4% with spouses, 16.2% with spouses and children, 7.4% with children and without a spouse, about 9% with one or both parents, and the remaining 11% live in other types of families (dati.disabilitaincifre).

It is worth considering how accessible tourism may contribute to both social inclusion of people with disability and an improvement in their knowledge and personal skills, by also influencing the quality of their free time. Thus, accessibility can be considered as a step toward full social inclusion of people with disabilities or other special needs, as well as a source of significant economic benefits.

The use of innovative IT will be of critical importance. Innovation is perceived as a process that results from various interactions among different actors and has emerged as a key factor concerning many functions of business activity. Moreover, the ability to continue to innovate has a great influence in the field of sustainability, in creating real value and providing products in the way customers need and require.

When innovation improves sustainable performance, including social criteria, it is defined as eco-innovation. In this case, it is considered as a process that integrates environmental, social, and financial sustainability within the whole company system (Charter & Clark, 2007).

According to Carrillo-Hermosilla et al. (2010, p. 5), "Basically, innovation refers to the change in the way something is done." It arises from a systemic process that refers to the interconnectedness and dynamic interaction between different actors and internal and external factors (Carrillo-Hermosilla et al., 2010). The economic system's ability to create and maintain the sustainable economic process, which does not involve short-term value creation at the expense of long-term wealth, is a fundamental aspect of the long-term survival of economics. Eco-innovation can contribute to reducing the environmental impact, even if the main reason for this harmful impact does not directly stem only from consumption or production activities. Consequently, the extent of the area of eco-innovation also encompasses broader social arrangements that generate changes in existing sociocultural norms and institutional structures. Thus, adopting new values and behavior both on the producer and consumer side is one of the essential conditions for such innovation. This more radical form of eco-innovation is becoming the key to enabling a sustainable transition (OECD). Among the several dimensions contemplated in the eco-innovation field, which are of direct interest for this paper, it is worth referring to one particular aspect that regards users' eco-innovation in the meaning of individual consumers that expect to benefit from the use of a product or service (Carrillo-Hermosilla et al., 2010). According to Hienerth et al., (2006, p. 1291), "user innovation begins when one or more users of some good recognize a new set of design possibilities – a so-called design space – and begin to explore it."

This considers a company's ability to involve users in the development of a new product or service in order to be confident that they will have a benefit from its use. Thus, companies have to be aware of the different kinds of users that can contribute to the phases of the innovation process and how to interact with them (Carrillo-Hermosilla et al., 2010). Growing importance is being given to the field of web accessibility (Directive (EU) 2016/2102) not only regarding technical standards and/or web architecture and/or design but also as a moral obligation. Given the constant evolution of technology, web accessibility, as a way of making websites and web applications inclusive and usable by people with all levels of abilities and disabilities, requires essential implementation of innovative interventions. Including innovation in the field of the web, accessibility is the right way to answer the need for inclusivity and usability by people with all levels of disabilities.

3 Methods and Data

To explore the significant implications of a co-innovation project in the field of tourism, as outlined in the conceptual framework, a qualitative-based approach based on a case study research methodology was adopted (Eisenhardt & Graebner, 2007; Flick, 2009; Grafton et al., 2011; Yin, 2009, 2014).

This methodology is considered suitable for the study in that it allows a more precise, detailed examination of the subject matter compared to other methods. Moreover, it allows the understanding of a real-life phenomenon in depth and in a real-life context (Yin, 2014), highlighting the complexity identified in an activity where multiple sources of evidence are used and much information is gathered.

The *Turismabile* project is deemed a typical case concerning the implementation of sustainable development in the field of tourism. This case was considered a suitable setting for the investigation for two main reasons. First, since 2007, it is the only Italian project engaged in improving tourist accessibility for everyone in an Italian region territory (Piemonte) and in promoting this place as a destination for all. *Turismabile* was also one of the first projects in Italy to consider accessible tourism in a new meaning: not only a hotel without architectural barriers but also an entire territory that considers good accessibility to its resources as a fundamental element of the quality of its own supply. The second reason is related to the ease of finding primary documents for in-depth analysis. Indeed, it was possible to explore the phenomenon thanks to easy access to the website of the project and also to the information gathered from the in-depth interviews carried out with Mr. Andrea Accortanzo, in charge of communications for the Council for People in Difficulty (CPD) and with Mr. Ferrero, CDP Director and General Director of the Project Thus, the research is based on combined data collection tools making use of diverse types of materials, methods, and investigations (Denzin, 1978). Different data sources were used, such as (a) official documents, Internet documents, internal company material, (b) academic papers, (c) semi-structured interviews with key informants, and (d) informal follow-ups based on e-mails and short phone calls (Denzin, 1978).

Interviews were considered as the principal source-gathering instrument for the research, in the form of a semi-structured interview. Major questions were developed as a general statement which was then followed by other questions to provide suitable information for the study. The choice of semi-structured interviews was deemed useful as they offer flexibility in approaching the respondent, assuming the form of guided conversations rather than structured questionnaires (Yin, 2009). Moreover, as they are based on a limited number of topics or issues or prompts, with the emphasis very much being on encouraging the respondents to talk around a theme (Rowley, 2012), this kind of methodology offers much flexibility.

The selection of those to be interviewed was targeted toward gathering information regarded as key in the value network. The first interview was addressed to one of the experts of the project, able to offer useful insights and comments on the research topic, willing to discuss its inner motivations, mechanisms, and developments over time. The second interview was addressed to the General Director specifically regarding administrative and social aspects. Moreover, both interviewees were willing and available to dedicate their time to provide information on the project (Rowley, 2012).

A total of four interviews were recorded between March and April 2021, lasting about one hour each. The interviews were later transcribed (Gibbert et al., 2008). To better analyze the data derived from the interviews, information was integrated and triangulated with other secondary data both to increase the information flow and to allow control of the opinions provided by the two interviewees (Gibbert et al., 2008).

By investigating the *Turismabile* single case study, the expected aims are an increase of the body of knowledge on the competitiveness of tourism also for people with disabilities and a suggestion for further research on related topics.

In the following paragraph, first, we outline the case study context by describing the general aim of the value network (4.1), and then the Piedmont territory to emphasize the diverse typology of territory and of the environment in which the

Turismabile activities are located (4.2). The following section (4.3) presents the *Turismabile* project, and in Sect. 4.4, we provide an overview of the website as an example of IT, which can be used by all.

4 The Case Study Context

4.1 Turismabile Profile

In 2006, the IX Winter Paralympic Games took place in Piedmont (Italy). On that occasion, 486 athletes with disabilities were hosted. This event represented a challenge and an important input aimed at beginning a course of progressive improvement of the quality of the touristic offer with a particular view to greater attention toward the multiple needs of tourists. The positive experience of the Paralympic event, together with ethical reasons and social responsibility, led the Piedmont region to continuously and concretely invest in the accessible tourism sector with the idea and subsequent implementation of the *Turismabile* project. It is a nonprofit project funded by the Council for People in Difficulty (CPD), Department of "Tourism for All Sector," and the Tourism Department of the Piedmont Region. This is the only initiative in Italy which, since 2007, first with the name "Piedmont for all," has been engaged in several activities aimed to improve Piedmont tourist accessibility and promote Piedmont as a touristic destination for all. From 2009, the project was formalized and renamed *Turismabile*. It was one of the first projects in Italy to consider accessible tourism not only in the meaning of a hotel without architectural barriers but also about accessibility in an entire territory, and it is often cited as a "best practice" in planning documents of tourism policies of other Italian regions.

Today, the project proposes a series of initiatives dedicated both to tourists and to tourist operators.

It concerns:

- An Internet portal constantly updated with newsletter services
- A database with records of usable tourist resources allocated in the Piedmont territory characterized by accessibility and usability of accommodation and catering facilities, together with tourist routes that allow any type of user to fully enjoy the tourist experience
- Organization of days dedicated to raising awareness and conferences on tourism issues for all (to date more than 90 realtors and more than 700 participants)
- Studies, research, and insights on the theme of accessible tourism
- Creation of thematic workshops for specialized tour operators
- Creation of educators for journalists and opinion leaders of disability
- Production of videos and information and promotional materials
- Carrying out studies, surveys, and research on accessible tourism
- Participation in trade fairs

4.2 Piedmont Territory

The Piedmont territory, in the northern part of Italy, is a predominantly mountainous land, surrounded on three sides by the alpine chain, which includes the highest peaks and the largest glaciers of Italy. Piedmont is the second largest of the 20 administrative regions of Italy, after Sicily, and its countryside is quite varied: one passes from the rugged peaks of the massifs of Monte Rosa and Gran Paradiso (National Park) to the damp rice paddies of the Vercellese and Novarese areas and from the gentle hillsides of the Langhe and of Monferrato to the plains, often polluted and studded with a mixture of farms and industrial enterprises. Numerous ski areas welcome winter sports enthusiasts. In the background, there are the Alps which open onto large, picturesque valleys, including Val di Susa, Valsesia, and the Val d'Ossola.

Another kind of landscape is offered with the panorama of the Langhe and Monferrato: a chain of hills cultivated with vineyards, dotted with villages and castles. It can be said that nature is just one of the many attractions in Piedmont. There are many other faces of the region: from Turin, the capital with its history and remarkable artistic heritage, to medieval castles, precious architecture, and historic spa resorts, which provide treatments for well-being and relaxation.

Given the variety and beauty of the area and the numerous cultural attractions that it offers, Piedmont is a region with a strong tourist vocation suitable for welcoming all types of customers with a varied, high-level offer. It is in this context that the tourism project was developed.

4.3 The Tourismabile Project

Turismabile could be considered an approach and a key concept that developed around the concept of territory, in accordance with what was said by the General Director of the project, Mr. Ferrero:

> Today, tourism is increasingly referring to the usability of an entire territory and is based on the concept of hospitality. It is no longer just a hotel or restaurant to establish the customer's choice, but the territorial system that becomes serviceable. Another focal point is represented by the idea of welcome as basically training, as a way of thinking. Today the customer knows exactly what he wants and realizes how to choose what he wants. Tourism based on pre-packaged catalogs is now dated. The various operators must exhibit and declare their availability, their capacity, and their reception level according to which all users can choose according to everyone's needs.

Accordingly, Turismabile can be considered as a project for raising awareness of the culture of hospitality. Hence, Turismabile aimed at considering people with disabilities in the same way as any tourist who wants to live their experience in a satisfying way regardless of their specific needs. It is based on four pillars:

- All tourists have the same desire for living a tourist experience.
- Accessibility must not only be linked to compliance with the rules but is a qualitative element of tourism planning, and this principle applies to everyone.
- Working in the supply chain of accessibility means making every tourist location in the area usable for everyone.
- The concept of tourism for all also represents an important economic value. Widening the target means creating more value.

Therefore, the notion of accessibility becomes a quality element of high usability of the whole territory. The accessibility chain refers to a set of possibilities that go beyond simple accommodation but also includes getting access to the following activities:

- Catering facilities
- Services
- Sports facilities
- Places of worship
- Historical-cultural places
- SPA solarium

Among the various proposals, it is worthwhile mentioning the so-called virtuous proposals, for example, to food and wine tours. From the Turismabile website, it is possible to discover various initiatives concerning visits to wine cellars (Wine corner) and, on request, it is possible to organize a route for people with specific needs specially created and designed for everyone.

The same type of viewpoint also applies to outdoor activities. In this case, for example, it is possible to take advantage of another initiative called the SciAbile Project connected to Turismabile. This project is a nonprofit organization, too, founded in 2003 thanks to the collaboration between BMW Italy and the Sauze d-Oulx (TO) Project Ski School. It aims at giving people who are affected by any kind of disability a chance to go skiing and snowboarding free of charge. The SciAbile project supplies the participants with all the necessary gear according to the kind of disability. The instructors are all specially qualified for teaching disabled people, and they all have an admirable passion and dedication for their work. In the last few years, they have taken over 800 people skiing (from Italy and abroad) and given 9000 lessons.[1]

4.4 Turismabile Website

Given the awareness of the growing importance of digital accessibility, which has become even more important due to the information and interactive services

---

[1] https://www.sauzedoulxproject.it/sciabileonlus/en/about-us-sciabile. Accessed: June 20, 2021.

provided through the web and mobile devices, and with the aim of not denying anyone the possibility to access the *Turismabile* services, great attention has been given to its website.

The website is strictly linked to the effective philosophy of the project by offering a clear vision of the touristic possibility in the Piemonte territory. Moreover, it is also organized with an accessibility helper BAR that makes using and surfing the website easy for disabled people. It can also convert text and image content to speech mode: indeed, screen readers are essential for people who are blind and are useful for people who are visually impaired, are illiterate, or have a learning disability.

The objective of making every kind of touristic offer accessible to all kinds of people has been achieved by a particular scheme that has to be filled out in an online version. In doing so, the tourist can independently assess the characteristics of the services offered according to his or her own needs: the offer is tailored to the various necessities, contemplating not only the specificities of persons with disability but also those of the elderly, children, those suffering from various food intolerances, or pregnant women.

On filling in the required fields of the *Turismabile* website, (www.turismabile.it), the information provided is automatically published on the website in the "Accessibility" section. A link is generated so that each operator can benefit from it to promote its level of accessibility on his or her information channels (site of the structure, social media, etc.).

This novelty represents a useful tool to have a complete "picture" of the accessibility and usability of the various offers, to obtain useful information on the quality of the welcome, and to facilitate complete and effective customer information.

With the aim of better understanding the style of the established information that is required to fill in the information sheets to render travel and tourism accessible to all travelers regardless of their physical limitation, disabilities, or age, some types of questions in the cards are presented in Table 2.

5 Discussion

As mentioned above, the in-depth information sheets on the accessibility and usability of tourist facilities are organized so as to allow the client to select the offers that best meet their personal needs for better use of the touristic facilities. This could be considered as one of the most important strategies regarding both web quality improvement and the particular aspect of eco-innovation concerning the dimension of individual consumers (Carrillo-Hermosilla et al., 2010) who expect to benefit from the use of a product or service.

As regards the website, as seen, it is possible to choose the type of tourist resource, select the subtype, select the province, and then access the cards of the various resources available. For example, if you are looking for a sports facility, you can find sports halls, swimming pools, playgrounds, or others. For each of these

Table 2 Example questions

1. Guest with physical and motor disabilities
Will you travel alone, or will you be accompanied?
If you are traveling with your companion, would you appreciate having two connecting rooms or neighboring rooms (unless they ask to sleep in the same room)?
Do you have a wheelchair with manual push or motor/electric drive?
What is the weight and dimensions of your wheelchair (width and length)?
Do you need a parking space nearby or near the entrance?
Do you need to have a shower seat? Do you need other aids?
2. Guest with sensory disability - blind or visually impaired
Will you travel alone, or will you be accompanied?
If you are traveling with your companion, would you appreciate having two connecting rooms or neighboring rooms (unless they ask to sleep in the same room)?
Are you traveling with your guide dog?
Do you have any specific requests for the dog?
Do you need a parking space near the entrance?
Would you like to receive a map of the facility in advance?
3. Guest with sensory disability - deaf or hearing impaired
Will you travel alone, or will you be accompanied?
If you are traveling with your companion, would you appreciate having two connecting rooms or neighboring rooms (unless they ask to sleep in the same room)?
Are you traveling with your guide dog? Do you have any specific requests for the dog?
Do you need a parking space near the entrance?
Would you like to receive a map of the facility in advance?
4. Guest with intellectual disability
Tourists with intellectual disabilities generally experience difficulties in understanding, communicating, and/or making decisions. These are people who depend on others for assistance and support. They are tourists that travel mainly with a companion. We recommend: Assume a relaxed and helpful attitude, be available for longer reaction times, use respectful forms of communication, do not address with a generic "you," if necessary, contact the tour leader to inquire about any specific needs of the tourist accompanying.
Does the guest have specific needs?
Do you need specific services? (e.g., we need a quiet room)
5. Guest with specific food needs
What kind of intolerance/allergy do you have?
Would you like to receive the menu for the period of stay in advance?
Do you need specific services? (e.g., we have menus for celiacs; we can give you indications about restaurants with menus for people with food intolerances, etc.)
6. Elderly guest.
Do you have any specific needs? (e.g., possibility of hiring - also external - aids/carers?)
Do you have difficulty walking long distances?
7. Families of tourists with children
Do you need a cot/crib?
Do you need to have a bottle warmer or kettle in the room?
How many beds should the room have?
8. Numerous families

(continued)

Eco-Innovation as a Tool to Enhance the Competitiveness of "Tourism for... 185

Table 2 (continued)

What type of room could suit your needs?
How many beds should the room have?
Do you need connecting rooms?
9. **Pregnant woman**
Would you like an additional pillow?

possibilities, it is possible to check the characteristics responding to the specific needs of the consumers through the single presentation cards.

Other than offers of accommodation facilities such as hotels, agritourism, or bed and breakfast, the most widespread type of offers concerns services such as tourist guide services, excursions, outdoor activities, mountain biking, tracking, experiences in thematic farms, ski courses, and more.

To fully understand the guests' needs and offer quality service and also to immediately identify the specific need of guests, the cards that correspond to each of the offers are all structured according to the same scheme. They provide practical indications that can be used in the case of a telephone conversation or an e-mail request if the guest has not explicitly or clearly defined his or her own disability/specific need. The systematic involvement of users in the *Turismabile* project, considering the different kinds of accessibility or usability requests made to the touristic facilities, demonstrates how user behavior plays a crucial role in the application of eco-innovations and the resulting impact on society (Carrillo-Hermosilla et al., 2010). Moreover, eco-innovation has improved *Turismabile* both in better understanding the different needs to satisfy and in understanding what the most useful tools are to better satisfy them.

Due to the impact of the coronavirus (COVID-19) pandemic, recently, there has been a sharp decline in mobility, which has caused a slump in tourism trade in all travel services and consumption also by nonresidents. Lockdowns and social distancing measures have led to steep declines in otherwise stable services consumption. It was estimated that Italy recorded a decrease of approximately 67 million tourist arrivals in 2020 over the previous year.[2] Table 3 shows lost visitor spending due to the pandemic and restrictions on travel and tourism, both in domestic and international visitor spending (World Travel & Tourism Council).

As a result, also with regard to *Turismabile* activities, there was a significant fall in the number of touristic activities proposed and a consequent decrease of access to the website. After another lost winter season and another lockdown in early spring, which has further depressed the touristic sector, to date, thanks to the measures adopted and especially to the vaccination campaign, Italy is looking at opening the country to tourists, introducing a range of measures aimed to protect visitors from the coronavirus as it tries to rescue a sector devastated by lockdowns and restrictions on movement. Thus, starting from the early days of March, the tourist resources of

---

[2] https://www.statista.com/statistics/1101025/impact-of-coronavirus-covid-19-on-tourist-arrivals-in-italy-by-region. Accessed on June 20, 2021.

Table 3 Lost visitor spending. Source: own elaboration from World Travel & Tourism Council

Visitor Impact		
2019	2020	
International		Change in international visitor spending:
EUR 45.6BN Visitor spending	**EUR 17.3BN** Visitor spending	−62.0%
Domestic		Change in domestic visitor spending:
EUR 142.8BN Visitor spending	**EUR 71.9BN** Visitor spending	−49.6%

Piedmont officially received the first invitations to fill in the new forms on the *Turismabile* website. Until now, they have registered about 350 tourist resources divided as follows:

- Accommodation facilities: 30%
- Catering facilities: 20%
- Cultural and historical places: 20%
- Places of worship: 10%
- Business and service providers: 10%
- Sports facilities: 5%
- Spa and solarium: 5%

These are still provisional data, constantly updated in relation to the response coming from the territory, but, in any case, they indicate a resumption of activities. Furthermore, during the interview with Mr. Ferrero, there was ample opportunity to expand on information relating to the project. Indeed, with the aim to cover the lack of quantitative data relating to *Turismabile* touristic activities, starting from the next year, social reporting will be published and will also improve other quantitative information.

6 Conclusions

Through analysis of the *Turismabile* project, this study examined a pivotal example of the accessible tourism segment, starting from the idea that, as Wu et al. (2014, p. 2093) have pointed out, "accessible tourism is not the only niche in the tourism market, and accessible facilities can also be of benefit to non-disabled individuals, including the elderly, young children and pregnant women." From a theoretical point of view, it was observed how the project has developed and spread an evolutionary perspective of innovation according to which innovation results from a systemic process that concerns interconnectedness and dynamic interaction between different actors and internal and external factors influence the process. This new vision enhances users as a key dimension of the eco-innovation concept. Accordingly, the capacity of eco-innovation to provide new business opportunities and contribute to a transformation toward a sustainable society is in this case study deemed as depending on a dimension that is strictly linked to the users that are engaged as key stakeholders in the innovation process. The *Turismabile* project was able to foresee the acceptance of an innovative service also by involving users in its development and thus ensuring its overall acceptance. The capacity to understand which users can contribute to the different phases of the innovation process and how to interact with them was crucial to the project (Carrillo-Hermosilla et al., 2010). In this regard, *Turismabile* has, over time, improved the special skill set needed to obtain valuable inputs to its innovative project from various users. Many significant benefits of the innovative project come from the involvement of potential users who, by choosing the opportunities offered by the project, can give more information regarding their real needs and desires, and in doing so, contribute to the development of the project itself.

From a managerial point of view, this chapter has shown how, starting from the described accessibility of the digital platform, the *Turismabile* project has enhanced interaction among interlocutors, operators, and partners, becoming a leading example in the panorama of Italian "tourism for all."

However, it is important to highlight that the ongoing COVID-19 pandemic marks an extraordinary global crisis unseen in this century, with its rapid spread worldwide and associated mortality burden, which is leading to profound economic consequences. In such an unprecedented scenario, most firms were not ready to deal with the resulting significant large-scale perturbations. Consequently, almost every sector of tourism has been affected by this pandemic that is also likely to change tourists' lifestyles, travel behaviors, and patterns.

Thus, it was impossible to obtain useful data to update the analysis of the project until today. Further studies will be addressed to deepen the analysis also with a comparison with other similar realities in Italy.

Acknowledgments The authors would like to thank Giovanni Ferrero and Andrea Accortanzo for their invaluable collaboration, sensitivity, and help in providing us with the material necessary to develop the case analysis and share our reflections.

References

Carrillo-Hermosilla, J., del Río, P., & Könnölä, T. (2010). Diversity of eco-innovations: Reflections from selected case studies. *Journal of Cleaner Production, 18*(10–12), 1073–1083.

Carter, J., & Markel, M. (2001). Web accessibility for people with disabilities: An introduction for web developers. *IEEE Transactions on Professional Communication, 44*, 225–233.

Cass, N., Shove, E., & Urry, J. (2005). Social exclusion, mobility and access. *The Sociological Review, 53*(3), 539–555.

Charter, M., & Clark T. (2007). *Sustainable innovation: Key conclusions from sustainable innovation conferences 2003–2006*, organised by the Centre for Sustainable Design. In Sustainable innovation, 2003–2006, University College for the Creative Arts, Farnham, Surrey.

Cobigo, V., Ouellette-Kuntz, H., Lysaght, R., & Martin, L. (2012). Shifting our conceptualization of social inclusion. *Stigma Research and Action, 2*(2), 75–84.

Denzin, N. K. (1978). *The research act: A theoretical introduction to sociological methods.* McGraw-Hill.

Disability and Development Report. (2018). Accessed March 10, 2021, from https://social.un.org/publications/UN-Flagship-Report-Disability-Final.pdf.

Eichhorn, V., Miller, G., Michopoulou, E., & Buhalis, D. (2008). Enabling access to tourism through information schemes? *Annals of Tourism Research, 35*(1), 578–600.

Eisenhardt, K. M., & Graebner, M. E. (2007). Theory building from cases: Opportunities and challenges. *Academy of Management Journal, 50*(1), 25–32.

Flick, U. (2009). *An introduction to qualitative research.* Sage Publications.

Gibbert, M., Ruigrok, W., & Wicki, B. (2008). What passes as a rigorous case study? *Strategic Management Journal, 29*(13), 1465–1147.

Grafton, J., Lillis, A. M., & Mahama, H. (2011). Mixed methods research in accounting. *Qualitative Research in Accounting & Management, 8*(1), 5–21.

Hienerth, C., von Hippel, E., Baldwin, C. Y., & How User Innovations Become Commercial Products: A Theoretical Investigation and Case Study. (2006, January). MIT Sloan Research Paper No. 4572-06, HBS Finance Working Paper No. 876967, Harvard NOM Working Paper No. 06-13. Accessed March, 24, 2021 from SSRN: https://ssrn.com/abstract¼876967 or https://doi.org/10.2139/ssrn.876967

Kastenholz, E., Eusébio, C., & Figueiredo, E. (2015). Contributions of tourism to social inclusion of persons with disability. *Disability & Society, 30*, 1259–1281.

Pulsiri, N., R. Vatananan-Thesenvitz, K. Tantipisitkul, T. Htoo Aung, A.A. Schaller, A.M. Schaller, K. Methananthakul, and R. Shannon. 2019. Achieving sustainable development goals for people with disabilities through digital technologies. In *Portland International Conference on Management of Engineering and Technology (PICMET)*, Portland, Oregon, USA, pp. 1–10.

Ramesh Babu, J., & Chandra Sekharaiah, K. (2014). Accessible computing for sustainable and inclusive development, international conference on computing for sustainable global development (INDIACom). *New Delhi, India, 2014*, 156–160. https://doi.org/10.1109/IndiaCom.2014.6828120

Rowley, J. (2012). Conducting research interviews. *Management Research Review, 35*, 260–271.

Siano, A., Conte, F., Amabile, S., Vollero, A., & Piciocchi, P. (2016). Communicating sustainability: An operational model for evaluating corporate websites. *Sustainability, 8*(9), 1–16.

Stucki, G. M. D. (2005, October). MS international classification of functioning, disability, and health (ICF). *American Journal of Physical Medicine & Rehabilitation, 84*(10), 733–740. https://doi.org/10.1097/01.phm.0000179521.70639.83

Westcott, J. (2004). *Improving information on accessible tourism for disabled people.* Office for Official Publications of the European Communities.

Wu, Y. C. J., & Cheng, M. J. (2008). Accessible tourism for the disabled: Long tail theory. In M. D. Lytras, J. M. Carroll, E. Damiani, & R. D. Tennyson (Eds.), *Emerging technologies and information systems for the knowledge society* (Vol. 5288). WSKS 2008. Lecture Notes in Computer Science. Springer. Accessed March, 18, 2021 from https://doi.org/10.1007/978-3-540-87781-3_61. http://www.tourismforall.eu

Wu, Y. C. J., Chang, C. L., & Hsieh, Y. J. (2014). Enhancing learning experience of the disabled: An accessible tourism platform. *Journal of Universal Computer Science, 20*(15), 2080–2095.

Yin, R. K. (2009). *Case study research: Design and methods* (4th ed., p. 2014). Sage.

Yin, R. K. (2014). *Case study research design and methods* (5th ed.). Thousand Oaks, CA, USA.

Conclusions

Tindara Abbate, Fabrizio Cesaroni, and Augusto D'Amico

The objective of this book is to examine strategies, policies, and activities aimed at fostering and sustaining forms of accessible tourism for people with disabilities. Assuming different levels (regional, national and international) and lenses of analysis, the studies reported in the book have mainly highlighted the wide range of constraints—such as social, cultural, legal, and information impediments—that are relevant obstacles to the welfare, inclusivity, full integration and participation of people with disabilities. By adopting a multidisciplinary methodological approach, the scientific contributions collected in this book have effectively explored both demand and supply of the problem at issue. On the one hand, studies included in Part I analyze the dynamics and determinants of tourism flows of people with disabilities by primarily highlighting the role that national and regional policies may have in boosting this specific type of tourism. On the other hand, studies included in the second and the third parts of the book debate the actions that firms and organizations involved in offering tourism products and services directed at people with disabilities should take to meet the requirements of this category of customer and, thus, to improve the likelihood of the success of their initiatives. In doing so, real-world examples have been analyzed and discussed, and practical managerial tools have been presented and examined.

A common element that emerges from most of the contributions of this book is that, in order to address the specific needs of (potential) tourists with disabilities, a "tourism for all" (Europe for All, 2007) approach should be adopted with the aim of developing tourism for inclusive growth (UNWTO, 2015). In fact, an effective application of the basic principles of "tourism for all" implies that, in order to fully and completely solve the problems of people with disabilities, the analysis should avoid what could be defined as "the market segment trap," which considers

---

T. Abbate · F. Cesaroni (✉) · A. D'Amico
Department of Economics, University of Messina, Messina, Italy
e-mail: abbatet@unime.it; fabrizio.cesaroni@unime.it; damicoa@unime.it

© The Author(s), under exclusive license to Springer Nature Switzerland AG 2022
T. Abbate et al. (eds.), *Tourism and Disability*, Tourism on the Verge,
https://doi.org/10.1007/978-3-030-93612-9_12

tourists with disabilities as simply a specific segment of the broader tourism market. Rather, the offer of tourism proposals should be designed to meet and satisfy the needs and preferences of each person (people with disabilities included), irrespective of their individualities, characteristics, and specificities. For instance, the adoption of such a holistic view would overcome the problems that providers of tourism services (i.e., accommodation, transport, hospitality, entertainment) face when seeking to re-design their facilities to reduce barriers for people with mobility, visual, hearing, or cognitive issues. The more disability categories considered, the more modifications are required, thus giving rise to a never-ending process of incremental modifications, rather than an ex-ante, comprehensive architectural design that disregards the type of disability to be met.

In this perspective, Smart Tourism Destinations is an emblematic case strongly oriented to design, collect and provide a large amount of dynamic and heterogeneous data (e.g., data arising from different sources and different tools/platforms), potentially used by all people, which can remove informational barriers that still exist in many circumstances, by enhancing tourism experiences (Gretzel et al., 2015). In turn, such smart destinations facilitate the transformation of massive data into meaningful information for potential tourists with the aim of increasing tourist satisfaction and the attractiveness of tourism and hospitality ventures. Additionally, the concept of smartness (intelligence) is strictly related to the ability to understand, discover solutions and solve problems by using knowledge, thus also having a major impact on universal accessibility, sustainability, and innovation.

Certainly, the goal of inclusive tourism is a challenging objective whose pursuit builds on the co-existence of a set of differentiated conditions. Firstly, in designing tourism proposals that also address people with disabilities, it is necessary to consider all the different attributes of the proposed product and service. In particular, there are not "more important" and "less important" attributes (according to the traditional marketing "importance-performance" perspective—Martilla & James, 1977; Oh, 2001; Azzopardi & Nash, 2013). Each attribute acquires the same importance, and what may be an irrelevant element for some may be of crucial importance for others. This means that tourism providers must define value propositions characterized by a wide set of attributes—addressing health, cultural, recreational, emotional, and many other aspects—to orient and develop valued experiences for all customers. In this perspective, such comprehensive tourism value proposals may improve the propensity to travel, permit tourism accessibility to more people as well as explore new business opportunities.

Secondly, the wide range of actors participating in the tourism industry (hotels, restaurants, museums, providers of entertainment services, transportation, public services, and so forth) cannot limit their focus only to their own specific activity, as the success of their business depends on the presence and performance of neighboring initiatives—in economic terms, positive and negative externalities arise from the various tourist actors operating in each area. A systemic approach is strongly recommended. However, do individual actors have sufficient incentives to behave cooperatively? Or, rather, will opportunistic forces bring all actors into the classic prisoner's dilemma conditions? The examples provided in this book underline the relevance of collaborative models and forms that are likely to emerge in narrow and limited locations, where the different actors involved in the tourism offer share the same culture, knowledge, and objectives. Were such examples replicated in other (wider) locations, the fragmentation often characterizing the tourism sector might be overcome, and collaborative networks for enhancing value through co-creation of products and services might be developed. In turn, cooperation and collaboration in a variety of ways are imperative for individual actors, which may lead to remarkable potential opportunities to gain a competitive advantage by improving the attractiveness and competitiveness of territories. Where the tourism offer is aimed at addressing people with disabilities, such opportunities appear even more relevant.

An interesting case in point is that of the *Turismabile* project (which has been extensively analyzed in the chapter "Eco-Innovation as a tool to enhance the competitiveness of 'Tourism for all'—the Italian project 'Turismabile'"), which has enhanced the interaction and participation among different interlocutors, operators, and partners, becoming a leading example in the panorama of Italian "tourism for all." Similarly, this case reveals the importance of the complementary commitment of all actors, both private and public organizations, to deliver holistic experiences to tourists. In fact, people with disabilities need appropriate solutions to their specific needs in terms of public services as well as other public sector spheres (barrier-free environments in tourist attractions, public information, and communication), but these must be complementary to corresponding satisfactory solutions in the private sector facilities they may employ (accommodation, restaurants, private information and communication).

Thirdly, as a consequence of the previous point, a radical shift in mindset is necessary to bring about an inevitable transition: from "tourism for all" to "tourism *from* all." In fact, the effectiveness and success of a tourism offer that is able to meet the expectations of tourists with disabilities is also and often the result of active engagement of those agents who are not usually considered relevant actors in the tourism industry. Such actors can become essential parts of the emergent ecosystem, characterized by the sharing of (material and immaterial) resources and competences necessary to redefine traditional business models, explore new opportunities for innovative products and services as well as activate innovative paths aimed at creating dynamism in the tourism sector. Mainly, included in this residual but complementary category of agents are citizens of tourist destinations who are not directly involved in the tourism market but who offer a fundamental contribution in the creation of a common and shared culture of openness and innovation. Some destinations that are activating a series of completely new and technologically advanced tourism services, providing benefits to all tourists, laying the foundations for increasingly innovative and immersive experiences can be identified through these interpretative lenses.

Fourthly, new technological solutions, mainly exploiting the possibilities offered by information and communication technologies (ICTs), may facilitate and sustain the development of a tourism offer addressing the real needs of people with disabilities. In this perspective, digital platforms, providing different services and using advanced ICT solutions, are assuming an important role in defining and planning complete tourism experiences for people with accessibility and inclusivity needs, thanks to the existence of network synergies. In fact, these digital platforms may become a suitable *locus* for sharing not only experiences among tourists but also for co-creating highly personalized products and services by stimulating the interaction between individuals and service providers. The wider set of social interaction tools captures the real feeling of tourists for what they want, expect, and experience in real-time, creating and delivering emotional experiences that go beyond simple tourist satisfaction.

Finally, one must bear in mind that all these changes involving a broad plethora of differentiated stakeholders require a necessarily long time to be implemented and become effective. The significant changes involved imply long-term investments in facilities, technological solutions, organizational arrangements, and also cultural mindset. In turn, the main issue becomes how to align the short-term behavior of the various actors involved in the process into a common path that meets the common long-term goal. This time issue underlines the relevance of new strategic thinking that is expected to emerge in the current business environment in order to face the global transformations that involve three main dimensions: scale, scope, and speed. Such a scenario is particularly challenging, especially for managers operating in the tourism industry who are required to possess and exploit proper dynamic capabilities (Eisenhardt & Martin, 2000; Camisón & Monfort-Mir, 2012) in order to stimulate the regeneration of their traditional strategy, the identification of new capabilities to anticipate future changes, and the development of necessary complementarities between profitability and social responsibilities.

All these considerations that have been explored in the different chapters of this book produce obvious strong managerial and political implications. The final outcome of inclusive tourism, which also meets the legitimate ambitions of potential tourists with disabilities, can be realized only through the necessary convergence of public policies and private competitive strategies of companies operating at different levels of the tourism value chain. Moreover, the content of this book also has relevant implications in terms of academic research. Mainly, studies aimed at addressing the problems of tourism for people with disabilities would benefit from an interdisciplinary approach by means of constructive cross-fertilization among scientific disciplines such as management, economics, health, psychology, architecture, etc. In fact, the fruitful combination of knowledge and insights from such different approaches and the ability of each discipline to focus on issues and problems specific to their scientific domain would facilitate the adoption of the holistic view mentioned above, which is implicit in the "tourism for all" perspective. In time, this may also become the first step of a process that proliferates the idea that tourism for people with disabilities is, indeed, simply tourism for people.

References

Azzopardi, E., & Nash, R. (2013). A critical evaluation of importance–performance analysis. *Tourism Management, 35*, 222–233.

Camisón, C., & Monfort-Mir, V. M. (2012). Measuring innovation in tourism from the Schumpeterian and the dynamic-capabilities perspectives. *Tourism Management, 33*(4), 776–789.

Eisenhardt, K. M., & Martin, J. A. (2000). Dynamic capabilities: What are they? *Strategic Management Journal, 21*(10–11), 1105–1121.

Europe for All. (2007). *Europe for all – better information discerning travellers*. On www.Europeforall.com.

Gretzel, U., Koo, C., Sigala, M., & Xiang, Z. (2015). Special issue on smart tourism: Convergence of information technologies, experiences, and theories. *Electronic Markets, 25*(3), 175–177.

Martilla, J. A., & James, J. C. (1977). Importance-performance analysis. *Journal of Marketing, 41*(1), 77–79.

Oh, H. (2001). Revisiting importance–performance analysis. *Tourism Management, 22*(6), 617–627.

UNWTO. (2015). *Manual of accessible tourism for all: Public partnership and good practices*. World Tourism Organization (UNWTO) and Fundación ACS.

The 12-Hour Author

The 12-Hour Author

Everything You Need to Know to Get Published and Become a Successful Writer

Noah Charney

ROWMAN & LITTLEFIELD
Lanham • Boulder • New York • London

Published by Rowman & Littlefield
An imprint of The Rowman & Littlefield Publishing Group, Inc.
4501 Forbes Boulevard, Suite 200, Lanham, Maryland 20706
www.rowman.com

86-90 Paul Street, London EC2A 4NE

Copyright © 2025 by Noah Charney

All rights reserved. No part of this book may be reproduced in any form or by any electronic or mechanical means, including information storage and retrieval systems, without written permission from the publisher, except by a reviewer who may quote passages in a review.

British Library Cataloguing in Publication Information Available

Library of Congress Cataloging-in-Publication Data

Names: Charney, Noah, author.
Title: The 12-hour author : everything you need to know to get published and become a successful writer / Noah Charney.
Description: Lanham : Rowman & Littlefield, 2025. | Includes bibliographical references and index.
Identifiers: LCCN 2024042911 (print) | LCCN 2024042912 (ebook) | ISBN 9781538187302 (cloth) | ISBN 9781538187319 (ebook)
Subjects: LCSH: Authorship—Vocational guidance. | Authorship.
Classification: LCC PN151 .C48 2025 (print) | LCC PN151 (ebook) | DDC 808.02023--dc23/eng/20241001
LC record available at https://lccn.loc.gov/2024042911
LC ebook record available at https://lccn.loc.gov/2024042912

♾️™ The paper used in this publication meets the minimum requirements of American National Standard for Information Sciences—Permanence of Paper for Printed Library Materials, ANSI/NISO Z39.48-1992.

To Boylan, with thanks for having been the only
writing teacher I ever had (or needed)

Contents

Acknowledgments	xi

PART 1: ON PUBLISHING   1

1 The Big Surprise: Don't Write the Book or Article—Write the
   Proposal   3
   No Editor Wants to Read Your Full Book . . . Yet   4
   Do I Need an Agent (and How Do I Get One)?   8
   Picking a Publisher (Then Hoping the Publisher Picks You)   19

2 Book Proposals   29
   Lite Book Proposal   29
   Book Proposal for Rowman & Littlefield   31
   Part One: On Publishing   34
   Part Two: On Writing Well   35
   Academic Book Proposal Template   37
   Image-Heavy Book Proposals   39
   Edited Collections   40
   Translation Book Proposals   40
   Trade Nonfiction Proposals   42

3 Behind the Scenes at the Publishing House   51
   Contracts   56
   Working with the Publishing House   60

4 Writing and Publishing Articles   73
   Truffles, Goat Cheese, and XXX in Istria, Croatia's Forgotten Coast 75
   What Makes for a Good Article?   76

vii

How Not to Scare Them Off: Letter Template for Pitching Articles and Chasing Editors		79
The Prince and the Looted Statues		81
In the Beginning Was the Word: Inside the Collection of the Forthcoming Museum of the Bible		82
The Hacker's Code: How Computer Programs Are Decoding Mysterious Manuscripts		84
Chasing Editors		85
Getting Paid (Finally)		87

PART 2: ON WRITING WELL (ENOUGH)   91

5	Tips on Article Research and Writing	93
	Research and Writing in the Age of AI	93
	Article Writing Tips: Great Openings	95
	Structuring Articles	99
	Anglophone Versus European Essay Styles	102
	Outline Versus Drifting	103
	Clarity Versus Intellectuality	104
	Conclusion	107
6	Story Mapping	109
	Big Rule 1: Make Your Reader Feel Smart	110
	Big Rule 2: Simplicity and Clarity	110
	ABAB Story Structure	112
	Story Mapping	113
	Character Mapping	115
	Story Structures	118
	The Sitcom Code	121
7	Writing Tips (and What to Avoid)	127
	Character Sheet	127
	Don'ts and Dos	128
	Don't	128
	Do	130
8	The Importance of Great Openings	133
	Nonfiction Openings	135
	Fiction Openings	140
9	Promoting Your Book	143
	Sales Expectations	144
	Organic Marketing	145
	Split Testing Social Media Ads	146
	Getting Reviewed and Interviewed	148

Paid Reviews	148
Becoming an Amazon Bestseller	149
Landing Pages and Promotional Videos	150
Publicity Versus Marketing	151
Book Events and Tours	151
Inside Book Tours: Analysis of an Endangered Species	152

10 The Two-Hour Workday: Tips to Maximize Efficacy in

Minimal Time	159
Portion Out Your Work and Time	160
Designate Your Workspace	162
Check Checklists	162
Control Your Email	163

11 Map Your Writing Plan 165
Getting Started: A 12-Day Plan 165

12 12 Steps to Success 173
Your First Book: A 12-Week Plan 173
Publishing Success: A 12-Month Plan 180
If You Need Assistance 184

Notes 185

Index 187

About the Author 189

Acknowledgments

I only ever had one formal writing teacher, whom everyone knew simply as Boylan, during one semester at Colby College. The experience certainly made an impression. The rest of this business I learned on the job, and it's important to keep in mind that writing is fun, and if you want to make a job out of it, it truly is a job. You have to work at it. Because I had to teach myself, learning by the slow, trial-and-error method, I thought it would be helpful to others to have it all laid out. So I began teaching the sort of courses I didn't see offered, with information that many creative writing programs leave out. There are plenty of good books on how to write well, but there is almost nothing on how to become a writer—how to pitch articles, propose books, submit novels, find an agent, read a contract, get paid, get published, promote your book. I taught these things for many years in many formats: as part of a Guardian Masterclass in London (taught by those of us who write for the *Guardian* newspaper), at the University of Ljubljana, in various online workshops, and in person. I have a slight neurosis in which I only feel like I have completed something if I write about it—and publish the text. So why not write about how to write, publish those lessons, and achieve a sense of completion? And here we are.

This book is my ninth with my ace editor, Charles Harmon, at Rowman & Littlefield, and is part of a growing series of books with "The 12-Hour" in the title. We've had *The 12-Hour Art Expert* and *The 12-Hour Film Expert* and now *The 12-Hour Author*. The idea of each work is to break down any sense of intimidation and present a one-book, all-you-need-to-know dive into a subject. It's been such a pleasure to publish with Rowman & Littlefield, and I'm delighted for this series to continue.

I've learned from fellow writers, editors, agents. I've learned from reading. When I read, I'm often deconstructing to peek behind the ink and try to understand what the writer is doing (even if the writer wasn't consciously thinking about what they were doing). I am like a mechanic popping the hood of every sweet car I see. This is what I've learned. My hope is that the trial and error I went through means that you don't have to.

Part 1

ON PUBLISHING

Chapter 1

The Big Surprise

Don't Write the Book or Article— Write the Proposal

I was sure that this was a great move.

I'd published my first book, a novel called *The Art Thief*. My agent had scored me a big advance—six figures—which allowed me to become a full-time writer. It had been a bestseller in five countries, translated into fourteen languages. I was ready for my next book, and I thought I'd surprise my agent with it. And I'd do so with my "brilliance"—or so my twenty-eight-year-old self, writing his own career script, imagined. So I wrote a full draft of a non-fiction book. It was the story of the world's most frequently stolen artwork, *The Ghent Altarpiece*.

It seemed like an ideal fit. My first book was a clockwork heist full of double crosses and twists, fiction set in the midst of the art world. In research-ing it, I'd become known as the leading expert on art crime. I'd made a name for myself through the good fortune of publishing a much-noted novel while, at the same time, a *New York Times Magazine* article came out about my aca-demic work in establishing the study of art crime ("To Sketch a Thief," *New York Times Magazine*, December 2006). Years before I'd even finished my PhD, I was "the art crime guy." So it made sense to me that I should turn my attention to a true crime involving art and tell that story with my next book. Fiction, nonfiction, what's the difference, right?

So I wrote a full draft of the book that would become *Stealing the Mystic Lamb: The True Story of the World's Most Coveted Masterpiece*. I sent it to my agent at the time.

She liked it. In retrospect, that was perhaps what should have been Surprise No. 1.

But then she replied, "This looks good, but what I need is a book proposal."

"What's a book proposal?" I thought, but decided it was uncool to write that in response.

Thankfully, she explained to me what she needed in order to shop this book of mine to publishers. She was aware that almost no young writers know about the world of book proposals and the art of making them well. So she set me to work studying successful book proposals so that I could write my own. I learned, in the thick of it, what I wish I'd learned long ahead of time. I would have saved a year or so of work. I've never studied writing, so perhaps I would have known all of this, had I enrolled in a creative writing program. But no, most writing programs will teach you how to write well, but they won't tell you the mechanics of how to become a paid writer. Book Proposals 101 is not among the course offerings. And that's why this book is necessary for anyone wishing to become a writer. It fills a gap that most formal writing programs skip over.

These are the sort of lessons that I want to share with aspiring writers. The job of a good professor is to inform while entertaining and to make the lives of their students or readers easier by providing useful knowledge.

That's the plan for this book. All the tricks, tips, lessons, and experiences that I've learned over my years, as the author of now more than twenty books, I'm delighted to pass on to you. I hope that in the process, you'll be inspired to write, that you'll make more effective use of your time, that you'll skip the queue when possible, and that you'll maximize your chance of success. I've spoken to so many graduates of renowned creative writing programs who have not been taught the basic tools of the trade. I don't mean how to write—that is taught well. I mean the logistics of how to be a professional writer. How to write proposals, how to pitch to editors, how to read contracts, how to build your portfolio. In short, how to get published and make a living. That's what this book will present. I hope that it will be a good complement to any writing course you may take. I never took one, but rather learned "on the job," from trial and error, from agents and editors. I'm delighted to lay it all out for you, in hopes that I can make your writing life a little easier and your writing dreams arrive a little more swiftly and smoothly.

NO EDITOR WANTS TO READ YOUR FULL BOOK . . . YET

No one will read a full nonfiction manuscript if you send it to them. Don't bother writing it ahead of time.

That was my biggest surprise. For fiction, things work differently. Editors and agents want you to have written the whole novel, and they want for it to be amazing—perhaps just one draft away from publication readiness—so when it gets published and you get paid for it, you're effectively being paid retroactively. Most of the work has already been done. You have to write the

The Big Surprise   5

novel on spec, in hopes of someone wanting to publish it. Depending on your pace and efficiency, that could easily mean a year's worth of work (if not significantly more) all running on the fumes of hope, without any guarantee that someone will publish it, and with no income generated from writing. That's the approach that I had assumed was a risk a writer had to take, as I had when writing *The Art Thief*. I was lucky in that I was a student when I wrote it, so as long as I could steal time away from my postgraduate degree program, I could find time to write. But once real life arrives, with bills to pay and a family to feed, then the luxury of taking a year to write a novel, perhaps some faraway fantasy novel involving dragons and wizards, might seem like a faraway fantasy.

In practice, agents and editors still won't read the whole novel, even if you send it to them. For new works of fiction that you'd like them to consider, they want the first three to five chapters, or roughly the first fifty pages, plus a summary of the rest. Only if they LOVE this will they want to read the rest. We'll circle back to how to get fiction published shortly. But back in 2008, I thought this was the approach for nonfiction as well. When my agent explained to me what this whole "book proposal" thing was, I had truly never heard of it. I'd soon realize that it's an author's best friend—if you know how to embrace it.

A book proposal is a document outlining what a future, as-yet-unwritten nonfiction book will be about. It is short enough that an editor or agent can read it in one sitting and make an informed decision about whether it would be of interest to publish. Based on the proposal, and the proposal alone, the editor will bring the project before their team at the publishing house. The job of an ace book proposal is to (a) engage the editor and make them feel that yes, this is a great book for the publishing house to publish, (b) convince the editor that this is the right writer to write it, and (c) help the editor convince their colleagues that the publishing house should make an offer for it.

Let's break down those three steps. All these critical decisions are made based only on the potential shown in the proposal.

Point A is the most obvious. You need to get an editor excited about the book you propose to write. We'll take a deep look at how to do that, what sort of approach is best to use, and how to "hook" an editor. There is also a degree of luck involved. Maybe the editor is having a bad day when they read your proposal. Or maybe they just contracted a book on a similar enough topic that yours will overlap too much in terms of target market, so they pass for that reason. It's important to know that it's not just about whether an acquisitions editor likes it. The editor also has to feel that it's right for their particular publishing house.

There are some ways to maximize your chances and minimize wasted submissions. If you want to write an academic book, then submit it to an academic or university press, not a trade press. If you want to write about archaeology, then make sure that this is a subject that is covered by the publishing house to which you submit your proposal. If the publishing house doesn't do archaeology books at all, then don't bother. Also check what is already published by that publishing house so you don't offer something that it has already covered in subject or theme.

You also need to demonstrate point B: Showing that you're the right writer for this particular project is important. I may be an established writer, but I'm established in the field of art, art crime, and perhaps more broadly, culture. If I were to pitch a book about, say, astrophysics or engineering, then I wouldn't likely pass muster as the "right writer" for that project, no matter how good the book idea might be or how good a writer I might be. To be honest, I'd bet I could write a great book on astrophysics, but I'd likely never get past the initial proposal phase because I don't seem to be the proper writer for such a book, given my background, expertise, and previous publications.

Acquiring books based only on the potential shown in a proposal is a risky game for the publisher, too, because they have no guarantee that the book that results from contracting the project outlined in the book proposal will be as good as the proposal promises. Sometimes the book proposal sounds far more exciting than the book turns out to be.

There is also much guessing involved—informed guesses, to be sure, but speculation nonetheless. The publishing team will look at "comps"—other books that they think have a similar audience—and based on how those have sold they estimate how many copies of this new book they imagine they could sell. Parts of your book proposal will help the potential publisher understand the market and audience.

Now we get to point C. The job of the book proposal is to make it as easy as possible for the editor who received the proposal to summarize it in a compelling way at their meeting with the rest of the team. The acquisitions editor is the only one likely to have actually read the full book proposal. They will probably have forwarded it to their colleagues, but did anyone read it or do more than a cursory scan?

The real test of a winning proposal is whether it makes it simple for the acquisitions editor to stand up at the meeting when their turn arrives and give a short pitch about the book proposals they've considered that they think would be great for the publisher to take on. Your book, or rather the proposal that you carefully wrote, should make it as easy as possible for the acquisitions editor who is interested to give a two-minute pitch summarizing you, your book idea, and why it's a good choice for the publishing house. A more easily "elevator-pitched" concept will have a greater likelihood of success.

When we turn to a deconstructive analysis of winning book proposals, we'll focus on the proposal first engaging the acquisitions editor, and then facilitating the acquisitions editor's spoken pitch at that meeting (usually every other Monday at 9:00 a.m., with the entire team seated around a large oval table spiked with Starbucks takeaway mugs, or so I imagine them).

Can the big idea proposed by the book be summarized in a tight one-liner? Take the proposal for my *Stealing the Mystic Lamb*. The one-liner might go something like this: "The true story of the world's most stolen artwork, which is also arguably the most influential painting ever made." That's a pretty good one-liner. If we expand it a bit, it gets better. "Anything bad that can happen to an artwork has happened to this painting: it was stolen six times, looted by Napoleon and the Nazis, forged, dismembered, smuggled, partly burned, nearly blown up, saved by the Monuments Men, and far more. One of its twelve panels is still missing. The story has never been fully told. This book will be written by the world's leading expert on art crime." That sounds pretty compelling as a thirty-second pitch. It's full of superlatives. It offers hints that leave you wanting more. ("Saved by the Monuments Men"? OK, cool, but how? Nearly blown up? Tell me more. How can a single artwork be stolen six times?")

That brief spoken pitch at that Monday morning meeting will determine whether your book will be offered a publishing contract or not. And if so, how much of an advance (if any) will you be offered in order to take the time to write the book? How much of a commitment to the book's success will the publishing house make? With only a little room for exceptional surprises, how well your book will do is determined from the proposal alone, long before you actually write it and the publisher sees if the end result is as good as the proposal promised—or any good at all. Because no one expects you to have written a nonfiction book ahead of time.

This brings me back to my email with my agent.

"This looks good, but what I need is a book proposal."

"What's a book proposal?"

I'd sent her the full draft of the manuscript, some sixty thousand words long. I thought I was mostly done. Now she informed me that even if she sent this along and it was ready for publication (which it wasn't yet), no one would read it. The problem is one of time. A past agent of mine told me that she gets around three hundred inquiries per week from aspiring writers hoping she'll represent them. She takes around two to three new writers *per year*. Even if she wanted to, she couldn't possibly read three hundred full manuscripts per week—that would be over fifteen thousand books in a year! Instead, agents and acquisitions editors want proposals of a length they can reasonably read through. Book proposals are usually between five and forty pages long, and most of that is a sample chapter (more on that later). Book proposals are a bit like TED Talks. The now-famous TED format requires that your dynamic, engaging, informative talk be no longer than eighteen minutes. If you can't

8 *Chapter 1*

convey your big idea in eighteen minutes, your services are not wanted. Book proposals should convey the excitement, novelty, intelligence, and market for a future book in just a few pages. This is what agents and editors want. The limitation of twenty-four-hour days requires concision. There aren't enough hours in the day to read through entire sixty-thousand-word manuscripts on spec, taking the time to consider whether to acquire them. And so, with much instruction from my agent, I had to take my sixty-thousand-word, nearly complete manuscript for *Stealing the Mystic Lamb* and "translate" it into a winning proposal for a future book that was no more than forty pages long—and preferably far shorter.

In order to show me what a winning book proposal looks like, the agent passed me ten proposals that had become legendary among agents and editors. They represented the diamonds. Each had received at least a six-figure advance (which is very unusual in nonfiction), and one forty-page proposal had produced a million-dollar advance for its author, who had been unknown at the time and had never published a book before. I was to study them, deconstruct them, and produce something that would, it was hoped, approximate their success.

All of them were different, but each contained certain key elements that I recognized were required. I deconstructed the heck out of those proposals, particularly the million-dollar one. I'll tell you everything I learned and have now put to use for the past twenty or so books I have written.

This book is your guide, handbook, and cheat sheet to becoming an author, or to leveling up your books if you already write.

DO I NEED AN AGENT (AND HOW DO I GET ONE)?

Everyone wants an agent. It sounds cool, right? And in principle, once you have an agent, everything should be easier for you as a writer. They do the hard work for you, don't they? The answer is "sometimes" and "hopefully."

Literary agents are a necessary filter for the biggest publishing houses, which would otherwise be inundated with submissions, most of which would not be at a level that would interest them. To separate the wheat from the chaff, the big publishers accept only submissions from licensed agents. With an agent, in principle your work—fiction or nonfiction—can be submitted anywhere.

What Should an Agent Do for Me If I Have One?

Have a look at the subheading above. Since you're a writer, you'll have spotted a conditional thrown in there: "should." Because having an agent, alas,

The Big Surprise 9

does not mean that all your problems are solved. But here is what an agent will—or at least should—do for you.

An agent should help you develop your book proposal, shaping it from the idea phase (you should be able to bounce ideas off your agent) through the proposal (they should read drafts of your proposal and give you both general comments and, ideally, a close-read redline edit as you approach the finish line) or manuscript of a novel.

An agent will then do the submissions for you. The real reason you may need an agent is that only licensed agents can submit to the Big Four publishing houses and their numerous imprints. The Big Four are Houghton Mifflin Harcourt (with notable imprints Clarion and John Joseph Adams), Hachette Livre (with notable imprints Grand Central; Little, Brown; and Mulholland), HarperCollins (with AvonBooks, Harlequin, Harper, and William Morrow), Penguin Random House (with imprints Knopf Doubleday, Crown, and Viking). Penguin Random House just got even bigger because in 2020 it bought Simon & Schuster, with its imprints Howard, Scribner, Touchstone, and Atria (which published my novel, *The Art Thief*), which used to be the Big Fifth trade publisher. These four umbrella companies now own the lion's share of the anglophone book market, and they are the ones who will accept only submissions via agents. There are countless others that you can submit to without an agent (of which more later), but these giants have the most money to pay authors advances, anticipate the biggest sales, and invest the most in promoting their books to ensure those big sales.

Do keep in mind that just because your book may be published by a big trade press doesn't guarantee it will sell well, or even do better than if it had been published by a smaller one. We'll return later to how and why books sell well and get critical attention. Suffice to say that the only way to have your books considered by the big guns is via agented submission. So that's the major advantage an agent can offer.

Agents are also going to negotiate better than you ever could. One of my agents (I've worked with four to date) was so good at negotiating that she managed to convince (or perhaps the better word choice is "trick") a publisher into thinking that there was a bidding war over one of my nonfiction book proposals—when in fact no one else had expressed interest yet. The publisher made an offer that was, at the time, its highest-ever bid for a nonfiction book. When I was working on another book, that same agent, contacted me and said, "Good news, we've got a publisher interested and they're offering $60,000." I was ecstatic. Then she called back. "Now it's $75,000." Then a few days later: $90,000. I'm not sure what magic she was working, but she was workin' it.

Sometimes an agent will help you shop an article to a big magazine or newspaper, but this is rare, simply because there isn't much money in it for the agent to do so. Agents will also help with foreign rights: selling your book for publication and translation in other countries. Most anglophone publishers will want to acquire world rights, in which case someone at the publishing house tries to sell foreign rights to as many languages and territories as possible. But if you've got a proactive agent, the agent can do this, or they may work with a subagent who specializes in foreign rights, like Andrew Nurnberg Associates, which is the one I hear about most frequently. They'll also seek to sell other rights related to the intellectual property you produce for your book: film rights, stage adaptation rights, audiobook publication, even rights to likenesses of your characters—things that rarely come up (unless you've written the next *Harry Potter*), but your agent will help you get the best deal if the situation arises, and the agent should help the situation arise by being proactive on your behalf.

How Does an Agent Work?

Most agents employ a fairly standard modus operandi. They will usually specialize in a certain genre, particularly if they work for a large agency, where the agents divide up potential and actual clients by genre. One agent might specialize in romance novels, another in true crime, or another in art books. If you browse an agent's website, they often list the types of books they tend to like, so you needn't waste time sending a romance novel to an agent who likes nonfiction science books, for instance.

Agents consider new submissions, but in practice these usually go initially to assistants or even interns who may be found on a chair in the corner of the agency, in the shade of a ficus plant, pouring through unsolicited submissions from those hoping to be taken on by the agency, when they are not making coffee runs or doing other interny activities. So the first "line of defense" of the agent is to have someone else read through new submissions and separate them into "no" and "maybe" piles. The "no" pile will likely never be seen by the agent. A template "thanks but no thanks" letter will be generated and sent to the writer submitting, and it will probably be generic enough that the writer won't even know if anyone actually read their submission at all.

The "maybe" pile will then be bumped up the literary ladder at the agency to be read by either a higher-up assistant or an agent. Thus, in order to move forward, you need the first reader (intern or assistant) to love your submission *and* the agent to love it.

Some agents will not offer a new client a contract with the agency until they have a book deal lined up for them. Your contract will specify that you will work exclusively with this agent or agency, who will be your representative in submissions and negotiations for either (a) the single book in question, or (b) generally for this and all future books. Initially the agent will likely

The Big Surprise 11

start with the one book you submitted and then see how it goes. If they are able to generate good interest in the book, they'll remain your agent for future books. The agency contract will cover all rights related to the books they represent for you. So your agent will be involved if someone wants to make a movie out of your book, or an audiobook, or even action figures. My novel had a contract that included a clause about how profits would be shared if an amusement park created a ride based on my novel or characters.

The best agents get things done the old-fashioned way: they socialize. They'll go to a lot of working lunches, dinner parties, cocktail events, and book launches. They will be ninja schmoozers. They'll get to know acquisitions editors at publishing houses personally, learn what those editors like and dislike, and cultivate personal acquaintanceships (if not true friendships) with them. This gives their clients a huge advantage, because the editors will feel that the agent knows them and what they like and won't waste their time. So when the agent sends a submission to the editor, that submission receives the benefit of the doubt and the editor will really pay attention to it. That doesn't mean that they'll go for it, of course, but it maximizes chances.

This is why it is very difficult for a literary agent to be good and effective if they do not live in New York or London, the two hubs of the anglophone publishing world. If you're living in a log cabin in the Montana Badlands, it'll be hard to keep popping up at cocktail parties in Manhattan. You might be a licensed agent, but you'll effectively be submitting "cold," by sending email to editors who don't know you personally or know you only via past email correspondences. This is decidedly less effective.

If there's a downside to agents submitting to editors with whom they've developed a positive, personal dynamic, it's that they will be *very* cautious about what they submit. Let's say that my agent (we'll call her Sophie) has a good vibe with an editor at Random House (we'll call her Danielle). That's a valuable vibe that is likely the fruit of many years of socializing. Sophie will want to be 99 percent certain that what she submits to Danielle for consideration will be something Danielle will like. If Sophie sends Danielle submissions that Danielle doesn't like, Danielle will start to think, "Sophie doesn't really know me at all," and will no longer prioritize reading her submissions. I've had agents who were painfully slow and cautious about actually submitting proposals that we both thought were strong, for fear of not quite getting the match right and losing the positive vibe developed with an editor.

This has been the most common complaint I hear from fellow writers regarding agents. They move at a glacial pace. You think that once you get an agent, you've done the hardest part and the rest is easy. Well, you have done the hardest part (we'll get to that next). But it doesn't guarantee anything, unfortunately. I've had writer friends with agents complain of having to wait months, and of having to send numerous emails, texts, and follow-up calls, before their agent—who already had signed them, mind you—actually submitted anything to publishers. I've heard of several agents who almost "disappeared" on their clients, not returning emails or calls for months at a time. I tell you this not to scare you off but to say that forewarned is fore-armed. It's good to know that getting an agent does not guaranteed entry into the promised land.

The financial deal with agents is simple and completely universal. A literary agent receives 15 percent of any money that comes through contracts they negotiate on your behalf. In practice, the publisher pays the full amount owed to the author to the author's agent. The agent keeps their 15 percent and then wires the remaining 85 percent to the author. The agent is also the recipient of the sales statements, which are then passed on to the author. These usually come in twice a year (in April and December) and list how many copies of your book were ordered, how many were sold, and in which formats and territories. Bookstores have the right to return unsold copies to the publisher, and this is why the number of books ordered usually exceeds the actual number sold. So the agent becomes the financial middleman, gathering money and book-related information on behalf of clients.

It is a strict rule that an author never pays a literary agent out of pocket. If someone claiming to be an agent requests this, you should immediately be suspicious. It's simply not how things work. Agents only make money out of money they've made for you. This incentivizes them. And their 15 percent cut is absolutely standard. The only exception is if they work with a subagent—for instance, selling foreign rights. In that case, the author receives 80 percent of income, and the primary agent and subagent split 20 percent.

Agents can be great as buffer zones. Since they're submitting on your behalf, you don't have to receive the inevitable avalanche of "no thank yous" before you get to one yes. Keep in mind that even with an agent submitting to friendly editors, almost all submissions will fail. There are no statistics kept, but I'd guess that something like nineteen out of twenty submissions—that is, 95 percent—are rejected. That's the nature of the industry and it's why you should submit to multiple publishers at once—even though many publishers will specify that they "do not accept simultaneous submissions," you can ignore this because life is too short. I always tell my agents that I'm not interested in hearing the many noes but just want to be contacted when they have good news. Same for reviews and press around my books. I'm not interested in reading if someone didn't like my book. Instead, I ask my agent to pass on constructive criticism for future reference and to send me clippings that were positive.

The key thing you won't get without an agent is an advance, or at least a significant one. That's really what distinguishes the major professional non-fiction writers from the less established ones.

How Do Advances Work?

An advance is money that goes to an author in exchange for exclusive rights to publish their book in specific territories, languages, and formats. It is a risk that the publisher takes on, because they never really know how well a book will sell. Advances are usually calculated based on the estimated royalties for the first year of book sales. The publisher guesses how much money the book would make in its first year. Author royalties are usually between 7 percent and 15 percent per book sold (we'll return to royalties later). For a standard book that costs $20, this would mean that around $2 per book goes to the author. So if a publisher thinks it can reasonably sell two thousand copies of your book in the first year, it might offer an advance of $4,000 dollars.

Authors do not receive any more income until the publisher has recouped the advance. So in our example, if I were given a $4,000 advance, I wouldn't receive any more money until the publisher had sold two thousand copies, thereby recovering the advance. The word "advance" refers to an advance on royalties, paying those royalties long before the book is out. Once the publisher sells copy 2,001 of the book, I'd start to get royalties.

The big advances that a good agent can score for an author come only from major trade publishers. These publishers are so much bigger and stronger than all the others that they feel confident they can sell far more copies, particularly given their promotional capabilities. Publishers may bid against each other, thus increasing advances, because of the excitement that's been generated by the agent over a book project. Rights for the autobiographies of Barack and Michelle Obama, for instance, were bid on by all the big publishers and drove the advances skyward—the couple got a combined advance of $65 million (hat's off to their agent).[1] That's an outlier, of course, but the short of it is that agents simply won't be interested in putting effort into a book that they think will get a small advance—even if the book is excellent.

Recall that your agent gets a flat 15 percent of any money they make for you. If they sell your book for a $100,000 advance, they pocket $15,000 and all they did was get one or more editors excited about the book proposal or novel draft you did all the work writing. Especially in the world of nonfiction, when it can be a year or more before an author completes a book that was proposed and contracted, the agent won't make any money, aside from the advance, for a very long time. In practical terms, I've learned that agents won't want to represent a book if they don't think it will get at least a $20,000 advance. Many an author friend has bemoaned receiving a no from an agent along the lines of, "What a beautiful book, I love this, but sadly I don't think there's a big enough market for it, so I'll have to pass."

This can be infuriating and disheartening, but keep in mind that a no does not mean there is anything wrong with your book. I mean, it could be lousy,

14   *Chapter 1*

of course, but that's not what a no means. It is most often a sign that the agent or editor doesn't see enough of a market for it, even if the book is wonderful. This might be cold comfort, but you're welcome to use it, as I have, as an ego defense mechanism. A no should never prompt you to throw away your idea. A no can mean many things other than a book not being good enough.

To live and work full-time as an author of books, you likely do need an agent because you'll likely live off of the advances. Advances are meant to provide the author with money to live off of while they actually finish writing the book and wait for the book to come out. Keep in mind how very slowly the traditional publishing world moves.

Take a nonfiction book proposal. I write it, and it takes me a few weeks to get it right. My agent submits it and we get a yes! Sweet. We're offered an advance of $60,000. Sounds awesome! And it is. But there's a schedule to keep in mind.

Advances are usually paid out in three parts: One-third when you sign the contract. One-third when you submit the complete book manuscript. And one-third when the book finally comes out.

For a work of nonfiction that isn't written until after it is contracted (which has been the case for all my books since *Stealing the Mystic Lamb*), you need to take time to actually write the darn thing. So of that $60,000 advance, I get $20,000 immediately. But actually I get $17,000, because 15 percent goes to my agent. So I need to live off of that $17,000 while I write the book because I don't get more until I've submitted the complete manuscript and it's been approved by my editor at the publishing house that acquired the rights to it. Then the next third of the advance has to tide me over until the book comes out. That can take a year or more, depending on the schedule planned by the publisher. Publishers often plan one to two years in advance which contracted books come out when (books usually come out in the spring or the fall). So I might need only six months to write a book, but the book might not come out until eighteen months after I've finished it.

Still, advances are great and make for an easier life for us writers of non-fiction, because I can write a killer book proposal in a matter of weeks (or even days), and then I don't lose any more time on that project unless I get a contract and advance to actually write the book. This is the main reason why my career to date has been writing trade nonfiction rather than novels. I actually enjoy writing fiction more, but logistically the book proposal system of nonfiction is easier to live from. I write a proposal, the proposal is sent to publishers, I get a contract and advance, and only then do I write the book. I also try to have my next book proposal ready, and *sold*, before I finish whatever book I'm currently working on. By overlapping I can make a reasonable, if modest, income as a full-time writer. Were I to write fiction, I'd have to write an entire novel on spec and then hope that someone would want to publish it and pay more for it. That's a dangerous approach if you've got a family to feed and bills to pay.

So if you want to make a meal out of being a full-time writer of books, you'll need an agent. However, if you can earn your keep elsewhere and want to write for reasons beyond income alone, you certainly do not need an agent.

How Can I Get an Agent?

This is the eternal question, and the answer is that it's a pain in the butt. I wish I could tell you otherwise, but this is probably the single most difficult thing to do in the realm of writing. A dear friend of mine who is the most famous writer in his European country embarked on a project-cum-sociological investigation to get himself an anglophone literary agent. I specify anglophone because most countries in the world do not use literary agents. The United States, Canada, Australia, and the United Kingdom are the mainstay locations for agents. There are some in Germany, too, and a smattering elsewhere who help authors. But in other countries they are not the necessary middleman that they are in the anglophone world. Abroad you just send your book proposal or novel excerpt directly to acquisitions editors at publishing houses. But my European writer friend wanted to get an agent in New York or London.

He'd had one who was based in North Carolina, and that was immediately suspicious. You just can't be that effective if you're not in the heat of the social scene in New York or London, and so it was with this agent. She was well meaning but largely ineffective. Now this friend of mine had won prizes abroad for translations into English of his books. He'd also won his country's highest literary award. And yet he wound up submitting queries to over two hundred literary agents over a period of two years—without a single yes.

Why do I tell you this tale of woe? I think it's important to be aware and have measured expectations. I also think it's important to decide if you really need an agent at all. If not, then it's best not to undertake the long and winding road to (hopefully) finding one.

To get one, it's a matter of luck, attrition, and quality of your idea—probably in that order. You will certainly need a cover letter in addition to your book proposal (for nonfiction) or the first three to five chapters (approximately fifty pages) of your novel plus a synopsis of the rest of it.

I'm including here a sample cover letter to an agent. It is invented but based on real letters that I've used to success.

The main rule is do not give the agent (or intern by the ficus plant in the corner) a reason to stop reading. This is less about wowing someone than about ensuring that they don't stop reading prematurely and throws your letter in the literal or digital recycling bin, moving on to the next among the several hundred unsolicited inquiries they've received that week.

I've had agents tell me all sorts of stories of people trying to get their attention. Someone sent a lock of their hair (at least, one hopes it was theirs). Another sent a photo of himself in a Speedo bathing suit. Another sent a handwritten note. Do none of the above. Basically, don't do anything weird and potentially creepy. Keep it simple. Let a snapshot of you and your accomplishments (if applicable) and your idea for a book be the stars.

You also want to keep things short. Eyes will glaze over if an agent opens an email and sees lots of text. Do send an email (the days of snail mail queries are long gone). Do not send a query via social media (it's not considered professional, even if the social network is LinkedIn).

You'll want three paragraphs: (1) who you are and why you are writing; (2) what you write about, a shorthand of distinctive attributes that help flesh you out as a three-dimensional human being of interest, and the subject of your next book; (3) a thank-you and how to contact you. Always provide a direct salutation with the name of the person to whom you're writing (for example, "Dear Georgina," not "Dear Agent" or "Dear Sir/Madam"—you'd be surprised how often people accidentally leave that placeholder in emails they send—or "To Whom It May Concern"). Always email a specific person's address, not a generic mailbox (so email Georgina directly, don't send it to info@ her agency or submissions@, because these go into a slush pile for that intern next to the ficus). There are some tricks to figuring out specific email addresses that I'll go over in the article submissions section.

Here's my sample cover letter to an agent.

Dear X:

My name is Noah Charney and I'm an American writer, presenter, and professor of art history living in Slovenia. I'm looking for an agent to represent my books. A number of colleagues recommended you as an ideal choice for me.

I write about art history and art crime, both fiction and nonfiction. My work has appeared in the following magazines: X, Y, and Z. I have won the XX Award. I've just finished my first book, entitled XXX. It is a novel/history/biography/ etc. about A, B, and C.

Please let me know if I might send you a book proposal or part of the novel with a synopsis. I'd be pleased and honored to work with you. You're welcome to contact me.

Thanks for your time and consideration,

Noah Charney

(contact info)

Let's break this simple cover letter down a bit. In paragraph 1 you want to give a sense of who you are as a unique individual. It could be that you mention something unusual ("I'm writing to you from prison" or "I'm a retired Olympic artistic swimmer" or, in my case, "I'm an American professor of art history living in Slovenia"). Unusual means memorable, and you want the reader to remember you—but in a positive way, hence the need to refrain from sending body parts or topless photos. You are welcome to borrow my strategic phrasing "A number of colleagues recommend you." This does a few things. First, it compliments the agent, and compliments earn you points. It also indirectly compliments you, the writer, because these unnamed colleagues recommended you for this agent. But you're being nondescript enough that it is unlikely to prompt a follow-up question as to which colleagues these are. So if you write this but no one actually recommended you . . . well, you might be a writer of fiction anyway, right? You certainly must not include anything in a cover letter that is demonstrably untrue. But this sort of harmless wordsmithery is innocuous. If you do happen to know a writer who the agent will have heard of, and if they're willing to actually recommend you, then do drop their name. If they are willing to write you a recommendation letter that you could include in your submission, even better. The goal is to get the agent to take your submission seriously, not to dismiss it.

Paragraph 2 has more going on in it. I recommend including some "fun facts" about you that help flesh you out as the unique person that you are, which isn't easy to do in a few sentences. Those fun facts should ideally be relevant to what you want to write about. We mentioned how a book proposal should convince an agent or editor that not only is this book a great idea but that you are the ideal person to write it. This is where your very short bio in the form of fun facts comes in. If I mention that I'm a specialist in art history and art crime, then it stands to reason that these should be the subjects of my books. If I'm a veteran walrus trainer from an aquarium and I'm pitching an art history book, then my personal story isn't relevant (though how cool would it be to be a walrus trainer?).

You'll want to include some references. If you've already published a book, you should include the titles, publishers, and dates. If you've won any award or gotten good critical recognition in any publication of note ("*The New York Times* wrote that I was 'walrus trainer of the year'"), this is where you mention it briefly. Many aspiring writers will have had work published in magazines before they have a book, so if that is the case for you, you can list three publications here. Three is a good number—it shows breadth, but it's

18 *Chapter 1*

manageable to wrap your head around. Include hyperlinks when applicable to your articles. This will also show the agent that some editor has said yes to you in the past, reassuring the agent that you know how to write well enough. Then include the working title of your book, its genre, and one to three sentences about it. Be minimalist. You just want to whet their appetite and not scare them off, so they'll reply, "Yes, please send it over, I'll consider it."

Then you end very simply and include your contact info.

Don't be afraid to toot your own horn in the letter. If ever there were a time to toot your horn, it's now. Your cover letter is introducing you to an agent who does not know you at all. Now is the time to explain how amazing you are, but in brief, intriguing bites, not at length.

The good news is that you can write one cover letter and reuse it, updating it as needed, indefinitely. You can and should also submit to multiple agents at once. They take a long time to get back to you (if they ever do), and you'll likely have at least a 95 percent rejection rate. Life is too short to wait and submit to one agent at a time. Whoever gets back to you with a yes first wins.

I also have a rule when submitting anything, whether an article pitch or a submission to a publisher or an agent. Each time I get a no, I immediately send out several fresh queries. This takes the negative response and flips it into multiple possible yeses. The immediacy of the action—in the same sitting that I read the rejection letter I'm emailing out several new possibilities—makes it impossible for me to dwell on the rejection. Publishing is 95 percent rejection or being ignored, which is no fun and risks thoroughly bumming you out. So spin any no into hopeful new options.

Now go and draft your own cover letter. And don't forget to toot.

What Can I Do Without an Agent?

You don't need a literary agent to get published and find success with your book. There are hundreds of good publishers in the United States alone who accept what are called "unsolicited submissions," which is to say that anyone can send them a book idea. It is rare to find a publisher outside of the biggest trade presses that require submissions via an agent. You can submit directly to all university presses, academic presses, art presses, independent or literary publishers, and the list goes on. These books can and sometimes do become bestsellers or receive the highest critical praise and visibility.

You'll still want a cover letter, and the template for an agent can be slightly shifted into a cover letter for an acquisitions editor. It should have the same three-paragraph structure, but you can likely already attach your book proposal or novel excerpt to the initial email. The request should just be changed from asking an agent to consider you as client to asking an editor to consider your book proposal or novel.

The Big Surprise 19

Without an agent, you'll have to develop your proposal or novel on your own, submit to publishers solo, and then negotiate and read the contract offer. The benefit? You'll earn 15 percent more. The downside? We're usually our own worst editors, and also our own worst negotiators, and it can be demoralizing to receive the barrage of rejections that inevitably precedes any "yes, we'd like to publish you." I've included a section on how to read contracts, and there is usually little wiggle room for negotiation unless you are already an established writer with a strong track record of sales and critical acclaim, but I'll point out in that section some wiggles to attempt.

Part of what an agent does is hype up the publisher that's acquiring your book, not only regarding the advance, but also to convince them that they'll sell a lot of copies and should budget a lot for promotion. Without an agent as your lobbyist, it's left to the acquisitions editor to get excited about your book, and there's not much you can do beyond submit a killer proposal or novel excerpt. We'll later also discuss what the publishing house does and plans behind the scenes, things that authors never get to know about but that dramatically affect a book's chance of success.

In short, without an agent you can still get published and find success doing so. But it will certainly result in a smaller or nonexistent advance, in which case you only start to earn money from your book in the form of royalties once the first copy is sold. Also, the chance of a publisher deciding that your book is one that it will put "front of catalog" (more on that later) is lower.

That said, unless your goal is to earn your living from book-related income, I actually wouldn't recommend even trying to get an agent. The process is slow, tiresome, and fraught, and even if you get an agent, as so many of my writer colleagues have experienced, it is no guarantee that your frustrations will end.

PICKING A PUBLISHER (THEN HOPING THE PUBLISHER PICKS YOU)

If you have an agent, they'll choose which publishers to submit to for you. This will be guided both by knowing what kind of books different publishing houses are after and by knowing specific editors at those publishing houses who your agent thinks have the best likelihood of digging your book.

But in this section, let's assume that you're looking for a publisher without an agent. There are far too many publishers to choose from. The process can be confusing and even intimidating, but it needn't be. I'm here to help.

Let's begin by separating how books are published into the three categories you'll want to deal with. The three main options are traditional publishing, self-publishing, and hybrid publishing.

20   *Chapter 1*

Traditional Publishing

Traditional publishing is the focus of this book and the goal of most writers. You come up with an idea, you approach a publisher. If they like it, they contract you to write it, paying you and also covering all expenses. You pay nothing at all through traditional publishing, with one exception that took me by surprise but that is traditional: unless it is negotiated otherwise or it's an art publisher, the author covers the rights costs for images they'd like to include in the book. I was confused when I was asked to cover image rights for what was planned as a sixteen-page color insert in my *Stealing the Mystic Lamb*. The rights to a single image for reproduction in a book vary based on size on the page (quarter, half, or full page), color versus black-and-white, and the preferences of the creator of the image or their estate. Rights to an artwork technically need to go to two people: the creator of the image if it's an artwork, and the photographer who took the picture of the artwork. Agencies such as Art Resource will handle this for you, and many publishers subscribe to image agencies (such as Bridgeman Images or Getty Images), but in most cases the cost comes out to around $100–$200 per image. When I heard this, I thought, "Who really needs sixteen pages of images? An eight-page insert is plenty!" But other than this little wrinkle, and ordering copies of your own book to give as Christmas presents, no money should ever go from the author to a traditional publisher.

But the traditional publisher is a business, and your book becomes a coproduction once you contract with it. Traditional publishers get loads of submissions and are usually looking for a reason to say no rather than to say yes, just by virtue of the quantity of material (much of it lousy) that they receive and must sort through. As a result, they are slow to respond and don't give authors they've not heard of the benefit of the doubt. Expect at least six months to find a publisher if you go the traditional route, and it can take that long just to hear its response.

If they contract your book, then you'll be assigned to an editor who will work with you. This editor is usually someone other than the acquisitions editor, but it depends on the publishing house structure and size. The final manuscript will be written by you, but with significant input from your editor. This means that it is no longer exclusively your baby, and it doesn't work to be precious about what your book includes at the end of the day. Editors usually know best, and your editor needs to sign off on your final manuscript, so you must consider it a coproduction, even if you're doing more than 90 percent of the work. The publisher will design the cover and the interior layout, but you will rarely be able to influence this. For *The Art Thief*, I was shown the final cover and essentially told, "You like this, don't you?" which fortunately I did. My editor specifically said that he doesn't want to show options to the author because they might like a cover design that differs from what he and the promotional teams prefer. I've occasionally been asked for ideas for a cover, but this is rare and is the mark of an extra friendly editor. The publisher feels that they know best what to do to maximize your book's chances on the market, and they're not really interested in your ideas on it. It's good to bear this in mind so you won't be surprised or disappointed.

Traditional publishers also handle promotion (publicity and marketing, of which more later) and distribution. Distribution is important because without it brick-and-mortar bookstores can't carry your book, nor are libraries permitted (in most cases) to buy it. Bookstores and libraries order from publisher catalogs, and libraries are usually not allowed to purchase self-published books.

Self-Publishing

Self-publishing used to be a naughty word. A few decades ago, it was what people fell back on if they couldn't get a traditional publisher interested. No longer. For many years now, self-publishing has been an empowering option for many authors, both known and unknown. It is essentially free to do, though you will need someone to design your cover and do the interior design and typesetting unless you are skilled with software like InDesign and can do this yourself, and it's always good to hire an editor and a proofreader. In a separate section I'll walk you through the logistics of self-publishing, but it's quite straightforward.

Most of the world's books are bought online, with Amazon having the lion's share of the market, so the most common way to self-publish is directly through Amazon. They have a platform called KDP (Kindle Direct Publishing) through which you can self-publish print and ebook editions. However, your book will be for sale only on Amazon. This is usually fine, because that's where the anglophone world tends to buy books, but Amazon insists on exclusivity. IngramSpark is probably the world's biggest self-publishing platform, and it does offer distribution, which is a distinct advantage. Self-publish with it and your book will be available not only on Amazon but also at all major online bookstores. Plus it publishes a catalog, which means that brick-and-mortar bookstores and libraries *could* order your book, though that's no guarantee that they will.

I'm not including specific prices, as these can vary and should be checked online, but the rough breakdown for self-publishing looks like this: You upload the final manuscript in two files—one PDF of the whole interior and one PDF of the front and back cover, both made according to the layout specifications of your self-publishing platform (where you can choose from numerous book sizes and options). Your books are printed on demand, meaning that there's no large outlay of money required to print, say, one thousand copies, and no storage requirements. When someone orders your book, a robot somewhere prints it, binds it, packages it, posts it to the buyer, and accepts the buyer's payment. At the end of the month, the self-publishing platform sends you your cut. You don't have to think about anything, store anything, or preorder anything—it's all automated. Shipping fees are added afterward, so that doesn't cut into your profit.

The profit share goes something like this: There's a fixed wholesale price that the self-publishing platform charges based on the size of the book, format (hardcover, paperback, ebook, paper weight, etc.), and page count. For a standard book of around 250 pages with no images this might come to around $4 per book. You, the author, pick the cover price. Let's say $14, because I'm bad at math. Someone buys your book. The platform keeps the first $4—that's the wholesale cost. Of the $14 cover price, you're down to $10. Then they also take a cut of the profit, usually 40 percent. That's $4 more. You get the rest, or usually 60 percent of the profits, in this case $6 per book.

That's far better than you'd get from a traditional publisher for royalties on a book that's the same price. Royalties are usually between 7 and 15 percent of the cover price. For a $14 book, that would be between $0.98 and $2.10 per book sold. You'll earn between three and six times as much money per copy sold. You do need to factor in expenses, but for many authors self-publishing is preferable because (a) you earn so much more per book, so even if you sell fewer copies than you might with the promotional assistance of a traditional publisher, you still end up with more money, and (b) you're in complete control of all aspects of your book—how it reads, how it looks, when it comes out. Your self-published book can be released within a matter of days of your completing it, whereas a traditional publisher will plan a year or more in advance, and you may have to wait that long before receiving the book you finished a year prior.

You can also order author copies of your own book for the printing cost alone (in our example, $4 a copy), whereas authors usually get a 40 percent discount from the cover price when ordering copies of their own book. So if you want to sell your own book directly, it's preferable to pay $4 per copy and sell for $14 than pay $5.60 per copy and sell for $14 (yes, I'm using a calculator, can you tell?).

The main reasons not to self-publish are (a) it's still considered cooler to have your book come out with an established publishing house, even if self-publishing is no longer uncool, and (b) it's extremely difficult and exhausting to get attention for your book. There's a tidal wave of new books published every month, and the real trick is getting anyone to notice your book—whether it's brilliant or mediocre. Traditional publishers will at least help

The Big Surprise

with that, though the extent to which they'll put in an effort and the resulting success vary widely.

I'm leaving out "vanity presses" as they are very 1980s and not really worth considering at this point. Vanity presses are boutique publishers that for a large fee will publish your book, regardless of how good it is. You can expand that fee if you want them to have an editor work with you or for them to design the cover and the interior (the interior design and layout is called "typesetting"). Vanity presses aren't cool. And they include a chunky profit for themselves to provide services (proofreading, editing, cover design, typesetting) that you could outsource freelance for a fraction of the price. But there is a variation on a vanity press that is cool, and that offers the best of traditional publishing combined with the best of self-publishing.

Hybrid Publishing

Some established, traditional publishing houses will offer a hybrid publishing plan, which effectively lets you fast-track your book to publication and lets you control all aspects of it. It offers the benefits of traditional publishing (the prestige of having your book with an established publisher, promotional assistance, distribution) and of self-publishing (you largely decide when it comes out, you have final say on the text, and you can control the cover and interior design).

In exchange for this seemingly ideal situation, the author has to pay the publisher a certain amount that allows the publisher to start the book "in the black," essentially without taking on any financial risk. A truly traditional approach requires the publisher to invest a lot of its own money in the book production (editing, design, layout, printing) and promotion (publicity, marketing, distribution). This goes far beyond any advance an author might receive, and can run into the tens of thousands of dollars (or more—just think of that deal the Obamas got!). Publishers are highly selective because they are taking on risk for each book they opt to publish. There is also a statistic bandied about that I've heard often but I'm not sure where it comes from: that 80 percent of published books lose money for the publisher, but those 20 percent that earn money earn so much that the publishing house profits each year. A *Forbes* article suggested that 99 percent of all published books lose money.[2] If a publisher can offset the expenses related to publishing a book, then the book will earn a profit. This usually takes the form of the author agreeing to preorder a set number of copies of their own book when it comes out.

I ghostwrite one or two books a year for clients, and they far and away prefer the hybrid approach. To illustrate how this works, I'll give one real-life example. A client wanted to control all content and design of their book, working with an award-winning designer of their choice. They also wanted to specify when the book came out, in time for an event. They agreed to buy five hundred copies of their own book at full retail price, which was $35, since the book was in full color and lavishly illustrated. Upon signing the contract, they paid this $17,500 to the publisher.

The publisher then put the book production into motion as it would a traditionally published title. It just allowed the client (working with me as ghost-writer) to complete the book without its involvement, although it did have to approve the final manuscript to ensure that it would not make the publishing house look bad or be subject to being sued for libel, for instance. It also required the submission of a "lite" version of a book proposal to ensure that the book would be of sufficient quality and interest that it would represent the publishing house well. A vanity press will publish anything for a fee. A hybrid approach is more selective because the publishing house's reputation is based on its output. The client provided the correctly formatted, typeset files according to the publisher's requirements, and the book was sent to print. The initial expenses of the publisher had been covered (in whole or in part, depending on the book and the publisher's enthusiasm for its sales potential), so any sales at all would be in the profit margin.

When the book came out, the client received their five hundred copies, which they could give away or sell—selling would recoup their initial investment. If they wished to order more copies, they could get them at the standard author discount of 40 percent off the cover price.

From the public's perspective, there is no distinction between a traditionally published book and a hybrid. This means that no one will know if your book was the product of a hybrid approach or not.

Is there a downside to this? Well, you do need enough capital to buy hundreds of copies of your own book (five hundred is actually a modest number to have to buy; one thousand is more common in hybrid deals). You can opt into having the publisher assist with editing, proofing, designing, and typesetting, but if you want to handle that yourself and maintain total control, you'll need to cover those expenses too. So rather than getting an advance or at the very least not having to pay anything to get published, you have to pay quite a bit—much more than if you went with self-publishing. But if that initial expense is acceptable, this is a pretty great—and quite new—option.

To Whom Do I Submit My Book?

For self-publishing, there's no submission to speak of. You simply upload your finished manuscript to the platform of your choice. It will need to be correctly formatted according to the instructions of the platform, but anyone versed in software like InDesign will be able to do this for you.

The Big Surprise 25

For traditional publishers, it can be more complicated to figure out (a) which publishers to approach, and (b) who at the publishing house should receive your query.

Considering publishers to query is a fraught process because you're actually hoping that they'll choose you, and you should be aware that each query is a very long shot. It doesn't make sense to be too selective, since the chances of getting a yes from each publisher to which you submit is only around 5 percent or less. It's a waste of time to slowly, carefully research and consider each publishing house in search of perfect matches. Better to cast a wide net. Research options to avoid wasted submissions rather than seek an ideal. Allow yourself to be selective and thoughtful about publishing houses only once some say yes, should you be lucky enough to have more than one get excited about your book.

In our section on book proposals, we'll distinguish between academic books and trade books. If you are writing an academic book—one that would be read in a university course, one that includes new research and citations—then that will help dictate where you submit. You'll want to aim for university presses (just about every university has a "press" or publishing house attached to it) and academic presses (there are also many good ones not directly affiliated with a university). For trade books and fiction, you can find independent presses and small literary presses. Some university presses have trade divisions featuring books they hope will sell well to general audiences, as opposed to academic books for students and libraries but with limited interest for the general reader. There are also art presses that specialize in books that are image heavy.

It's good to check the catalogs of presses at least briefly to be sure that they publish in your field but more specifically to be sure that they do not currently have in print a book that overlaps too closely with the one you plan to write. If a publisher already has a book on art forgery, it doesn't make sense to submit a proposal for a book on art forgery unless your book is demonstrably, substantially different.

A good thing about books is that competition doesn't really exist. If someone is interested in art forgery, or the Civil War, or bicycle repair, then they'll buy multiple books on that subject if they're all supposed to be good. A book isn't like a vacuum cleaner, for which you'll read loads of reviews and only ever buy one. But publishers don't like to duplicate in-print books within their own catalog.

Once you've identified a promising publisher, figure out to whom you want to send your submission. Small publishers may just have one or a few editors. Large publishers may have dozens. The more editors there are, the more specific their fields will be. So be sure to pick someone to write to who is likely to be interested in the subject of your book. Try to write to someone who can make a decision independently. This means you probably don't want to submit to any "junior assistants," because even if they like what you send, they'll need someone else to read it and like it in order for it to move ahead in the publication process. Likewise, don't write to the president or publisher, because reading book proposals is likely below their pay grade. Some websites make it obvious who to submit what to, while others obfuscate and require you to problem-solve a bit.

Finding an editor to whom you can submit your work isn't always straightforward. Some publishers want to funnel unsolicited submissions into a single catchall email address (usually submissions@ . . .), but you don't want your proposal to get stuck there. You want to go directly to an editor who you think has a chance of liking it based on their interests, which are usually listed on the publishing house website. If the website is straightforward and lists the email addresses of editors, then there's no riddle to solve. But a large percentage of publishers don't offer up everyone's email. Yet there's a way to figure it out.

Most websites have a consistent formula for email addresses. All publishers want to make it easy for bookstores to order their books. So even if the emails of editors may be hidden away on some remote subpage, or not listed at all, you can always find the email of someone in the sales department. Take Harvard University Press, for example. As of this writing, its website lists key members of staff but does not include their email addresses. There's just a generic contact@ and info@ pair of addresses. You want to avoid these. But you can find the names of editors (just not their email addresses), and you can easily find the names of people in the sales department, along with their email addresses. So we can see the formula for the Harvard University Press email addresses: first initial last name @harvardup.co.uk (for the UK office) and first name underscore last name @harvard.edu in the United States. Almost all websites have a consistent formula for their email addresses: some combination of first name or initial, followed by a dot or an underscore or nothing, followed by the last name. From seeing the formula in the sales department listings and knowing the name of an acquisition editor, you can conclude what the editor's email address must be. If you get it wrong, it'll just bounce back. If you get it right, you have the benefit of being one of the few people who took the time to figure out the elusive email address, so it's more likely that you'll grab the editor's attention. I've used this trick frequently and always to success. That is to say, I've never had an editor reply, "How did you find my email? You're creeping me out, Charney." I suppose there's always time for that.

The Big Surprise

Now that we've gone over how to prepare your cover letter and to whom you should submit your work, let's look at how to write the book proposals themselves for nonfiction books. I've divided this next part into sections, so you can skip to the one relevant to what you're writing (trade nonfiction, academic, translations, edited collections, or image-heavy books) or you can read through it all to get the most complete eye view.

Chapter 2

Book Proposals

Book proposals can take a variety of forms, but the most straightforward is the academic book proposal, so this is the best place to begin. Different publishers will have their own variations, and many have either questions online or a template, or they will send you one upon request. But all have the same basic questions that the acquisitions editor will want answered. It is perhaps less intimidating to think of this as a Q&A sheet you fill out about your book idea, and that's really what it is. The trade nonfiction proposals can be far more creative and free-form, and can get very long—a friend's agent encouraged him to prepare a twenty-thousand-word proposal plus a sample, which meant that by the time his book was contracted, he'd already written a third of it!

In order to best understand how to make a proposal, we'll first present a "lite" version that is actually the template provided by Rowman & Littlefield—and the one I filled out to propose the book you are now reading (thanks for giving it the thumbs-up, Charles!). First, we'll lay out the questions, with some notes on what to include. Then I'll include the actual proposal that got the book you're reading green-lit.

Note: Anyone who buys *The 12-Hour Author* can get a circa one-hundred-page bonus pack PDF of full, successful book proposals of various types (academic, for a book in translation, for an art book that is full of images, and for trade nonfiction).

LITE BOOK PROPOSAL

-Book Title and Subtitle
-Author Name

30   *Chapter 2*

*-Why is the book needed? Who will want to buy it and why? How is it differ-
ent from other books on the same topic (what's <u>unique</u> about your idea)?*
*-Imagine that your book is in our next catalog. Begin with a <u>title</u> that captures
the tone and spirit of your book. What would the ideal catalog copy be?
Emphasize special features or sections using bullets where appropriate.*
*-Identify titles on the same topic published in the last 5–7 years. These will
be your book's competition. Can you give us a sentence or two that would
make us want to publish your book even though those are out there?*
*-May we have a 1–3 paragraph biographical statement about you written in
the third person? Emphasize your education and experience that's relevant
to this book topic. Please include other articles or books you've published
related to this topic. The point here is to position you as an expert in this
area.*
*-Please let us have a tentative table of contents. Include page number esti-
mates for each chapter. Please also include an estimated number of photographs, figures, tables, or other graphic elements you think you would
want to include in each chapter.*
-What is your target date for completing the manuscript?

This short-form proposal is a good place to begin when you are developing an
idea for your book. The questions will help you hone your concept. Frankly,
this is a good idea even for fiction. As mentioned, you don't need a book
proposal for a work of fiction. An editor or agent will want the first three
chapters (or roughly fifty pages) plus a summary of the rest. But filling out a
lite questionnaire like this can help sharpen the focus of fiction too.

The questions are detailed enough as to be self-explanatory. The gist
of what the editor needs from you is: Who is your book for? What's new
about it? How does it differ from other books either on the same topic
or with a similar audience? How would you pitch the book to a reader?
What other books might have a comparable audience? Who are you (and
why are you suited to write this book)? Does the book need images (and
if so, color or black-and-white, and how many)? How long will the book
be and when do you expect to finish it? And what will the book consist
of?

This last question requires the most time, research, and thought. The others you might be able to fire off in one sitting, but creating a tentative table
of contents with summaries of each chapter means thinking deeply about the
project. This question is there in part to give the editor a strong understanding
of what they'd be commissioning, but also in part to ensure that any proposal
they receive is deeply considered, not fired off in one sitting. I will use this
short-form proposal as a sandbox to develop book ideas, and five of the six

questions I can usually answer straightaway. But then I'll need to develop the chapter-by-chapter outline.

To see what a proposal like this can be in practice, here is the actual proposal for *The 12-Hour Author*. As you'll see, the final book doesn't need to precisely match the proposal. That is for you and your editor to decide as you go. So you shouldn't feel pressure to be "locked into" the proposal. It really is just a tool for you to convey your ideas to the editor, and then for the editor to take the idea and, if they like it, pitch it to their colleagues and hopefully get you a contract offer.

BOOK PROPOSAL FOR ROWMAN & LITTLEFIELD

The 12-Hour Author:
Everything You Need to Know to Get Published and Become a Successful Writer

By Noah Charney

For many years I've taught a masterclass on writing for publication, in which I teach all the nuts and bolts about getting published and earning money as a writer that usually aren't taught in creative writing courses. I'd like to put this course into book form, and I think it would fit nicely in our *12-Hour* series (having already published *The 12-Hour Art Expert* with Rowman and with *The 12-Hour Film Expert* under contract and to be completed in June). This requires no images at all and will be quick for me to write, as I've been teaching the material for so long, including as part of the Guardian Masterclass series (run through the *Guardian* newspaper), and at the University of Ljubljana.

1. *Why is the book needed? Who will want to buy it and why? How is it different from other books on the same topic (what's <u>unique</u> about your idea)?*

There are countless books and courses on how to write well. They are valuable. But almost none go into any detail about how to be a professional writer. The writing itself aside, there are all manner of tricks of the trade that I had to learn as I went, and wish I'd had knowledge of ahead of time. It seems to be something of an industry secret, for instance, how to write a winning book proposal, how to pitch to newspaper editors, how to read a book contract, and other nuts and bolts of getting published and becoming a successful, paid writer.

This book will fill this void. It will appeal to any aspiring writers, from high school age on up—anyone who would like to get published and earn

32 *Chapter 2*

money as a writer, but who has either not started, or has just started and isn't sure what to do next.

They should still take creative writing courses and can buy the "how to write well" books—this book will include some elements of these topics, so that it can be truly marketed as an "everything you need." But its strength and distinction is in my lifting the veil and telling all that I wish I'd been told ahead of time about how to achieve success as a writer in addition to the actual writing itself.

2. *Imagine that your book is in our next catalog. Begin with a title that captures the tone and spirit of your book. What would the ideal catalog copy be? Emphasize special features or sections using bullets where appropriate.*

The 12-Hour Author:

Everything You Need to Know to Get Published and Become a Successful Writer

Are you interested in getting published and earning money as a writer? Whether your focus is books or articles, there are all manner of tricks of the trade that most writers have to learn the hard way, on their own, through trial and error—if they learn them at all. From how to write a book proposal to pitching to editors, from great openings to how to get paid and read contracts, the logistics of how to be a writer are rarely taught, even in creative writing programs and in how-to-write books. *The 12-Hour Author* lifts the veil and invites the reader in on the secrets of successful writers, both from the angle of how to write well, but also—and almost uniquely among books on the subject—the practical elements of how to work as a writer. The author is a Pulitzer nominee who has published more than twenty books, including international bestsellers, and hundreds of articles for major publications, including *The Guardian* and *The Washington Post*. The book is divided into 12 chapters, and if you're willing to commit as little as 12 hours to learning this craft, you'll have all the tools you'll need.

3. *Identify titles on the same topic published in the last 5–7 years. These will be your book's competition. Can you give us a sentence or two that would make us want to publish your book even though those are out there?*

The closest comps are two series published by small independent presses. One is called Curl Up Press, with 13 books written by Joanna Penn—this is the main sponsor on Amazon searches for "how to be a writer." Their series is called Creative Business Books for Writers and Authors and includes *How to Make a Living with Your Writing* and *Your Author Business Plan*. These seem to do quite well, judging by the number of reviews, but they come from an unknown author and are published by a small independent press. It would be good to take a note from their promotional strategy, however, as they are the first sponsored hit on Amazon.com when you type in "how to be a writer" as most aspiring authors will do.

A similar series is published by another small independent, Compendium Press, written by James Scott Bell. Like Penn's series, this is a multibook series called Bell on Writing including titles like *How to Make a Living as a Writer*. Bell is a best-selling thriller writer, so this is a closer parallel to my profile, but the series approach makes one think that you'll need by buy the whole series to learn the tricks of the trade, whereas the appeal of ours is one book with "everything you need."

Other titles that have sold well include *Write a Novel in a Year* (which focuses on walking the reader through finishing a novel) and *How to Write a Book: An 11-Step Process* (which is about encouraging new writers to build good habits and get things done). Perhaps the most famous is *Story: Substance, Structure, Style, and the Principles of Screenwriting* by Robert McKee, which is the go-to tome on writing for the screen. But that is just about writing for the screen and plot development (what has to happen in each Act of a film), without any of the logistical elements in my proposed book. The same is true with the oft-assigned book, *On Writing Well: The Classic Guide to Writing Nonfiction* by William Zinsser, which has nearly 5000 Amazon reviews and has been through multiple editions, with over one million copies sold. It is a great book, but only deals with nonfiction and writing style, none of the aspects of becoming an author. It was also published first in the 1980s and so is somewhat dated (for instance, my book will have a chapter on using AI as a research assistant that older books will lack).

All of these books seem to sell well, but none directly matches what I propose.

From a marketing perspective, getting to the top of Amazon searches for "how to be a writer" is a key step, as well as encouraging creative writing courses to assign this book. It's an ideal addition to creative writing course syllabi in that it covers those nuts and bolts that are often left out of writing courses.

4. *May we have a 1–3 paragraph biographical statement about you written in the third person? Emphasize your education and experience that's relevant to this book topic. Please include other articles or books*

34 *Chapter 2*

you've published related to this topic. The point here is to position you as an expert in this area.

Dr. Noah Charney is the internationally best-selling author of more than a dozen books, translated into fourteen languages, including *The Collector of Lives: Giorgio Vasari and the Invention of Art*, which was nominated for the 2017 Pulitzer Prize in Biography, and *Museum of Lost Art*, which was the finalist for the 2018 Digital Book World Award. He is a professor of art history specializing in art crime, and has taught for Yale University, Brown University, American University of Rome and University of Ljubljana. He is founder of ARCA, the Association for Research into Crimes against Art, a ground-breaking research group (www.artcrimeresearch.org), and teaches on their annual summerlong Postgraduate Program in Art Crime and Cultural Heritage Protection. He writes regularly for dozens of major magazines and newspapers, including *The Guardian, The Washington Post, The Observer*, and *The Art Newspaper*. His other books published by Rowman & Littlefield include *The Devil in the Gallery: How Scandal, Shock and Rivalry Shaped the Art World*; *Making It: The Artist's Survival Guide*; *The 12-Hour Art Expert: Everything You Need to Know About Art in a Dozen Masterpieces*; *The Thefts of the Mona Lisa: The Complete Story of the World's Most Famous Painting*; and *Gold Wine*. He lives in Slovenia with his wife, children and their hairless dog, Hubert van Eyck. Learn more at www.noahcharney.com.

5. *Please let us have a tentative table of contents. Please include page number estimates for each chapter. Please also include an estimated number of photographs, figures, tables, or other graphic elements you think you would want to include in each chapter.*

The book will be divided into 24 chapters, the idea being that each will take 30 minutes to read, hence the "12-hour" of the title. These chapters will also include some boxed text or guest advice from agents, editors and other writers, to bring in more voices than my own. Part One is the nearly unique content of this book, the logistics of getting published that are so rarely laid out in the open. Part Two borrows from masterclasses I've taught in helping to coach aspiring writers into how to level up their writing and also schedule a writing plan that feels achievable.

PART ONE: ON PUBLISHING

The Big Surprise: Don't Write the Book or Article—Write the Proposal
Do I Need an Agent (and How Do I Get One)?

Getting Fiction Published

Getting Nonfiction Published

Monetizing and Guerrilla Marketing: How to Get Noticed and Get Paid Postpublication

ARTICLES

What Makes for a Good Article?

How Not to Scare Them Off: Cover Letter Template for Pitching Articles and Chasing Editors

Your First Three Articles: A Shortcut

Befriending (and Not Misusing) AI Software

BOOKS

Trade Nonfiction Book Proposals

Academic Book Proposals

Variations: Translations, Picture Books, Edited Collections

From Contract to Publication: Each Step of the Process

The Fiddly Bits: Image Rights, Citations, Fair Use, Redline Edits and More

PART TWO: ON WRITING WELL

First Line, First Page, First Chapter: Great Openings and Their Importance

Plot/Story Mapping and the "Story" Structure

The Sitcom Code: What Writing for Sitcoms Teaches Us About Writing in General

Character Mapping

Tension as Your Power Tool

Style, Length, and Content

The Two-Hour Workday: Tips to Maximize Efficacy in Minimal Time

Getting Started: A 12-Day Plan

Your First Book: A 12-Week Plan

Publishing Success: A 12-Month Plan

This book is quite different from the others I've done with Rowman, in that it requires no images and no citations. One thing it does require is an appendix or sample book and article proposals. I have a 75-page course pack that I've given to students when I've taught this material in a classroom setting. This could be included within the printed book itself, or it could be made available on a website linked to the book. This is mostly a question to be determined by the publisher. The content of the book without the sample proposals is

36 *Chapter 2*

relatively compact—I'd guess 50,000 words. With the samples, it would approach 80,000 words. So the publisher can choose whether to include the appendix in the printed version or to direct readers to a website and opt for a slimmer volume. Either way I'd be producing around 80,000 words of text.

6. *What is your target date for completing the manuscript?*

I've taught this for so long that all the material is ready to commit to writing. I also have a 75-page course pack I prepared for students of my Writing for Publication classes, which includes successful book and article proposals, which act as examples and templates for the readers of the book. I would need around 4–5 months to write this book, so if we can get it contracted in May, I could file it in October or November.

You can also see that the final book you're reading doesn't precisely match up with the outline. That's fine. This is a general, gist-of-it plan, so don't feel pressured or bound by it.

My approach here is quite informal, since this is something like my eighth book with the same publisher and same lovely editor, whom I now consider a friend—hence the more conversational tone. But it's fine to consider the proposal a one-sided dialogue with an editor who doesn't know you yet. An extended elevator pitch. Were I pitching to a new publisher and new editor, I would be a bit more formal, and I would also fill out the table of contents (question 5) in more detail, with at least a few sentences on each planned chapter.

The above is a streamlined proposal, and for your first book you'll want to prepare something more detailed and longer. A good length for the proposal would be around two thousand words, plus a writing sample of ideally another circa two thousand words at least. Next we'll look at a template for an academic book proposal, one that answers similar questions but with more information. This is a template that is quite universal—I doubt that any academic or university press would ask you to redo your proposal in a different format if you follow this one, though each may have its own templates.

Remember that academic books should

-advance scholarly understanding of their subject (as opposed to just explaining the scholarly status quo to a general audience);
-be the sort of text that a student would use for research or that would be assigned in a class; and
-include citations (footnotes or endnotes) and include a thorough bibliography and index.

And from the publisher's perspective, remember that

-your proposal first has to make it past an acquisitions editor, then past his or her board (a group meeting of decision-makers at the publishing house), and then must be sent out for peer review, receiving two positive reviews in order for the publisher to offer you a contract;

-academic books are primarily marketed to libraries and to students and researchers, so selling to general readers is a bonus and one that is not a given nor a target for the marketing department (though academic publishers sometimes have a "trade division" that publishes books also aimed at general readers and marketed as such);

-expect a small advance or none at all for your academic book, as publishers assume (rightly or wrongly) that academic authors have a day job (usually as a professor) and so publish in order to fulfill tenure obligations and to advance knowledge and their status in their fields, not as an income source. You can certainly make money off your academic book, but it would be a modest amount that comes mostly through royalties, and over the course of many years.

ACADEMIC BOOK PROPOSAL TEMPLATE

The template below is based on the real template used by Bloomsbury's academic division, a publishing powerhouse (of *Harry Potter* fame) that acquired Rowman & Littlefield while I was writing this book. So as not to take up too much of this book with sample full proposals, I'm including just some basic notes. See the hundred-page bonus pack for full proposals.

Book Title and Subtitle
   Author Name
   Summary: a one-line description of the book, summing up its scope and content.

   Description: a concise description of the book (up to 250 words). This needs to be clear, informative, persuasive, and suitable for us as the book's marketing copy. It should be written so that readers with only a basic knowledge of the field can understand what the book is about.

   Key Features & Selling Points: Highlight three key benefits the book offers readers. These should be short, pithy, and cover three reasons why someone should buy this book rather than other titles about similar subject matter.

   Table of Contents: Give chapter titles and subheadings for sections of each chapter. If this is an edited volume with multiple authors, then include the author's name and affiliation along with the chapter they are writing.

   Chapter-by-Chapter Summary: Provide details on each chapter, including a summary of the content, angle, purpose, and relevance. Think of the synopsis as a whole: there should be a logical progression. To appeal to the broadest audience, include a good mix of international examples, case studies, interviews, and contributors (if relevant). The summary should be 1–2 paragraphs per chapter, like an abstract for a journal article.

Teaching Features: If this is a textbook, for classroom use, then include this section. It should list pedagogical features you plan to include and a brief explanation of what they are trying to achieve. What competitive advantages do they offer? These could be discussion questions, exercises, learning goals, glossary, case studies, further reading. . . .

Ancillary Material: What additional material, if any, is planned for the book? This could include a companion website, app, instructor's manual, student workbook. . . .

Word and Image Count: How long do you expect the book to be, within a range of 5,000 words (including notes and bibliography)? Does the book need images and, if so, could they be in black and white or do they need to be in color? How many images? And would image rights need to be purchased or do you have rights to them?

Submission Date: When do you expect to be able to deliver the complete manuscript?

Peer Review Suggestions: Some publishers will ask you to recommend some colleagues who would be good choices to review your book. They usually ask this only if they really want the book—the implication is that you'll recommend people who think well of you and are likely to recommend the book for publication. If they ask for recommendations, they'll want the names, affiliations, and email addresses of three people.

Other Relevant Publications: List 3–5 other books that would compete for a reader's attention with yours. How does yours differ? Provide the title, author, publisher, and publication date of the other books. If no book is a direct comp, explain why there is no other book that compares to the one you are proposing.

Market and Readership: What are the primary and secondary markets for your book? Which institutions would be most interested in them? Which courses might assign them? Also specify the academic level you are writing for. Include any marketing ideas or plans you have that are distinctive.

Author Bio: List your bio, up to 50 words long, in the third person.

Websites and Social Media: List your website and any social media accounts with a usable number of followers.

Sample Material: Supply a sample section. It should be at least 2,500 words long and be indicative of the writing style and content that will appear in the book.

IMAGE-HEAVY BOOK PROPOSALS

For proposals for books that require lots of images—for instance, an art history textbook or a guidebook—the format is the same, but you'll need an extended section on images. What the publisher really wants to know are answers to the following questions:

-Does this book need to be in color (which costs much more to print) or could it be in black and white?
-If it requires color images, could they be in the form of a tip-in color insert (in clusters of 4, 8, or 16 pages, printed separately on better paper, with the rest of the book black-and-white on normal paper)?
-How many images does it need versus how many would you like it to have? There's a difference. If I'm writing about *Mona Lisa* then the book really needs an image of *Mona Lisa*, but I might want to have a few dozen others if I had my druthers.
-Do you (the author) own rights to the images in question?

That last question is the most important, because image rights aren't cheap. To license an image for use in a normal book (with a maximum print run of fifty thousand copies, which is a whole lot, but that's a standard threshold in image rights contracts), it'll cost you $100–$200 in most cases. There are ways around this—for instance, some publishers subscribe to image databanks, like Getty Images or the Bridgeman Images, and can therefore get these images at no extra cost. Some images are free on Wikicommons, but you've got to double-check, because some that look free actually turn out not to be (they were uploaded by someone who is probably not the rights holder).

The main difference between art publishers (like Phaidon, Thames & Hudson, Abrams, and Rizzoli) and others is that art publishers assume that their books will be full of images and take on the responsibility of paying for image rights themselves. In exchange, however, they usually offer much lower advances. General publishers usually expect authors to cover image rights costs, while they handle all other expenses (printing, etc.).

Images aren't just pictures or artworks. They might include charts, sketches, or graphs. If you make these yourself, then they are your intellectual property and you can include them in your book for free. But you still need to tell the publisher about them, because they are images and this is important to cost estimates, especially if you want them to be printed in color.

For books with a single artist or photographer as part of the proposal, also include their name beside yours as author, and include their bio, as well as sample images (usually via a hyperlink to their website or online portfolio).

When thinking of the number of images, consider whether you'll have to provide or pay for them, and what is really needed. An image-abundant Art History 101 textbook might have 250 images, but that's the far highest end of the spectrum. My book *The Thefts of the Mona Lisa* could have really had just one image, of the painting in question, but we ended up with twenty-six images. The basic rule is that it's easier for the publisher to say yes to a book that has no images, or only black-and-white images, than to anything with color.

When it comes to book production, you'll work with someone at the publisher on image rights, captions, and more. They'll likely provide you with an arts and permissions Excel file or the equivalent. You'll need to number each image, list its file name, including a caption if you'd like one, and include the credit line (the rights owner or copyright info).

It's good to sort out images early in your writing process, since which images you can include may determine what you write about and how. The estate of Pablo Picasso, for instance, is infamous for charging far higher prices for image rights than just about any other art library or estate, so including a Picasso may be out of budget—and that's good to know before you spend a few thousand pages writing about a Picasso painting that perhaps you can't include.

EDITED COLLECTIONS

Books that you are proposing but that involve multiple authors, such as edited collections that might have a different author for each chapter, can use the same academic proposal format. The main distinction is in your chapter-by-chapter summary. In an edited collection, your chapter outline should include

-the title and subject of the chapter;
-the author of the chapter and their short bio, particularly focused on their professional affiliation (for instance, where they teach) and expertise that is relevant to the chapter's subject matter;
-a short description of what the chapter will include (the equivalent of an abstract in an academic article).

TRANSLATION BOOK PROPOSALS

Proposals for a book in translation aren't what they used to be. In the 2000s and before, publishers might have bought foreign language rights to a book (the right to publish an English translation of a Slovenian novel, for instance)

based on a translated sample section and a summary of the rest of the book, plus some context about why the book is important. These sample translations could be done on spec by a hopeful translator or, in some cases, would be sponsored by the government in order to promote its country's literature abroad.

In recent decades, however, publishers want fully translated books in most cases, as well as proposals. This is understandable from the perspective of the publisher—if they can't read the whole book, then they're sort of acquiring rights to a black box. They don't really know what they're getting. On the other hand, it's a huge amount of time and expense to translate a whole book on spec and hope a publisher goes for it.

Publishers will employ readers in common languages to read books of note and recommend which ones they should perhaps acquire translation rights to. Common languages are the most populous or ones with the richest literary tradition in anglophone translation: French, Italian, Spanish, Arabic, Russian, Chinese, German. If you're talking about literature from a more "exotic" country, like Slovenia, then a potential translator or the publisher in Slovenia that owns world rights to a book will have to propose a translation.

Translation rights are mostly sold during prearranged meetings at the annual Frankfurt Book Fair. I've been there and can assure you that authors have nothing to do there at all in terms of getting deals done. I've sometimes heard an author say, "Maybe I'll go to the Frankfurt Book Fair and shop my book around to publishers there." No, you won't. All the meetings are publisher to publisher and were reserved months before—they are usually meeting to close a deal on a book they already know they want, and the publisher's foreign language rights person will try to upsell them on a few other books from their list in the process.

But you can provide a written proposal for a book in translation, provided you know you can get (or already have) the rights to it in the target language.

This is the one exception to the rule about fiction not requiring a proposal. Novels proposed for translation should have a book proposal attached, because the anglophone publisher needs to know about the book and the author, how they succeeded in their home country, and why this book would be good to translate and publish in English.

The proposal format can mirror those above, but instead of an outline of a nonfiction book, a novel would include a chapter-by-chapter summary of the plot. There should be a bio of the author of the original text and a bio of the translator. You'll need to include a section about the importance and reception of the work in its original language and argue why it would be good to have it available in English. Then you'll need to provide a sample translation.

Proposals for books in translation are long shots unless you are working alongside the publisher that holds the rights. You'll need a publisher to be

42   *Chapter 2*

the in at the Frankfurt Book Fair, who will send the proposal to anglophone publishers six months ahead of time and hope someone is interested enough to meet and do the deal in Frankfurt.

TRADE NONFICTION PROPOSALS

Here's where it gets harder to teach and explain. Trade nonfiction proposals offer far more freeform. I've seen some weird ones, like a nonfiction, prose book of which the proposal was made in the form of a theatrical dialogue. I've seen eighty-page proposals, but I've also written a fifty-page proposal myself (which I thought was killer) and then got feedback that it was way too long and could I reduce it by three-quarters please? A longer proposal shows how much you've researched a subject and how passionate you are about it, but unless the acquisitions editor just adores the material, it's going to eat up a lot of their week just reading the proposal, and they've got forty-seven more proposals in their inbox. Editors will decide if they like a proposal within the first thousand words, for sure, perhaps even sooner. So do you really need another nineteen thousand words if they're already "in"? Some agents will say, yes, the longer the better, while others will recommend something more concise. I'm in favor of the life-is-short philosophy and would prefer to maximize efficacy with minimal word count. I'm not convinced that a longer proposal is necessarily better, and I am convinced that no editor will be on the fence and then decide, "Yeah, I'm gonna go for this," on page 32 of a proposal. If you haven't convinced them by page 2, it's not going to happen.

With that in mind, I'd point you to the variety of book proposals available in the bonus pack that all buyers of *The 12-Hour Author* can get for free by contacting me through my website, www.noahcharney.com.

For your trade nonfiction proposal, the acquisitions editor (or agent, if you're trying for one) will want to know answers to the same questions as those posed in the academic book proposal. The main difference is that the template, the Q&A format, is optional, and as long as you answer the questions they want, you can provide the responses in a more creative, less formulaic way.

Keep in mind that a trade nonfiction book should be

-targeted at a general readership without any required a priori knowledge of the subject matter;
-written in an engaging, entertaining way first (that's paramount), with the qualities of informative and educational in second place;
-enjoyable to the reader. They are reading it by choice, out of interest, hoping it will be fun. Understand that and reward this expectation;

Book Proposals 43

-the one book on a subject that a reader might need. This means that it explains anything the reader might need to know about the world of its subject. It also means that it's not a problem if a trade nonfiction book breaks no entirely new ground. It can be a book that effectively gathers already published information and sifts it together into a single, engaging story;

-the book that you, the author proposing it, are meant to write. Your personal and professional background should indicate that this is a book that only you can write. Since I'm an art historian, it's a tough sell if I want to write a book about space exploration, for instance. So aim your author bio so that it logically leads the reader of the proposal to conclude, "Yes, this is the right author for this project." And when choosing a topic, you'll make the strongest case if it's something that your experience and expertise qualify you for.

In terms of format, I think it's wisest to kick off a trade nonfiction proposal with a writing sample, a narrative that ideally begins in medias res—in the middle of the action—and then stops just before that action is resolved. This could provide enough text to be your writing sample, or it could be something shorter. But it should function as a narrative hook, like the opening riff of a song that forces you to stop switching the radio stations and give it a listen.

By way of example, I'll include a few opening paragraphs from my own book proposals. The test is to ask yourself if, upon reading these opening lines, do you (a) think well of the author and the project already, and (b) want to eagerly read on? If the answer to these questions is yes, then it's a good opening.

From my book proposal for *Stealing the Mystic Lamb* (2010):

Captain Posey and Private Kirstein stood inside a cottage nestled in the dark German forest—the hiding place of an SS officer and art expert who had deserted the Nazi army. Though the front line raged mere kilometers away, the cottage was a tranquil contrast to the chaotic final months of the Second World War. The home in the forest was full of flowers, books, and photographs pinned to the walls—black-and-white prints of French Gothic art and architecture: of Notre Dame de Paris, Cluny, Sainte-Chapelle, Chartres.

Posey and Kirstein were American officers of the Monuments and Fine Arts Division, a group of art historians, architects, and archaeologists assigned to the various Allied armies, charged with protecting art and monuments in conflict zones. They were war-zone art detectives assigned to General George Patton's Allied Third Army, gathering clues as to the whereabouts of the stolen art.

Since the start of the war, Posey and Kirstein had heard rumors of the wholesale looting of artwork from Nazi-occupied territories. It was clear that thousands of works of art had been seized by Nazi troops, but they did not know whether there was an overall plan or destination for the loot, nor had they

44   *Chapter 2*

recovered any of the major stolen treasures: works by the likes of Titian, Rembrandt, Leonardo, Michelangelo, and Jan van Eyck.

For all its financial and cultural ramifications, the theft and rescue of artistic treasures has a far greater symbolic value to the countries and individuals involved. Since ancient Rome was looted, first by the Goths and then by the Vandals in the fifth century, the ability to defend art has been seen as an indication of one's strength or failure as a person or nation. When King Genseric and his Vandals approached the city gates in AD 455, Pope Leo I negotiated the surrender of Rome's treasures with the promise that the city would not be razed. Possessing the artistic treasures that had made Rome the wealthiest city in Europe was sufficient for the Vandals to demonstrate their superiority and conquest. Occupying the city, or knocking it to the ground, was unnecessary, provided they stripped Rome of its art and gold. Art and monuments carry a symbolic weight for their owners: the destruction of Westminster Abbey by an enemy would strike more psychological damage to the British than the cost of its stone and glass. The loss of art shatters morale: its theft is like the kidnap of a princess. The story of the theft and recovery of art is a history of the attempt to retain or steal the object that humans value most, both monetarily and symbolically. Since the looting of Rome, great artworks have been the battle flags of warring factions, captured and recaptured by individuals and armies. And during the Second World War, an unprecedented number of battle flags simply disappeared from the homes, castles, churches, and museums of Europe. It was the job of the Monuments Men to find them.

From *Collector of Lives: Giorgio Vasari and the Invention of Art* (2017, written with Ingrid Rowland):

> As you step out of the blinding Florentine sunlight and into the terracotta-scented Palazzo Vecchio, it will take a moment for your eyes to adjust. But when they do, and the Sala dei Cinquecento leaps into clarity, you may be surprised to find yourself surrounded by giants. The soaring walls of this vast meeting hall (12,750 square feet) are painted with larger-than-life-size frescoes of riding and ranting warriors. Four enormous battle scenes show the military triumphs of the Medici family, painted in 1563 by Giorgio Vasari. His soldiers bulge out of skintight armor as they assault a fortified city by lamplight.
>
> The Mannerist style of painting, with its steroid-popping musculature and neon armor-clad warriors, is not everyone's cup of tea. Even fellow Mannerists mocked each other: the great sculptor Benvenuto Cellini got it just about right when he said that Baccio Bandinelli's *Hercules* looked "like a sack full of melons." Developed by the followers of Michelangelo in sixteenth-century Florence, with its intentional contortions and refusal to adhere to the laws of physics and anatomy, Mannerist paintings look to many like piles of bodybuilders in Day-Glo spandex while engaged in an overzealous round of Twister. Yet the colossal frescoes that cover the walls of the Sala dei Cinquecento in

Florence's Palazzo Vecchio are undoubtedly awe inspiring, and are considered masterworks of sixteenth-century painting.

They are also intriguing for another reason. Buried beneath one of the four frescoed walls there may lie a treasure of far greater importance—one that, should it still exist, has not been seen for five centuries. Beneath Vasari's fresco could be a lost painting by Leonardo da Vinci, one that tells the tale of a battle between the two greatest painters of Renaissance Italy.

The known facts are these: In the fourteenth century, the Sala dei Cinquecento, with its theatrically tall ceilings, functioned as the reception room used by the Medicis when hosting visiting dignitaries whom they wished to awe. In 1505, during a brief period when the Medici family was expelled from Florence, Leonardo began the monumental wall painting (54 x 21 feet in size) in the sala called the *Battle of Anghiari*: a torqued battle scene of riders and swordsmen, larger than life-size. The Medicis also commissioned Michelangelo to paint a second battle scene on the opposite wall of the sala, called *Battle of Cascina*. Michelangelo made a preparatory sketch but never executed the fresco, as he felt that Leonardo's side of the room had better light, and that he would be at a disadvantage in this intentional duel between the two greatest living artists. While Michelangelo never began his side, Leonardo began but did not finish his. Leonardo's partial *Battle of Anghiari* is known only by a number of copies, the most famous of which is by Rubens, which was painted around 1604, and which itself must have been made based on a drawing, since the original had been covered over four decades prior by Vasari. Based on the Rubens copy, it seems that Leonardo painted only a small portion of one wall, but the beauty and dynamism of his embattled warriors made the unfinished work a point of pilgrimage for artists who traveled to Florence.

While Michelangelo felt that he was put at a disadvantage, and therefore withdrew from the commission, the question that remains is this: Why did Leonardo give up on what seemed like a promising project? Possibly the abandoned painting was the victim of his genius. The notoriously impatient Leonardo rarely completed anything—he wrote that one of his greatest regrets was that he never once finished a single painting. He was exaggerating, but not by much.

But there's another plausible reason that the project was abandoned, beyond Leonardo's high-level attention deficit disorder. According to Leonardo's own notes, a portentous disaster struck when he was just at the start of painting his battle scene. His diary, dated June 6, 1505, reads, "Just as I lowered the brush, the weather changed for the worse and the bell started to toll . . . the cartoon was torn, water poured down and . . . it rained very heavily until nightfall and the day was as night." Melodramatic weather, as well as Leonardo's habit of rarely finishing anything he began, both led to his deserting the commission.

There are only twenty-two extant paintings by Leonardo, and eight more that are mentioned in archival documents but have never been found. Should this unfinished battle scene resurface, it would become the twenty-third.

From an as yet unpublished book of mine:

46   *Chapter 2*

The sky turned iron as we pulled up to the gates of the Pratolino. Rain was due, but perhaps we still had time? Somehow I'd never gotten here before. It's only fifteen minutes north of Florence, and I'd lived in Florence and taught art history there. This was finally my chance. My wife and daughters, nine and eleven, were with me as we passed the gate and walked the path. We'd been driving for hours from our holiday house in Umbria back home to the Slovenian Alps, so we skipped to stretch our legs. I was skipping for joy, the anticipation of seeing a much-studied masterpiece in situ for the first time propelling me forward. I couldn't wait. That childlike, Christmas morning rush was upon me.

We wound along the path through Pratolino, now called Villa Demidoff. It was once the summer getaway for the Medici family, during those long, hot months when the center of Florence is weighty with heat and ladles of sunlight. The forested garden estate would have been refreshing, airy, green while Florence is all tans and yellows. But today, we were bundled up and also realized we'd left our umbrellas back in the car.

A sign indicated that it was just ahead, around the bend. The *Apennine Colossus* by Giambologna. It's a work I'd seen in books, but somehow never had registered its size. I'd thought it was man-size, perhaps two meters tall. It's a sculpture of a personification of the Apennine mountain range, imagined as an old man three-quarters carved out of a huge boulder, with one-quarter of the original stone remaining, cragged and organic. But on our way here, I checked the details and realized that *L'Apennino*, as it's called in Italian, is eleven meters (thirty-six feet) tall! It's the size of a two-story house.

And then I saw it.

From another unpublished book of mine:

The success that would make Allan Pinkerton's career came when, in Baltimore in February 1861, his agents saved the newly elected president, Abraham Lincoln, from an assassination attempt. Pinkerton's agency was hired by the rail company to investigate suspicions of a threat to the president during his planned route by train from Illinois, via seventy towns and cities, to Washington, DC. The main concern was Baltimore, Maryland (a proslavery state at the cusp of the Civil War), one train stop before Washington. Pinkerton had learned from one of his agents, Kate Warne, who was working under deep cover, posing as a wealthy Southern socialite, that a plot was afoot to attack Lincoln in his railroad carriage between the two stations in Baltimore, on February 23. Pinkerton was extremely cautious—it would be a regular criticism of him, but then again, if you want someone to care for your security, presumably caution is a plus—and he tried to get Lincoln to alter his program, but to no avail. Lincoln's friend, Ward Hill Lamon, wanted Lincoln to ride armed with a revolver and a bowie knife, but Pinkerton famously stated that he "would not for the world have it said that Mr. Lincoln had to enter the National Capitol armed." On February 22, Pinkerton had telegraph lines cut to keep conspirators from communicating. Lincoln, disguised, boarded a special compartment on a normally scheduled train at Harrisburg, Pennsylvania, to Baltimore. In order to avoid being noticed, Lincoln did not ride with a formal bodyguard, but instead had his "sister" with him—Kate Warne, who sat beside him, pretending to be his sister, but was secretly well armed. The other passengers never knew that Lincoln was riding with them, and while he slept through the night, a Pinkerton detective, the world's first female detective, kept watch. Meanwhile, the train the president was meant to arrive on, the one that Pinkerton had learned from Warne would be swarmed en route by knife-wielding assassins, was a decoy. The crowds waiting to greet Lincoln when that train pulled in went away confused, but Pinkerton and his employers, the railroad company, considered it a job well done. He telegraphed them from Washington with the coded phrase "Plums delivered nuts safely." The Pinkerton Agency used new techniques that they developed and codified—female agents, deep cover intelligence gathering, plainclothes detectives, disguise, and decoy—to protect the president's life. It was the start of a system that would eventually lead to the organization of the Secret Service, the FBI, and the CIA, and would help develop the field of criminology, changing forever the way crime was investigated and thwarted, how presidents would be protected, and how intelligence agencies and police departments would function the world over.

And one more:

August 6, 2010. Stockholm, Sweden. The fog-draped evening quiet is suddenly ripped apart by a series of car bombs set off at various points around the city. The burning cars perfume the still air with the scent of scorched petrol. Sirens scream and spin. A phalanx of police cars wheels through the city, converging on the bomb sites—surely this is a terrorist attack.

The police, patrols diverted to the bombings, arrive and survey the charred carcasses of the cars. They cordon off the city streets a safe distance from the smoldering black bent metal, all that remains, if you can spot it through the gray smoke.

By the time they realize this was all just a diversion, it's too late.

On the other side of the city, a team of balaclava-clad thieves smashes through a set of double doors at the Chinese Pavilion, part of the Swedish royal residence, Drottningholm Palace. Sure, the alarms go off, but with the police still dealing with a presumed terrorist attack, who is going to respond in time?

Inside the museum, flashlights zag about the walls as the thieves move with purpose toward preselected antiquities. They break open three showcases and grab a red lacquered chalice with a lid, a wine goblet carved from rhinoceros horn, a bronze teapot, a green soapstone sculpture, a clay figurine of a woman lying on a divan, a lacquer box for holding cakes of ink, and a plate made of muskwood, all part of the Swedish state's permanent collection.

They're inside the building for just six minutes before they make their escape. They hop onto mopeds and shoot across the palace grounds toward Lake Malaren, one of the largest lakes in Sweden.

48   *Chapter 2*

There are no sirens approaching. The diversion worked. In the best-case scenario, police response time to an alarm in a city is two to three minutes. A heist from within palace grounds would take longer, even without the tactic of having set off the car bombs to focus police priorities elsewhere.

Off they go, the thieves leaving the mopeds to climb aboard a motorboat that is idling by the shore. The boat pulls off onto the lake, able to go traceless in any direction since the lake spans more than a thousand square kilometers.

So the thieves disappeared into the mist-bound night.

All the treasures are still missing.

The heist in Stockholm was carried out by a professional crew who left no trace and apparently knew what they wanted: Chinese imperial treasures.

The goal is just to get the agent or editor to want to read more. It's also showing off your ability to manipulate the reader in a pleasant way. I think it's good to "cut away" from the opening narrative hook when a question has been planted in the reader's mind but the answer to it has not yet been conveyed. For example, with the first, from *Stealing the Mystic Lamb*, I go on to describe how a commando team of Austrian double agents, led by Albrecht Gaiswinkler, defended the Altaussee salt mine stolen art warehouse against the local SS soldiers. But their leader, August Eigruber, was determined to destroy all the art in the mine if he could not keep it out of Allied hands, so he sent a flamethrower division to break through the line of the double agents and members of the Resistance and incinerate the thousands of masterpieces within. I end the opening narrative of the book proposal, which is seven pages long (I reproduced just the first page above), like this:

Meanwhile, the Allied Third Army was past Salzburg, closing in fast on Altaussee, but still perhaps a day away. Gaiswinkler and his Resistance fighters stalked through the dense forest to the mine's entrance, ready to attack the SS guards posted there. But they found no one at the mine. Rumor of the arrival of the Third Army had frightened the guards, who had fled in anticipation. But Eigruber's soldiers were on their way. The Resistance fighters set up a defensive perimeter around the mine's entrance, in anticipation of the arrival of Eigruber's flamethrower detachment.

By nightfall, Eigruber's men still had not arrived. Had they been recalled? Gaiswinkler knew that he would be hopelessly outnumbered. Only a thin line of brave Resistance fighters stood between the flames of the SS, bent on destruction, and the world's greatest art treasures, helpless like lambs in a field of wolves. Gaiswinkler and his men waited, rifles at the ready, for some sound beyond the wind in the trees.

That's it. Nothing more. I then "cut away" and introduce a section of the proposal called "The Book Proposal and My Path to It," describing who I am and my first encounter with the *Ghent Altarpiece*. I'm toying with the reader, implying, "Pretty good, right? You wanna know what happened next? I'll tell you . . . if you commission my book!" It's a cheeky move but it worked well. The reader should be slightly frustrated not knowing what happened with the flamethrowers and the Resistance fighters. Instead, I give them this:

> As the oak door to the chapel swung open, I was first struck by the scents. The cool, ancient stone of the walls of Saint Bavon Cathedral, the smell of frankincense, and then the surprising notes of old wood, linseed oil, and varnish. I'd waited years to view the painting inside.
>
> I had traveled to Ghent, Belgium, with one purpose: to see Jan van Eyck's masterpiece, the *Ghent Altarpiece*. I first studied this painting in my undergraduate art history courses. It was certainly on any art historian's list of the ten most important paintings ever made. But two comments made by an old art history professor of mine had particularly sparked my interest.
>
> He said that Jan van Eyck's masterpiece was the most frequently stolen artwork of all time. It had been involved in thirteen different crimes since its completion in 1432, including seven separate thefts. This dwarfed the next runner-up, a Rembrandt portrait, stolen from London's Dulwich Picture Gallery on a mere four occasions.
>
> I found this comment intriguing at the time. But in recent years, this observation about the altarpiece gained significantly in meaning for me. For since then, I've become an authority on the history of art crime—a field I fell into quite accidentally.

With a long enough opening narrative hook, you might not need a sample chapter. If your book idea began with a magazine article, as many do, then the article itself could serve as your opening hook.

You'll then go on to include all the material you would in an academic proposal: marketing and promotional ideas, other relevant publications, about the author, estimated word count, number of images, when you can finish it, and the chapter-by-chapter outline. But how you do this, to what length, and with what style is up to you.

You don't need to show off any particular writing chops to make a successful academic book proposal. The goal is to show you can convey material that you thoroughly understand in a clear manner. That's all. That's also OK for trade nonfiction: better to use clear, simple writing than try too hard and overwrite (something I've been guilty of in the past, particularly in my first book, *The Art Thief*). So always opt for clean over stylish in all writing aside from poetry and literary fiction. But the best trade nonfiction proposals will do it all.

Chapter 3

Behind the Scenes at the Publishing House

Looking ahead to when you get your yes, what actually happened behind the scenes that led to that joyous occasion?

The acquisitions editor actually read your email! And liked your proposal or novel excerpt! If they loved the novel excerpt, they will have replied with enthusiasm stating that they'd like to read the rest of it. You did finish writing it, right?

A friend from my days at the University of Cambridge got such a letter for her first novel, when she was still a teenager and had sent it to only one agent. That *never* happens, which is why it made headlines when it did. But the problem was that she'd said in her cover letter that it was an excerpt from a finished novel, figuring that surely she'd have to go through many months of waiting and many submissions to agents before anyone even replied, much less said yes. So she hadn't actually written any more of the novel! When she got the positive email, she panicked. The agent had written that not only did he want to see the whole novel immediately, but it was one of the best things he'd ever read.[1]

To buy time, she fibbed a bit and said that she'd lost the rest of it in a hard drive incident but would rewrite it and get it to him ASAP. Amazingly, she wrote the rest of the novel in a matter of weeks, while studying for her high school final exams. The agent adored it and wound up getting her a UK-record advance for a first novel.

I mention the story not to give anyone false hope but to illustrate how agents and editors expect you to have written a full novel when you submit the first section to them, and if they quickly reply with enthusiasm, it's poor etiquette not to have the rest to give them. However, this note should be balanced with the reality that in almost all cases their reply, if it comes at all, will take many weeks or sometimes months, giving you a cushion of time to

52   *Chapter 3*

do more writing. I wouldn't recommend waiting to have the novel finished before you submit the first section—life is too short. But make sure that opening section is as strong as you think it can be before you submit it anywhere, because you'll get one shot at grabbing the reader's attention.

Agents and editors no longer contract writers on potential alone. They want something that is one draft away from being ready to publish; otherwise they're not interested. Back in the 1970s, a writer with one really good short story (preferably published in *The New Yorker*) could get a novel contract on spec, but those days are long gone. In the one case out of a thousand that receives a swift, super enthusiastic reply, you'll figure out what to do with the good "problem" of having a yes without a finished novel. For the other 999 instances, it's fine to send out a novel partially written if the part you submit really sings, and then while waiting for replies, you can work on finishing the rest of it.

For nonfiction, you just need the book proposal and chapter sample. No one expects you to have written anything more.

So what happens when an editor likes what you submitted, but before the contract is signed?

Swift replies to your submissions are almost always negative. The exception I mentioned above aside, to say "no thank you," often in so generic an email that you're not quite sure if they actually read your submission or not, can come quickly. But to get a yes, the acquisitions editor needs to discuss the project with their team, and that takes time.

The process can be sped up if you are already a known commodity—for example, an experienced author with a good sales record who is submitting a new book project. That will likely be read sooner than a submission from someone a publisher hasn't heard of. If they haven't heard of you, but you have a friend who is a known commodity who would be willing to recommend you, either with a formal letter of recommendation or a simple one-line blurb that you can include in your cover letter, that can also help get your submission read sooner and with more optimism.

For fiction, you'll need the cover letter, plus a circa fifty-page writing sample and a synopsis of the rest of the novel. For nonfiction, as we saw in chapter 2, you'll need a thorough book proposal with a sample section to go with your cover letter. You send it to an acquisitions editor. What then?

Editors are looking for a reason to say no. This is not out of malice, just pragmatism. They get so many submissions that they need to be selective. They're looking for projects that either (a) seem to really break ground and therefore are candidates for awards and positive press, or (b) look like they'd sell well (or even better, both). Editors also look to "fill out their lists"—which is to say, ensure that there is no duplication of a topic (which can make the books redundant) and that the lists cover a wide array of subjects within their overall subject. So if you are pitching a book to an editor who covers history for a publishing house, they won't want multiple books on the Hundred Years' War (unless they approach the theme from sufficiently different angles), but they will want books on as many historical themes as possible in terms of geographies, cultures, and eras. Larger publishers will have more editors who are more specialized. Smaller houses might have only a few editors in total, who cover more subjects. Some publishers are small enough that they focus on niches. They may list their areas of interest and also book series on certain themes. It can be a step easier to pitch your book to fit into a preexisting series than to pitch it as an independent one-off.

When the editor looks at your proposal, they are considering what promise it holds in terms of advancing knowledge, garnering positive reviews, and potential sales. They have an eye out for diversity in terms of authorial voices and backgrounds. For academic books, the key is to demonstrate that the proposed book advances scholarly knowledge and thought on its subject. This doesn't mean that something new has to have been discovered, but the content or argument must differ in some way from the already-published literature on the subject. For trade nonfiction books, the requirement to substantively advance scholarship is not obligatory—these books can tell already-known stories in a new way, or for a general audience.

The editor may reply quickly with follow-up questions to cover an aspect not answered clearly in the proposal. But otherwise, if they like the proposal, they will pass it on to other departments for consideration, and then present it at one of those team meetings with the Starbucks takeaway cups. Remember what we discussed in chapter 1: The mark of a proposal with maximum chance for success lies in its ability to help the interested acquisitions editor summarize what makes it interesting in a concise manner at that team meeting.

Here is where academic publishers differ from trade or independent publishers. Academic publishers, most of which are affiliated with a university, will want to send your proposal out to two anonymous peer reviewers before offering a publishing contract. In practice, the author's name is removed from the proposal and the editor sends the proposal to two scholars who know the subject of the book well enough to be able to evaluate whether the book proposed would substantively add to scholarship. In principle, the readers will not know who the author of the book proposal is—it could be a famous figure or it could be a grad student with no publication history, so they are meant to judge the proposal objectively on its merit alone, without the weight of expectation of knowing who the author is. But in practice, academic fields tend to be so small and niche that peer reviewers can often guess who the author is.

The problem with peer reviews is the ego of so many reviewers. Asking experts in a field to weigh in on another expert's proposal can bring out a competitive streak. Rare are the peer reviews that simply say, "Yes, this sounds great, contract it!" It's also fairly rare for a reviewer to dismiss a proposal altogether as not worth considering, because the editor will not have let a proposal get as far as peer reviewers without having a pretty good sense that it's of merit. In most cases, the reviewers will produce written response along the lines of, "If the author makes the following changes to the proposal, or their argument, then I'd recommend publishing," followed by a list of items that would make the proposal more in line with the peer reviewer's own thoughts on the subject. Honestly, peer reviews can be super annoying.

But they are necessary, as academic presses usually will not offer a contract for your book without two positive peer reviews. This takes time, because the publisher usually gives the peer reviewers at least six weeks, and sometimes as long as three months, to read your proposal and respond. If they get two negative reviews, then that's game over. It's a bummer for the editor too, because the editor wouldn't have taken your proposal to the peer review level unless they were excited about it. In that case, you'll get a glum email from the editor saying, "Alas, we got two negative peer reviews so we'll have to pass on this." You can try with another academic press, of course, but they'll also need two positive peer reviews to offer you a contract, and so the process may repeat. If the editor receives two positive reviews, then you're good to go and the process moves forward. If you get one positive and one negative, the editor may look for a third peer reviewer to act as a tiebreaker. What happens most often is that you'll get reviews that are "yes, but . . ." The reviewers will list what they think the author should consider (or reconsider) for the book itself. The editor may then ask you to rework your book proposal with this in mind, or craft a short response letter addressing the reviewer's input (which the editor can share with the publishing team to show that you're taking the input seriously), or simply ask you to keep these notes in mind when you write the book.

Editors normally have to research and reach out to potential peer reviewers themselves. But if an editor *really* wants to acquire your book, they may do you a subtle favor and ask you to suggest some peer reviewers. In this case, they aren't really going to be anonymous. The editor is effectively saying, "Want to tell me who is sympathetic to you and your theories, who will likely give the proposal the thumbs-up?" Other presses will send book proposals to librarians, rather than peer scholars, to get notes on whether the librarian would acquire the book for their library. This sending out for external opinions takes place in academic presses but rarely elsewhere.

When it comes to sales, academic books are less focused on the money the book would make for the publisher. Academic books tend to be priced high (some are over $100 each!) and are sold primarily to libraries and, hopefully, to students assigned them as course reading. General readers are welcome but are not expected and are not marketed to. The price of most academic books is beyond what general readers will want to pay, anyway. So the focus is on how the book expands knowledge of a scholarly field and how interested libraries will be in acquiring it.

If the first meeting pitch goes well, then the proposal is considered by other departments at the publishing house. When I taught a Guardian Masterclass called How to Write About Art, my coteacher was my editor at the art publisher Phaidon. She brought in a document that I had never seen but that certainly intrigued me. It was the in-house worksheet for my own book, the one authors are not allowed to see, because it includes planned investment in promotion, the cost per page of printing the book, estimated sales and profits, and so on. Authors aren't shown this because it would likely either depress or annoy them ("They're only spending that much on marketing!"), and indeed I wasn't allowed to see the numbers even then. My editor had blacked out the numbers, showing only the categories covered in the document. But all those calculations—sales, costs, profits, investment in promotion, distribution—are estimated before the book is even contracted, much less finished. The publishing team will estimate how much money they expect to make in the first year's sales total, then they calculate from that the expected royalty payment to the author, and this is usually the quick calculation for the advance offered for the book. So if the publisher thinks that it can sell $100,000 worth of the proposed book in the first year, and the author would then get 10 percent royalties, it would offer a $10,000 advance. The word "advance" is short for "advance on royalties," after all.

This is all to emphasize how the proposal is actually *more* important to the sales of your book than the finished book itself. That sounds weird, I'm sure, but to a large extent the publisher decides how well a book will sell. There are always going to be external factors that can make for surprise bestsellers, and the publisher won't know how much press it can get for a book despite its efforts. But it can funnel money into marketing (paid ads or promotions or placements in pay-to-play review websites, for example), and so can largely determine which of the books will do best. The editor can only hope that the final book will live up to the potential of the proposal, and they'll help it to do so, through their editorial coaching and assistance. But the commitment of the publisher is based on the proposal alone.

If the publishing team is all on board with the initial print run, the retail price of the book, the cost to the publisher per copy, the cost of any images or other elements calculated, the marketing budget set, the estimated total sales in year one, then you get the happy email from the editor. They'd be delighted to publish your book!

56   *Chapter 3*

CONTRACTS

That happy email will be followed by a contract, and those can be tricky to read. In my experience they are not usually written in an obscure "legalese," but they do look intimidating. If you have an agent, they'll check it over for you. You can always hire a lawyer to check it, but this is expensive and usually not necessary. There are various clauses that most publishing agreements will feature.

THE AUTHOR SHALL GRANT TO THE PUBLISHER

The lead clause is normally the one that lays out that you, the author, are giving the publisher exclusive right to "publish, sell, and distribute" your book. You can give it world rights in all languages, which is recommended unless you have an agent or your own direct connections to foreign publishers. If you give it world language rights, then a staff member at the publishing house will do their best to sell your book to foreign publishers for foreign language editions. This usually involves your book being part of a catalog prepared by the publisher that it sends directly to the relevant people at scores of publishing houses the world over, who then plan meetings at the annual Frankfurt Book Fair, where the deals are done. You will be paid for all such editions sold via the primary publisher, but the primary publisher gets a cut, so you'll earn less than you would if you could sell your book to foreign publishers directly. But if you don't already have connections to foreign publishers, then it's best to let your primary publisher handle it. It doesn't work well to cold-email foreign publishers and pitch your book.

There are other rights to consider, such as audiobook, and some books are published in English by different publishers in different territories. My novel, *The Art Thief*, was published in the United States by Atria (an imprint of Simon & Schuster), but in the UK it was published by Simon & Schuster itself (not one of its imprints). The United States and UK had entirely different covers for the same book and the rights were handled separately. The shorthand rule is to only withhold rights if you already have a contact that is likely interested in publishing. For instance, since I live in Slovenia, I withhold Slovenian language rights for my books because I can call up publishers here whom I know personally and make a deal myself, but I give other world rights to my primary publisher.

THE AUTHOR SHALL DELIVER TO THE PUBLISHER

This lays out a due date for you to email a copy of the full manuscript, including any notes (citations), bibliography, and permissions (for example, for image reproductions). But this delivery date is for the full *draft*, and it will then go through your editor, so it's a long way from being finished. You don't need to worry about the date when the publisher needs the finished manuscript ready for layout—or rather, it isn't in the contract. Your editor will be in touch with you about that after you submit the full draft.

This clause usually also lists the total word count (check carefully whether this includes or excludes notes and the bibliography). An average book length would be 60,000–80,000 words. You can never go wrong with that length. Image-heavy books can be shorter (as short as 40,000 words) and big, fat books can be longer, but publishers generally don't want a book that's longer than 120,000 words.

You need to be careful to stick to the word count. Some editors are flexible, but others will make you trim to get under the contracted count. Publishers calculate down to the estimated number of printed pages when they make budgets, and while you might not think that a few thousand words more will make a difference, your editor may think otherwise.

Do note that unless you are publishing with an art press (like the sort I often do, including Phaidon, Thames & Hudson, and Rowman & Littlefield), it is normal for the responsibility of providing images, tables, charts, and so on to fall on the author. This means that authors will have to pay for their own image reproduction rights, which can cost $100–$200 each, so do keep that in mind. This part of your publishing agreement should list the total number of "tables, art, and figures"—meaning nontextual components that will be laid out as images in the manuscript when it's typeset. For my art books, this can include, say, a maximum number of images (for example, sixty) and a maximum budget that the publisher has set aside to cover these images (say, $2,000). If the publisher is covering image rights, then you will work with someone from the publishing house and together reach out to image rights agencies or rights holders and negotiate image use and payment. The publisher will then complete the deals that you set up. If you need to cover any image costs yourself, then you'll be advised by the publisher but are otherwise on your own to sort this out.

This section of the contract will have some basic protections for the publishers baked into the language—for instance, that the author guarantees that the work "must be factually accurate and original and must acknowledge all intellectual debts," common phrasing to mean that it's up to the author to make sure they aren't plagiarizing and are properly citing sources. The publisher can also terminate the contract if the author is late (usually by more than thirty days) submitting the full draft, or if the manuscript is deemed "unacceptable." That "unacceptable" is rather nebulous—who's to evaluate it? In practice it should never come to that, because you should be submitting sections to your editor as you go so there's no big surprise at the end and you do not submit a "finished" book that is substandard. You'll also have to take care not to include anything in your book that could be libelous, as the contract will state that you'll have to cover legal fees if the publisher deems that it needs to hire a lawyer to vet the text.

THE PUBLISHER SHALL PUBLISH THE WORK

The publisher usually agrees to publish the book within eighteen months of the manuscript being accepted. If for whatever reason it takes too long, the author can request that the rights be returned and the contract voided. This clause also specifies in what formats the publisher will release the book (hardcover, trade paperback, mass market paperback, ebook). Unless this is a hybrid contract, the publisher takes on all expenses related to publishing (the only exception being image rights, as mentioned above).

There may be a clause in which the publisher and author agree to "take such steps as necessary to preserve a valid United States copyright." Sometimes the publisher does the copyright paperwork; sometimes the author is meant to. Copyright is not something to be concerned with for books because of a few facts: (a) if your book comes out in ebook format there will likely be a pirated version available online, whether or not you've filed copyright— that's the nature of the Wild West web, and (b) a book without an author to promote it isn't of much interest to most publishers (those experimenting with AI-written books aside). Publishers want the book plus the author as a package. And you and the publisher will work as a team to make sure your book's rights are upheld.

If your book is out of print for more than eighteen months, you can formally request that rights be reverted from the publisher. In that case, you as the author can republish the book elsewhere if there is interest in doing so. If your publisher releases an ebook edition, then effectively your book is forever "in print" because anyone can buy and receive an ebook version without any action on the part of the publisher.

THE AUTHOR ALSO GRANTS TO THE PUBLISHER

There may be some oddball clauses that will make you think, "Why are these in a contract at all?" My novel contract included clauses on how payments would be divided in the unlikely event of toys being produced based on my story or characters, amusement park rides, and so on. TV and film rights are sometimes separate from the book, or sometimes included with it. Same with theatrical development rights. Keep an eye out for whether these are included in a contract you are offered. They should be specifically referenced if they are included. You might also find some remnant clauses that no one bothered to remove but that are technologically extinct (like CD-ROM rights). You may spot a catchall clause like this one: "The author grants to the publisher the exclusive right to license, sell, or otherwise dispose of the following rights in the Work: publication or sale of the Work by publication of a reprint edition of the Work by another publisher in any edition or format whether print, electronic, audio or broadcast . . . electronic rights of every kind and nature, dramatic and motion picture rights and performance rights of every kind or nature, including but not limited to feature length motion picture, television, cable, and internet rights." And the clause just keeps going. This is a way of saying, "We've got the rights to everything." But keep in mind that everything in a contract is negotiable. This is a clause that my literary agent would probably attack with a virtual or literal pen, blacking out certain sections for rights we wish to retain. You have the right to request any changes to your contract. The publisher may say, "Sorry, it's either this way or not at all," and you can decide at that point. But most publishers begin with standard, boilerplate contracts that are weighted in favor of the publisher having as many rights (and therefore ways of earning) from your intellectual property as possible, and it's up to you to politely request changes to their standard.

THE PUBLISHER SHALL PAY TO THE AUTHOR

This is where the royalty payment system is outlined. The amount you receive may differ from print to ebook editions, and it often rises in brackets based on sales. For print copies, it would be normal to receive, for instance, 7 percent for 1–3,000 copies sold, 10 percent for 3,001–6,000 copies sold, and 12 percent for 6,001 or more copies sold. And for electronic editions (ebooks), 20–25 percent as a flat royalty percentage is common. There may be other clauses, such as how royalties will be paid if the publisher sells remaindered copies at a heavy discount, for instance. No royalty is paid for copies sent for free—for instance, review copies.

Within this section or elsewhere, the contract should specify when it sends sales results and remittance advice to authors. This is often twice a year (once in June and once in December). This document will list all copies ordered by bookstores in the last six months and in the lifetime of the book, all copies sold in all formats, and copies returned. This "returned" is potentially confusing, but bookstores have a good deal. They can order copies and return to the publisher whatever they don't sell. So Barnes & Noble might order 500 copies of your book, but if they only sell 411, then 89 copies will be returned to the publisher.

One thing that American contracts usually do not include are print runs (this does appear in some European contracts). So you might not know how many copies of your book are being printed in one print run. Publishers will prefer to err on the side of caution, and it's better to have to do more print runs than to have extra unsold books sitting in warehouses. But a normal print run for a trade nonfiction book that they hope to sell a lot of might be 5,000; for a more niche or academic book, 3,000; and for purely academic books,

60   *Chapter 3*

1,000 or fewer. Novels tend to sell in far greater numbers than nonfiction and so will have higher print runs.

There are a few other common clauses worth mentioning.

The author usually must approve any request or plan to publish more than 10 percent of the work. This is the maximum permitted without copyright infringement.

There may be a noncompete clause along the lines of "the author agrees not to author, co-author or serve as general editor for a full-length print book on the same subject matter or one that would directly compete with the sales of the work named herein . . . for one year after publication of the initial edition of the work."

The publisher can use the "likeness, biography, and photograph of the author in all media . . . in connection with advertising, publicizing, licensing, promoting and selling the work."

The author will be owed a set number of free copies that the publisher will provide (ten is a standard number to receive), and has a set author discount (usually 50 percent off the publisher's retail price) to buy as many extra copies as they would like.

Then the last section of contracts often switches to "legalese" and deals with nondisclosure, what happens if the author dies, and other elements that can be found in most contracts, regardless of whether they are for book publishing.

If you are offered an advance, that sometimes is placed as an addendum to the standard contract. Advances are usually paid in three slices: one-third within ninety days of signing the contract, one-third within ninety days of having filed the full manuscript, and the last third within ninety days of the publication date of the book.

If you have an agent, all payments go to them first, they retain their 15 percent, and then they send you the rest. If you do not have an agent, payment is made in full directly to you.

Contracts are signed and dated by the author and a representative of the publishing house (usually the person with the title of publisher).

WORKING WITH THE PUBLISHING HOUSE

Your contract is signed, your book is accepted, and now it's time to get to work on actually writing the thing. If it's a novel, then the assumption is that a full manuscript has already been written, and you can begin to work on it with your editor. The timeline will be tighter, as you don't need to write the whole

Behind the Scenes at the Publishing House 61

book from scratch. For nonfiction, at least nine months is usual, from contract signature to manuscript due date, and up to around two years may be fine.

Either way, you'll be assigned an editor for your book. This might be the same acquisitions editor who championed your project from the start, or it could be someone else at the publishing house. Your job is to satisfy them as to your progress, and their job is to help you make the best possible book—which for the publisher means the best possible sales. Decisions will be made that are geared toward selling the most possible copies. This should be understood as having precedence over artistry in all genres of books except poetry and literary fiction.

Your Editor

Some authors are prima donnas about their text. "It must be just so, not a word or comma but where I decide to put it." This doesn't go over well. It's important to understand that a book, unless you self-publish it or are in the pantheon of literary gods already, is a coproduction. You're the author and you get all the credit, but it's a collaboration between you and the editor to determine the final content, from the ideas and concepts conveyed within to the words themselves.

My policy is to go with whatever my editor suggests in every case I feel I can. It's very rare that I take a stand on something editorial or content related, and even rarer on style. I know that the editor is there to help me and is certainly far more experienced than I am in terms of books produced and shepherded through to market. Chances are they know what works best.

Just what they may suggest you change can vary, but it can begin with the conceptualization. When I filed my proposal with Phaidon for *The Art of Forgery*, the original idea was to have a book in two halves: the first would be a chronological history of famous forgers, and the second would be a playful how-to of forgery, with techniques and recipes that worked for past forgers. After the book was already contracted, over conversations with the acquisitions editor and the hands-on editor who worked with me (two different people), we shifted gears. The book would be structured in a totally different way, though most of the stories and research would remain. We opted for a book with a through line on "the minds, methods, and motivations" of forgers, so the psychology was what propelled the reader through the case studies. The book was the better for it.

That book also went through a process that my editor at the time joked was to make it "British critic-proof." Being an American, I have a tendency toward hyperbole and superlatives: the first, the biggest, the best. British critics and readers tend to be humbler and more subdued, and such hyperbole can rub the wrong way. This is perhaps best exemplified by a simple article change that will occur in biographies. An American biography of, say, Winston Churchill would likely be titled *Churchill: The Biography.* The British edition would be called *Churchill: A Biography.* The difference between "the" and "a" may seem subtle, but there's a world of pomp and self-confidence hidden behind it. "The" biography suggests that this is it, the only one of merit, the only one you'll ever need. "A" biography suggests that it is one of many, but we think it's rather good and we hope you like it. Phaidon, though owned by Americans, is a storied British publishing house, and the editor there understood that it is preferable to tone down the hyperbole and edit with a potentially annoyed British critic as the ideal reader in mind. If you can satisfy them, which is to say not rub them the wrong way, then it'll be good enough for anyone.

Making a book British requires being attuned not just to content but also to grammar and spelling. Most of the world learns British English as a second language, so many writers will default to UK grammar and spelling rules. The problem with this is that many Americans don't know that there is such a thing as UK grammar and spelling rules: they see a British approach (single quotation marks, commas outside of punctuation, program spelled with an extra *me* at the end, color with a *u* tucked in there) and think it's a mistake. The general rule is to write with whichever grammar in English is easiest for you. The key is to maintain the same rules within any given manuscript. It will be up to the publisher to decide which grammar it prefers (this will be made clear during an early meeting with your editor, and you may be given a house writing style sheet), but any professional publisher will have your manuscript edited and proofed as part of its process, so changing the grammar from American to British or vice versa is doable. You should just be consistent within your own writing. The fact is that it's not just from country to country, but from publisher to publisher, that the house rules can change. Don't get bogged down in your writing by worrying too much about the house style if it's not what comes naturally to you. Write however it flows best, and then fix the grammar style on a later pass through the manuscript.

Your editor may ask you to provide your preferred writing calendar, choosing how much of your book you plan to submit by which date, provided that the final draft is submitted before the date on the contract. It's usually good to plan to file a smaller section fairly quickly so that early on, and without you putting in too much work, you can be sure that you and your editor are on the same page in terms of writing. You don't want to write one hundred thousand words, send it to your editor three days before the contractual deadline, and have her say, "This ain't working." I like to file a first chapter, or up to ten thousand words, pretty quickly if I'm working with a new editor. This reassures the editor that you're on the right track and reassures you that your

Behind the Scenes at the Publishing House 63

editor thinks you're on the right track. If, by chance, you're on the wrong track, you've got loads of time to right the ship.

Your editor, at this point, may give you general notes in an email, or might give you a marked-up manuscript with comments in the margins of a Word file. It's too early for what's called a "redline draft" (of which more later). These are general notes for you to apply on your own in your next edit of this section and sometimes in future sections. The notes might be something like "tell less, show more" or "remember to cite all quotes" or "too many run-on sentences" or "think about referencing X, Y, and Z." You'll know more about your book's subject than your editor, but that's a good thing. The editor isn't there to help with your research but with how you present your ideas, arguments, or story to the reader.

The calendar you make with your editor helps the editor know when to "chase" you—if you file the sections on the dates you select for your schedule, then you won't need chasing at all. A reasonable schedule for an 80,000-word manuscript contracted January 1 and due December 31 might be 10,000 words filed by March 1, then another 30,000 by June 1, 30,000 by September 1, and the last 30,000 by November 1. That leaves two months for a final edit of the entire manuscript before you even have to give it all to your editor. You can always file earlier—no one will complain about that if it's good and you're early. And recall that the contract due date is for the full manuscript as a draft—or rather, when you feel it's done. At that point the clock begins anew as your editor reads the whole thing and the editing process begins. Ideally that will have been ongoing, with your editor reading sections as you file them, so that the manuscript can go out for a redline edit once it's all submitted.

The redline edit is hands-on, with your editor suggesting rewrites of sentences, swapping words, querying facts that sound off or aren't properly cited. Not that long ago (for my first book, the novel) it was still done with an old-school approach. I was living and teaching an art history abroad program in Florence, Italy, when the package arrived. It was the whole manuscript for *The Art Thief*, in a very fat folder, along with a green pencil. The manuscript had been marked thoroughly by my editor with a red pencil—literally a redline edit. Queries and rewrite suggestions were written in by hand. This wasn't the Mesozoic Era; this was 2005! The green pencil was enclosed for me to use in either accepting or rejecting the edits made and answering queries in the margins. I had to reply within two weeks, then mail the manuscript back from Italy to New York.

Today you'll get something like a Word file with track changes used and the document locked, so that you can reply to the changes but not undo them. You'll be asked to respond to marginal comments and accept or reject the editor's suggested, hands-on changes that have already been applied to the text.

64   *Chapter 3*

The manuscript you receive may also already be formatted in a house style, the way the production team would like it. This varies from one publisher to the next. This book manuscript included the notation each time I wanted a line to be skipped (such as between subsections) as a note to the typesetter. I've never had a publisher who wanted that, but each house will do whatever works best for it. You'll be given instructions if there are specifics like that which the editor would like you to include. There are also some "fiddly bits" that are worth mentioning here, as they should be included in your manuscript at this point—before the final edit and typesetting.

The Fiddly Bits: Image Rights, Citations, Fair Use, and More

There are parts of piecing together manuscripts that I wished I'd known more about ahead of time. This is especially the case with bits of work that are *far* harder to fix after the fact than if you keep track of them as you go. I'm looking at you, citations.

Unless you are David Foster Wallace or some other postmodernist novelist, fiction doesn't involve footnotes. But nonfiction does, even trade nonfiction books that are meant for general readers. You might think that you only need to keep track of citations for academic books, but let me tell you, your life will be much easier if you keep track of them for any work of nonfiction.

I know this from the unfortunate experience of having written a nonfiction book thinking it would be for the general public, so no citations would be needed But then the editor and I decided after it was finished, "You know what, we should really include citations." It is fairly quick and easy to keep track of sources as you go. You find a quote or a fact, type it into your manuscript, and throw in a footnote. But imagine looking back at one hundred thousand words of manuscript and having to remember where you found those quotes and facts. That's infinitely fiddlier.

There are different ways to cite. Footnotes are really just for academic books, with the assumption that no one is really reading "for fun" but to gather information, and such info hunters will want to easily see the source of a quote or fact. For most nonacademic nonfiction books, endnotes are preferred. This gathers all the citations at the back of the book, so they are accessible but don't interfere with the reading flow. You, as an author, don't need to worry about this—the publisher will decide how best to include citations. What you need to worry about is keeping track of sources as you write so you don't have to work backward after the fact. And the easiest way to do this is to keep on footnoting as you write. Don't worry about getting the citation formatting right. You just need to remember the source and page number. The publisher will have a preferred house style for citations (following the *Chicago Manual of Style*, or the Modern Language Association format, or doing its own thing), so you can sort that out later. The same goes for when to use indented block quotes. I was always taught that you use them whenever there is a quote longer than two lines, but I've heard other rules too. It's generally best to get all your ideas down on paper and record their sources however is easiest and quickest for you, then much later, near the end of the writing process, you can go back over and synthesize the formatting.

Citing can extend to fair use and bibliographies. Fair use is generally acceptable when quoting less than 10 percent of another text, and all quotes must be cited. If you want to reproduce more than 10 percent of the length of any text you did not write yourself, you'll need written permission from the author.

The bibliography should be a list of all the works you referenced during the research process. This will include everything you cited in a footnote, plus many more texts that you read (all or in part) even if you didn't directly cite them. It covers books, of course, but also articles, websites, documentary films—all media. But in practice you'll almost always include a "Selected Bibliography" rather than a complete one because of the number of pages a full one would take up. So consider the few dozen books that you found most useful in researching your own book to include in the bibliography. Stickler readers will flip to the bibliography to make sure you've referenced all the key books that come to their minds when considering your subject, so think of what to include from that perspective.

If your book will contain any images, it's good to be forewarned that unless you're publishing with an art press of the sort I write for—since my books are largely about art history and art crime—you'll have to pay for rights yourself. This came as a surprise to me when I was finishing *Stealing the Mystic Lamb*. I thought that I would want to have a lot of images, and the publisher was willing to include a sixteen-page color insert. Unless your whole book is in color, books are printed in grayscale (black and white) on cheaper paper, and inserts are used to provide some color images. These inserts are printed separately, usually on glossy, higher-quality paper that will most cleanly present the color images. The inserts come in four-, eight-, or sixteen-page clusters, which you can imagine as A4 (standard-size) pieces of paper folded. If you were to fold a piece of paper in half lengthwise, you'd be left with four surfaces on which to print. Add another folded page to this, and you'd have eight surfaces to play with. Each surface can take a full-page vertical image or two half-page horizontal images, for example. These color inserts are "tipped in," pasted, or sometimes, with fancier editions, sewn in along with all the other pages when the book is bound.

What's important for the author to know is that unless it's stated otherwise in your contract, you'll be responsible for paying for image rights. When I heard this, I quickly decided that an eight-page color insert would be just fine, thank you. Who needs sixteen pages anyway? Image rights can be acquired via companies like Art Resource, Bridgeman Images, Getty Images, and others. They can be tricky because, in principle, someone has to pay both the person who created the artwork (if it's an image of an artwork) and the photographer who took the photo you are using of the artwork. In other cases you might want to include a journalistic photo, a drawing, or a chart. Unless you made all the images yourself, you'll need to clear rights to use them in your book. These image rights companies can sort it out for you, but it's normal for an image to cost $100–$200 each for rights to print it in a book with a print run of up to fifty thousand copies (which will cover any nonfiction book aside from the very biggest bestsellers). This can add up. You might think that some images are free, such as those found in Wikicommons. But this isn't always the case—it's often unclear, as I've learned from experience—so it's safest to always clear rights so you've got a file of digital paperwork showing you've done your part.

You can sort out image rights as a final step before you finish the book, so as not to slow yourself down. But in my case, I like to be sure that I can get the images I want as I go, because if, for instance, rights to a Picasso painting are too costly, then I might not be able to include it in my book at all, so it's useful to know ahead of time if there are any images that really must be included or if you'd have to write your book in a different way.

If all your images will appear in an insert, then you will need to provide the images (usually as JPEG files of at least 300 dpi in quality) to the publisher, as well as any copyright information and a caption to accompany the image. If images should appear throughout your book, then you'll be asked to give each image a number and to put "image callouts" in your manuscript. Images of any sort are usually referred to as "figures," so you might be asked to place roughly where you'd like an image to appear the note INSERT FIG. 1 or INSERT FIG. 27. The typesetter won't always be able to put the image exactly where you want but will do their best to place it close to where your callout is in the text. This is also useful when you're writing, because you can refer to the image in question in the body text—for example, "Noah had a big nose, as seen in figure 12."

There is some additional material that should appear in books, particularly nonfiction. One is the acknowledgments. This is a chance to thank anyone who needs thanking, but it should be brief—about a page. It is optional but nice to include. You might thank family, friends, your editor, friends who read early drafts and made suggestions, anyone who went above and beyond to help you during the writing process, in work, or in life. You can also dedicate your book to someone. This dedication usually appears before the book begins. It's particularly meaningful to have a book dedicated to you, so think carefully about your dedication.

Behind the Scenes at the Publishing House 67

You may wish to include a note from the author section. This is useful if there's anything unusual about how you researched or wrote the book, something that could do with explaining. It's a chance to step aside from the narrative itself, turn directly to the readers, and tell them a bit about your process and why you made certain decisions regarding the book.

The last thing you'll want to gather, once the manuscript is done but before it's been laid out for printing, are blurbs. Blurbs are short quotes in support of the author or the book in question. They are usually written by people who have more name recognition than the author, the idea being that if potential book buyers have heard of the blurber but haven't heard of the author, then maybe they'll take the blurber's recommendation. The bigger the name, the better. If you can get Stephen King to say, "This is the best book ever," that can go a long way to reassuring potential buyers that it must be good, even if they've never heard of the author or the book. If not a famous name, then someone with a bio that reassures a reader of the quality of the book's content can also help. For instance, if it's a book about the human body, it might be good for a doctor to provide a blurb.

Blurbs are provided for free—there's no tradition of paying people for them. It's a mutual favor done by one author for another. To get a big-name author you don't know personally will be tricky. You can write to them directly or to their agent, but this is hit or miss in terms of success. Your publisher can also write for you and may have more luck. Still, a personal connection is your best bet. Ideally you'd have three or four blurbs for your book. These can be placed on the front cover (if there's one particularly good one), back cover, or inside the flaps of a hardcover book with a dust jacket. They also go on your book's landing page on the publisher's website and on the Amazon page.

A bigger ask than a blurb is a foreword, afterword, or introduction. These can add value to your book, and anyone who writes one for inclusion in your book is taking a strong stand in support of your work. These are also written as favors between authors, not for pay. These are short texts, around one thousand words or less, but it is a commitment to write one, much more so than a one-to-three-sentence blurb. It's up to the author to invite someone to write such a text, while your publisher can help you get blurbs.

And Then You're Published

Your text is done, edited, and ready for production into a book. Your role as author ends but you've got a few more things to do before the book is printed and proudly clutched in your hands.

Once the manuscript is finished, your book will go to a copyeditor who is usually someone other than the editor with whom you worked. A fresh set of eyes is always helpful—we are our own worst editors, since we've been through our own thickets of text so often that we tend to skim over our words and not look at them with clear, analytical eyes. The copyeditor should also help format the manuscript if there are final things to do, like ensuring that all citations are in the correct, consistent format.

At this point, the publisher will be developing a cover for your book. They may ask you if you have suggestions for a cover image or concept, but this is rare. For *The Art Thief*, I was shown the final cover and effectively told, "You like this, don't you?" To which I nodded in affirmation. My editor specifically told me that he'd chosen not to show me the other designs they were considering because he didn't want me to fall in love with one that, in the end, they weren't going to use. The covers are chosen by your editor and the marketing team, and they usually aren't interested in the author's "vision." If they seek any author input, that should be considered a pleasant surprise.

Covers can vary wildly. *The Art Thief* had three different covers in the English edition alone. The trade paperback cover I suppose just didn't work at all, but sales were much better for the mass market paperback version. What are the differences?

Print books tend to come out in three formats. Hardcover books are the sort that libraries want, and they come out first. They cost the most to buy but also the most to produce. They are made of quality paper and are well bound and meant to last a generation, with many read-throughs. Not all books come out in hardcover. Your publisher will decide in which formats to print your book (this will be in your contract). Trade paperbacks have the same quality paper, ink, and binding of a hardcover, but the cover itself is soft. These are likewise meant to last a generation, but the soft covers can lead to the books being beat up more easily, and so libraries tend not to stock them. The cheapest to print and to buy, but with the significantly highest profit margin for the publisher, is the mass market paperback. These are printed on cheaper paper and are meant to last a few years and perhaps just two or three read-throughs. This is what you'll find at airport bookshops, the sort of books that might cost less than ten dollars. The ink may smudge if you touch a page with a finger that was recently in touch with a glazed doughnut, and the pages tend to rip out.

In addition to being printed, nowadays most books are also released as ebooks, which download directly after purchase to be read on an e-reader, like a Kindle or iPad, or right on your smartphone. This has the benefit of costing nothing at all for the publisher once the master file has been made (this requires a separate layout from the print books and a little bit of programming, since ebooks tend to have some features like a built-in dictionary to define words, underlining key passages, embedded hyperlinks, the ability to jump to the start of chapters, etc.).

Audiobooks are also common today, but they are usually made by specialized publishers and the author is rarely involved. There are instances when the author is also the reader of the book, but this is usually only if the author is a celebrity. Otherwise, professional readers are used by the audiobook publisher. The audiobook tends to function like a foreign language edition. The rights are sold separately, and authors rarely have any contact with the publisher, aside from receiving a few copies of their own book in the mail (for audiobooks this might still be in the form of CDs).

Most of the time one designer will specialize in book covers while another will do the interior layout as well as the typesetting. This involves the design of the interior of the book plus the actual laying out of the text and images. "Typesetting" is an old-fashioned term that hails back to movable type printing, so it's a charming anachronism to use it today, when books are "typeset" using Adobe InDesign.

You'll provide no feedback at all in the interior design process. The designer will choose the font, the size, various elements (like drop caps to start chapters, for instance) alone. The publisher will have budgeted to the precise number of total pages for your book, and so there is little wiggle room. If your publisher budgeted for your book to have 247 pages, then it must have a maximum of 247 pages when laid out. This is up to your typesetter to manage, but there may be some situations where you'll have to lend a hand. For instance, if your bibliography goes on for pages and pages, trimming it might be a way to keep the page count down. The maximum page count will also be a factor when it comes to making your index (of which more later).

It's important to understand that the typesetting process is not automatic. I'd thought that you just press a button and your Word document magically appears in InDesign, a few things are touched up, and that's that. *Au contraire*. The typesetter has to lay out each page individually, and the process for a normal book takes a week or more. This is a precise activity in which the typesetter will seek to avoid having "widows" or "orphans." A "widow" is a lone word or short group of words that appears at the bottom of a paragraph, column, or page. An "orphan" is the same idea but appearing at the top of a new page. They are considered unsatisfying to the eye, and they make typesetters itch, so they must be removed. But each time one block of words shifts so that a page is clean, with no widows or orphans, text gets bumped on other pages, which can cause new widows and orphans. Typesetters are like fishermen, constantly reeling in text or letting the slack out until it settles just right.

This is why your last chance to change your text in any significant way is *before* it is typeset. Your contract may actually state that if you as an author insist on changing text significantly after typesetting, then you have to pay the typesetter to redo their work. The typeset version of your book won't "flow" the way you think it would, because those widows and orphans may appear. This is why any changes you make in the final proofing—that is, working off the typeset, fully laid-out manuscript that you're usually given as a PDF just before it goes to print—must be small enough not to require repagination. This means that if you want to remove a word, you may have to replace it, for example. Keep this in mind as you go through the two final passes. The penultimate pass is before the book is typeset. You're still working in Word or the equivalent word processor, and you can make even large changes (adding a chapter, chopping three paragraphs). The final pass is through the typeset book in PDF format (gone are the days of being mailed printed versions with accompanying green pencils), and here it's just about last-minute commas, a lone typo your proofreader missed, a decision to swap out one adjective for a preferred one.

I'll add one note to be understanding about the proofreader. I've proofread many a book not my own and I know that there is inevitably a typo or two that everyone who checked the book missed. A good proofreader should guarantee that the book is 99 percent perfect, but even some of my big books that were professionally proofread have had numerous typos, some quite egregious. I was thoroughly annoyed until I myself started proofreading for other authors. Now I always tell clients that 99 percent perfect is the goal. Software checks do not catch everything nor do even the most well-meaning eyes.

That typeset version has all the pages in place. This means that you can prepare your index. There are professional indexers you can hire, but they charge a considerable amount, particularly because they don't know your book at all. They have to read it thoroughly and guess what is important enough to be included in the index. You're really better off making the index yourself. This is not the place to explain what an index is, but suffice to say that for general readership books, you don't have to go nuts. The index should contain proper names (of people, places, events) and some keywords and themes that a reader is likely to want to look up. But don't worry about being exhaustive. For an academic book, more detailed indexes are helpful, because they are there to assist researchers and students.

The index is prepared in two steps, and the first one you can begin anytime you like, even before you've finished the book. This step is keeping the list of keywords and names that you think should go in the index. If you keep this in alphabetical order as a running file that you add to as you go, you'll save time at the end. You'll also be more likely to remember the words you want to index if you add them slowly during the writing process, rather than trying to recall them on the final day.

The second step is boring but easy. You have the typeset PDF open on your computer, and the Word file with your index keywords beside it. For each index word, you use the "find" feature to seek out every instance of the word

Behind the Scenes at the Publishing House 71

inside the PDF. You write down each page on which the word appears, and in this way you fill out your index. This can be done while you're wearing a beer helmet watching *Simpsons* reruns (I say possibly from experience). It's mindless and takes a half day but needs to be done. Be sure to check the number at the bottom of each page that the keywords appear on, not the number that the "find" feature shows you when using Adobe software to read the PDF. This is because these numbers can differ. If you have, say, five pages of preface, which are marked with Roman numerals (i, ii, iii, iv, etc.) rather than Arabic numbers (1, 2, 3, etc.), as is sometimes the case, the "find" feature will read the preface's first page, which is indicated as "i," as page 1, while the actual page with a 1 in the footer will be considered by the software as page 6.

In addition to the index, you'll prepare a table of contents (TOC) to go at the start of the book and indicate the page on which each new section or chapter begins.

And that should be it. Your book goes off to the printer and is magicked into an ebook. It will still be a while before it comes out officially. Many months, in fact. But that's good, because it gives you time to prepare for promotion.

Chapter 4

Writing and Publishing Articles

Books are full meals. The proposals alone can take many days if not weeks to craft, and a book is usually a 60,000–100,000-word commitment. Depending on your pace, that could mean a year or even more of research, writing, and editing. As we've seen, if you add in the time it takes to get a book proposal green-lit and for the book to actually come out, it's likely a two-year odyssey.

But if books are full meals, articles are snacks. They bring swift satisfaction, moving from pitch to writing to publication more often in a matter of days than any longer duration. If the article's subject is time sensitive and linked to the news cycle, then you might pitch an article, get a green light, and be asked to file it within hours for it to come out the next morning.

Articles bring swifter satisfaction and are more concise, punchy ideas than expansive explorations. But how they are pitched is very similar to how books are proposed, just in a much shorter format.

Articles are pitched to editors at publications. These could be websites, magazines, newspapers, or academic journals. Academic journals should be considered separately, but magazines and newspapers, online or in print, follow a simple template, as do their pitches.

Pitches for articles in most cases should be just one or two paragraphs in length. The ideal number of pitches to send to an editor in one email is three. Sending just one implies that "this is my only idea, I hope you like it, take it or leave it." Sending three ideas for articles that would suit that publication shows a thoughtful, flexible writer. More than three feels like overkill (no editor wants to open their email Monday morning and see "Dear Sir and/or Madam, here are 37 ideas I have").

Give each article pitch a catchy, intriguing title—but I can guarantee that this will not be the title of the article if it is commissioned and run. Editors choose the titles based on what they think will draw the eye (and, with it, the click, which is how most publications make money). I pitched an article about what the United States could learn from how Slovenia is governed. An editor at *The Washington Post* went for it. It was originally titled "20 Things the US Could Learn from Slovenia." Then the editor told me that we had only six hundred words of space in the print newspaper, so "20 Things" became "6 Things." When the article actually ran, the title (which I'd never been told, much less approved) was "6 Great Things About Slovenia That Have Nothing to Do with Melania Trump." Whatever.

The title should not be too artsy. It should tell the editor exactly what they are going to get, or it should prompt a question in their minds. I once published an article called "Is This the Microbrewery Beer Capital of the World?" That title literally includes a question. The answer, when you read the article, was "probably." My adopted hometown of Kamnik, Slovenia, at one point had seven microbreweries for a population of around two thousand people, which I believe was the most per capita of any town in the world. But if you google that now, only my article comes up as testament to the superlative. The point is that the title was intriguing, but it did not contain anything less than factual. If I'd titled it "This Town Is the Microbrew Capital of the World," the article would have had to contain proof, or some authority beyond me as author stating that it is the case. Since the title asked a question, it was acceptable to have the answer be, "Well, I think so . . . it'd be cool if it were the case, wouldn't it?"

Marketing researchers have found that article titles with numbers in them are more appealing than those without. My article "5 Tips from Running a Successful Crowdfunding Campaign" sounds more inviting than "Some Tips from Running a Successful Crowdfunding Campaign" or even "How to Run a Successful Crowdfunding Campaign." The number (provided the number is not too high—three to twelve seems to be optimal) gives the reader an assurance that the ideas offered in the article are finite, with few enough that you can wrap your head around them. Reading this won't feel like work, it suggests. The reader knows what to expect. This is reassuring and lays the groundwork for engaging with the article better than an indefinite number does (as is implied by a title with "Some Tips" in it rather than a specific number of tips).

Newsier titles should be more straightforward, as in a *Guardian* article of mine, "Marina Abramovic Ex-Partner Claims Victory in Lawsuit," or an exhibition review in the same newspaper, "Restored and Ravishing: The Ghent Altarpiece Gives Up Its Centuries-Old Mysteries."

Your working titles should be followed by around one sentence that acts as a narrative "hook" to draw in the reader, followed by a paragraph—or two at most—explaining what the article will be. The pitch should include some explanation as to why you are a good person to write this article. If I'm an art historian then I need to explain why I would want to write about, say, planning a mission to Mars. There may be a good reason (my photographer buddy has been documenting projects on Earth in anticipation of the eventual colonization of Mars—he got a *National Geographic* commission and they recruited me as a last-minute writer to go with his amazing photos). These reasons don't need to relate to expertise. It can boil down to access—you happen to know an actor in a new film and can get an interview with them, for example. It can be geographic—you're going on holiday to Croatia and can research and write an article about your trip. In fact, as I write this (June 2024), I just got back from visiting a friend in Istria, the peninsula in northern Croatia between the Dalmatian Coast, Slovenia, and Venice. While I was there, I wrote a quick article pitch (let's be honest—I'm trying to get a commission to recoup my holiday expenses . . . nothing wrong with that!). Here's what I sketched:

TRUFFLES, GOAT CHEESE, AND XXX IN ISTRIA, CROATIA'S FORGOTTEN COAST

Dalmatia, Croatia's storied coastline, studded with over one thousand islands, is packed with pale tourists all summer long. But the Istrian Peninsula, tucked between Dalmatia, Slovenia, and Venice, remains relatively quiet, despite its spectacular beaches, charming coastal towns, and rich history. From a Roman amphitheater in Pula (where James Joyce once lived) to Rovinj (the "second most picturesque port in the Mediterranean"), from truffle hunting in Paladin to ancient printmaking in Motovun to art gallery hopping in Grožnjan and tasting the world's best goat cheese in Kumparička, this article will introduce the Istrian Peninsula as a less crowded holiday destination.

That's a decent article pitch. You'll notice that I haven't figured out yet what the third item listed in the title should be, after truffles and goat cheese. I'll throw something in later. I don't have much of a hook in the first line. I might insert: "By the time we'd found our fourth black truffle, or rather the highly trained dog had while we'd enjoyed a walk in the woods, we were ready for a feast of truffles piled so high that they disguised the scrambled eggs they were meant to accompany." Or "Nothing says 'Welcome' like a goat skull impaled on a pole, I thought as we pulled into a remote farm near Pula that is said to make the world's best goat cheese." At the moment, the pitch begins with the explanation of what the article will be, and a hook of a first line kicks it up a notch.

I recommend including three of these in your email. Below are some more examples of winning article pitches. Big, researched feature articles for which

76   *Chapter 4*

you hope to be paid can warrant more robust pitches—up to half a page, but rarely longer than that. Editors don't have the time (or don't think they do) to read long pitches.

But here's the thing to know: You are doing the editors a favor. It won't feel like that. Their approach is to make you feel like they are doing you a favor should they deign to commission an article from you and publish it. But in fact they need content. Magazines and newspapers make money off of ads or subscriptions or both. They have pages, virtual or real, to fill. The content must come from somewhere, and most do not employ enough full-time writers, so freelancers are needed. Go into your pitch with an alpha attitude: It's the editor's lucky day because you have some cool ideas for their publication, and you'd be happy to write them up as ace articles!

So what makes for a good article, and how is it different from a topic that requires a full book?

WHAT MAKES FOR A GOOD ARTICLE?

Articles can take a number of forms, and there are some standard approaches. In part 2 of this book, we'll look at some tricks and tactics for writing winning articles. But at a basic level, the difference is that you have around one hundred times as much space to write in a book as you do in an article. This means that articles must be really tight and focused on conveying a single idea well, without meandering or covering too much.

Online articles are usually 800 words long. This isn't much, and I often find it harder to write more briefly than to write at length. A long article for online reading will be around 1,200 words. Most editors feel that readers have a shorter attention span for online reading, while they can stay with articles longer in print. A print feature article will be around 1,500 words long. Rarely you'll encounter a "long-read" of around 3,000 words, but aside from a big feature in, say, *The New York Times Magazine* or *The New Yorker*, long-reads are a rare breed. If you're new to writing articles, you'll likely be looking at the 800–1,200-word range.

What can you do with a text that short? The best way to understand it is to read a handful of articles in publications of the sort you'd like to write for, now that you are thinking in more deconstructionist terms: What is this article I'm reading *doing* and how can I apply it to articles that I write?

We'll include some sample articles in part 2, but the basic idea is to ask a question and answer it. Don't ask a "big" question. "What's the meaning of life?" is not a good article-length question. "How a Philosopher Used AI to Crack the Meaning of Life" could be, however. Most articles are about a single thing: a person, an event, an invention, a place. They focus on a single

Writing and Publishing Articles 77

newsworthy or particularly interesting aspect of that single thing: a person who made a world record, an event that has never happened before, an invention that will revolutionize something, a place with a unique story. To tell everything about a person's life would require a book-length biography, so in an article you'll focus on a single aspect, with a light explanation of the rest of the life in question. A 1,200-word article can't cover the story of a place like Rome—that's book territory—but you could write an article about a neighborhood in Rome, or a special event there.

We can lay out some types of articles in brief, from which you can draw inspiration for what you might enjoy researching and writing.

What's described above is a **feature article**. This is an in-depth piece that covers a single topic in a comprehensive way—at least, as comprehensive as the word count allows. The "best" journalism comes in feature articles. This is where writing shines, and the best writers are usually assigned them.

News articles are time sensitive and cover something that just happened or is about to happen. They are meant to inform in an objective way. They are almost exclusively assigned to staff writers, because the turnaround time for freelancers submitting pitches is too long. To pitch a news article you'd need to plan ahead. I once pitched an article about my favorite basketball player, Luka Dončič (go Mavs!), who would be doing a special event at Lake Bled, near where I live in his native Slovenia. I had a VIP pass to the event so I could be there, while most NBA reporters based in the United States could not. I offered to report on this and write a news article.

Interviews offer a good way to access someone with a public profile, which has multiple benefits. These can either be in a Q&A format or written as a narrative of your experience with the person of note, including numerous quotes from them. The benefit of this is that the person of note, the interview subject, is likely to be of interest to an editor, but you need to be sure you'll be able to get the interview. Notable figures, such as authors or filmmakers, are contractually required to give interviews to promote a new release, provided the interview is for a reasonably exciting publication that will result in good exposure. I once interviewed actor Bill Murray for *Esquire* magazine. He accepted because he was promoting Slovenia Vodka, a vodka he co-owns. He wound up calling me for the interview (sorry, I don't have his phone number), and he then spent most of the call interviewing me about why I live in Slovenia, my love for the Boston Red Sox, and whether he could get invited to a Slovenian village schnapps-making competition.

You usually have to know where the interview will run before someone will say yes to it. But how can you know where it will run if you don't know if the person of note will accept your interview? It's a bit of a catch-22. This is a line I've used successfully in the past: "I'm not yet sure where I'll place the interview, but I'll do my best to get it in a high-profile publication." Then

78   *Chapter 4*

it's up to the subject (or their publicist or agent, if they're really a big shot) to say yes or no.

An instructional article with step-by-step guidance is called a **how-to article**. This could be about cooking or home maintenance or life hacks, for example. The goal of this article is to teach someone without specialized training a new skill they can immediately apply.

Opinions and editorials are usually written by nonstaff writers in response to a news event or an article written by a staff writer. They are sometimes called **op-eds**, for two reasons: these are abbreviations for op(inions) and ed(itorials), but it also means "op(posite) the ed(itorials)," which refers to where in the newspaper these were published—on the page facing the editorials. Opinions from readers were often published on the left side of a broadsheet with editorials by staff writers on the right. These can be a good way to get into a major publication, but they require lightning speed. You need to hear of an event or read an article in the publication in question, then immediately pitch your response article. Unlike with all other types of articles, editors often want the whole opinion piece written—not a pitch first. This comes mostly down to time. Responses are usually published the day after the event or article to which they respond, otherwise the news cycle has moved on and it's no longer of interest. These are often, then, "hot takes"—a very quick, almost instinctual response to the news or article that you pour out in one sitting and then send off.

Reviews are a good way to get an article out without requiring extensive research. You see a film, read a book, watch a TV series, or eat at a restaurant and then review it, offering your opinion, critique, and recommendation. A review of a single thing (album, movie, diner, novel) is a good article subject.

Travel articles likewise can be a benefit to a trip you're already planning to take. Off to San Antonio for the weekend? Why not pitch an article titled "48 Hours in San Antonio" and see if you can get a publication out of it? You'll usually need to specify what you plan to do, and it should feel non-generic. Something unique, covering a festival, getting a behind-the-scenes look, taking an unusual angle ("Las Vegas for Families with Young Children," for example)—these are more likely to excite an editor. My sample pitch above is for a travel article.

Stories about people can be called **human interest** stories if they focus on a particular event (usually heartwarming, sometimes chilling). If they are about a single person in significant detail, someone of note or a celebrity, they are called **profiles**.

Trends or **lifestyle** articles are about something that is newly of note, an aspect of daily life, from fashion to technology, from business to health, from nutrition to relationships.

Writing and Publishing Articles 79

Listicles (also called roundups) are perhaps the easiest of all articles to pitch, but they are appealing to readers (and therefore to editors). These are collections of related items, ideas, or tips usually presented in a list. They could be "Top Ten Sandwiches to Order in New York" or "Around the World in Cookies" (the latter is an article I actually wrote—why haven't I gotten a Pulitzer in journalism yet?).

These categories are those most likely to be assigned to a freelancer who is relatively new to writing. **Essays** are big, meaty thought pieces that are rarely assigned to new writers. And **columns**, which are series of articles on a single general theme, are only the realm of veteran writers. But consider any of the above categories as potential to pitch.

HOW NOT TO SCARE THEM OFF: LETTER TEMPLATE FOR PITCHING ARTICLES AND CHASING EDITORS

When considering where to pitch articles, it's good to check whether the publication you are considering has already covered the subject you plan to pitch. If *The Guardian* has already run a feature on "Where Footballers Eat in Manchester," then it's a waste of your time and the editor's for you to pitch that subject to that publication. However, if *The Guardian* ran an article on that, you can pitch the same concept to a different newspaper that hasn't run anything on it. You can't copyright a topic for an article, and of course your article will be different from any other (it may include the same restaurants, since those are objectively, factually, favorites of Manchester football players, but you'll be writing it afresh, in your own voice, and hopefully with different leads and elements to highlight).

Also think about the writing style. When I write for *Esquire*, I'm familiar with their American hipster-ironic voice, and it's very different from how I write an article for *The Guardian.* It's about more than US versus UK grammar, punctuation, and phrasing. You should be familiar with the "house voice" of any publication you'd like to write for, and do what you can to if not match it, then ensure that your article doesn't feel out of place in terms of how it's written.

Who to pitch to is the next question. Some publications list their mastheads, while most don't. They figure that those in the know will know how to reach the right editors, and they don't want to make it overly easy for the general public to write (they're not afraid of article pitches but they don't want random people complaining to them). So it can take a bit of detective work.

Depending on the size of the publication, there may be a single editor who covers everything and accepts pitches, or there could be various departmental editors: one for the travel section, one for food, one for arts, one for television, and so on. Pitch to whoever seems most appropriate to your topics of interest.

But there's a twist! Even if you find a masthead listing who is in charge of which section, email addresses might not be listed. Not to worry, there's a trick to untwisting this twist. While some publications play hard to get when it comes to their editorial staff, every publication wants to make it as easy as possible for advertisers to reach them. This means that whoever is in charge of promotions, publicity, or ads (however it may be listed) will have their email address listed. This can be your path to the email addresses of anyone else at the publication, because it will almost certainly be formulaic. Email addresses are usually firstname.lastname@ or firstinitial.lastname@, or something to that effect. So if you can find any email address within a company, you can unlock the template for them all.

A word of warning about emailing. Don't send anything to a generic address, like submissions@ or info@. These go into a slush pile administered periodically by interns who cannot make any decisions. Always email a specific person who you refer to by name in the salutation, so that it's clear that this is a real email from one real person (not a bot) to another.

I've prepared a basic letter-to-an-editor template, which you're welcome to use or adapt. The key is not to do anything to make an editor stop reading. It's the opposite of what you might think. You don't need to dazzle them. They get a lot of email pitches and they're looking for a reason to stop reading yours and move on to the next one. Don't give them a reason to do that.

To this end, I recommend a formula that begins with a simple salutation but always specifically addresses a named person. Not "Dear Sir/Madam," not "Dear Editor," but "Dear Gwendolyn" or whatever their name is (first names are fine, less formal).

Your first paragraph should be no more than a few sentences and should tell why you're writing (to pitch some article ideas) and who you are. The who you are should be brief and highlight only what's relevant to writing on the subjects you're pitching. So if you're pitching articles about cycling, you should mention that you're a cyclist. If it's articles about Sri Lanka, you might mention that you're an expat there or that you're planning to visit in two months. Ideally, you'll have some obvious in or expertise in the subjects you're wanting to write about.

The next paragraph should explain that you're already a published writer. How to do this if you're not already a published writer? There are some tricks below to getting started, but your main goal is to convey to the editor to whom you're pitching that other editors have already said yes to you.

Editors have very little time (or at least they think they do). You can send writing samples, but they're unlikely to read them. What they want is to

Writing and Publishing Articles 81

see that other editors have already commissioned and published your work, which means that you must write well enough. For article writing, you don't need to be a Great Writer. You just need to write clearly and readably.

A shorthand way to convey this is one you are welcome to copy. It's a phrasing that is not lying but that reassuringly implies that you're more of a veteran writer than you might actually be. The line is: "My recent publications include . . ." and then you list three magazines or websites in which your work appears, with a hyperlink to your article in each. It's important not to lie. You do need to have actually written the articles to which you include hyperlinks. But the chances are small that the editor will bother reading them. They just want the reassurance that someone else decided that you know what you're doing.

So here is a template for an initial pitch letter to an editor—one actually sent by me—as well as several article pitches that were accepted, so you can get a sense of what they might look like, as you prefer your own.

Dear [INSERT FIRST NAME OF EDITOR],

My name is Noah Charney and I'm a best-selling author and professor of art history. My recent articles include features published in *The Guardian*, *The Washington Post*, and *The Art Newspaper*.

I would be pleased to be considered as a writer for [INSERT NAME OF PUBLICATION]. I've included three brief article pitches for you to consider. Please let me know if any of them are of interest, or if you'd like to see others.

Thanks and best wishes, Noah

THE PRINCE AND THE LOOTED STATUES

This is the story of an exiled prince, three statues stolen from ancient Cambodian temples, and the successful fight to win them back. It is the story of Prince Ravivaddhana Sisowath Monipong (Ravi to his friends) and how the tale of three lost statues demonstrates the connection between looted antiquities, organized crime, and terrorism, not only in Cambodia but around the world.

In November 2012, Sotheby's placed on the front of its auction catalog a gorgeous, life-size statue of a Hindu warrior called Duryodhanna, which, meaningfully, had no feet. It was valued at some $3 million, and was to be the centerpiece of the Sotheby's auction. Sotheby's argued that when the statue was imported, its owner submitted a form to US Customs specifying that this masterpiece was "not cultural property." This was obviously untrue, and yet the object entered the United States all the same. Not only is it cultural property, but it is one of the most beautiful statues to emerge from Cambodia, a product of the majestic Koh Ker temple complex, built by the Khmer kingdom in the fifteenth century. Not only was it obviously a great work of cultural heritage, but it had obviously been looted. Its feet were missing because the sculpted feet that

82   *Chapter 4*

precisely matched this sculpture were still in situ at Koh Ker—they had been sawed off by tomb raiders to facilitate the removal of the statue.

Sotheby's refused to withdraw the statue from the sale. But it eventually succumbed to pressure. The statue was withdrawn and only now returned to Cambodia. During this same period two other similarly grand statues, also from the Koh Ker temple complex, were likewise removed from prospective sale: the Balarama and the Bhima. While Christie's quickly cooperated in removing works that appeared to have been looted from sale, Sotheby's (with its long history of questionable practices, detailed in Peter Watson's *Sotheby's: the Inside Story*) resisted as long as it could. What finally swayed it, and ultimately resulted in the return of these three statues, was the concerted efforts of Prince Ravi.

Ravi is a kind, soft-spoken but passionate child of the exiled Cambodian royal family, who have been obliged to live abroad since the 1970s. He grew up in Paris and now lives in Rome, balancing a *Grande Bellezza* lifestyle among his friends and fellow aristocrats with his love for his homeland and fighting spirit to curb the rampant looting of Cambodia's cultural heritage. Thanks to his campaigning, and the on-site fieldwork of criminologists like Dr. Simon MacKenzie of the University of Glasgow, not only have three magnificent statues been returned, but the elaborated, highly organized network of antiquities looting in Cambodia has been exposed. It is now clear that in Cambodia, as elsewhere, looted antiquities fund terrorist activity. The story of Ravi and the three looted statues provides a view into the hidden cocktail of stolen art, organized crime, and terrorism.

IN THE BEGINNING WAS THE WORD: INSIDE THE COLLECTION OF THE FORTHCOMING MUSEUM OF THE BIBLE

In 2017 a high-profile new $500 million museum will open its doors in Washington, DC. The Museum of the Bible has made most of its headlines through the prominent and questionable actions of its patrons, the Green family: self-made billionaires thanks to the Hobby Lobby chain of arts and crafts shops. Patriarch David Green is best known for having brought a suit against the United States in which, for fundamentalist religious reasons, the Greens object to their tax dollars going, due to healthcare reforms, to pay for contraception. But Green's pet project is what looks to be the world's largest collection of biblical artifacts, primarily in the form of text fragments from ancient Bibles and biblical apocrypha. Green sets aside half of his annual income (part of a net worth of an estimated $5 billion) to charities and evangelical networks, and is now the money behind a multimillion-dollar private collection of biblical material that will become a major attraction in DC when it opens in 2017.

While the media has made much of Green's politics and the lawsuit against the United States, relatively little has been written about the contents of this new museum. This article will look in-depth at the 40,000+ biblical artifacts that will fill the museum. For there are questions about where they come from, their authenticity, and whether they were legally excavated and exported. At a recent conference on art crime, a speaker detailed her concerns about the provenance of the Green Collection, as well as how it is being handled. One curator is touring the world (and indeed recently did a show at the Vatican, despite the Greens' fervent Protestantism) and can be seen in YouTube videos handling ancient objects in what appears to be a careless manner, as well as preaching to crowds and the camera more like a used car salesman than a professor specializing in biblical history.

Our view into the collection will come from an outsider within the inner circle of the Green project: Dr. David Trobisch. Trobisch is the son of missionaries, born in Cameroon and raised in Germany. He is a widely respected, serious, intelligent scholar (and he is *not* the fellow in the YouTube videos), and he brings a level of thoughtfulness, calm, and expertise to the Museum of the Bible that the project seems, on the surface, to lack. He is the director of the Green Collection, meaning that he is in charge of the objects that will populate the future museum (as opposed to being the director of the museum itself, which is more of a public relations role). He joined the project only in 2014, and his first task is to see what exactly the Green Collection, currently based in Oklahoma City, consists of. He is employing a team of a dozen researchers who are looking not only at the pieces in the collection, with an eye toward how the Museum of the Bible will be curated, but also at their history, authenticity, and the legality of how they were acquired. According to Trobisch he has yet to find a questionable piece, but other scholars are concerned. Some have identified specific papyrus fragments that were advertised on eBay from unscrupulous sellers (some of whom were later banned from eBay), and a number of works in the collection appear to have been harvested from mummies. There is a tradition of papyrus with text on it being used in mummy wrapping. Sometimes this text itself is valuable (though it was considered a mere form of recycling in ancient Egypt). But to harvest mummy papyrus, one must dismantle the mummy. Trobisch chooses to refrain from commenting on his patrons—for him, this is the opportunity of a lifetime to be at the center of what is probably the world's largest private collection of ancient biblical material, his area of expertise. Though he has taught in the United States (including at Yale Divinity School), he is something of a fish out of water in Oklahoma, but he is surrounded by thousands of artifacts, all of which need examination, as he prepares for the 2017 launch of this major new American museum.

This article will focus on Dr. Trobisch and the contents of the Green Collection—just what the Museum of the Bible will showcase, whether it will eschew other faiths in favor of the evangelical Protestantism of its patrons, and just where all these artifacts came from.

84   *Chapter 4*

THE HACKER'S CODE: HOW COMPUTER PROGRAMS ARE DECODING MYSTERIOUS MANUSCRIPTS

For six centuries code breakers have attempted to crack a particularly stubborn and enigmatic medieval manuscript that rests in Yale's Beinecke Rare Books Library. The so-called Voynich Manuscript is written in an unknown, coded language, and is full of bizarre hand-painted illustrations, including many of naked women frolicking in what looks like alchemical apparati. The manuscript was first recorded in 1665, as part of the collection of natural and man-made wonders owned by Emperor Rudolf II of Bohemia (he also collected Arcimboldo paintings, hosted the magician John Dee, and kept both penguins and a giant octopus in a tank). When Rudolf acquired it, the manuscript cost 600 ducats, which was significantly more than any work of art—Caravaggio paintings sold for around 100–200 ducats, and the most expensive painter of seventeenth century Rome, Claude Lorrain, would command around 400 ducats for his finest work. No one knows how to read the book, why Rudolf II would pay so much for it, or even what it is about. It was carbon-dated only last year, and found to have originated around 1420. That's as much as anyone knows.

While medieval scholars, Jesuit linguists, and military code breakers (including those who cracked the Enigma code) have all tried their hand at deciphering the Voynich Manuscript, none have succeeded. But now, computer programmers may have the best shot at unlocking this real-life coded book. Kevin Knight, a computer scientist at USC, is interested in how coded texts like the Voynich Manuscript might both be cracked by computers and can also help to teach computers how to perform complex translation tasks. Knight is at work on "translating" this manuscript, and has assigned each symbol within it a digital equivalent—no small task, since there are 170,000 characters in the book, excluding paintings. Initial analysis suggests that the text is organized around specific topics, and that the text better resembles a language than an assemblage of random information.

There is a precedent to the success of computer programmers deciphering historical mysteries. The Copiale Cipher, a manuscript dated to around 1760, is 105 pages long and written entirely in code. It was Kevin Knight, now tackling the Voynich, who led an international team of code breakers in solving the Copiale Cipher—but it was only in 2011 that he did so. But that text was far easier than the Voynich. It turned out to have been written in a complex substitution code, but one that used a combination of abstract symbols along with Greek and Roman letters. The Voynich is entirely in an unknown symbolic language, making it that much harder to solve.

This article will discuss how computer programmers trained in code breaking and linguistic programs managed to crack the Copiale Cipher, and how they will approach the unbreached Voynich Manuscript. We will follow Kevin Knight as he tackles the Voynich, and also consider the application of his techniques to other famous art historical mysteries, such as the complex allegorical illustrated

Writing and Publishing Articles　　　　85

poem "Hypnerotomachia Poliphili" and the mysteries *Sacred Allegory* by Giovanni Bellini.

Those three article pitches are longer and more detailed and were meant for high-end publications. Pitches can be far simpler—I include more advanced pitches because they are good learning tools. The first and third were commissioned for *The Guardian*, the second one for *The Washington Post*. The third was commissioned but in a different way: The editor there asked for an article about "digital discoveries," including several examples of how cutting-edge technology was solving age-old art historical puzzles. This is good to keep in mind. You might pitch something, but the editor replies, "Well, not this, but how about that?" and will ask you if you're up for a variation on what you pitched. I've rarely had a pitch accepted by my editor at *The Guardian* travel section, but when I pitch I sort of remind him that I'm out there, and he's often come back to me with his own idea of what I should write for them. Then it's up to you to say yes or no—but if you say no, understand that the editor will be unlikely to want to work with you again. Pitching is like the improv performance rule: whatever your improv partner does, your reply should be "yes, and" and pick up from there. The moment you negate, the relationship is at an end. It's entirely your right to say no thanks to a counter-offer of an article idea, but understand that editors want people who say yes to their writing requests.

CHASING EDITORS

Editors will mean to get back to you. They just are slow and forget—sometimes they forget even when they mean to say yes! So I have a system in which I mark my calendar to send a gentle follow-up once every two weeks until I get a response (or until a response would no longer be relevant—for instance, if my pitch has been commissioned by a different editor). Not once has an editor replied grumpily that I should leave him or her alone. They mean to write back and it's not a problem to inquire if you've not heard back in more than a week. I usually send something like this:

Dear [FIRST NAME],
　　Noah Charney here, the author who pitched you some ideas a few weeks back. I just wanted to follow up and see if you were interested in any of them, or might like to hear others. Thanks and have a good day.

86 *Chapter 4*

This is simple, quick, and not too pushy. I just keep sending this same follow-up until I get a reply. It's their responsibility to answer (eventually), so don't be shy about chasing an editor in a nonintrusive way like this.

Along with the dos there are some don'ts in your correspondence with editors. Don't hit them up over social media (aside from perhaps LinkedIn, which is business focused). Social media is for entertainment and wasting time, not for pitching business. Don't try to wow the editor with your writing. The danger of overwriting is too great. Articles aren't meant to be great literature; they're meant to clearly explain even complex stories in a way that all readers will (a) understand, and (b) be engaged by. You've got to get the facts right and write them coherently. That's all for now (as you gain more experience you can throw in the occasional writerly turn of phrase, but focus on function over style at the start). Don't try to stand out through quirkiness in a cover letter (for instance, don't send a photo of yourself or a lock of your hair). Don't send too many pitches at once (three is a magic number). Don't pitch something that shows you haven't done any homework (make sure that the publication to which you're pitching hasn't already run an article that overlaps too much with what you're offering to write). And finally for now, don't expect to be paid until you've published a reasonable number of articles and so can be considered no longer a novice. I'd say to expect to publish at least ten articles before you should expect a paid commission.

Your First Three Articles: A Shortcut

I mentioned that your pitch should include three hyperlinks to articles of yours already published. But how can you get those first three if you've never published before? There are innumerable ways, but here is what I usually tell my students.

There is a world of publications, particularly online magazines and blogs, that will be happy to publish writers, provided they don't have to pay you anything. All internet publications are in constant search of content, and you can provide it. So the goal is to get at least three articles out there. Ideally the publications will be of note, ones the editor to whom you're pitching will have heard of, but don't expect too much too soon. I've directed students to the following, for instance, to get the ball rolling.

Honest Cooking is one of scores of good online food magazines. You have to eat, right? So you might as well use that as an opportunity for an article. Food article approaches can include an interview with someone in the food industry, introducing an exotic food to a new readership (this includes the cultural history of the food and a recipe for it), reviewing a restaurant or food event, reviewing a cookbook or food-related book, a food-related listicle

Writing and Publishing Articles 87

(remember my magnum opus "Around the World in Cookies"), or a quest ("Finding the Best Burger in New Jersey").

You will wish to be entertained and will watch TV or a film to do so. That can be your portal to another article. Consider an online film magazine like *Film International*. The print quarterly version is highly respected and most libraries with film studies sections subscribe to it. The website is also very good, but much less selective. It's also much less prestigious, but in your cover letter you will just say, "My recent publications include *Film International*," and you needn't specify that it's the website, not the quarterly. Browse the magazine so you're not overlapping with something already published there, and consider pitching an interview with someone in the film world, reviewing a new film or TV series, introducing the readers to a classic or foreign film they likely haven't seen, writing an analysis of the whole oeuvre of a director or actor, covering a film festival, and so on.

Book reviews or interviews with authors of newly released books are also a good way to get started. They do not require extensive research, beyond reading the book in question. Reading a book takes an average of around ten hours (while watching the film that you'll write about for *Film International* takes only about two hours), and that's really all you'd need to do. There are numerous literary or book review websites. You can always check resources like pw.org (the website of the magazine *Poets & Writers*) or even ask AI software to recommend online magazines that accept "unsolicited submissions," the fancy word for a willingness to consider any pitches that are sent their way.

GETTING PAID (FINALLY)

Once you've broken ground on your article-writing career with some free articles, you should feel empowered to pitch to magazines that pay. It's often difficult to tell which pay and which don't. Most pay for print articles, which are considered more prestigious than online only, and it's not a given that payment is offered for online-only articles, aside from the big-name magazines and newspapers, which pay for everything (aside from op-eds). You should not plan to mention payment at all until an editor replies that they'd like to commission an article from you. At that point, the editor should tell you how much they are willing to pay for it. If they don't do so, you can assume that they are hoping you'll do it for free. It's up to you if you're OK doing it for free to beef up your résumé. If not, you can reply with something like, "I'd be delighted to write this for you. May I ask if there's a fee for doing so?"

How much one gets paid shifts and varies, so there may not be much point in laying out prices here. But to give an example from my past gigs, around ten cents per word is probably average. That means you might make $150 for an 800–1,000-word article. Making $250 for an article of that length was considered pretty good. You get twice as much if your article is in a print edition. I've gotten $250 for an online *Guardian* article but $600 for one that was in the print newspaper. Only big-name writers will make much more than this. Since you may be as curious as I was, the highest-paid writer of articles in the world is mega bestseller Michael Lewis, who gets $10 per word. If I got that, I'd be slipping in a great many, nay, I daresay a plethora, or rather a cornucopia, of additional words to expand my lexicon and optimize my earnings (which might well lead to run-on sentences).

Whether this is good money is up to your circumstances and how long it takes you to write. At this point, I can write a solid article in about two hours, which means that $150–$250 is excellent. If it took me two days to write it, maybe that's not so excellent. I spend *far* more time chasing editors than I do actually writing articles. This is what can be frustrating about the otherwise delightful practice of writing articles. There's a great satisfaction and endorphin rush in getting that elusive yes from an editor, and the adrenaline of writing quickly and seeing your article published within a matter of days. Books can't beat that, because they are a long game. There was a time when I wrote between ten and twelve articles a month because I needed the quantity in order to earn enough money to live off of. That was a time when I was primarily writing articles. If I could get my ideas green-lit swiftly and regularly, I could easily write between ten and twelve a month, but I found the time chasing editors—even those who have said yes to me in the past and will likely do so again, but because editors are the way they are, they can go weeks without replying—tiresome enough that I wound down my article writing. I mention this only for you to be aware that most of your time will be spent chasing editors, even when you become an established author. The only exceptions come when you secure a regular column—for instance, I was the art columnist for *Salon* for several years, writing once a week about art and culture—or if you become a staff writer at a publication.

You can reuse your material, but only once per language. If you've already written about, say, wine tasting in Burgundy, for one publication, no other publication will want an article on the same subject by the same author. You'll have used that "bullet." However, you can publish the same article in different languages, the assumption being that each language has its own audience independent of any other languages. So that article of yours about wine tasting in Burgundy could run in English, but also in French with a French magazine, Italian with an Italian newspaper, and so on.

The exception to this rule of one article only for one writer per subject per language is when there is something newsy that requires an update of the previous narrative. For instance, if you covered the Cannes Film Festival last year and did a good job, you could write about it this year too, and it wouldn't be considered too much of a repetition. I've written about the *Ghent Altarpiece* probably a dozen times, all in English, but each time I've tried to take a different angle and respond to something new in the story of the artwork—that's fine to do.

The takeaway from all of this is that writing articles is more immediately satisfying than writing books due to the quick turnover from green light (which gives me an endorphin burst) to writing (I love completing texts) to publication (another endorphin shot). But be aware that the pay is limited and the tedious part is getting to that green light.

Part 2

ON WRITING WELL (ENOUGH)

Chapter 5

Tips on Article Research and Writing

As an observant reader, you'll have noted that this part of the book is called "On Writing Well (Enough)." There are plenty of books out there about how to write, but part of my point is that it's worse to overwrite, to try too hard to be a Writer, which often means throwing in literary shenanigans where they distract rather than embellish, and that it's better, especially for writing articles, to keep it simple and clear. Take, for example, my previous sentence. It's all wiggly—lots of mini clauses that require numerous commas. It's okay, but it's not great writing. Great writing is clear. Simple. Hemingwayesque. No, that's not right either. Hemingway's style of paring down to the bone is cool for Hemingway but isn't good for articles. In this chapter, we'll look at some basic and easily applicable tips for writing well enough. Particularly when you're first starting out, the goal is to not write badly, rather than to write really well. But before you write, you should really research that article that you just got green-lit.

RESEARCH AND WRITING IN THE AGE OF AI

As I write this, AI software is just now becoming ubiquitous. It's an amazing and also creepy tool that is very helpful but cannot yet and shouldn't be used instead of old(er)-fashioned research and writing.

Technology moves at so swift a pace that it is likely fruitless to comment on it in a book, which takes many months to come out and could be years before it reaches the hands of any given reader. But in the spring of 2024, AI software writes articles the way a high school sophomore would. The grammar is correct. The research is probably mostly correct. But the articles are so without style as to be unreadable for pleasure. They convey information but

94   *Chapter 5*

do so in a way that reads like a student essay or, at best, a Wikipedia page. Neither of those will get you commissions.

So you cannot just get a commission, tell AI to write the article for you, and file it. There will be websites in particular that use AI instead of hiring writers, but those are just after clicks based on the inclusion of SEO (search engine optimization) keywords. You don't want to write for them and they don't think they need human writers. So we'll set them aside. You may be asked to include keywords as often as possible, because search engines are more likely to place an article higher in an internet search if the keyword entered by the user appears more often in the article. But that's not something to worry about at this point.

AI can already replace to some degree very basic copywriting, and it's good enough at translation to convey meaning well (though it still has to be checked by a bilingual human because it makes enough silly mistakes). But it cannot (yet) write engaging articles. The best it can do is develop listicles or Wikipedia-style biographies of people and summaries of places.

What I do use AI for is the initial research. Rather than using Google searches, which require combing through many hits, I've begun to ask AI the very questions I would Google. AI combs the internet for me and offers up the answer it thinks I want, based on how the question I asked is most frequently answered online. This is helpful, but with two caveats. First, just because an answer appears most frequently online doesn't mean it's the right answer. If I search for "What happens to people during a full moon?" the most frequent answer online might be "they turn into a werewolf," but that's possibly not the correct answer. Second, AI software doesn't provide citations (again, maybe it already does by the time you're reading this, but at the moment it does not). This means that you don't know where the information came from. For academic books and articles, you'll need to cite all facts and quotes, so researching without knowing sources isn't useful at all. For popular books and articles, citations aren't expected in footnote terms, but you are supposed to include where you got specific facts, as in, "According to the Pew Research Center, 37 percent of readers wouldn't trust an article written entirely by AI to be factual." And you need to name whomever you are quoting, as in, "Dr. Noah Charney said, 'Be careful when using AI as a writing tool.'"

The top publications will assign your articles to fact-checkers as well as proofreaders. If the fact-checker checks a fact and can't verify it, the fact-checker will ask you to check the fact and send him or her the citation (that sentence sounds like a Dr. Seuss tongue twister). So it's best for you to keep running track of where you get your information. This can be as simple as pasting a URL or the name, author, and date of a book or magazine from which you drew a fact or a quote. You probably won't need to refer back

Tips on Article Research and Writing 95

to it, but it's *way* harder to work backward and figure out where you read something than it is to just keep gentle track of what you're reading as you go.

I like using AI to find answers to googleable questions, but then I need to also look deeper. I'll ask AI, "Name me ten types of cookies from around the world," and I'll get a short list. That's not enough to write a good article, but it can point me in helpful directions. I'll then search for each cookie that sounds like it could be of interest.

Know this: Neither editors nor grown-ups trust Wikipedia as a source. It's not permitted as a cited source in many cases. This is because anybody can add, remove, or edit Wikipedia pages. So remove Wikipedia from your research vocabulary. If you want an encyclopedia, Britannica is very reliable. It's also always better to trust a written source that contains citations (like an academic or medical article) than one without. More renowned publications are also generally more trustworthy. Print articles are considered preferable to online only, and books tend to be more trustworthy than articles. AI cannot yet search books, so its pool of information isn't maximally reliable, since it draws from billions of websites (millions of which could be packed with false information).

Interviewing people and getting quotes for articles adds a lot and is worth the effort. Most people are delighted and flattered to be interviewed. If you want to quote someone but didn't do the interview yourself, be sure to cite where the quote first appeared, as in, "In an interview with *The Wall Street Journal*, Jon Butterfield said, 'I like to eat beans on toast.'"

Read at least three sources per article to ensure that you have a reasonable breadth of sources and to compare the facts. If facts are facts, they should be consistent across several articles and are likely safe to include in your own.

ARTICLE WRITING TIPS: GREAT OPENINGS

The opening of your article or book is the most important part. It will immediately determine whether your reader reads on, and whether they do so with optimism. In our age of shrunken attention spans and infinite other options, an uninteresting opening will mean that you'll lose your reader before they've even gotten started. You have a sentence or two, perhaps a paragraph, with which to convince them to read all of your article. If they've not opted in by the end of the first paragraph, they'll move on to another source of information or entertainment. Neuroscientists have demonstrated that human attention is divided into three-second slices. Every three seconds, your brain needs to proactively opt in to another three-second slice. This can be seen in the duration of time people spend on average looking at an image online (or an ad or an Instagram post), or even looking at a real painting in a real museum.

96   *Chapter 5*

Your initial goal as a writer is to compel your reader to choose to keep reading after the first three seconds. Three seconds is about as long as it takes to read two sentences.

Kind of pathetic, right? Human attention spans have been steadily shrinking, most sharply in the "screen era," when first television, the internet, and now smartphones ruled our entertainment lives, and our patience dwindled as options to jump around to other entertainments proliferated. This isn't a good thing, but it is a fact. I often joke to my students that Balzac, one of the greatest novelists in history, would never have found a publisher today. His novel *Père Goriot* opens with more than a dozen pages just describing the outside of a country inn. No matter that *Père Goriot* is one of the masterpieces of nineteenth-century literature. It just starts too slowly for today's readers. Almost no one who doesn't already know its reputation would be patient enough to read through all that description. This is why so many films, TV series, books, and even articles begin with a bang: someone chased, in danger, being killed in an exotic manner, engaged in an outrageously surreal activity. We have to grab readers by the throats (metaphorically, please) from the start, otherwise they'll move on to other things.

I've spotted a formula for openings of high-end feature articles, profiles, and reviews that is used so often that once it's pointed out to you, you'll start to see it *everywhere*. As an exercise, I'll bring to class a randomly selected issue of *The New York Review of Books* or the *London Review of Books*, two of the most prestigious and best-written anglophone publications. For any given issue, more than half of the articles will open with the same formula. This is it:

> Describe a specific, named person, in a specific place, in a specific year, engaged in a specific activity that is relevant to the topic of the article.

Here are some examples of opening lines that match this description or have the slightest variation on it.

> In November 2012, Sotheby's London office placed on the front of its auction catalog a gorgeous, life-size statue of a Hindu warrior called Duryodhanna, which, meaningfully, had no feet.

In this example, instead of a named person we have a named institution (the auction house Sotheby's) and the place (London). The date (November 2012) situates the action in our minds. The action itself isn't so remarkable—"[placing] on the front of its auction catalog"—but it becomes more vivid, more cinematic, and imaginable when I describe a "life-size statue of a Hindu warrior," and it's got a surrealist kicker, if you will, since the statue "had no

Tips on Article Research and Writing 97

feet." That "had no feet" functions both as a visual hook and as foreshadowing, because the fact that the statue was looted will be explained in the article as having been proven because the feet were found at a Hindu temple in Cambodia, and they matched the legs perfectly.

> On December 29, 1984, three people dressed as workmen strolled into a cathedral in Malta and robbed it of a Caravaggio.

This is the opening of an article about how a Maltese priest recovered a stolen Caravaggio painting. We have the date and location ("December 29, 1984" and "a cathedral in Malta"). We don't name the people yet, but we have the action that is relevant to the story: robbing a Caravaggio.

> A tall, bearded old man with the weathered, craggy face of a handsome, kindly sea captain stands in a pale pink negligee in a gallery in Amsterdam's Stedelijk Museum. As part of his January 15, 2015, performance, portentously titled *A Skeleton in the Closet*, he inscribes clusters of numbers onto a pale pink square on the wall: 252, 253, 288, 289.

Here we have the time and place ("January 15, 2015" and "Amsterdam's Stedelijk Museum"). We don't name the "tall, bearded old man with the weathered, craggy face of a handsome, kindly sea captain" yet—it is the conceptual artist Ulay. But we do have a very surreal, memorable image of him "in a pale pink negligee" inscribing "clusters of numbers onto a pale pink square on the wall."

If we want to get a little more fancy, we can approach the opening in a cinematic way. From the second half of the twentieth century forward, we humans have read in a different way. The televisual era is upon us. We used to read for the sake of reading, words conjuring images in our minds that we would sink into slowly. Lengthier texts were preferable to shorter ones (see all those doorstop nineteenth-century novels as examples). Now our minds are trained to imagine in the form of videos spinning in our mind's eyes. We read words and "translate" them into a movie.

With this in mind, we can make that translation into a movie easier for readers, and this will win us points. Abstract, theoretical matters are hardest to transfer into film and are likewise unpopular. Readers generally don't like to have to work, to put in effort to follow an article or understand what the author is trying to say. (Those that do are philosophers, and they do not represent your target audience.) Your reader will love you if you facilitate this "cinematization" of text. This doesn't mean a dumbing down. It just means providing specific, vivid, ideally unusual or surreal imagery through your words. Here is an example:

98   *Chapter 5*

A sweat-smothered man in a wide-brimmed hat, knee-high leather boots and a khaki uniform machetes his way through lush jungle foliage. As thick tangles of vine fall beneath his blade, he pushes into a clearing, then suddenly staggers back. The fanged mouth of a primordial stone beast gapes toward him. Before him rises the crumbled ruins of an enormous portal of rock, black with age but with a colossal grandeur immediately evident—a fine example of what archaeologists call a "zoomorphic portal" or, more popularly, a "monster mouth gate." What was once the gateway to an ancient Mayan city, built circa 700 and mysteriously abandoned by 1100, stands before him. He has found the lost city of Lagunita.

This article is about how a Slovenian "Indiana Jones," a swashbuckling archaeologist, has discovered more than eighty lost ancient Mayan cities— and how, in this era of Google Earth, when our world has been thoroughly mapped, there can be entire cities still lost to us.

That's the "big idea" of the article. But big ideas are like mist, hard to grab hold of. Protagonists engaged in an action are easy to grab hold of and cinematize. Consider the second paragraph of this same article:

The world grows ever smaller. Through the internet and travel programs we can virtually voyage across the globe, from mountain peaks to subterranean caverns to the ocean floor. Google Earth allows us to instantly capture a bird's-eye view of any location we can imagine. The planet has been mapped, circumnavigated, measured, and tagged in all ways imaginable, from pole to pole and back again. The age of explorers discovering new worlds seems a quaint memory, a flash of a different century. But there are some adventurers who continue to explore forgotten corners of the globe, and some find astonishing things. One such explorer, part Indiana Jones part Magellan, is the Slovenian archaeologist, Dr. Ivan Sprajc. Since 1996, he and his team have discovered more than eighty ancient Mayan cities in the jungles of Mexico, few of which the modern world had known before. Lagunita is but the most recent example.

Had I begun the article with this second paragraph, it would have been OK, but it would have become more of a thought piece. It would be more theoretical, philosophical, playing with an idea. And it would have had far fewer readers.

By starting with the cinematic hook, I've grabbed the readers. They've opted in, and now will be patient with me for the thoughtful bits, because I've reassured them that I know how to entertain. Let's unpack this opening paragraph further.

I withhold the reveal of who the "sweat-smothered man" is because you won't have heard of him, even if you're Slovenian. He should be famous but isn't. You will get an Indiana Jones vibe from my description, however,

Tips on Article Research and Writing 99

which is what I'm after. He's been called "a real-life Indiana Jones" and not just by me.

I'm not really igniting any literary fireworks, but the first sentence is a bit more interesting because I've used a noun as a verb: "machetes his way through," which feels apt. We understand that he's carving a path by slashing with a machete, but I wrote it in a somewhat surprising way that felt "right." That's a great writerly goal to aim for.

I put the opening paragraph in the present tense even though the action happened in the past. This is a trick to add a sense of immediacy, to pull the reader in. We've gone back in time and are seeing this as it happens, *now*, and there's an excitement to that.

He "suddenly staggers back," but I make the reader wait a second before I reveal what surprised him enough for him to stagger back. The question is planted in the reader's mind ("What did he see?"), and I delay the reveal just a hair, to add tension. The cinematography is extended by the next sentence: "The fanged mouth of a primordial stone beast gapes toward him." It isn't until later that we learn that this is a "monster mouth gate." If we were to film this opening, you can imagine the shots. Close-up of the archaeologist's sweaty brow as he slashes through the jungle. Fear on his face as he sees the monster mouth gate. Then we see it suddenly and think it might be a monster. Then we recognize it as part of a ruin.

There are a few more facts that aren't immediately explained, but the implication is "keep reading with me and I'll tell you about it." This is particularly the case for "mysteriously abandoned." This plants the question "Why was it abandoned?" without overtly asking it. And we end with "he has found the lost city of Lagunita." It's not something readers will have heard of, but the implication is there: "a lost city." Sounds cool.

Having dipped into strategies for opening articles, let's turn to how they can best be structured.

STRUCTURING ARTICLES

Every article will benefit from a good opening. The above approach is tried and tested, but there are other ways to go. All articles are essentially asking a question and seeking to answer it, so you might open your article with the question, either overtly asked or implied. An overt opening question might be "What are the best beaches in Dalmatia?" or "Where is America's best burger?" or "Why did Leonardo da Vinci make so few paintings?" or "Is the new Christopher Nolan movie any good?" Implying the question involves tricking the reader into thinking the question without actually writing a sentence that ends with a question mark: "These are the best beaches in

100   *Chapter 5*

Dalmatia" or "There are ten highest-rated burgers in America" or "Leonardo made only a few paintings during his long life, despite being one of the most acclaimed artists in Europe" or "If you like solving Rubik's Cubes, you'll love Christopher Nolan's new movie." Each of those sentences plants a question without asking a question. The "deal" that you, the author, are making with the reader is that you'll go on to answer that main driver of a question over the course of the article.

Asking a question and delaying the answer produces a pleasant tension in the reader. If I tell you that at the end of this chapter, I'll reveal the best way to structure your article, then you're likely to hang in there with me till the end because the tension has been raised and the question inserted ("What is the best way to structure an article?"), and you won't want to stop reading until the tension is relieved, the question answered.

In terms of the overall structure of an article or essay, I'll introduce the basics, which form a point of departure for variations. Back in third grade, in Mrs. Chen's class, I learned a super simple version of how to write a compelling essay. It was based on the advice that the ancient Roman senator Cicero wrote in *On Rhetoric*. He was describing how to make a compelling spoken argument, but this has ever since been applied to texts as well. The third-grade version of it is to begin with an introduction that presents the question that you hope to answer, or your hypothesis (what you guess is the answer to the question). This is followed by three points in favor of your argument. Then the conclusion reiterates the question or hypothesis, as well as the points in favor of your argument, so there can be no possible confusion. Back in Mrs. Chen's class, it went something like this:

Introduction: I think that ice cream is the best food.
Point 1: It's refreshing on a hot day.
Point 2: It comes in a cookie cone.
Point 3: You can get lots of flavors.
Conclusion: In conclusion, ice cream is the best food because it's refreshing on a hot day, it comes in a cookie cone, and you can get lots of flavors.

Super basic, right? But at an early age this is what we were taught often enough that it sunk in. Fast-forward two decades and I'm writing peer-reviewed academic essays. It's not so different. We still begin with an introduction, which includes the primary question or hypothesis. Add in a literature review, bringing the reader up to speed with published material on your subject. But then we still have points in favor of your argument. You might have a methodology section, explaining how you approached whatever it is you're studying. There might be datasets if this is science rather than the humanities. You might also include some counterpoints. But then you end with a conclusion that reiterates the question, the points in favor of it (or against it), and what you concluded. Add on a bibliography and throw in some citations, and Mrs. Chen's third-grade essay has become Dr. Chen's postdoctoral thesis submission.

For popular articles, you can still use this structure, but it will be less formal, less academic, more flexible. It's important to end your article in such a way that the reader will be clear as to what your point is (see the next section for when articles can get a bit too artsy, which doesn't work for anglophone and world readerships).

It's good to include other voices beyond your own as author. Your opinion is less valuable than you think it is to readers who don't know you. With this in mind, it's good to find a few people who appear to be authorities whom you can quote. For a 1,500-word article, bringing in quotes from two or three authorities will both show the work that you put in and give your argument more weight, since independent people with impressive-sounding pedigrees have said things in support of it. For example, your article might be about how Louis' Lunch is the best burger restaurant in America (my hometown favorite, not that I'm biased). It's one thing for an author to say it. But if you can find a hamburger historian (this is actually a profession, and one that I now wish I had trained for) to back that up, so much the better: "Dr. Pickles von Burgerstein from the University of Hamburg said, 'Louis' Lunch is the best burger in the United States.'" For a shorter article (around eight hundred words), a single external quote is enough.

Do your best to show, rather than tell. This is a general rule in writing, but it goes something like this: Instead of writing, "Louis' Lunch is the best burger in America," you could write, "The line at lunchtime wound around the corner and down the adjacent street—the only question was whether Louis' Lunch would run out of burgers by the time I got inside." The latter sentence is better because (a) it paints a scene, allowing the reader to cinematize the text, and (b) it shows the popularity without stating it directly.

We professors know that students who we can lead to come to their own conclusions will remember things better and longer than they would if we just told them something and asked them to memorize it. It's the same with readers. If I, as a writer, can lay things out in such a way that the reader will come to a conclusion I want them to reach themselves, it's more powerful and effective. The reader is asked to be proactive and is made to feel smart. This is a big key we'll get to in our summary of good writing strategy for books: Your job is to make the reader feel smart. It can start with the basics: Write in such a way that you're laying down a trail of clues for them to solve and thereby reach the conclusion you want them to reach.

In summary, just to be a Ciceronian as possible: Use a hook of an opening, include quotes from authorities, help your reader cinematize your story, be

102   *Chapter 5*

clear in your conclusion what your main point is. Because in some cultural traditions, writing clearly and making the reader feel smart isn't the norm. And those traditions tend not to translate well to anglophone or even global audiences.

ANGLOPHONE VERSUS EUROPEAN ESSAY STYLES

I was once asked to edit the English translation of a collection of essays by leading intellectual and cultural figures from throughout central and eastern Europe. As I read the thirty-odd essays, I at first thought that the translations were flawed. But then I realized that this was not possible, since the essays had been translated by a variety of people, from a variety of languages, from Bulgarian to Serbian to Polish to Slovene. It was not the translators' fault. And yet the majority of the essays—a good 90 percent of them—were all but incomprehensible. The problem was not from word to word. Sentences were for the most part grammatically acceptable, if not strictly correct. The issue was that after having read each essay, I had no idea what the essay was about. What point had the author made, or tried to make? The essays drifted from one idea to the next, without clearly stated theses, without clear conclusions, bereft of any evident buildup of an argument. If asked to summarize in one sentence, the point of each essay, I would be at a loss—and this made me think that the authors themselves would be too. Were these authors "bad" writers? None of their peers seemed to think so. They are all renowned thinkers and writers, at least within their countries of origin. So if these are considered "good" writers, were the essays "badly" written? This was a more complicated question, for I soon realized that the answer was part of a sociocultural phenomenon. From an anglophone perspective, yes: These essays *were* badly written. But from a central European perspective, no: The essays were just fine.

Struck by this, I decided to investigate. Was there really such a difference between what is considered "good" essay writing in the anglophone world, versus central and eastern Europe? This article will examine my findings, while a second, related article, published next month, will go on to discuss teaching styles in the anglophone world versus central and eastern Europe.

Cicero on How to Write

As we mention above, there is a "right" way to write nonfiction essays in English. Americans are taught how to do so in elementary school, and the system used is one that was codified by Cicero, who used it both for writing and for public speaking and debate. Good essays begin with an introduction that clearly states your thesis: What is this essay about, and what is the point you intend to make in it? For example, you can write:

> This essay is a comparison of preferred essay-writing styles in anglophone versus European nonfiction. I will argue that there are two distinct styles at play, and while the anglophone style is considered "good" and acceptable in both anglophone and European contexts, the same is not true for the European style, which is considered "good" and acceptable *only* in Europe.

There you have the thesis of this essay that you are now reading. There is no mistaking what I'm trying to say. Whether you agree or not is a different question, but anyone can read that statement and know what the point of my essay is. Good writing begins with clarity. In the anglophone system, almost all readers should clearly understand *everything* in a good essay the first time through. If something is confusing or unclear, it means that the author wrote poorly. This is not the case in European essays, as we will see.

Good, Ciceronian writing, after a clearly stated introduction and thesis, moves on to make three points in support of the thesis. Three seems to be some magic number, as may be seen with jokes (where the punch line always seems to come in the third attempt at something) or fairy tales (in "Goldilocks and the *Three* Bears" it is the third bowl of porridge that is "just right"). Two points feels too few, and four feels like more than you need. This three-point argument is very basic—in fact, it is taught in elementary school throughout the United States—but it is a useful rule of thumb and point of departure.

In keeping with our old friend Cicero, here are the three points of comparison that I will discuss in this essay: the preferences for (1) anglophone outlining of one's arguments versus European drifting through arguments more organically, (2) anglophone clarity versus European intellectuality, and (3) anglophone arguments through specific anecdotes that practically demonstrate ideas versus European discussion of theories in the abstract.

OUTLINE VERSUS DRIFTING

I live in Slovenia, and so asked a Slovene writer friend about this phenomenon I had noticed. He explained that it is not something I imagined but is based on two different teaching traditions. He described the Franco-Germanic style of university lectures, which dates back many centuries—at least to the Enlightenment—as the origin of the European method still used today. Brilliant thinkers are not always great teachers, and this is a case in point. He mentioned philosopher Jacques Derrida by way of example. Derrida would lecture to university students like this: He would be given a philosophical

104   *Chapter 5*

theme—for instance, "jealousy"—and would be asked to talk about it for ninety minutes. He would have no notes, nothing written beforehand, essentially nothing prepared at all for the immediate task at hand. But he would simply be asked to stand up before the audience and begin speaking about the subject.

No one doubts his genius, but many would argue over whether he was good at conveying his ingenious thoughts to students and readers. He would launch into a lecture that was more akin to theatrical improv than a proper rhetorical argument. Without an outline or plan in mind, he would circle around his subject. Surely there would be nuggets of wisdom within that ninety-minute lecture, but it would be up to the students, frantically taking notes, to scoop up the most important points from the stream-of-consciousness words of the lecture.

By contrast, American professors and essayists are taught to create thorough outlines for their lectures and articles, mapping out ahead of time what they plan to say, when, and how, so that they make the strongest and clearest possible arguments. The chart of good anglophone essays inevitably resembles a straight line, or a constellation in the night sky: Each point made, or star, makes it easier to see the ultimate entirety of the argument at hand. Each point is clearly linked to the previous one and builds to a single, strong conclusion. If we were to chart European-style essays, the chart might resemble a random cluster of stars in the night-sky: Each star is a point that the author makes, but it takes a serpentine route to connect the points, and they do not necessarily build to a single, strong conclusion, but instead drift and sway and wind their way to the end. The strongest point might have been stated somewhere in the middle, where it is in danger of being lost to the reader.

CLARITY VERSUS INTELLECTUALITY

One of the very few Slovenian essayists whose style is considered good by anglophone standards is Miha Mazzini. Ironically, many Slovenes find him too blunt and too direct, almost offensively so—these are exactly the characteristics that make his writing a pleasure for foreigners to read. When I asked him about this discrepancy in style that I had noted, he made a few interesting observations. First, he noted that Slovenes, like most people, have always longed to belong to groups. The group responsible for the longest period of formative cultural influence in Slovenia was the Hapsburg Empire. This means that over the course of centuries, Slovene intellectuals sought to write in the way that the leading imperial authors wrote. Second, Mazzini cited a book by Frank Robert, *The Economic Naturalist*, which explains that many people feel that using exotic, esoteric words makes you look clever. For this reason, Slovene essayists like to employ an abstruse lexicon. This idea that sounding complicated makes you sound clever is not universally shared, however. Most American readers would say that anyone who uses exotic words, like "abstruse lexicon," are overcompensating for a lack of content, and looking up ten-euro words in a thesaurus makes you sound desperate, not clever.

Anglophone professors are taught that their lectures should be entirely clear to every student the first time through. If a student doesn't understand something, that means that the professor has taught poorly and should take the time to explain their point in a different way. In too many European classrooms, the opposite is true. Students are made to feel that they must sit and listen to the professor, and if they didn't understand something, then it must be because they are stupid—not because the professor might have been unclear. They are also discouraged from asking questions, because floating about the room is the implication that you *should* understand everything the first time through, otherwise you are stupid.

European essays, alas, seem to follow this pattern of European teaching. While anglophone essays are all about clarity—every reader should understand clearly everything stated in the essay, otherwise the essayist has failed—one has a sense from too many European essays, particularly those on philosophy or other high-intellectual matters, that the author is *trying* to be complicated. Many European essays I've read, including most of them in the collection I mentioned at the start of this article, left me with the sense that the author was nervous that if the writing were *too* clear, then the author would not sound smart enough. As if writing in a complicated way about complicated things made the author seem smart, that the author was trying hard to sound smarter than the reader. The result for me was that I wasn't even sure the author knew what he wanted to say! Anglophone readers, writers, and students think that this is very silly. The smartest people, and the best writers, are the ones who can make a *complicated* idea seem *simple*, not the other way around. Life, particularly intellectual life, is complicated enough already. The sign of a truly great teacher or writer is the ability to make the multifarious seem straightforward. That is how you teach well, whether to students or readers.

Miha Mazzini points out that Slovene essayists tend to write for what they think their audience expects. "If the state is giving money [to fund a project]," he says, "then some bureaucrat will say yes or no, so we have to look clever and unfathomable. The bureaucrat will say, Wow, I don't understand anything, so it must be science. Here is your money!" But likewise Slovene writers can adapt, and they do. They simply feel that Slovene readers appreciate, and expect, the European model of essay. It takes a conscious effort on the part of the Slovene author to switch to the anglophone style. When they

106 *Chapter 5*

do switch, their writing is as enjoyable to anglophone readers as any—it's just a question of writing to one's audience.

Anecdotes Versus Theories

While we have described what constitutes "good" anglophone writing, there is also a formula for what constitutes the *best* of anglophone essay writing. Read enough articles in leading magazines and newspapers, especially *The New Yorker* and *The New York Times*, and the formula becomes clear. The best essays, by today's popular intelligent periodical standards, are told anecdotally, with narrated stories about real people and events used as a conduit to explain theories or ideas.

People remember interesting anecdotes far more easily than abstract theories. So when you are trying to explain abstract theories, keep in mind that it is easier for other people to ingest them, and remember them, if those theories are "attached" to interesting, memorable anecdotes. The very strongest feature articles begin with a memorable image, introduce a protagonist who is relevant to the topic at hand (a real person who becomes the center of the story), and then follow the protagonist, who serves as a vehicle for explaining the idea behind the article, as he or she undertakes some action that is relevant to the subject at hand.

For example, I am writing an article about how national identity can be achieved through specialty foods, dishes unique to a region. In order to tell the story in the *New Yorker* style, I first introduced a protagonist, Dr. Janez Bogataj, the Slovenian food ethnologist. He is my protagonist. The action relevant to the subject at hand is his effort to get EU recognition and protected status for the special Slovenian sausage Kranjska Klobasa. The story of Bogataj and his lobbying on behalf of Kranjska Klobasa provides a lens through which I can discuss the larger subject of the article: how a nation like Slovenia can become more recognizable internationally through a local food specialty. As Dijon is known for mustard, Bavaria for beer, and Valencia for paella, Slovenia can become known by foreigners for Kranjska Klobasa. Protagonist + action = theoretical argument. Whatever theory is present in the article is fed to the reader through anecdotes and is always as clear as possible.

We mentioned that brilliant people are not always good writers. Philosopher and mathematician Ludwig Wittgenstein was famously incapable of explaining his theories coherently to anyone, even philosopher friends like Bertrand Russell. Georg Hegel is a fine example—no one doubts that he was a genius, but anyone who has tried to read his books will soon realize that the man was a terrible writer. You need a map, a compass, and a tent to hike your way through his dense thickets of prose, and there's still no guarantee

Tips on Article Research and Writing   107

that you'll end up, seven hundred pages later, with any idea what the heck he was talking about.

Hegel fan Slavoj Žižek is another, less extreme example. His books are incredibly dense and difficult to understand. They are also hugely long, and the writing resembles the drifting swirls of Derrida's lectures. But Žižek lecturing live is an entirely different story. His lectures, and especially his short YouTube videos, are far clearer, more fun, and memorable. Žižek is the *only* Slovenian intellectual to achieve world fame and particular popularity in the English-speaking world because however difficult his writing is, his spoken persona is just what the anglophone world likes. He is his own protagonist, a wonderfully odd character with infectious enthusiasm, and he speaks in anecdotes and specifics, and he is particularly good about bringing in pop culture examples to illustrate complex abstract concepts in a way that is as easy as possible for his audience to understand. In this way, Žižek represents a bridge between the two styles: his writing is European, his personal presentations are anglophone.

CONCLUSION

Cicero teaches us that the three points of argument are followed by a conclusion, in which the major points are summarized, the introduction and thesis are reiterated, and an ultimate conclusion is made based on the material covered in the essay. This section is often lacking in European essays, as authors convey a sense that the reader is on his or her own to "get" the point of the essay. Even if the point is clear, it should be reiterated in the conclusion to ensure that those who finish reading feel more enlightened and smarter than they did when they began. That is the main intangible difference between the anglophone and European essays that I read. The reader has a sense in the European essays that the point of the essay is for the author to demonstrate how smart he or she is, often at the expense of readers, who feel confused and dumb by the end if there's anything that they didn't understand. The best anglophone essays demonstrate the intelligence of the author through the clarity of the writing—the author is considered good and smart if *readers* feel smarter after having read the essay than they did before.

While the anglophone writing style is considered good, interesting, engaging, and admirable in both anglophone and European contexts—indeed for readers worldwide—the same is not so for the European style, which does not function well for anglophone readers. Those used to anglophone-style essays find European essays in general boring, slow, difficult to follow, poorly structured, and not much fun to read. There are numerous exceptions to this generalization, but it is, alas, true in the vast majority of cases. Of the

108   *Chapter 5*

thirty-odd essays in the collection I edited recently, only a few of them would
be considered "good" or even readable by intelligent anglophone readers.
Most of them would never find a publisher in the United States or UK unless
they were entirely rewritten to suit the anglophone style. I've read scores of
European-style essays, from throughout central and eastern Europe, and have
found this to be a consistent problem. It is only the European writers who
write in an anglophone style who find popular success in the United States
and UK.

We mentioned that most Slovene writers are entirely capable of writing
in the anglophone style—they simply are not encouraged to do so within the
context of Slovenia. But since the anglophone style is considered "good"
around the world, and the European style has a more limited audience who
appreciate it, it is a wise tactic to choose the anglophone style when in doubt.
For young writers, or veteran authors wishing to find a larger audience
beyond the confines of central and eastern Europe, it is the anglophone style
that they should cultivate, practice, and strive for.

A friend of mine who is an accomplished writer, editor, and teacher was
told by European colleagues that her writing was not good enough to write
academic papers since her articles were "more interesting than scientific." Of
this she said, "My colleagues think that science should not be well written,
we only have to point out facts." It is a sad fact that within Slovenia, scientific
writing is associated with boring writing. Good writing is *always* interesting,
and it must be all the more so when it is scientific or academic. European
essays would find a lot more happy readers if they looked to please the reader
more than the author, to be all-inclusive instead of exclusive, to be interesting
always, and to strive for clarity.

Chapter 6

Story Mapping

Whether you're writing fiction or nonfiction, an article or a book, you are telling a story. The story must inform the reader and entertain them, or at least engage them to a level where it doesn't feel tedious to read. You want tedious? Go read an academic article. There's no rule that something of intellectual merit shouldn't also be engaging to read, even fun. The only people who think that are those who can't write well. You are not one of them.

It can help to think of yourself as a storyteller. The story can be true (nonfiction) or invented (fiction). It can be a means to convey an idea or a story for story's sake. An example of story for story's sake—what might be considered "human interest"—is a *New York Times* feature published on June 15, 2023, called "Hey Dad, Can You Help Me Return the Picasso I Stole?" It's the story of an accidental art theft—a worker at Logan Airport took home a box without knowing what was in it and discovered that it contained a Picasso painting. He then learned that the Boston mob was after the painting and so, of course, was the FBI, since now it was stolen. He had to figure out how to return it without getting arrested or killed.

It's a great story, but it's a story for story's sake. It's meant for you to enjoy reading and think, "Wow, what a story!" It isn't there to convey a big idea or theory or philosophy or to teach you about something. And that's fine.

If this incident were the opening of a book about art theft in America, then the story would become a narrative hook to draw the reader in and then teach them about a subject. That subject can be fun—learning about the criminology of art theft through good stories about heists and chases—but it becomes a way to teach people so that they don't really notice that they're learning in the this-feels-like-work sense. They are entertained and then, by the end of the article or book, they know much more than they did when they began.

110   *Chapter 6*

This is a theme I'll repeat more than once. Your job as a writer is to make your reader feel smart. If your reader feels smart, then you've won. They'll love you. They'll think you're a good writer. They'll want to read more by you. You'll have empowered them.

BIG RULE 1: MAKE YOUR READER FEEL SMART

If you overcomplicate, use thesaurusy words, and present complex ideas in a complex way, your readers will not just dislike your writing but will also dislike you. You'll have made them feel dumb. Rarely will a reader, upon struggling with a text, think, "Man, I'm not smart enough." Instead, they will think, "Man, this writer is so bad they can't even write in a clear way!" or "This writer must not understand their own material if they can't write in a way that's understandable."

Where I live, in central Europe, there's a tradition of, frankly, overcomplicated writing. Long, run-on sentences, paragraphs that go on for a page, assuming an extremely high level of a priori knowledge on the part of the reader (which means that almost nothing is defined, to help the reader out), and so on. I once was interviewed by a literary critic who reasoned that the critic's article should match the level of what he's writing about. If it's fancy literary fiction, his review should be written in a fancy literary voice. This is ridiculous. The last thing I would ever want to do is read an article about a book that's written in the voice of the book. I'm a regular reader of the *London Review of Books*, *The New York Times Book Review*, and *The New York Review of Books*, the most prestigious critical publications in the world, and none write in a complicated manner.

BIG RULE 2: SIMPLICITY AND CLARITY

The mark of a great mind and a great writer is the ability to convey even the most complicated idea in a simple, clear way that 95 percent of readers will understand the first time through.

That's a good Big Rule to write by. You'll never be able to please 100 percent of readers, but aiming for 95 percent being able to understand everything in your book is a good thing to aim for. Part of this is knowing the audience. If you're writing an academic article for peer professors, you don't have to define all terms. But if you're a professor writing a popular magazine article for general readers, you should define all terms that don't feel obvious. This can be tricky to gauge, but it's always better to define too many terms than too few. If I encounter a term or person I already know about, and the author briefly explains what or who they are, I'm never bothered as a reader—I just skim over it and move on. But if I encounter a term or person I'm not familiar with, and the author assumes that I am and doesn't explain the reference, then I'm stuck. I feel dumb but mostly I feel annoyed with the writer for not doing their job properly.

It's tough to know what to define. If I'm writing about the Second World War, it's safe to say that I don't need to explain who Hitler, Churchill, Stalin, or Roosevelt were. But after that, there's no guarantee. I would guess that I don't need to introduce Tito or Mussolini or Emperor Hirohito, but we're already at a level where, depending on the reader, these other major figures might ring a distant bell, but it would still help to briefly explain who they were. Go any deeper (Himmler, Göring, Patton, General Montgomery) and it's safest to be sure the reader is with you, rather than risk losing them.

This explaining can be light and breezy, oh-by-the-way definitions. For example, "It was my first time in Ljubljana, Slovenia's teacup capital city, and I was hungry." I just threw in a potted explanation of what Ljubljana is, in case a reader doesn't know, but did so in a way that is unobtrusive, feels organic (as opposed to being overt exposition), and isn't going to bother someone who already knows what Ljubljana is. It's always better to define more terms and names than too few.

This is linked to Big Rule 1: By defining things, you're ensuring that your reader won't feel dumb for not knowing something when the phrasing of your text suggests that they should. By not making them feel dumb, you make them feel either neutral or smart—and both of these qualify as wins if you're a writer.

Big Rule 2, focus on simplicity and clarity of writing, is also about making the reader feel smart. I don't care how complex a concept is, even if you're writing about chaos theory or bicycle mechanics or neurocognition. The mark of an intelligent person and a good writer is the ability to convey even these challenging ideas in a way that all your readers will understand. The only exception to this rule is in philosophy (but how many people are really reading that for fun?) and for peer-reviewed academic articles and niche academic books. For any text intended to reach a general audience, this rule is hard and fast.

It's an anglophone approach. Much of central Europe has grown up with a pathological fear of not sounding smart enough, and so they subconsciously—I imagine—overcomplicate their texts, reasoning that if a reader can't understand it, then at least they'll think the author must be much smarter than they are. What a stupid tactic. This is a quick way to get worldwide readers to think badly of you. And it's so easy to avoid. Just focus on clarity. Being clear, concise, not repetitive, and simple is *far* more important than any sort of literary fireworks you might want to throw in. Consider writing

112   *Chapter 6*

a text without a single adjective or adverb. Of course you can use them, but avoiding them forces you to keep things simple.

And simple makes your reader feel smart, which makes them think that you're smart. And a great writer.

ABAB STORY STRUCTURE

The million-dollar book proposal mentioned in part 1 of this book, *Moonwalking with Einstein*, uses a structure that I've found works very well with trade nonfiction or fiction. I call it an "ABAB structure." In fiction, it involves creating two parallel storylines that meet around two-thirds of the way through the book and remain together until the end. A straightforward example of this is in Dan Brown's *The Da Vinci Code*.

Chapters alternate, one following the story of an albino assassin working for a secret religious organization, the other following our hero, Robert Langdon, who is called to investigate a bizarre murder in the Louvre that seems somehow symbolically related to Leonardo da Vinci. Let's call the Langdon plot Story A, and the assassin plot Story B.

Odd-numbered chapters (1, 3, 5, etc.) follow Story A, while even-numbered chapters (2, 4, 6, etc.) follow Story B. Brown's writerly trick is that *every* chapter ends with a cliff-hanger. A cliff-hanger is a moment of high tension and drama, usually with someone in mortal peril (as in our hero is hanging by his fingers from a cliff—will he fall?). The resolution of this tension is delayed. In film, we "cut away" from the hero in danger and focus elsewhere, not sure how the danger was resolved until later. The lack of immediate resolution provides a pleasant tension. Cliff-hangers are nothing new, but this is a technique that effectively pummels the reader into reading on when you have every single chapter end with a cliff-hanger. In *The Da Vinci Code*, chapter 1 (Story A) ends with a cliff-hanger that is only resolved when we come back to Story A in chapter 3. Meanwhile, as we read chapter 2 (Story B) we're wondering how the hero got out of the jam from the end of chapter 1. But wait! Chapter 2 (Story B) also ends with a cliff-hanger. Eek! We have to wait for chapter 4, when we get back to Story B, to find out what happened. But meanwhile, we're back to Story A, and we see how our hero escaped certain death—only to be faced with certain death at the end of that chapter too!

It's kind of exhausting just to write about it, and reading it can feel like you're being manipulated by the author. But you know what? It works. We feel like we can't stop reading because there's no pause to exhale at the end of a chapter. We would need to stop reading in the middle of a chapter to catch a breath. Toward the end of *The Da Vinci Code* Robert Langdon comes face-to-face with the albino assassin and the two storylines become one through the climax.

Hats off to Dan Brown, who is no one's idea of a great writer, for using an obvious trick to such winning effect that we recognize that we're being manipulated, but we're having such fun that we don't mind. By the end of the book we think, "Wow, Brown is a really good writer since I couldn't stop reading." In fact, he's a really clever writer.

This same ABAB approach can be used in nonfiction. Here two narrative storylines, both true stories, can be plaited together. Chapters can end with cliff-hangers, provided they are historically accurate since this is nonfiction. But as was the case in *Moonwalking with Einstein,* there's another nonfiction version that works very well.

It involves alternating a narrative "hook" storyline (each chapter of which ends with a cliff-hanger) with informative chapters that teach you things but don't advance a plotline. *Moonwalking with Einstein* is driven along by Story A, in which the author, Joshua Foer, decides he's going to go from a guy who can never find his car keys to a trained memory champion. Story A follows his path, training, and competitions in a narrative, engaging manner where we're invested in his success as a protagonist. Story B, in the even numbered chapters, is a series of short, almost stand-alone essays about aspects of the main subject of this book: memory. There's a chapter on the history of mnemonic (memory developing) techniques, like the memory palace. There's a chapter on the neuroscience of memory. And so on. Each one of these informative chapters could function as a stand-alone article. They are written clearly and well. But they don't have enough drive alone to propel a reader through the book. If this were an academic book on memory, it might consist only of those Story B chapters. But because we have the nonfiction narrative, complete with cliff-hangers, in the Story A chapters, we zip along, content to read the good-for-us information in the even chapters because we're eager to find out in the odd-numbered chapters how Joshua did in his quest.

STORY MAPPING

Whether you are writing fiction or nonfiction, it's useful to map out your story. This involves planning major points of action and drama, incidents along the path of the story you plan to write. You can, of course, just wing it and improvise as you go, but this is not recommended for inexperienced writers—or experienced ones, for that matter. It tends to lead to a text that feels like it's drifting, uncertain. And without knowing what will happen next, at least to some extent, you can't insert things like foreshadowing that make a text far richer.

114 *Chapter 6*

I find that mapping by hand works better for me than on a computer. Using software is easy, but there's a tendency to want to use the order in which you first write things down. There's also something more thoughtful and organic about the analog use of pencil or pen on paper.

I like to take an oversized blank sheet of paper and write out, intentionally in no particular order, key moments, incidents, actions, or set pieces that I plan to include. If you're telling a true story you can write these out chronologically, but it isn't necessary to do so. When I was writing *Stealing the Mystic Lamb*, I mapped out thirteen criminal incidents or misadventures that befell Jan van Eyck's *Adoration of the Mystic Lamb* painting. Each one would become a work package, or a chapter that I would write. But I didn't have to write them in the order in which they happened, nor did my book have to be chronologically oriented. You can jump around in time. For example, maybe it's best to open the book with the most exciting of all the incidents (the near destruction of the altarpiece during the Second World War, or the theft of one panel from it in 1934), then once that hook has been established, go back to the beginning.

For fiction, it's especially useful to map out of order. You might envision a set piece of, say, a chase through the canals of Venice. That's one item on your map, but you don't yet know who is chasing whom, and where it will come in the story. So just write it down briefly, as a reminder to yourself, and move on. Maybe you can picture a sword fight on the roof of the Houses of Parliament in London? Don't worry about where it goes and who is dueling yet. Just jot down the idea on your mind map. You can also include character elements as mind map notes, or title ideas for your book—anything relevant. Think of it as a commonplace book, a cluster of ideas that you can see all on one surface, without the need to scroll or flip pages. I like to use a color-coding system, preferably with one of those multicolor clicky pens. Blue could be plot points, red could be character notes, green could be turns of phrase you like the sound of—whatever you like. The idea is to outline first (as described in the previous chapter) because this is so helpful to writing clear, well-considered texts.

Don't remain married to every idea you have. It is empowering to opt out of some things that seemed like a good idea before. Perhaps you bump them to some other project. Or just cut them altogether. I have two ideas for books: One is on colossal artworks, where size is the key "wow" factor. The other is about what is arguably the most influential sculpture ever made, *Laocoon and His Sons*, an ancient marble statue at the Vatican. I thought to connect these two ideas by writing about a colossal statue that I'm quite obsessed with, *The Apennine Colossus* by Giambologna, a follower of Michelangelo. I also once wrote an article about the Colossus of Rhodes, so I threw that in as well. And I also thought to write a popular biography of Michelangelo. I

Story Mapping 115

mind mapped all these ideas on one sheet. But I'm not sure they all fit in the same book. That's OK. It helps me see, envision, and decide when I see it all out there on one sheet.

When it comes to actually writing, I like to use the same mind map in two ways. First, I play connect the dots (in pencil, so I can change my mind) to link up what happens when. I use arrows to go from one note to the next. I also might link up a setting that I think would be cool to use (like the roof of the Houses of Parliament) with an event in the story that I'd like to incorporate (a sword fight). So I'll connect the note on the location with the note on the event, and I've got a sword fight on the roof planned out—a scene to write.

Once I have my mind map clustered into scenes, I move on to the next preparatory step.

In addition to connecting the ideas on the mind map into scenes and then linking them with arrows, to put them in a possible order for the plot, I'll also place two small blank squares next to each scene I plan to write. When I've drafted the scene, I'll check off the first blank square. When I've written a second draft, I'll check off the second one.

It's super satisfying to check off these boxes. They provide a sense of accomplishment, a feeling of working toward the goal, and they slice up the seemingly huge project of writing a whole book into feasible, bite-sized pieces. When you use them, your mind map transforms into a practical worksheet that also maps your progress toward the finish line.

You can use a similar approach with mapping characters, too, whether fictional or real.

CHARACTER MAPPING

I use mind maps for characters as well as for plot and story structure. I got the idea from Dungeons & Dragons, the dice-based role-playing game of the 1980s that I'm just old enough to have grown-up playing. Players create imaginary *Lord of the Rings*–style characters who they will "play" in a spoken-word adventure designed by a Dungeon Master, a narrator who designs the adventure and its obstacles that the players, each with their own imagined character, will encounter. Players fill out character sheets, which include physical and mental attributes (intelligence, strength, dexterity) that are determined by rolling dice. They also can be equipped with weapons and armor, spells, magical items, and personal characteristics that aren't critical to game play but that make it more vivid and fun.

I do a version of these character sheets for my books. If the book is fiction, everything is invented. If it's nonfiction, the "characters" are historical or contemporary real people with attributes, qualities, and quirks already present. If one of my characters in a nonfiction book is Abraham Lincoln, say, the character sheet can include his unusually tall height, the beard he developed when he turned to politics to look more serious and older, his early work as a rail-splitter, the trauma of losing his son, and so on. If it's a work of fiction, I'll want to invent character details that may or may not be directly referenced in my book. But if I'm cognizant of them, they will subtly make their way into the text. For example, let's say that I design a character who had a formative trauma in which she was bitten by a spider while at summer camp. I might not state this in the text, but I would know it as I write the book, and I might make her skittish around spiders, so that the reader will infer that she's afraid of them, and further infer that this may have come from an early trauma involving one.

You can make Dungeons & Dragons–style character sheets, or you can use your mind map to note down character traits that you think would be quite cool to incorporate, and only later decide which traits will be applied and to which character. Want someone arachnophobic but not sure who yet? No problem, just jot down "afraid of spiders" and you'll later decide how to use that. Think it would be cool to have a character proficient in capoeira? Note it down and you'll later decide which character it should be.

Character maps can become character sheets if you want to be that organized. Or they can remain maps with some arrows linking who is who, just to gently fix the concept in your mind before you start writing.

I've sometimes encountered real-life characters so larger than life that if you read about them, you would assume they were fictional. I've got a real-life friend who was a covert agent engaged in black ops for a major government, was trained by the secret police, joined the French Foreign Legion, and was also world champion of an illegal cage-fighting ring. If I read that I'd assume this was a made-up character, but he's actually a real-life Jason Bourne type. I'd still have trouble convincing a reader that he's real because his true story is so outrageous.

The more common problem is how to make a character, whether fictional or real, stand out on the page and enter the memory of the reader, not just blend into the scenery or meld with other characters in your book. There are a few quick tricks to doing this.

First is to decide how extensive a name to give your character. We readers understand that if you the writer tell us a character's full name—first name and last name—this is someone important to the story whom we should remember. It's like pushing a pin in the name and affixing it among the Main Characters in our imagined cast list for the story. The next level down is when you call a character by one name (either first name or last name). We readers interpret this to mean that the character is of mid-to-low-level importance.

Story Mapping

They serve a function and we'll see them in more than one scene, but they aren't among the main characters. The lowest level is a character who isn't named at all, but is just described, often by their occupation: the policeman, the woman in blue, a lawyer, and so on. These unnamed characters are like pawns on the chessboard. They're mostly scenery dressing, of no importance to the overall plot, just filling out the scene and not reappearing elsewhere.

The only characters you'll want to make feel more three-dimensional are those whom the reader needs to pin in their memory. It's good to have a reasonable number of such characters. If you have one hundred, it's too much for one book. *War and Peace* aside, you don't want to have so many characters that your reader needs a cast list to remember who's who. It's easiest for the reader to focus on one, two, three, maybe four protagonists—main characters, and probably fewer than twenty other named characters whom they're meant to picture vividly and recall. Those numbers aren't fixed, just an estimate, but one to keep in mind.

The writing rule of show don't tell is the case with building character if that character gets enough space in your book to show who they are in such a way that the reader will understand their depth. If a character appears only for three pages, then it might be hard to squeeze in showing their personality traits and backstory. So you can occasionally tell, but the clunkiest way to do so is to have your narrative voice state it plainly. Better to have a character mention it, if it must be told rather than shown. Here is an example:

Let's say we want to convey that a character, we'll call her Ella, has a neurotic level of obsessive-compulsive behavior, is afraid of spiders, and is a former secret agent. The most leaden way to convey that is for me to write, "Ella, a former secret agent, was known to her colleagues as suffering from a comedic level of OCD and for freaking out every time she saw a spider." That's OK, but clumsy. One step better would be to convey this in dialogue:

"Psst, Jamie, have you seen the new boss, Ella?"

"Yeah. We met when she called me into her office, because she'd been cornered by a daddy longlegs and asked me to remove it for her. I guess former secret agents aren't as tough as I thought."

"I spotted her arranging all the pencils in her desk drawer by length. I think we're in for a rough few months with her in charge."

In this example, I put the exposition into dialogue, and it comes across as less expositiony. But the best of all would be to, over the course of many pages (so it doesn't feel squished in) show Ella arranging her pencils, and cowering from a daddy longlegs, and doing something secret agentish that we, as readers, "observe" through the story, rather than seeing it stated directly.

118   *Chapter 6*

The shorthand for conveying a three-dimensional character, fictional or real, is to pick three details about them, their personality, preferences, profession, or backstory, the Venn diagram of which creates a unique character. When I teach I have my students do this for themselves. Here's what my character diagram might look like, with three fun facts about me that are unusual:

> Noah was (a) a top-level squash player in high school, (b) he won a playwrighting contest in college, and (c) always wears a silver ball-bearing wallet chain that he received for his sixteenth birthday—it's his most notable affectation, and he even wore it with his wedding suit.

If you were to map this as a Venn diagram, you'd put each attribute in one circle (squash, playwrighting, wallet chain). There are plenty of people in the world who were very good at squash, plenty who won playwrighting contests, and plenty who still wear wallet chains (even the exotic ball-bearing kind and even though it's no longer the 1990s), but the union of the three is me. There is likely almost no one who embodies all three of these attributes. Thus, I'm made to appear three-dimensional.

It's funny because every real human being is a three-dimensional person with all sorts of quirks and unique attributes. The problem is when you have to make them *feel* real just by writing about them. In that case, consider using this rule of three as a shortcut to creating three-dimensional-seeming characters—even when they're actually real people.

STORY STRUCTURES

Books can take all sorts of forms. But if you're just starting out, it's wisest to gain experience in a more straightforward format, because the weird ones really only work well in the hands of the masters. How long it takes to really get into the writing groove depends on you and how you work. The cliché about needing 10,000 hours of practice to achieve mastery depends on how you use those 10,000 hours, but when I think back on my own writing career, it was probably at around the 10,000-hour mark of writing that things really clicked. I felt a lurch into a new gear and was suddenly able to sit and write thousands of words in a day that were usable, if not great. It's been smooth sailing since then.

But on your way to your own level of mastery, it can be useful to consider basic story structures to follow. Story structures are frameworks that outline the way a narrative is organized. Different structures can guide writers in developing their plots and characters.

Story Mapping 119

The simplest is a three-act structure, which traditionally was used in theatrical plays. We can use the term "act" even for prose, because it's really just a synonym for a part of the story.

Act 1 is the "setup." We meet the characters, get to know the setting and the "rules" associated with it (if it's Middle Earth, we need to know what sort of creatures live there, if it's the Galapagos Islands when Darwin was visiting, well, we need to know what sort of creatures live there). We also are introduced to the main conflict: What is the action we are witnessing, the quest, the obstacle to overcome?

Act 2 is the "confrontation." The protagonist faces obstacles that deepen the conflict as the protagonist works toward their goal.

Act 3 sees the "resolution." The obstacle is overcome (or not), there is a climax to the action, and it is resolved—happily, if this is a comedy, or unhappily but with catharsis if this is a tragedy (or unhappily and with flying body parts, if this is a zombie horror story).

Many writers have weighed in on what makes for good stories. I admire and highly recommend Stephen King's *On Writing*, a book that most writers I know consider the go-to manual. While it is not a book about how to write, a key book on how to look at stories is Joseph Campbell's *The Hero with a Thousand Faces* (1949), which describes a structure found in innumerable world myths, the "monomyth." He calls it the "hero's journey" and it consists of twelve stages:

1. "Ordinary World"—The hero's normal life before the adventure.
2. "Call to Adventure"—The hero is presented with a challenge.
3. "Refusal of the Call"—The hero hesitates to accept the challenge.
4. "Meeting the Mentor"—The hero meets a guide.
5. "Crossing the Threshold"—The hero commits to the adventure.
6. "Tests, Allies, and Enemies"—The hero faces challenges and meets friends and foes.
7. "Approach to the Inmost Cave"—The hero prepares for the central challenge.
8. "Ordeal"—The hero faces a major crisis.
9. "Reward (Seizing the Sword)"—The hero achieves a victory.
10. "The Road Back"—The hero begins the return journey.
11. "Resurrection"—The hero faces a final test.
12. "Return with the Elixir"—The hero returns home transformed.

That may seem awfully formulaic, but it's amazing how many stories, myths, films, and novels follow it. It's also totally fine, even a good idea, to use it as a template for your own writing if you aren't otherwise sure how to structure your story, particularly if it's a novel. For someone new to writing,

120   Chapter 6

it works well because you can mind map your story and then slip in your character and ideas into these twelve steps.

The hero's journey was simplified by television writer and director Dan Harmon into eight steps, which he calls the "Story Circle." This isn't substantially different from Joseph Campbell's construction, but it feels more modern and more easily applicable to stories that don't involve swordsmen, magic, and monsters. It goes like this:

1. "You"—The protagonist in their comfort zone.
2. "Need"—The protagonist desires something.
3. "Go"—The protagonist enters an unfamiliar situation.
4. "Search"—The protagonist adapts and faces challenges.
5. "Find"—The protagonist gets what they wanted.
6. "Take"—The protagonist pays a price for their goal.
7. "Return"—The protagonist returns to their comfort zone.
8. "Change"—The protagonist has transformed.

This eighth step is important. Readers want to see the protagonist changed in some way by the end of the story. If the protagonist is exactly where they started, the entire journey of the story feels like a waste. Consider how the protagonist will change (emotionally, physically, circumstantially) and what will bring about that change. This requires deciding how the protagonist begins to understand how wherever they end is different from their start. It could be mild-mannered Bilbo Baggins not wanting to go on an adventure but being recruited as a burglar to join a treasure-hunting party of dwarves in *The Hobbit.* And by the end, Bilbo has become the hero. Change must happen to the protagonist. This is perhaps the only fixed rule. Without that change (ideally a change for the better), the story will feel unsatisfying.

These structures provide writers with various frameworks to construct their stories, each offering unique strengths for different types of narratives. Just about the only formula in which characters don't change at the end of the episode is in the television sitcom. Part of the appeal of this format is that every episode, we get them roughly back where they started—and we like it there. The Simpsons are always the same age, and whatever happens during an episode, the next episode is right back at the drawing board. There are some sitcoms that have storylines developing over seasons, like *The Office* or *Brooklyn Nine-Nine* (two of my favorites). But from episode to episode the characters don't really develop. It's only over the course of an entire show that we see change, such as Michael Scott in *The Office* going from an annoying but secretly sweet boss to a sweet boss who still has annoying moments, or from Jake Peralta of *Brooklyn Nine-Nine* going from being an energetic man-child who never brushes his teeth to an energetic man-child

Story Mapping 121

who never brushes his teeth but is in a loving marriage and is a great father to his newborn son.

THE SITCOM CODE

A version of this article was published way back in 2014 in *The Atlantic* magazine, and it remains the article of mine about which I receive the most emails. It's hard to believe that I hit on something that still helps people, whether they are just enjoying televisual entertainment or trying to write for it. I include an updated version of the article here, because it is relevant to our discussion of deconstructing texts, breaking stories into slices that we can map and plan out. This happens to be for television sitcoms, a highly specific medium that follows a template, but learning how to see this form for what it really is will open your eyes to other media and formats.

As happens to so many of us, I was asked to write a sitcom for Croatian television. I'm an American expat living in Slovenia, and I know next to nothing about Croatia, besides the fact that it is Slovenia's southern neighbor, a fellow ex-Yugoslav republic, and that their language resembles Slovene accept with a lot more *j*'s in it. I am a writer of books and articles, and I used to write a lot of plays, but I've never written for television. So I immediately said, "Sure, of course I can do that," before rushing off to google "how to write a sitcom."

In addition to much googling, I spent a good deal of time watching sitcoms. I was after tips on how they are constructed, and I watched actively, looking to crack open their laugh-tracked shiny exterior to get at the goopy mechanism within, to see how they functioned. What I found out surprised me and changed the way that I watch television.

From *The Simpsons* to *Seinfeld*, from *Everybody Loves Raymond* to *Everybody Hates Chris*, from *Taxi* to *Arrested Development* to *Parks and Recreation*, there is a highly specific, minute-by-minute recipe used to write the vast majority of sitcoms out there. And once you know the formula, it makes it much easier to write them, and much harder to watch them without seeing that formula, the "sitcom code," everywhere you look.

My giddy-panicked googling actually produced fruitful results. With little idea as to where I should begin, I turned to the confidence-inspiring blog *Wise Sloth*, whose author, like me, has no TV writing experience, and which provided a fifteen-page breakdown of sitcom formats, which I used as a point of departure for my own study. And by study, I mean hopping into my pajamas, cuddling up to my Peruvian hairless, and watching TV with a notebook in hand. My *Atlantic* colleague Talib Visram recently wrote about his experience counting jokes per minute in favorite TV shows. My approach was more

122   *Chapter 6*

deconstructionist, and directly applicable to my new gainful employment. I had to figure out how such shows were built, and fast.

The answer presented itself very quickly.

First of all, word-processing programs often come with screenwriting templates. FinalDraft, the most popular software for those penning scripts, even has a sitcom template, which of course makes life much easier. But as for how to construct an episode, various bloggers, from the Wise Sloth to helpful folks at the BBC, noted a basic structure that I immediately recognized in *every* sitcom episode I tested. This structure is so formulaic that you would think it would suck the fun out of writing and watching such shows, but it does nothing of the sort. Instead it changes the way I watch TV, but only increases my admiration for the good writers who do so much within relatively strict confines.

To demonstrate how this "Sitcom Code" works, I've chosen an episode of a favorite show, somewhat at random, because it ideally exemplifies the template: episode 4 of season 1 of *Parks and Recreation.*

The Sitcom Code breaks down what needs to happen in each episode, by the minute. As Dan Richter of Demand Media notes, "Sitcoms, minus commercials, are typically 22 minutes longer [with] a script of 25–40 pages. Every sitcom episode has a main plot (story A), as well as one or two subplots (stories B and C)." There are three main acts, divided by two commercial breaks (in most American TV), with 3–5 scenes per act. One of the distinguishing characteristics of sitcoms, as opposed to other forms of television, is that the main protagonist(s) barely change from one episode to the next, let alone from season to season (Maggie Simpson has been sucking on a pacifier for nearly thirty years). Therefore whatever happens in the episode, the situation must end largely where it began. The Wise Sloth points out that 22 minutes is "not even really time enough to tell a full story. The whole story has to be on fast-forward," so simplification is key.

Poet Philip Larkin described all plots as "a beginning, a muddle, and an end," which is as good a description as any. Each episode begins with the protagonist stating a goal or problem that must be solved, and which we understand will be solved by the end of the episode. If the problem is solved too quickly, then the episode won't stretch out to 22 minutes, so the first attempt at reaching the goal or solving the problem must fail ("the muddle"), requiring a new approach, before the episode ends and the protagonist either does, or does not, achieve what they set out to do. The goal might be Homer trying to make a fortune by selling recycled grease in *The Simpsons*, or Job Bluth setting out to sabotage the family's banana stand in *Arrested Development*, or the *Seinfeld* crew looking for where they parked in a vast lot. Another hallmark of sitcoms is that the protagonists frequently fail, and we often want them to, because we do not want our favorite characters to change too much.

Story Mapping 123

If Leslie Knope ever left Pawnee for a career as a DC politician, we would be distraught. If Kramer got married and moved to the suburbs—whoa now!

When writers sit around and prepare a new episode, many literally map out what will happen, minute by minute, in the main storyline and substorylines, filling in jokes later. Let's see how this played out in the *Parks and Recreation* episode entitled "Boys' Club."

The Teaser (Minutes 1–3)

A short, introductory sketch that often runs before the credits. It is little more than a setup, delivery, and reaction: a single joke. It introduces the protagonist and shows some aspect of their personality (for viewers new to the show), and ideally it introduces viewers to the main obstacle to be overcome in the episode. But as often as not, it is simply a quick joke to get the ball rolling.

Leslie Knope and her assistant, Tom Haverford, arrive at a park where they are checking on reports that kids are having fights with dog poo. The rumors are confirmed. Noble Tom hides in the car, while moral Leslie first tries to confront the kids, is fired on with a barrage of dog poo, and then fires back, admitting that this actually is a lot of fun. We see Leslie's role as a local government authority, and her strong (but porous) moral stance—morality as steel sieve.

The Trouble (Minutes 3–8)

We meet the protagonist(s) and see that they are just where we left them last episode, but a new problem or goal has come to their attention, which forms the main plot (Story A) of the episode. A plan must be made as to how the goal is to be achieved, or the problem overcome. Around the 6th minute we might be introduced to a subplot (Story B). Subplots must be even briefer than the main plots, and feature one of the minor or secondary characters. It's great if the subplot can somehow link to the ultimate conclusion of the main plot, but this is not necessary. Think of each subplot as a main plot in miniature, likewise with a beginning, a muddle, and the end.

Trouble arrives in the form of a gift basket of wine and cheese that Leslie thinks is a bribery attempt from a local firm. She reprimands her colleagues for wanting to dive into the basket's goodies. They complain that she's a Goody Two-shoes, and we see her as self-righteous—a beautiful setup for a fall. We also see the Boys' Club: Every Tuesday some guys in another government department drink beers in the courtyard, including Mark, who Leslie has a crush on. She grabs her friend Ann and determines to "shatter the glass ceiling" by infiltrating this men's club. They are welcomed immediately, and join the fun, but they quickly run out of beer. Trying to keep the party rolling

124   *Chapter 6*

and impress Mark, Leslie breaks open the gift basket that she had previously sequestered and opens the bottles of wine. Trouble will surely follow.

The Muddle (Minutes 8–13)

The plan drawn up a few minutes ago to tackle the main plot is put into action, but it can't work—otherwise the episode would be over already. There must be another obstacle, a spanner in the works that requires an alternative plan or some amusing delay to the success of the initial strategy. As the Wise Sloth writes, the characters must "confront these obstacles according to their own personal style," meaning that Leslie will approach the problem with her boundless enthusiasm for government and abiding by rules that the little girl inside her sometimes wants to break. With subplots in play, minutes 8–9 establish where we left off with Story A. Minutes 9–12 provide the middle muddle of Story B (the secondary character overcomes a minor obstacle toward their goal), and then minutes 12–13 return to Story A, and see the main plan diverted.

Distraught at having broken the code of ethics that she so firmly sought to uphold, Leslie confesses to her colleagues. We are then introduced to Story B, in which a secondary character, Andy, despite his leg being in a cast and his slovenly personality, plots to secretly surprise girlfriend Ann by cleaning the house, and himself, while she is at work. Back at the Parks and Rec office, Leslie "whistle blows herself" and confesses to her boss, Ron, who merely tells her not to make a big deal of the situation. This could be the end of the show, but it is coming too soon. Where's that spanner? Back at Story B, we see Andy hobbling along and cleaning the house, then throwing the garbage in the neighboring pit that has been a recurrent theme of past episodes. And then there's the spanner: Underage intern April is bored at work and films herself drinking leftover gift basket wine, then puts the video on the official, Leslie-sanctioned website of the aforementioned pit. Ron confronts Leslie, who is now called before the disciplinary committee.

The Triumph/Failure (Minutes 13–18)

By this time, the protagonist is getting desperate and the stakes are high— they've already tried once and failed. They turn to a last resort, put it into play, and it works . . . or it doesn't. Remember that failure is frequent and fine in the world of sitcoms, unlike feature films and dramas. Failure is humorous rather than frustrating, because we don't want our characters to change. Minutes 13–15 reestablish the action of Story A, but pause before the payoff of whether the backup plan will work. Minutes 15–17 conclude Story B: the secondary character either does, or does not, accomplish what they set out to

Story Mapping 125

do, and this may, or may not affect the outcome of Story A. Minutes 17–18 show whether the protagonist succeeds or fails in Story A.

Ron sits beside Leslie at the disciplinary committee hearing. Leslie reads out a passionate confession. Meanwhile, back at Story B, Andy cleans himself in a kiddie pool, but a neighbor steals his boom box. Naked and soapy, he gives chase. Returning to Story A, Ron defends Leslie against the committee. His anti-government, anarchic stance (despite working for the government) gets her out of a jam. His intervention means that Leslie will only receive a letter in her file and will not be fired. Leslie confesses to Ann that she opened the gift basket not just to "shatter the glass ceiling" and allow women into a boys' club but because she has a crush on Mark. Story A is resolved, as is Story B. Ann returns home to a clean house and clean Andy, who has succeeded in his goal, despite the mini muddle of the neighbor stealing his boom box. He announces to us that he will "get gently laid tonight."

The Kicker (Minutes 19–21)

Like the teaser intro segment before the credits, there is usually an "outro" (sometimes while the credits are rolling), which shows the protagonist in the aftermath of that episode's action. We find it comforting to see that nothing has really changed, and life has reset, back to where it started and primed for the next episode. It might end with a nice punch line at the end that brings back a joke from earlier in the episode.

In "The Old Boys Club," the kicker is not a joke but a propulsion into the next episode, fleshing out the budding romance between Mark and Leslie. Mark brings Leslie a beer at her office, after hours, saying, "Welcome to the team." She is in the boys' club, and Mark may reciprocate her feelings for him. Roll the credits.

This deconstructionist approach to sitcoms was truly helpful when it came time to write my own, as I had minute-by-minute slots to fill and a strong idea of this endlessly successful and recycled series of plot arcs. But I still had to write the darn thing. The Croatian public were waiting.

Next time you settle in to watch a sitcom, keep this code in mind, and an eye on your stopwatch. You'll be amazed at how tight and to the minute the formula is, yet you'll marvel at the variety that TV writers conjure within this straitjacket literary form. Now, I'd better start googling "what Croatians find funny."

Chapter 7

Writing Tips (and What to Avoid)

Book proposals and mind maps help you to conceptualize your book. But what about individual characters? We've talked about how to develop them, to make them appear three-dimensional to your reader—even if they are real people, they must read as three-dimensional via your text. One way to help is to develop a character sheet. I borrowed this idea from Dungeons & Dragons, but you don't need twenty-sided dice and a character who is a half-elf ranger called Finnegan Arrowhand to find character sheets useful. Here is a character sheet for one of my own inventions, the protagonist of my only published novel, *The Art Thief*, to see what a character sheet might look like. You can then make your own for primary or secondary characters in your own book, whether it's fiction or nonfiction. If it's nonfiction, research will tell you how to fill out the sheet. If it's fiction, you can do whatever you like. Remember that you don't really need to mention all the characteristics that you've designed. Sometimes just knowing them yourself will result in a beautifully subtle inflection of them in the text. For instance, my character below is Catholic, but I don't need to say that. I can just describe him at some point genuflecting in front of an altar in a church and his religion will be implied.

CHARACTER SHEET

Full name: Gabriel Coffin
Age when story begins: 44
Distinctive physical characteristics: Salt-and-pepper beard, dresses formally whenever out
Country of birth: USA
Residence when story begins: Rome

Languages spoken: English, Italian, French, Spanish, German

Education: PhD in the study of art theft, police academy graduate, art academy

Names of important relatives: Jacob Coffin (father)

Names of important friends: Daniela Vallombroso (girlfriend)

Profession and professional history: freelance art crime specialist investigator working primarily for the Italian Carabinieri, but behind the scenes he's an art forger and thief

Socioeconomic status: upper middle class

Ethnicity and religion: Caucasian, born Jewish, he converted to Catholicism for the art

Favorite things: painting, Caravaggio, Rome, the puzzle exercise of planning crimes and the delight in solving them, cappuccinos from Tazza d'Oro in Rome, Da Luigi restaurant in Rome

Dislikes: salty, bony fish

Distinctive abilities: highly proficient in canne de combat (stick fighting)

Quirks and affectations: strongly opposed to violence that involves bloodshed much less death, so when obliged to turn to violence, seeks to subdue opponents, and uses a gun loaded with rubber bullets

Now try your hand at making your own character sheet. A good exercise is to make one for yourself, to consider which attributes of yours might make for the most vivid representation of you as a character in a book.

DON'TS AND DOS

Over the years I've taught writing for publication courses, both solo and with editors. There are some standard tips that seem to always be useful and applicable, and that I sometimes need to remind myself of, even now that I'm past twenty published books. What follows are 12 things to do and 12 things to avoid when writing.

DON'T

1. **Don't allude to things**—state them.
2. **Don't discuss what you are going to do**—do it. For example, don't write, "In this book, I will. . . ." Just do it.
3. **Don't jump around to different topics and times**—address each point clearly and in full before moving on to the next point. When you

move the multiple mentions of the same topic in different paragraphs together, it shows how much repetition there is.

4. **Don't write in a way that sounds too much like you're giving a talk.** There are several elements that can make the text too lecture-room-like, rather than for the page. Avoid first person plural where possible (avoid "we see that" or "now we turn to"), don't comment on what the book is going to do (avoid "in this chapter we will"), don't overuse rhetorical questions (avoid phrases like "But was it really too late?"), don't include anecdotal asides that don't offer new information (avoid "Incidentally, New Haven is also the US pizza capital").

5. **Don't describe too much.** Writing about art is most boring when it is describing art. It's the same for any topic. Use your subject as a lens through which to discuss everything around it. Keep descriptions to a minimum and assume that readers will see an image of the object anyway, if it isn't fictitious. Most readers will search online for anything they can't picture, and describing too much slows down the reading experience.

6. **Don't keep anything that makes your eyes glaze over when you reread.** If your eyes glaze over and you want to skip over any section, that is a sign that it is boring and should be removed.

7. **Don't jump around to different authorial voices**, even if the book is coauthored. Readers are most comfortable with a single authorial voice per book (the exceptions are fiction with multiple narrators or edited nonfiction volumes). The style of writing needs to be more consistent in order for the reader not to feel disoriented. Write the whole book in a continuous voice.

8. **Don't mix colloquial and formal/academic language.** The tone should remain consistent (midway between the two is ideal, depending on what your topic is and who your intended audience is).

9. **Don't use too many adjectives and adverbs.** Descriptive words are useful when implemented selectively and only when necessary. Only bother describing distinctive, important elements. If someone is "medium height with no distinguishing features" then we don't even need to know that—it has told us nothing (unless your point is how generic and uninteresting the character looks).

10. **Always illustrate theory.** Theory alone is boring and difficult to grasp. Start with an anecdote that proves a point and then circle back to cast a net of theory over it, rather than presenting theory first and then examples.

11. **Don't jump around and circle back.** On the page, it's easier to read and follow when topics do not jump around between examples—for example, avoid "and that brings us back to," and similar wording.

130   *Chapter 7*

12. **Don't assume that what you wrote in your first draft is ready for publication.** Ask for the opinions of other people who will read and honestly tell you what could be better. Not even the best authors produce perfection in their first drafts. Expect to do many drafts, of whole manuscripts or parts of them. If you go into it expecting to have to do, say, at least three drafts before it's ready for showtime, it will be easier for you.

DO

1. **The title can be artsy and abstract but do pick a subtitle that should tell you exactly what you're getting in the book.** Fiction doesn't have subtitles, so you can choose whatever you like, but it should be memorable (naming a novel after its main character is not memorable unless the book is already famous and the main character iconic).
2. **Write out clearly, in one to two sentences, the argument you are making in your book.** Ask yourself, Why am I writing this? Why should someone bother reading it? What is the main idea that I hope readers will come away with (being entertained and learning some historical facts is not sufficient)? How does this book differ from others on a similar topic? Keep the answer in mind throughout the writing, but especially the editing, process.
3. **Write out a single paragraph (one to four sentences) about why each chapter or case study is important to the overall argument of the book.** That paragraph can be your introduction to each chapter, but it also forces you to ask yourself, Do I need to include this? Is this important? Does this benefit the overall argument of my book, or is it an add-on?
4. **Throughout, ask yourself whether each section adheres to your cohesive narrative or argument.** To do this, once you've written the whole book, go back and write short summaries to each chapter, linking the chapter's contents back to the original argument of the book. If any chapter or case study struggles to support to core argument, consider removing it.
5. **With each case study, ask yourself why** you are including it in this particular chapter, and what its inclusion tells the reader. This will help draw together the narrative thread of the book, which still feels loose and bitty.
6. **Cite everything as you go**, even if you might remove citations later on. It is always easier to trim citations than to go back through and search for your sources.

Writing Tips (and What to Avoid) 131

7. **Keep a running bibliography as you go** so you needn't make one later. Also keep a running acknowledgments page so you don't forget anyone.
8. **Less but more detailed, fresh, and relevant information** is better than lots of bits of information, which can be tiring to read, like a list of events.
9. **Stick to your main story or stories.** Throwing in fun facts or extra bits rarely improves and often distracts from the focal story you are telling.
10. **Flesh out any character who is worth introducing**, even with a few words, choosing what makes him or her most colorful and memorable for the reader.
11. **Include as much specific detail as possible**—dates, names, and places. It will not do to be vague and refer to "recently" or "thousands of years"—this sounds like you don't know exactly when. "A city" is less interesting than "Boston," and someone "eating breakfast" is less interesting than someone "eating toast cut on a diagonal with peanut butter and sliced pear."
12. **Stop chapters at cliff-hangers** to force the reader to . . .

Chapter 8

The Importance of Great Openings

This book is about beginnings: how to get published, in most cases for the first time if you've bought a book on how to get published. There are other good books on writing, but I've never come across a book like this one on how to get started. We've mentioned how important the start of your text is, whether it's a proposal, article, or book. It colors the way your reader will think about everything they read next in your text. It's like the saying "You never get a second chance to make a first impression." So it is with an editor or reader reading the first words of a new author's text. If we were to make a pie chart of the time you should be spending in deep thought about what to write and polishing that writing, your first sentence, first paragraph, first page, and first chapter should receive the biggest piece of literary pie. The first sentence is like your fishing lure, to hook the reader's attention and enthusiasm to read on. That enthusiasm should grow through the first paragraph, and at the end of the first page, they should be eager to turn to the next one. Your first chapter, which may be your writing sample, should lay a foundation of positive thoughts in the reader about this book and its writer. And if you can end your first chapter with a cliff-hanger—actual or metaphorical (with a question and therefore tension raised and not yet resolved)—you've won.

This chapter looks at some examples of good openings. As with the rest of this book, I'm using my own examples, not because I think they're any better than those of many fellow writers, but because I didn't need to ask anyone's permission to reproduce the texts. However, for educational purposes, I can quote short bits of text, if properly cited, so while most of this book includes examples I've written, here are some famous first lines of books or articles that exemplify this idea of the first line begging the reader to read on.

134 *Chapter 8*

"It was a bright cold day in April, and the clocks were striking thirteen."

—*1984* by George Orwell

"It was the best of times, it was the worst of times, it was the age of wisdom, it was the age of foolishness, it was the epoch of belief, it was the epoch of incredulity, it was the season of Light, it was the season of Darkness, it was the spring of hope, it was the winter of despair, we had everything before us, we had nothing before us, we were all going direct to Heaven, we were all going direct the other way."

—*A Tale of Two Cities* by Charles Dickens

"You don't know about me without you have read a book by the name of *The Adventures of Tom Sawyer*; but that ain't no matter."

—*The Adventures of Huckleberry Finn* by Mark Twain

"Frank Sinatra, holding a glass of bourbon in one hand and a cigarette in the other, stood in a dark corner of the bar between two attractive but fading blondes who sat waiting for him to say something."

—"Frank Sinatra Has a Cold" by Gay Talese, from *Esquire*

"All happy families are alike; each unhappy family is unhappy in its own way."

—*Anna Karenina* by Lev Tolstoy

"The sun shone, having no alternative, on the nothing new."

—*Murphy* by Samuel Beckett

"It is a truth universally acknowledged, that a single man in possession of a good fortune, must be in want of a wife."

—*Pride and Prejudice* by Jane Austen

"It is a truth universally acknowledged that a zombie in possession of brains must be in want of more brains."

—*Pride and Prejudice and Zombies* by Seth Grahame-Smith

These first lines likely need no analysis to see why they are good. They vary in style dramatically, but all invite us to keep reading, and all show off the skill of the writer, assuring us readers that we are in good hands. That's what we're after.

NONFICTION OPENINGS

Experiment with numerous potential first lines before you choose what to run with. For my first book, and only novel, *The Art Thief*, I began with what I thought was an epic first line: "And then the strangest thing happened." This, I thought, was impossible to deny, a first line that insisted, with a white-knuckle fury, that you read on. But it wound up being cut by my editor. He argued that what happened next wasn't "the strangest thing," and so while it was a good first line, it didn't suit the novel to which it was attached. The moral is that it can't just be good, it has to be apt for the story you're telling.

What follows are some of my first lines and first paragraphs, each with a short note as to what I was trying to do and why (hopefully) it works as a good opening. By throwing out a variety of examples this may inspire you in your writing.

> We're supposed to think that Jackson Pollock invented drip painting, and with it the American branch of Abstract Expressionism. He did, didn't he? So say *Life* and *Time* magazines and countless art history books and professors in dimly lit lecture halls, their brows tinted by the light from the projector, their words backed by the windy hum of its motor. The first drip, or all-around painting—made by the revolutionary technique of splattering and dripping paint on the fly while approaching the canvas from all angles, as it lay on the floor—was Pollock's 1947 *Galaxy*. Wasn't it?

The reader is confronted with something they assume to be true (that Pollock invented drip painting), but phrased in such a way that they will doubt this "fact."

> If you stand before Rubens's majestic *Adoration of the Magi* in King's College Chapel, you will see a gorgeous painting, colossal in size and accomplishment. But you will not yet see its scars. In order to do so, you must maneuver over to either side of the painting, and view it in a raking light. If you do so, you will see that the canvas bears the remnant scars of three letters that were carved into it during the tumultuous 1970s. Those three letters are *I-R-A*.

The second sentence implants the question "What scars?" The "if you stand" and "you must maneuver" give a cinematic effect, as if you can imagine yourself in a documentary film examining the painting in person. Naming the three letters tells you that the scars are the result of an IRA act of terrorism

136   *Chapter 8*

without actually stating it overtly. The reader is permitted space to fill in the blanks themself.

> You enter the cave. The walkway you traverse winds around spotlit, saber-toothed stalactites and stalagmites, and the rough-skin texture of the stone walls, slick in the perpetual dark damp. Your flashlight picks out first one, then more, of the prehistoric paintings on the wall. A deer, bison, a rhinoceros, painted onto the wall in charcoal black by hands that were protohuman. We are in the Chauvet cave, thirty-five thousand years old. Or are we? Something is missing. Even the blind could tell that. The scent is all wrong. Instead of damp and darkness, it smells of, well, tourists. For we are not in the Chauvet cave itself, which is closed to the public, since the atmospheric conditions that preserve the fragile paintings inside must be maintained. No, we are in the Caverne du Pont d'Arc, a just-opened replica of the Chauvet cave, accurate down to the last undulation of the stone wall, to the last stalactite (with an added catwalk and lighting, of course), but patently false.
>
> Now travel, blindfolded, to some anonymous, freshly built art museum. Down goes the blindfold, and you stand before van Gogh's *Almond Blossoms*. Surely you must be in the Van Gogh Museum in Amsterdam, you think. Why, it's obviously a van Gogh, with his globular, three-dimensional application of vast, snotty quantities of oil, so much so that his paint casts a shadow. But no. You're looking at a work from the Relievo collection, an odd package offered (for a quarter million) by the Van Gogh Museum itself to extremely wealthy collectors and institutions that would quite like nine of the Van Gogh Museum's greatest hits paintings on their walls, but cannot get them, thanks to the inconvenience of most art being unique (and prohibitively expensive). These reproductions are pinpoint accurate as they are made with sophisticated three-dimensional scanning and three-dimensional printing, so every brushstroke is just as van Gogh made it. Only van Gogh did not make it. A printer did.
>
> Welcome to what we might call "art in the age of digital reproduction." We are riffing on the famous essay by Walter Benjamin titled "Art in the Age of Mechanical Reproduction," which argued that great, and authentic, artworks have a certain, undefinable "aura" about them that makes them great. Reproductions, whether mechanical (as they were when Benjamin was writing) or digital (in our own era) are missing this. We might even risk calling this the "soul" of the work. But it is a key component that art lovers find missing when they see a digital copy.

This is a full first page, and there's a lot going on. The use of the present tense and second person ("you enter") brings an immediacy to the action. It's a nonspecific "you" used instead of "a person" or "someone," but it tricks the reader into imagining themself undertaking the action. This brings them right

The Importance of Great Openings   137

into the moment and turns them into the protagonist, immediately making them care about the protagonist because, for this sentence at least, it is they.

The next paragraph begins with "now travel, blindfolded," which continues this reader-made-protagonist, and using the imperative verb gives a sense of urgency. The reader will wonder why "blindfolded," and when the reader wonders something, but feels they are in safe hands and that the author will reveal the answer to them, that's a good thing.

> On April Fools' Day 1998, the crème de la crème of the New York art scene gathered for a party in the studio of Jeff Koons. David Bowie played host, and while a who's who of the art crowd mingled over canapés and cocktails, the mastermind behind what would be (perhaps overzealously) dubbed "the biggest art hoax in history" prowled the perimeters of the party. It was the key event to launch an elaborate practical joke concocted by Bowie and his friend, the Scottish novelist William Boyd, multi–award-winning author of numerous novels, most famously *Any Human Heart*. Bowie and Boyd met while both were members of the editorial board for *Modern Painters* magazine, and quickly hit it off. Both were outsiders in the sense that they were art lovers but not involved in the art world directly, as a rock star and a star novelist. After a meeting in 1998, they bounced the idea around of introducing a fictitious artist into the magazine. Rolling with this idea, Boyd developed a fictitious history of a "lost American artist" by the name of Nat Tate.
>
> With a novelist's flair, Boyd developed a complete backstory for Tate: An orphan born in New Jersey in 1928, adopted by a family on Long Island, sent to art school and established in Greenwich Village in the 1950s. Tate met Picasso and Braques in France, but this triggered self-doubt, rather than inspiration. Returning to New York, Tate burned most of his oeuvre. Substance abuse and depression led to his suicide on January 12, 1960, aged only thirty-one. It was a dramatic tale but one in touch with the history of art, which is unfortunately full of tragic stories of early deaths, from Giorgione and Raphael to Basquiat and beyond. It also conveniently allowed for the lack of documentation about the life of Tate, as well as the paucity of surviving works. But coming up with the story was the easy part. Building physical evidence to back the story proved much trickier.

There's a whirlwind of activity going on in the first sentence. We're thrown in medias res, into the midst of a party, in an exotic time and place, and there's David Bowie! The fact that it's April Fools' Day should foreshadow that something funny is going on. Then we wonder what the deal is with this intriguing "biggest art hoax in history." Then we learn that a pair of celebrities invented a painter and tried to trick the art world into thinking he was real. I'm certainly curious to read on.

138   *Chapter 8*

In 2014, Matisse's *Odalisque in Red Trousers* was recovered after an FBI sting operation and returned to the Caracas Museum of Contemporary Art in Venezuela, from which it had been stolen in 2000—though it had never gone missing. At least, that's how it appeared. The real Matisse had been swiped back in 2002, but no one—no curator, no guard, no visitor, no staff member—had noticed, because the thieves had swapped a very good forgery in its place. It was only after two years, in 2002, that museum staff noticed that the switch had taken place. In retrospect, curators noted that the forgery was already in place in a September 2000 photograph of President Hugo Chávez, standing proudly in front of the museum's prized possession.

In August 1545, Duke Cosimo de'Medici of Florence requested that his court painter, Bronzino, paint a copy on panel of the pala, the centerpiece, of his frescoes in the chapel of Eleonora di Toledo in the Palazzo Vecchio, to be sent as a gift to a French diplomat who had just awarded Cosimo with the prestigious Order of the Golden Fleece.

Ely Sakhai, a respected art dealer with a swanky gallery in Manhattan, hatched a scheme to buy authentic paintings, have them secretly copied by Chinese forgers, and then sell the copies, with the provenance that had accompanied the originals. The real paintings stayed in his home. He would have gotten away with it had he not grown hubristic (or some might say stupid) and tried to sell the original when, at the same time, a gallery that had bought the forgery tried to sell that—both in New York. Christie's and Sotheby's both had Gauguin's *Vase de Fleurs* in their May 2000 catalogs, Sotheby's with the original, Christie's with the forged version. They only noticed when the catalogs came out.

What do these stories have to do with Alec Baldwin?

More than you might think.

By now you'll have spotted my frequent use of my own advice, starting your story with a person, in a specific location at a specified time, engaged in an action relevant to the story. In this case the place is the Caracas Museum of Contemporary Art in Venezuela, the time is 2014, the action is the recovery of a Matisse painting. We don't have a person per se, but we do have the FBI. But then there's a twist. The painting that was recovered "had never gone missing." Huh? But I'm tripling up on my own tactic, because I've got three such openings in a row in the first three paragraphs of this story. Venezuela, Bronzino, Ely Sakhai. Then I throw in a confusing curveball, which should make the reader do a sort of double take, when I write, "What do these stories have to do with Alec Baldwin?" It feels like they have nothing to do with him, but since this is the opening of an article, there must be some connection, you think. I'm not sure the article needed "More than you might think." This is optional. I could see an editor cutting it as unnecessary. It's implied, so doesn't really need stating, but I also don't think it detracts.

The Importance of Great Openings   139

Imagine a Museum of Lost Art. It would contain more masterpieces than all the world's museums combined. From the treasures of Rome to the library of Alexandria, from the religious art smashed in the Reformation to the masterpieces taken in the Gardner heist, from the looting of the Iraq Museum and hundreds of thousands of archaeological sites to the ancient structures and statues smashed by ISIS, from the hundreds of thousands of treasures seized by the Nazis to the millions of objects stolen, hidden, or destroyed throughout the modern era and never found, a Museum of Lost Art provides a cutting reminder of the fragility of the world's treasures. Many of humanity's greatest artworks have been lost to theft, vandalism, iconoclasm, misfortune, and wilful or inadvertent destruction. Still more have disappeared, at the mercy of thieves, with only a sliver eventually recovered, often after dramatic investigations. It is important to study what has been lost and why, to understand how art can best be preserved in the future, to appreciate what has survived, and just how delicate is that miraculous fraction of mankind's creative history that has endured for centuries or even millennia. It is important, also, to recognize that the art blessed with survival is not necessarily the art that was most important or influential when it was first displayed. Just because an object had the bad luck to have been lost or destroyed, by man or by nature, does not mean its place in history was insignificant.

This is meant to make the reader think. Presumably they'll never have imagined a "Museum of Lost Art," and I want to surprise them by describing the extent of what it would contain. Eye-opening fun facts are good to include, the sort that make you want to turn to your spouse and say, "Hey honey, did you know that . . ." The best piece of writing in this opening is the phrase "miraculous fraction." It tells a lot and has an echoing sound to it (the *ac* in "fraction" echoes the *ac* in "miraculous"). This isn't important, but including little flourishes shows the reader that you know what you're doing. Grace notes of writerly style like this are better than trying too hard. Write like a scalpel, not like a machete.

The heist went down like this.

So simple, but many of us are fascinated with capers and heists, and this opening line lets you know that you're in for a good story, an inside story.

Count Jan Potocki (1761–1815) is one of Poland's most revered writers and intellectuals. His masterpiece, *The Manuscript Found in Saragossa*, is considered among the greatest works of prose storytelling, in the vein of *1001 Arabian Nights*. Hailing from one of Poland's wealthiest aristocratic families, he was a world traveler and polyglot, having written his masterwork in French. He was educated in Switzerland, served as captain of the engineers in the Polish Army, and was recruited as a Knight of Malta and Freemason. On December 23, 1815, this brilliant, worldly man absconded with one of his mother's silver teapots, made out of it a bullet, had this silver bullet blessed by a priest, and then shot himself in the head with it. Jan Potocki was entirely convinced that he was doing

140 *Chapter 8*

the world a great favor and saving many lives by taking his own, because Jan Potocki believed that he was a werewolf.

This is a setup. You're meant to think that it's going to be a fairly straightforward bio piece about a Polish writer. But then the rug is pulled out from under you when this paragon of reason and intellectuality does something entirely irrational and surprising.

This "rug-pull" effect resonates with readers as "good writing" and delights the way eureka moments do in film. If you've seen *The Usual Suspects* through to the end, you'll know what I mean. There's a twist that makes you smile, admire the storyteller, and want to see the whole film all over again straightaway. It's not easy to pull this off, but it's a crowd-pleaser. What is probably the best piece of journalistic writing I've ever read does this halfway through the article. It's a feature called "Mark of a Masterpiece" by David Grann that ran in *The New Yorker*. That's prose that I aspire to.

FICTION OPENINGS

The above examples were all openings for nonfiction texts, but the same strategies can be applied to fiction, as in the following:

> "Where is the stake?" he cried. "Where did you hide the stake?"
>
> He turned to the thing before him. "What have you done with my boy? Give me back my son!" As he spoke the blood sizzled out of his face, making him as pale as the creature at which he screamed. "The stake, where is the stake?! I'll have the head of whoever hid it!"

This example and the next start in medias res and force the reader to catch up with the story. This provides a sense of urgency (the reader's subconscious says, "Uh-oh, I missed something, gotta catch up, what's happening here"). This is a werewolf story, and we can work out at least that it's supernatural, possibly about vampires, thanks to the reference to a "stake." We are showing rather than telling.

> As the clubs and hoes and threshers and rakes hailed down upon him, and the last of his breath was bludgeoned from his body, his mouth gaped open a final time and into it flew a black butterfly.
>
> Sava Savanović was dead.
>
> For now.

The Importance of Great Openings 141

In medias res, yes, with a few surprises. One, that a black butterfly would fly into someone's mouth. And then the zinger at the end: "For now."

> Wander, my child, across three times nine kingdoms, thread the links in a chain of mighty mountains, and you will come to a remote Tsardom where a merchant once dwelled. Twelve years had he been married, but in all that time, no son was born, but merely a single daughter. But like you, my child, this little girl was as beautiful as the moon, and so they called her Vasilissa the Beautiful.

This example and the last one below come from Slavic fairy tales that I rewrote. The above passage is meant to evoke the oral tradition of telling folktales and fairy tales, which were traditionally told by old women to children. This is intentionally archaic ("across three times nine kingdoms") and has a little literary flair ("thread the links in a chain of mighty mountains"). The goal is to lull the reader into the feeling of being told a story by an elder, reverting them back to their own childhood experience, and with a poetic, songlike rhythm at play. And finally:

> There once lived a sorcerer-tsar with thirteen adopted daughters and thirteen adopted sons, for he could never have any of his own. They all dwelled in a castle, but no ordinary one. Sure, it was embowered by thick stone walls, but only ringing round the keep. For the keep itself was shaped like an egg and made entirely of glass, which his magic upheld against hail and lightning. The glass was there to capture the fire of the sun to keep warm the sorcerer-tsar's prized possession, a tree that bore golden apples.
>
> Golden apples that someone had been stealing.
>
> The sorcerer-tsar set his guards to watch the golden apple tree in the orchard all night, but they found no one. After all, how could someone from outside get into the enchanted glass castle?

We're clearly in fairy-tale mode, but there are some surrealist elements that will make the story stand out and fix itself in the memory. The castle made of glass and shaped like an egg is certainly distinctive. The plot really begins when we get to the phrase "that someone had been stealing." And the question is planted directly: "How could someone from outside get into the enchanted glass castle?" Oh, my child, you'll soon find out. . . .

If you have some turn of phrase in your mind that won't leave you alone, write it down in a commonplace book and see if you can find a home for it or even build a story around it. I've wanted to write a children's book that begins, "A butterfly flutters by." But I have no idea what the rest of the book would include.

Maybe I can finally come up with a book that actually could begin with, "And then the strangest thing happened."

Chapter 9

Promoting Your Book

If we were to make a book development timeline, it might look like this:

Conceive of your book and prepare either the proposal (for nonfiction) or the sample section and synopsis (for fiction)
Find an agent and develop your concept with them or find a publisher directly
Get a publishing deal
Write the book with the input of the editor
Copyedit (usually with another editor)
Cover design
Typesetting (interior design and formatting, the book is laid out)
Proofreading (usually with yet another editor)
Prepromotion marketing
Printing
Distribution
Launch
Publicity and marketing

This section looks at prepromotion and publicity and marketing, right at the end of your book journey.

Your book is about to come out, so it's time to think about how to promote it. Ideally you could leave this to your publisher, but how much effort they put in is always a question. The answer has been determined since the moment they offered you a contract, but you don't get to know it. It's top secret, because no matter how much effort they put in, an author is going to complain that they're not putting in enough effort. So there's a lack of transparency between publisher and author that's understandable, if sometimes frustrating for the author.

144   *Chapter 9*

In practice, particularly now in the social media era, publishers expect authors to shoulder a great deal of the promotional burden. There's an expectation that authors will bring along their own following. That may be the case for some, but not for most, and new authors may have no following to speak of. By a following of note, this usually means at least ten thousand followers on any given social media platform. Fewer than that is not really considered noteworthy, because it's assumed that only a small percentage of followers will follow through and buy a book, even if they are fans of the author. I've heard the hopeful estimates of between 2 and 10 percent of an author's following as calculated to buy the book based on the author announcing it on social media or in a newsletter. You can do the math. Unless you have a whole lot of followers, then 2–10 percent of them isn't enough to excite a publisher in terms of sales.

SALES EXPECTATIONS

I often hear overly optimistic numbers when new authors talk about how many copies they hope to sell. Fiction usually sells many more copies than nonfiction, but here are some numbers for the very highest-selling books, those that make bestseller lists. Bestseller lists are usually calculated in two-week periods, so it's better to focus your promotional efforts than spread them out.

The *New York Times* bestseller list can be reached with 5,000–10,000 copies sold in a week, while the *USA Today* list can be made with 3,000–5,000 copies sold. Amazon's bestseller list is more complicated. To reach the top of all books, across the board, you might have to sell thousands of copies in a single day, because it's about total sales updated every few hours. In England, the *Sunday Times* bestseller list requires around 3,000–5,000 copies sold in a week for fiction, but for nonfiction sometimes as few as 1,500 copies can make the back end of the list. In Canada, the *Globe and Mail* list requires selling 1,000–3,000 copies in a week. Australia needs only 500–2,000. Germany's list requires 3,000–5,000 copies; France, 1,500–4,000; Japan, as many as 10,000 copies. In Slovenia, if you're curious, it can be as low as a few hundred copies. It depends on the reading habits of the country and its population, and it's all relative: the most copies sold in a finite period.

That's over a week or two. Over the lifetime of a book, strong sales for nonfiction would be 10,000–40,000 copies. For fiction, we're talking 100,000 copies or more for strong sales, but this is over a few years. Most copies will sell when there is proactive promotion, like an appearance on a TV or radio show or a review in a prominent publication (or a tweet from Oprah). Then sales tend to plateau. My two books with Phaidon, *The Art of Forgery* and

Museum of Lost Art, each sold around 20,000 copies in the first five weeks, then plateaued and sold just a few thousand copies a year thereafter. Other books of mine have sold a few thousand copies and were considered a great success by the publisher. To say "it depends" is certainly the case with books.

The goal is to be part of roughly 20 percent of books that make a profit for your publisher. However many copies you sell, if you're on that side of the ledger, the publisher will be delighted and then the book will be considered a success.

But keep in mind anticipated income so you can plan accordingly. Royalties come out to around one dollar, euro, or pound sterling per copy sold of your average book. If you got an advance, your book has to sell enough copies for the publisher to earn back the advance before you get anything more (the word "advance" is short for "advance on royalties," and it's usually calculated by the royalties the publisher expects to have to pay you through book sales during the first year).

You should also be rational about how many copies of your own book you can expect your organic audience to buy. If you're publishing a first book, there's likely to be enthusiasm. For more than the twenty-first book, I no longer even bother to expect anyone I know to buy it, much less read it. I'm always pleasantly surprised when they do. I assume that I produce too much for even friends to keep up with, and so my readers are always new for each book.

I mention this just so you don't feel disappointed at who doesn't buy your book. So how can you encourage people to buy it?

ORGANIC MARKETING

Getting the attention of people who already know you should be easier than enchanting strangers. So this represents your initial target audience. Newsletters, emails, and social media posts can be good, but think about how much attention you pay to those you receive, even from people you know. Not that much, I imagine. Plan to use all three tools. Draft posts and notes. But also think of sending unique messages to specific people, one at a time. It's fiddly but it makes a big difference. If I get a generic "Dear Friends" email I'm far less likely to act on a call to action within it (like preordering a book), but if I get a message or voicemail from someone I know sent just to me, leading with my name, then I feel I'm being personally addressed and I'm much more likely to respond proactively.

In practice, you can write a template message and just change the salutation and perhaps one sentence to make it personalized to each recipient. That's fine. The salutation alone makes a big difference in how committed a

146   *Chapter 9*

recipient will be to acting on what you're asking of them. "Dear Noah, my first book is about to come out. I'm hoping to drum up some good presales. If you're interested and would consider preordering a copy, I'd be much obliged. If not, no worries and have a good day. Be in touch!" That's enough for me to go ahead and make the preorder as a favor, whether or not I'm actually interested in the book.

SPLIT TESTING SOCIAL MEDIA ADS

Products sold via social media ads undergo A/B, or split, testing to determine which ads are most effective. This isn't hard to do yourself, but it is time consuming and requires organization. It's cost effective as a promotional tool, which is good because buying ads in big media is cost prohibitive. You can hire a firm to do this for you (I've worked with Pubvendo, for instance), or do it yourself. It's best used for self-published books, as it becomes your main tool in generating sales, but you can also use it to promote a book from a publisher, to expand your newsletter outreach, to get followers, or to get listeners to a podcast—anything that requires your drawing attention or getting a click-through on your ad, and then you have hope that the website the click-through sends the clicker to is engaging enough to make them answer your call to action.

Split testing is a method used to compare two versions of a social media ad to determine which one performs better. It involves creating two variations (A and B) of an ad, then showing them to different segments of your target audience simultaneously. By analyzing the performance of each version, you can make data-driven decisions to optimize your advertising strategy.

There are a few marketing-speak terms that are useful to know here. Key performance indicators (KPIs) are outcomes that will indicate the success of a campaign. When referring to companies, they are quantifiable measurements that gauge long-term success. This could be profits, units sold, or signatures gathered for a political campaign. For books, it's going to be units sold. Click-through rate (CTR) is what percentage of people who see your ad actually click on it. Call to action (CTA) is what you hope a potential target for the ad will do. This may mean buying a book, signing up for a newsletter, or "liking" a post. So when someone's interest is piqued by an ad, they click on it (CTR) and then they go to some landing page (which you must design, unless that landing page is, for example, the Amazon page of your book) and there hopefully follow through with your CTA. Your KPI in this case would be how many books are sold. Many more people will click through an ad than will actually buy your book. A successful ad campaign is usually measured in CTR—the ad has garnered lots of attention and clicks. But what the ad sends the clicker to must do the rest of the work and encourage the clicker to buy your book. You'll also need to consider return on investment (ROI), also called return on ad spend (ROAS), if the money you spent on ads is really your only expense. Social media ads can be charged by the number of imprints (how many times the ad appears) or clicks (you pay only for each time someone clicks on the ad). Let's say an ad set on Facebook or Instagram costs eighteen cents per click. Your book costs eighteen dollars. If your only expense is ad spend, if you can sell at least one book per 1,799 clicks, then you're profiting (even if only by one cent).

When you create and test multiple versions of an ad for split testing, the versions can vary in terms of headlines, images or videos, ad copy (the short text beneath the image or video), call to action button ("buy" or "preorder" or "sign up"), target audience segments, or ad placement (for instance, Instagram Stories versus Facebook Feed).

To do this, first you come up with several different ads for the same product—in this case, your book. A/B testing refers to two versions in play. You could have more—A/B/C testing with three, for instance. Maybe one is a 3D rendering of the book itself, another is a fifteen-second video of you pretending to be a dragon, a third is a picture of a dragon (because of course you're writing about dragons, right?). Then you can come up with three possible headlines for each of the three images or videos. That gives you nine possible ad combinations with varying headlines and lead images or videos. You'll try some ads on Facebook and some on Instagram. That means eighteen variations on your ad.

You can try all of these with the same target audience segment. This could be "women, ages thirty to fifty, who speak English, are university educated, and live in Boston, Chicago, or Des Moines, and have the word 'dragons' listed among their interests." (I'm not sure this description actually matches any real humans, but the point is you should do some research into who is most likely to be interested in your book and focus the ads on that target audience segment.)

Now try to run eighteen ad variations all targeting that audience segment. You don't need to put a lot of money into them. How about $5 for each campaign and the campaign runs just one day? That'll cost you 18 x 5, so $90. Facebook, Instagram, and similar platforms are designed to facilitate data gathering from such ads. So run all the ads for a day and then see which were most successful. Put more money into those that seemed successful—the ones that generated clicks—and cancel those that didn't.

Keep the ads that did best and play with the audience segment next. Maybe try "men, ages twenty-two to thirty-two, who have 'Dungeons and Dragons' among their interests and who live in London, Manchester, and Glasgow" and a few other potential audiences. See which audience segment reacts best. Add ad spend money to the ads and segments that seem to do well, and drop those that don't.

148   *Chapter 9*

Keep this up, experimenting with variations as needed and adding budget to successful ad sets as long as your ROAS is keeping you in profits. To keep track of which ad click-throughs actually result in books sold, you can make a unique URL for each ad. If you send all ads to the Amazon page of your book, you might generate sales there but you won't know which ads led to those sales. Implementing tracking software that can identify which ads led to sales and, ideally, can gather some basic info about who is buying your book will be valuable, because that characteristics of your buyers can be used to target audience segments. Maybe Belgians are your primary book buyers, but unless you can track where those clicks are coming from, you might never know that your ideal target audience was "women, ages seventy-seven to eighty-two, from Ghent, who have 'waffles' listed among their interests."

This is a good guerrilla marketing approach, but as you can see it requires being organized and creative, and it takes up a lot of time.

GETTING REVIEWED AND INTERVIEWED

Only your publicist has any hope of getting you interviewed in major venues or reviewed by major publications. There's really no point in your trying, unless you've already appeared there and have the direct contact info of someone who will fondly remember your last appearance. Otherwise, it's best to leave it to the pros, hoping for the best when it comes to the big platforms, while you focus on what you can potentially book yourself.

There is a world of blogs, podcasts, and under-top-tier websites, magazines, podcasts, and more that are always on the lookout for content and that are worth contacting. You can offer to be interviewed. You can offer a free review copy (usually an e-copy is fine). You can offer permission to run an excerpt from your book. Or you can offer to write something new for the platform, hoping that its readers will like your style and look into your book. All of this is hit or miss. You have to cast a wide net to catch a few fish. I'm never quite sure what helps. Rarely will you know that having done promotion Y has resulted in X number of books sold. The only metric for this is really online ads. In theory, the more you are "out there," either writing new material or being interviewed or being reviewed, the more people will know about your book and the more copies you'll sell. But it's an opaque alchemy and not even publicists know for sure.

PAID REVIEWS

Some publications will allow you to buy into a guaranteed review, but the good ones won't guarantee that the review will be good. *Kirkus* does this.

You pay a reasonable fee (in the low hundreds), and they guarantee that an independent reader will review your book. But the reviewer might not like it—that's the risk. But they make it easier for you. They show you the review before it's published. If you're happy with the review, it gets published, and voilà, you've been reviewed by the prestigious *Kirkus*. If you don't like the review, you click a different button and it disappears forever, never to be published. But you don't get your money back.

Paying people to positively review your book, on Amazon for instance, is no longer permitted (it used to be frowned on but you could still hire companies or individuals to do it). But there are ways around this. Pubby.co, for instance, is a subscription website populated by writers who are hoping other writers will review their books. At the time of writing, for thirty dollars a month, you can expect to get between five and ten new reviews by real people per week for each of your books. You can't control whether the reviewer likes your book, but people on the site are there to support one another, so it's a pretty safe bet that these will all be positive reviews.

Amazon reviews are hugely helpful. The problem is that anyone can write them. I've had some grumpy person who I've never identified who writes a single, unhelpful, very bad review of each of my books on the day they come out—which means that he or she has certainly not read the book. They're just eager to annoy. This can happen to anyone, and a single 1-star review can make your book look less than appealing, requiring at least ten 5-star reviews to crank it back to the 4–5-star range that one hopes for. It's fair play for you to ask ten to twenty friends and loved ones to each buy your book on day one and write in a glowing review, so you kick things off with more than ten 5-star reviews. This has two benefits: It encourages potential buyers, who see the good reviews and think the book must be good, and it discourages someone who read it and didn't like it—seeing all 5-star reviews can make them think they must've missed something, and perhaps they won't bother posting a negative review.

In practice, Amazon reviews don't tell you much. A small percentage of people will be enthusiastic enough to bother writing a positive review, and it's more likely that someone riled up with bile will seek passive-aggressive satisfaction by posting a bad review (whether or not your book deserves it). But if you can load up on friendly reviews that can only help.

BECOMING AN AMAZON BESTSELLER

I've been a No. 1 Amazon bestseller multiple times. This sounds great but upon further examination it doesn't mean all that much. Bestsellers are based on categories, and the categories get really specific. They are updated every few hours and it doesn't matter how many copies you've sold—you just have to have sold the most copies in that category over that period of time. So if I'm in the category of, say, bicycle repair, and I sold three copies in the last hour, and no one else sold more than two, then I'll be a No. 1 bestseller, but it won't exactly fund my retirement. Still, if you're quick enough to take a screenshot when Amazon has the "#1 bestseller" label next to your book, it's a good feeling and certainly encourages further sales.

You can sort of rig this. If your book is listed in an esoteric category it's much easier. One of my books, *Gold Wine*, somehow got categorized under "guidebooks–Western Balkans." That doesn't really fit. It's about an ancient white wine varietal called Rebula and the region it hails from, the border between Italy and Slovenia. But seeing as there likely wasn't much competition that day, it did make it to No. 1 in the category.

If you can coordinate your followers and ask them all to order your book within the same hour, there's a very good chance you can push your book to the No. 1 slot in its category through your own effort.

LANDING PAGES AND PROMOTIONAL VIDEOS

We live in a world that centers around short videos. The human mind has a three-second attention span and must opt in to continue its focus for another three-second window. Optimal online videos are fifteen seconds long, because studies show that this is how long most people will give a video before deciding to either click away or watch it to the end. With this in mind, consider making your own three-second and fifteen-second videos to promote your book. Fifteen-second videos live happily on Instagram Reels and TikTok, and in Facebook ads. You might opt for a longer video, but it must grab the viewer within the first fifteen seconds, or you've lost them. No slow development allowed.

A unique landing page for your book is a good idea, and one you control can be helpful. It's tempting to just send people to the Amazon book page, or the landing page on your publisher's website, but then those entities get the information about who is visiting your site and interested in your work, not you. Google Analytics linked to your own website gives you that info.

Consider making your landing page look like a Kickstarter page. Kickstarter is a proven template. It leads with a video—preferably one to three minutes long—that tells the story of the author and the product in some detail, and ideally it is quirky and memorable. Then there is some text and a lot of infographics and images. Most of us browse online on our phones, which means small screens and limited focus. It takes a commitment to read a long block of text. So a landing page with minimalist text, more images, and one or more videos is more likely to please. Be sure your call to action to buy or preorder the book

Promoting Your Book 151

is clear. Invite sign-ups for your newsletter, perhaps by offering bonuses—for instance, free unpublished chapters, extra essays, or your availability to answer questions or appear via Zoom for book clubs that read your book.

I know several people who slowly but surely developed newsletter lists of nearly ten thousand people and who make a living selling self-published books via Amazon KDP almost exclusively to their preexisting audience: those receiving their newsletter. (One of them writes in the category of "orc romance"; I think I'm in the wrong genre.)

PUBLICITY VERSUS MARKETING

In publishing these are different roles. Publicity involves the author directly (appearances, interviews, book tours), while marketing does not require the author to be involved (ads, announcements in a newsletter). Most publishers have separate publicity and marketing departments. You may be asked to fill out an author questionnaire in which you can suggest some promotional ideas.

You'll be assigned to someone in these departments who will do their best to promote your book. But "their best" was determined when you were offered a contract, and the amount of effort and optimism can vary. You'll hope to be "front of catalog," which means they will put the most effort into your book. But this still means sending out review copies, offering yourself as an interview subject, offering excerpts to publications, and hoping for the best. The top publicists cultivate personal relationships with people who are in positions of power to promote books, so they may have an in, but they will almost never know where traction will be gained. They also have a pile of books—sometimes dozens—to promote, and yours is but one among them.

Unless you are already very wealthy, you probably shouldn't bother hiring your own, independent publicist. They often cost $20,000 or more per book they help promote, and while they will certainly get you more exposure than you'd have gotten without them (with only the publisher's in-house team working for you), the chances of their efforts earning back their fee are slender. Still, this is why the rich get richer and the bestsellers are perennial. Someone who has sold a ton of books can reinvest some of that money in promoting the next book to ensure that it, too, sells by the ton.

BOOK EVENTS AND TOURS

It feels satisfying to have a book launch event, but you will probably have to organize it yourself. Publishers tend to splash out on the expense only for authors who are already earning a lot for the publisher. It's sometimes a safer bet to throw a party at which you'll offer drinks and snacks, give a talk, and charge a modest ticket price that includes a "free" copy of your book, as well as covers your expenses for the event, rather than to let people come for free and hope they buy a book.

Book tours used to be relatively common, but these days readers are used to virtual events, and the expense of sending an author on tour is high enough that publishers rarely do it anymore. The only people sent on book tours now are either celebrities, already mega bestsellers, or unusually strong public speakers. I qualify only for the third item on that list, but I've not been on a book tour since 2018. Here is an article I wrote for *The Atlantic* after one of my book tours.

INSIDE BOOK TOURS: ANALYSIS OF AN ENDANGERED SPECIES

I'm flying (Economy Plus!) from my home in Slovenia to New York for a week-long US tour to promote my new book. As I fantasize about the knishes and bialys I will consume while on tour (I don't get back stateside much), I am acutely aware that it is a rare privilege these days for an author to be sent on a book tour at all.

Especially since the recession of 2008, when author advances shrunk and publishing had to tighten its collective belt, one of the first things to go were book tours (and you can almost forget about the extinct beast called the "book release party"). They are expensive (covering transport, meals and nice hotels) and do not necessarily translate into a more successful book. It's hard to tell, in fact, what effect they have, as sales records don't show what prompted someone to buy the book—only where the book was purchased.

The main selling point on my current US tour is an appearance on *Fresh Air*, a nationally-syndicated NPR radio show. I've been on NPR many times before, but they don't really like to have guests by telephone, and are much more likely to book you if you are there, in the flesh. *Fresh Air* is the ne plus ultra of book-selling radio: Terry Gross is mistress of 4.5 million regular listeners who consume books like Tic Tacs. They are the target audience for all American publishers of nonfiction and anything literary. I'll be doing major live appearances (Kramer Books in DC, 92nd Street Y in New York, Museum of Fine Arts Boston), but each event will only reach a few hundred people, if we're lucky. *Fresh Air* listeners are the publisher's dream, as they comprise America's leading book-consumer demographic. This appearance alone could justify the considerable cost of paying my way over (not to mention that this author can eat his weight in knishes). Touring is expensive, and

Promoting Your Book 153

rarely shows direct corresponding evidence of an upturn in sales. So many interviews these days are by phone or Skype or email that it is not strictly necessary to have Author A in Location B in order to get media coverage. But for *Fresh Air* this is necessary. And there's a white whale out there that my Phaidon publicist, whom we'll call KGB, had been chasing for weeks, but which was proving slippery to harpoon: *CBS This Morning*, a nationally-televised morning show with some 3 million viewers. Getting authors who are not already TV personalities onto TV shows is very hard to do. I actually appear on TV semi-regularly, and I've got a Discovery/Nat Geo mini-series I'm hosting that films in the fall—but I'm a long way from a household name, and I'm a long way from the million-selling authors that occasionally sneak onto such programs. By the time I arrive stateside to begin my tour, CBS is still proving elusive, saying neither a firm yes nor no.

In this new, austere era there are only three types of authors who are regularly sent on tour at the publisher's expense: a) exceptionally good public speakers, b) writers with an established very large audience (the James Pattersons, Gary Shteyngarts, Nicholas Sparks and so on) and who are therefore guaranteed to sell well and therefore cover expenses, or c) writers with a high pop culture profile that extends beyond books (like actors, athletes, comedians) who readers would be keen to see in person but know via their television sets. Publishers might send the odd debut author, in hopes of more media coverage, but it's no longer a given. Of these author types, I am only (a), so I'm told, and I'm very lucky to be sent on tour—and I love it. Writing is great but solitary, normally undertaken in a dark room, alone, in my pajamas. I enjoy the adrenaline of performance, the bigger the audience, the better. I've spoken for audiences ranging in size from 700 to 3 (more on that later), and been interviewed on everything from local blogs with a readership in the low hundreds to US national television and the BBC. But it has always been clear to me that the very fact that I am sent on often arduous, often expensive tours by my publishers is a special privilege, because the vast majority of authors remain in their pjs back home throughout the publicity process.

There's nothing more boring than watching someone read from their own book, and most authors, I'm told, neither like public speaking nor are any good at it. As Tom Mayer, an editor at Norton (and editor of my next book) notes, "What many authors don't realize is that a book event is a performance. It's not enough to just read from your work; you have to put on a show and engage your audience. In fact, reading your work is sometimes the worst thing you can do." For authors who write for the solitary qualities of the profession, public speaking can be a stressful nightmare, and not everyone is good at it. Tom continues, "A great performance will lead to more book sales, further invitations, and general good feeling among writer, audience, and bookseller." On tour I learned that the number of people you read to, or

154   *Chapter 9*

directly sell books to at an event, is not the main point of touring. It's about developing positive vibes with bookstore managers, who have enormous control over how your book sells in their establishment, as they can display it however they like, recommend it to customers, and essentially determine your success—at least within the realm of their establishment.

Back in the day, publishers sent authors out on tour fairly regularly, with the more events and cities covered, the better. They used to send them off with a company credit card, and they were otherwise on their own to make their own way. This proved a bad idea. Authors don't always like touring, and often like drinking, and the unchaperoned use of a company card led to binges of epic excess, often accompanied by missing events while passed out on a hotel floor, possibly bleeding from the ear. My binging on knishes and espresso Frappuccinos is, it turns out, the least of all evils. Then publishers began to send publicists out with authors, which had a dual function: fixer (with a theoretically more mild use of the company credit card) and chaperone (to make sure hotel room floors were only walked upon). But this was double the expense—publishers had to fork out twice the plane and train tickets, twice the meals, twice the hotels. So a compromise was reached that I only learned about on my first tour, back in 2007 for a novel, *The Art Thief*. It peeled back the veil over this quasi-legendary concept of authors on tour (I imagined groupies, whiskey, cigarette smoke, typewriters), and exposed me to a new, and completely fascinating, profession that I never knew existed: the awkwardly-named "escort."

It's not what you think. Author escorts are local residents of the cities visited by those of us on tour, and are subcontracted by a variety of publishers to meet and act as fixer for each author as he or she comes into town. You can spot them at airports and train stations, because they're always carrying a copy of your book. And most of them are elegant middle-aged women with pearl necklaces and SUVs and husbands in banking who read vast numbers of books, love their cities, know them inside out and are thrilled to show authors around. They do have the company credit card, and anything you do while they are with you is free (free food is the siren song for writers, impossible to resist). But because they live in the city in question, the publisher doesn't need to fly them in or spring for their hotel. It's a more cost-effective way to get authors where they need to be.

And we need it. My tour for *The Art Thief* featured twelve cities in fourteen days. I'd get up each morning around 6, groggily pack up my bag at anonymous hotel number 47, and be driven to the airport for an early flight to the next city. There I'd be picked up by the next escort, smiling and brandishing my book and inevitably the most interesting person I could possibly meet that day, and bring me to interviews, radio stations, TV studios, hotel rooms where I might be locked in for press junkets in person or by phone, to meals

Promoting Your Book

(they always know the places to eat), and then to the book event. Blurry-eyed authors, uncertain of the day of the week, their current location or just who is president of the United States require hand-holding to maintain such a schedule. My current tour, for *The Art of Forgery*, includes 5 cities in 7 days, with one day featuring a 3-city ping-pong.

Escorts are often the most interesting part of a tour. In Chicago for *The Art Thief,* my escort was an aspiring writer planning to pen a memoir called "Super Jew," while my San Francisco escort was a novelist who had a hit about Beat vampires back in the 70s. That escort was one of three audience members (another was my dad) at a bookstore reading of mine, and I wondered why my publisher had flown me all that way (particularly since my previous event was in Houston and the next was in Austin). But then the manager wheeled out hundreds of books to sign for a signed first edition mail club, and all was clear. Arriving in Austin, Texas, the escort asked me what I'd like for lunch. I said that I'd read that a suburb of Austin, Lockhart, was the barbecue capital of the United States. Did we have time? Indeed we did! We ordered a portion at each of the three most famous joints in town and did a barbecue-crawl prior to my reading. Had I fallen over and passed out that night, a trail of barbecue sauce would have spooled out of my ear. For the Dutch edition of the book, I had a film-style press junket, locked in a hotel lounge in Amsterdam, as one journalist after another asked me variations on the same five questions over and over, while I pretended that no one had ever asked me them before. Pauses were permitted only to smoke doobies. One city stop was key to my romantic life: I'd preordered a wedding ring and had it waiting at the local Bulgari store, but I had only thirty minutes of down-time, so I had to sprint to get it before leaving for the next city, thereby securing the means to propose to my future wife.

When I arrive at JFK airport for my current book tour, I'm greeted not by an escort, as KGB will accompany me throughout, but by Waldemar, my Polish driver who couldn't understand why the Soviet Union and Yugoslavia broke up: "When you split up, you are weak. Like a pizza! If is whole, is hard to eat, but in slices . . . boom!" I learned all I wanted to know about his cholesterol problem ("I live only the once-time, maybe, so party hard!"). I arrive at 10pm at my hotel, which is 5am in my head, so of course I go straight to Katz's Deli for pastrami on rye and sour pickles. Having not been home to the United States in years, I feel like Crocodile Dundee when he comes in from the outback and meets a bold new world. I will eat a squagel (which I'm told is a square bagel), a French toast bagel (be still my heart) and be offered eleven different brewing methods when I try to order a coffee. After a talk at Kramer Books in DC, I party at the Buzzfeed office (which has much free beer and many, many bowls of free candy), and eat pulled pork with duck instead of the pork. In addition to the coup of KGB booking me on *Fresh*

Air, she had also found me about a dozen other interviews to build around the big gun, but is still working on *CBS This Morning*. Time was tight and they hadn't yet committed. For an art book, this sort of television appearance is just about unheard of. Could KGB pull it off?

In Boston, I speak to a full house at the MFA, and eat a croissant doughnut—my god, what has America come to in the few years since I last visited? Bars serve kombucha on tap (I'm still not sure what this is) and I was offered chia seeds in my morning OJ. I also wonder if anyone has ever actually dunked a Dunkin' Donut.

Then the call comes in. *CBS This Morning* is on. For the following morning. KGB and I are in Boston and have a gig in New Haven the next afternoon. Squeeze in a trip to New York between? You betcha. This is publicity gold, and could only happen if I was physically in a studio in New York, rather than on my couch in Slovenia. This is why publishers send authors on tour. My ninja publicists had rocked it. In other news, my book is listed as the #1 bestseller on Amazon in the category of . . . finance and stock market history. Hm. Algorithms may be a bit wonky, but it's still nice to see #1 next to your book.

We get up at 5am, snarf a cronut, fly to New York, film at CBS (I was on after The Tallest Man on Earth, which I was very disappointed to learn was not the tallest man on earth, but a band), then hop the train to New Haven for the next talk. All in a (very long) day's work. Let no one say that authors on tour have it easy. Or maybe we do. Giddy from lack of sleep and potential publicity, I set off with KGB and the Phaidon book rep, whom we'll call Neptune, into the New Haven night to do something I'd never done in my own hometown but have longed to try: a direct taste-test of the three famous pizzerias in town. Culinary explorers voyage to New Haven for the pizza, but locals are divided as to whether the ancient rivals, Sally's and Pepe's, or the more modern upstart, Modern, is the best. Eat at any one of them, and your eyes will roll back into your skull (in a good way). But I'd never done a direct taste test. So we order a single margherita pie at each place and stagger the pickup time in fifteen minute intervals. (Sally's won.)

KGB asked Keith Fox, the CEO of my publishing house, to weigh in on book tours. He gave a solid but rather press-release-y answer: "In a new and fragmented world, our books require a diverse mix of engaging activities from short videos, author events, and demonstrations to reader exclusives, all of which connect with potential buyers. Book signings and author tours are part of the dialogue and one of many initiatives that Phaidon employs to engage readers." Whether he also had in mind authors on tour engaging in pizza-tastings with their staff is a matter of speculation, but as long as the books are selling, I'm guessing he's down.

Promoting Your Book 157

By the end of the tour, whatever arcane book tour-y voodoo we've been practicing seems to be working. Either my book has righted itself, or Amazon's category algorithm has un-wonked. The book is now listed as the #1 bestseller among new releases in art history, finally the right category. This is why they send authors on tour. Good news, even before *CBS This Morning* and *Fresh Air* run. Who knows, maybe those programs will launch me to #1 in an entirely new and unexpected category? Soft-core erotica? Fine with me, as long as books are selling and the readers are happy.

Chapter 10

The Two-Hour Workday

Tips to Maximize Efficacy in Minimal Time

Some ten years ago, I wrote a book and a half, taught three courses, and wrote 66 articles (62 of which were published), not to mention the 52 installments of a weekly series on writing. I managed this despite the fact that my first child was born in April of that year, meaning that half the calendar was taken up with childcare and related domestic activities. Not everything postbaby remained as productive as I might have liked: I read less than half as many books that year as the year before, and my film-watching, TV-bingeing, and lying-on-the-couch-looking-at-magazines quota went down to practically nil. But I somehow managed to be more productive in my writing than ever before.

So many colleagues and strangers have commented with surprise and interest on my situation that I thought I should examine that qualifier: "somehow." How, exactly, did I pull it off, and is there a recipe that might help others? What follows is one man's guide to increasing productivity despite having markedly fewer hours per day in which to work. All or part of this "Two-Hour Workday" plan can be adapted to anyone keen to do more with less time, but it's especially useful for folks like me, who work in a portable way (i.e., writers with laptops) on creative matters (without data entry quotas and the like). But not to worry if you work in an office, like a normal person, and not in your pajamas like I often do. The lessons can be adapted to other sorts of work just as easily. This is most readily applicable to work as a writer. So roll up your proverbial sleeves (though I usually work in a T-shirt atop my pajama pants), and prepare to work less.

PORTION OUT YOUR WORK AND TIME

My work as a writer takes two major forms: books and articles. Nonfiction books are essentially very long articles, or collections of linked articles with a strong through line. The key is to divide your work into blocks of time—periods you can reasonably set aside each day, and for which you can concentrate without the need for pharmaceutical assistance. My system doesn't work for fiction, at least not for me. When I write fiction, I really need to be alone, in silence, and to have an extended period, ideally indefinite, ahead of me in which to plunge into the world I'm creating. I need that somewhat prima donna luxury of undisturbed quiet, lots of coffee, and my Peruvian hairless at my side. But with nonfiction books and articles, I think I've got this down to a science.

You don't have to be a writer to find this approach useful. Dividing any task, from data entry to doing your income taxes, into digestible portions makes you feel more productive (checking off more boxes, even if those boxes are sections of a single larger project) and makes the work feel easier (jogging four miles might sound exhausting, but a mile at a time—not so bad). Borrow a page from Pavlovian conditioning theory and reward yourself after you complete each portion: Grab a coffee, eat a gummy bear, watch a YouTube video of a cat falling off a table. You'll learn to work for the reward, and even enjoy the work more, as a means to a treat at the end.

With an infant to care for and a house to maintain, all I could count on when I began this system was one guaranteed two-hour block of genuine work time per day. With this in mind, I divided my nonfiction book projects into article-length slices. Most books are 80,000 to 100,000 words, which, sliced into 1,500-word segments, should take me about sixty two-hour blocks to write. Of course, books always take longer than one thinks (there's research to be done, outlining, interviews, and finally a whole lot of editing), but the basic premise is there: The rough draft of a book can be divided into however many two-hour blocks you might need, just like articles or any sort of portable work can likewise be subdivided into digestible, single-sitting "portions."

I first applied this to my 2015 book, *The Art of Forgery*. It took me two months of two-hour workdays to draft. When outlining, I mapped the project in terms of articles, breaking down the overall subject into nibbleable pieces of around 1,500 words each, pieces that I felt I could write in short bursts. While I use this technique for writing, it can easily be transferred to other activities and broken down into smaller time bites. Even logging data entry can be sliced into pieces that feel more digestible: 1,000 items to log sounds daunting, but 10 bursts of 100 feels more feasible, with built-in breaks to reward productivity and make a long haul feel shorter.

The Two-Hour Workday 161

Some techniques ask you to focus for only twenty-five minutes, followed by five minutes of downtime. This works for many people, but for me it was too short a work period. This short burst followed by reward is best suited to repetitive, boring work like data entry, where lasting twenty-five minutes focused is something of a miracle. For creative work like writing, you'll likely want longer sustained blocks of time, hence the two-hour segments, followed by downtime of any length you like.

Not all of you (probably almost none of you) will be planning to write while parenting a newborn. But the guarantee of no more than two hours of writing time per day is still applicable to anyone for whom writing is not the primary activity. If you work an eight-hour job each day, it's a luxury to take two hours for writing at the end of the day. Perhaps you can fit in a two-hour block only once or twice a week? No problem. The basic idea remains, and it's a form of scientific reductionism. Take a big, intimidating project and slice it into smaller "problems" that feel more reasonable to tackle and "solve." For a scientist, this might be attacking parts of an elaborate mathematical or chemical puzzle. For those with an overstuffed, hoarder house, it might be deciding to clean just one room a week. Bite-sized pieces. For those writing a 60,000-word book, it might be slicing it up into 60 1,000-word work packages, each of which you'll try to finish in one or two days.

If you can set aside more than two hours per day, so much the better. Likewise, if you (or I) need eight hours instead of two for the first draft of an article, or whatever project you're attempting, that's of course also fine. It's not about the speed, nor does it have to be two-hour blocks. It's about subdividing one's workload into lengths of time during which you can reasonably remain sharp and focused. I find that after two hours, my mind will drift. I'll want to look at Instagram, eat peanuts, take my Hubert van Eyck for a walk (that's my Peruvian hairless), or watch that cat video again. I would need a break every two hours anyway, otherwise my brain will risk melting out of my ears, so why not stop altogether and resume work in another two-hour block later on? Your blocks of time can be as long or short as you like, or your day can swing. Lawyers bill clients in fifteen-minute increments, so they wind up dividing their workload into blocks of that size almost without realizing they are doing so.

The concept works both ways—chopping a big project into several smaller ones or identifying a block of free time and seeing what you can fit into it. If you have a spare half hour, what can you do to make that time maximally productive? If you're a secretary moonlighting as a novelist but having difficulty finding time to write, consider any found block of fifteen free minutes to be a bonus, and see how useful you can make that time.

DESIGNATE YOUR WORKSPACE

It's important to have a designated workspace, wherever that might be, whether within the context of your office or at home. But it needn't be a room of one's own. It could be a corner, or a stool at a café, or a couch of one's own.

For a long time, I tried to get work done from home, but I was always half minding the baby and half typing, which is not fair either to my work or to Junior. I then started to go out to a café, or to lock myself into another room and wear headphones, for my two-hour work blocks. I like to vary my workspaces, even changing venues in the same room—such as moving from couch to dining table—with each new block of work time. Many modern office spaces, especially at tech companies, understand that sitting in the same place all day results in diminishing productivity. So they have open workspaces: You get a desk, but there are also comfy chairs, couches, and other areas available for you to shift locations. If there's any way for you to do this while at work, it will feel wonderfully refreshing.

The real key is to keep work time and space separate from relaxing, social, space-out, or family time. If you go to an office each morning, that's not a problem (you do work at work). But if you don't, you have to enforce such rules. When I'm working, I want to be 100 percent efficient, so that when I'm not working I can be 100 percent present with my family (or 100 percent spacing out on the couch eating peanuts). Mixing work, family, and leisure in the same space of blocks of time results in doing none of them fully, and none of them as well as you could.

If writing is not your main occupation, it's worth giving yourself a writing spot that is neither where you relax after work nor where you do your day job. Writing, if it's not your day job, is part work, part fun, so it deserves its own spot. Setting up in a specific, regular location subconsciously clicks you into "writing mode," and that will benefit you long term.

CHECK CHECKLISTS

If you know that you'll have, say, only two or five or ten secure blocks of time with which to work during the week (hopefully more, but any extra will be considered a bonus), you'll need to get organized. There are various obsessive-compulsive levels of organization available, but the one I use is low-key. At the start of each week, I write in my Moleskine weekly planner (I prefer the analog variety to its digital counterparts) and make a list of what I need to do. Before each entry I draw a small square box. My level of OCD is such that I *cannot* bring myself to turn the page to the next week in

The Two-Hour Workday 163

my planner and shift over the bookmark unless all those small square boxes are checked. Each time I finish a task, I eagerly check the box and also write what I did in the day-by-day section of the planner, with a word count for each writing project. This way I'm quantifying what I do, as well as seeing just how productive I can be, and this boosts morale.

If I have articles due in the future, I'll create boxes to check a few weeks in advance, including a box for "first draft" and another one for "final draft." I also make boxes for errands, deadlines, meetings, and so on. The more boxes I can check off, the better I feel. This method lets you see how productive you are, and plan things out accordingly. For *The Art of Forgery*, I created a list of around forty article-length sections of the book that I had to research (one box) and then write (a second box). By doing this, I clearly saw my progress and what remained on my to-do list.

I find this system hugely satisfying, and it makes it easier to plan ahead. It is also psychologically easier to feel that you have to write forty ten-page sections, checking them off as you go, rather than the daunting prospect of a single four-hundred-page swath of blankness to fill in. As before, this technique can be applied to anything—cleaning the whole apartment feels like a hassle, but tackling the six rooms in six ten-minute bursts? Not so bad.

CONTROL YOUR EMAIL

Much of one's workday, whether at home or in an office, is consumed by email and internet. This is no new concept, but my approach to email draws enough positive and wistful comments from friends and colleagues and strangers who read my email signature that it seems worth mentioning. If you get an email from me, it will likely contain a signature at the bottom that explains that I "check and write email only twice per week," apologizing for any delay in response and offering a separate email address for urgent matters. When I'm also filming something, I switch to "only checking and writing emails on Fridays." You wouldn't believe how many folks reply enthusiastically to this, wishing that they could do the same.

People seem to love this idea of controlling email rather than letting it control you, as happens so often in this age of being plugged in at all times. I find that when I do administrative work (emails, errands, invoices, phone calls) I'm in one zone, and I cannot easily shift into "creative mode" and get good writing done. I therefore try to limit and define when I do this admin so it does not tread on the toes of my real work, writing. I certainly understand that not everyone can afford to check email only twice a week. Or, as I write this, only on Fridays.

Most jobs require far more constant access, and so this system won't work for everyone. But there are things you can do to control your email while still keeping yourself available. One great trick is to create multiple email addresses that you check in different ways and assign to different tasks. One address should be reserved for time-urgent matters (emergencies, deadlines, messages from your boss), and it's a good idea to have this accessible on your smartphone so you'll get messages immediately. But you don't want a barrage of messages constantly beeping at you from your pocket, so be selective in giving out (and writing from) that email address. Then you can have one or more other addresses that are for work-related matters that are not time urgent and that you can afford to check just once a day (or twice a week).

Social messages, from your Aunt Gertrude or your college roommate, should be directed somewhere else entirely so you don't feel clogged by personal messages (or rushed to plow through them to get back to work). I actually prefer instant messages for personal correspondence and keep email exclusively professional.

These days you can ask a single email address to sort your messages for you. For instance, Gmail divides your inbox into "primary," "social," and "promotional" categories automatically, and you can produce more. This is fine, but it does not allow you to check each category of email in a separate way, or on a separate device. I use three addresses: One, for urgent matters, is on my phone; a second, for normal correspondence, is via Outlook on my laptop, and I check it about twice a week; and a third is for matters that I know can wait, that I can safely deal with only once a week, and this I check on my browser. I also check email only when in "offline mode," meaning that I receive and send emails when I press a button to do so, and I work on them offline. This saves the agony of clearing one's inbox only to have another five messages come in during that time. My neurosis extends to not being able to see that I have an email without immediately reading it and responding to it, so this system works wonders for me. As with checking boxes and dividing work into two-hour blocks, it's all about compartmentalizing and feeling like you're getting more done in less time. I interviewed author Michael Connelly about his writing habits and learned that he locks himself in a room with blackout curtains, no internet, with masking tape over the part of his computer screen where the clock is located, and a restaurant-sized tank of sweet iced tea. You don't have to go quite this all in, but isolating yourself from distractions is a good approach.

This article, now clocking in at 2,833 words, took me exactly 205 minutes to do, or two of my two-hour work blocks. I'm off to check a box in my Moleskine, eat some peanuts, and watch a video of a cat.

Chapter 11

Map Your Writing Plan

This book began in part 1 with information on the logistics of how to get published and earn money as an author. Part 2 has covered strategies on writing and promoting your work. Now that you are equipped with knowledge, it's time to put it into practice. The goal of this chapter, but really the whole book, is to make the intimidating idea of writing professionally feel less frightening and more doable. Everyone who wants to write can and even should do so. It's fun, introspective, and a great way to explore your interests and get to know yourself. And there's always the bonus that someone else might want to read it too!

To lay out a plan for you, we'll tackle a 12-day plan, a 12-week plan, and a 12-month plan that will end with your complete book.

GETTING STARTED: A 12-DAY PLAN

If you're as old as I am, you may remember the Choose Your Own Adventure books, in which chapters ended with two options that the reader could choose from. Each led to a different page, and a different outcome for the character in the story. One usually ended with success, the other with being eaten by a dragon. Thankfully, real life isn't like that, but I quite like the "choose your own adventure" approach to writing. I'll lay out the options and what you'd need to do to get started. You can then use it as a to-do list, or make your own based on it.

166 *Chapter 11*

Day 1

What do you want to write about? What sort of book? Choose from fiction, trade nonfiction, and academic. (There are other options, but for our purposes these three will guide you.)

If you opted for fiction, you'll want to develop characters and your story, as well as build the world your characters will inhabit (if it is not a realist novel taking place in the here and now). Even if it takes place here and is realist, if it is at all historical, you'll want to research the era so that your book feels accurate and transports your readers.

If you're choosing nonfiction, consider whether you want trade or academic. This questionnaire might help. Circle A or B.

-Is earning money from your book important to you (A) or would it be just a nice bonus (B)?
-Do you want to reach the maximum number of readers (A) or is speaking to a select, perhaps more prestigious few more your goal (B)?
-Is publishing a book a fun project (A), or do you need to publish in order to advance your career (B)?
-Do you have a job that doesn't involve teaching or researching or advanced degrees (A), or do you have a job that does involve those things (B)?
-Does it sound more fun to introduce an idea in an engaging way to people who know little to nothing about it (A), or would it be cooler to dive deeply into a subject and enrich the total knowledge of it, paving pathways for future research (B)?
-Do you want to sell to real people, the more the merrier (A), or do you want to sell to libraries and some students who will have to read your book and otherwise only to your mother and Aunt Gertrude (B)?
-Are you willing to proactively market your book and be engaged on social media (A), or do you want to just write a good book and then move on to the next project (B)?

If you answered mostly A then you should write trade nonfiction. Mostly B? You're a future academic author!

Day 2

Day 1 wasn't so hard, right? You just chose the type of book you want to write. Hopefully that got you thinking and, during the night, you dreamt of your ideal book project. No worries if it didn't manifest itself to you in a dream. Day 2 is for thinking deeply about it.

Here's the thing about thinking deeply. We rarely do it. We're always rushing from one project to the next. We're thinking, but mostly ahead rather than deeply. As a writer, part of your work is to slow down. To take the time to really . . . think . . . about . . . a subject. That can be hard to do. You probably wanted to speed-read past all the . . . in the previous sentence, because I was slowing down your groove. But books cannot be written well at high speed. Or rather the actual typing can be as quick as your finger-to-brain connection (I'm sure there's a proper term for this, but now you see why I'm a humanities guy) can communicate. The thought behind what you want to say, and the research that stirs the thoughts within you, must be done slowly. Taking time off between bouts of thinking and writing is also good. Let some fresh air in. Let things marinate. Between fresh air and marination, ideas bloom, while others you'll discard. Only start writing when you know what you want to say. It's rare for valuable insights to come out as you write. This approach leads to too much drifting as you try to find your thoughts, and you're forcing the reader to drift along with you. We readers feel in safer hands when the thought is clear and the writing provides a logical and mostly direct line to that thought.

So spend day 2 thinking about what you'd like to write on. It must be a subject that will hold your interest for six to twelve months. That can be tough to choose. It's a long time to have one's interest held. It also should be something that you already know at least enough about to be confident that it would hold your interest for that long. And the more you already know about it, the more of a head start you have and the more convincing you'll be as an ideal author for the topic.

Think also about whether you can reasonably do the research. These days so much is digitized that you don't often need to actually go to a new geography—a library or archive abroad, for instance—in order to research something. But sometimes you do, particularly for academic books that should be advancing knowledge and that require primary source research and scientific testing. If you live in Topeka, Kansas, but want to write about statue looting from temples in Cambodia, you'll probably have to go to Cambodia. Is that feasible in the next six months or so?

Your book will become a calling card. People who have never met or sometimes even heard of you will come across your book. What sort of a calling card would be most useful or appealing to you to send out into the world?

Day 3

This is a day to begin the mind map of your book, the one I described in chapter 6.

168   *Chapter 11*

For fiction, you can begin creating the world of your characters (mapping out the locations for the story, whether imagined or real, and considering what set pieces or scenes you might envision where). I like to make an actual map if it's an invented world, or a constellation of locations if the story will take place in the real world, or at least recognizable geographies of our planet (even if you want to throw in a magical entrance to a third dimension behind a passport photo booth at the corner of Seventy-Seventh Street and Madison Avenue).

Nonfiction projects can also begin with handwritten mind maps. Lay out all the ideas, characters (real people still qualify as characters), places, scenes—anything you already imagine you'd like to include. You can also develop a reading list—the start of your bibliography—which will be a required element of your finished nonfiction book, whether trade or academic.

Day 4

Revisit and adjust your mind map as you go. You'll find that some elements don't fit with the others, while after a few days an idea will come to you that you simply must include but hadn't thought of before. This is why you need to offer the gift of time to yourself and your book. You can loosely gather elements that you think will work well, ideally in pencil so it doesn't feel committal. By this I mean you might want a scene in which Albert Einstein and Niels Bohr meet to chat, and you might think a scene in a Princeton, New Jersey, diner would be good, and you might have a character who is a waitress who couldn't afford schooling but is actually a math whiz—and these three independent elements of your mind map naturally mesh together into a single scene.

This is also a day to consider whether any travel will be necessary in order for you to research your book. If so, it's not too early to start planning it. The same goes for taking time off other work or projects to write. I can write nonfiction during in-between moments, but I need multiple uninterrupted entire days to get into the fiction writing zone. Think about what works for you. Maybe taking a long weekend a month, for instance, devoted to writing would be more productive for you than trying to slip in an hour each evening during the workweek?

Day 5

Make your bibliography. You'll want one even if you're working on fiction, because reading is the best thing you can do to improve your writing short of, well, writing. For nonfiction you'll certainly need to read to conduct your research. For fiction, if the world your characters inhabit is any different from

Map Your Writing Plan 169

the one you inhabit as you write, there is research to be done. The more realistic and vivid your writing is, the better. That goes for realism or even fantasy. So if you've got a novel planned that takes place in Boston in 1969, you'll want to read to learn (or remind yourself) what Boston was like then. Remember the rule about specifics always being more interesting than something general. If you can describe the Citgo sign above Fenway Park as it looked in 1969 it'll be a better read than just stating that Fenway Park was surrounded by signs (without specifying which ones or describing them). Knowing that Bostonians would go to the North End to eat Italian is a better detail than not specifying what type of restaurant or where it was located within the city.

And if you're not reading to gather information and store it away for potential use in your book, you should just read good writing in the general style you'll be writing in. That means you should read fantasy novels if you're writing one yourself or read a hard-boiled detective novel if that's what you'll be penning. Reading good writing inspires good writing.

Day 6

Now you've got a book idea, a bibliography, and the start of a mind map. Expand and alter as you go and start reading. It's good to think about what you feel you need to read before you can start writing, versus what would be nice to read while writing.

Think about a good title. This will likely change, and the final title may be the fruit of a discussion with your editor, but it feels right to name your project. It makes it feel more real, gives it more character. Speaking of which, also name your characters. It helps them feel more three-dimensional, even before you start to design (or research and flesh out) their dimensions.

Think also about who your target audience is for this book. Is there a specific readership in mind? To say that your book is "for everyone" is the least useful thing you can do, so don't do it. Think specifically, because the narrower your primary target audience, the easier it is to market to it. A colleague once wrote a book about his own experience as an athlete engaging in sports even though he has epilepsy. That's a great concept with a very specific audience: first, those with epilepsy and their families, then honing even further, those with epilepsy who also engage in sports activities. Though it may seem counterintuitive, narrower audiences are easier to reach and market to, and more likely to buy your book.

Day 7

The first week has passed and it's time to start your "lite" book proposal following the template in chapter 2. Though you will probably need a full

170 *Chapter 11*

proposal for your nonfiction book, the lite one is a good place to start, as it's like a sandbox for developing your idea. The material in it can be used or expanded for a longer proposal, so it's effort put to good use. The simpler nature of it as a questionnaire makes it less intimidating and easier to play around with than making a full, ten-to-twenty-page proposal.

I suggest filling out a lite proposal even if you're writing fiction. Most of the questions are still relevant. What is your book about? How would you describe it in a catalog entry that would grab a potential reader? Who are you? If this is a first book, you may not know how long it would take you to write, so don't worry about that question, but the others are useful. At this stage you probably don't have a chapter-by-chapter outline in mind, so leave that blank. You can fill that in later. That begins with your mind map. It's key not to beat yourself up for any reason at all. You can do no wrong. You're not showing this to anyone yet. It's your playground. Enjoy.

Day 8

Write something that might actually go in your book. Anything. It can be a paragraph. It can be a page. It can be a few random sentences. You've spent a week thinking and sketching ideas out. That blank page must be inked to get the ball(point) rolling. Just get some text down. You probably won't use it (though you might). This is about initiating momentum. The inertia of the blank page is your enemy. Start writing without the pressure that it must be "good" or even usable. Just write.

Try to give yourself a block of time that feels generous enough that you're not checking the clock. So that if you get into a good groove, you can keep grooving. Mute your phone, don't look at emails, give yourself the gift of focus. Whatever you write is better than not writing at all.

Think of this time as a sketchbook. Sketch out a few lines here, a few paragraphs there. Write what feels most urgent, easier, most fun. At this point, don't do anything that feels like "work." There will be plenty of time for that later.

Day 9

From day 8 on, you should try to write something, even if it's just a few sentences, on any writing day you can give yourself. This is one of them. Ideally, you'd write at least a little every day, but that's just not feasible for many people, and that's fine. This is a fine day to make a writing schedule for yourself.

Consistency will really help. Don't expect to finish a project as involved as a book with a "I'll fit it in when I can" approach. It might work, but it's

Map Your Writing Plan 171

unlikely and not the best way to focus on a goal. Think of it like your fitness plan. If you say to yourself, "Eh, I'll work out when I can, we'll see what happens," then you're likely to be highly irregular with your fitness, which means mixed results. Writing is the same. Rhythm really helps, and some days you'll have to force yourself. It is work. It doesn't look like work to someone who's never written anything elaborate before. It shouldn't feel like work most of the time (especially not at the start). But for those of us who have this as a full-time career, we know you've got to treat it as such.

One option is to slice out a time slot each day, or four or five days a week. This should be at least thirty minutes long, but that's quite tight. It can take the first ten minutes to get into the zone. An hour is great. If you're feeling it, then you can follow my "Two-Hour Workday" system from chapter 10. Don't pressure yourself to do more than that. As with fitness, no one expects you to go pro right away and do four hours of workouts each day unless you're training for a lead role in the next *X-Men* film. If you can get an hour in there that's excellent. But it should be on consistent days and it should be on your calendar. Monday through Thursday from 7:00 a.m. to 8:00 a.m., or maybe Monday, Wednesday, Friday, Sunday from 9:00 p.m. to 10:00 p.m. Do whatever works for you, but keep it consistent.

The other approach is to do a lengthy session once or maybe twice a week. Maybe Sunday is your writing day, and you can fit in four to six hours? That's great. Really anything is great if it keeps you writing and keeps the momentum going. So make your schedule and do your best to stick to it.

Day 10

Today you should try to finish all the parts of the lite book proposal aside from the chapter-by-chapter outline. Fill in whatever you can, but with no pressure to complete it. Keep in mind that at this point, the proposal is only to give the editor or agent a sense of what the book will be. Everyone understands that details (number of chapters, what happens in them, the order of events) can change. The book theme needs to remain whatever was in the contracted proposal, but the outline and specific contents are flexible. You're still in the sandbox period so fill out the lite proposal as much as you can today.

Day 11

Unless you're a veteran writer, you'll need a writing sample to include with any proposal (lite or full). Since we've got the proposal well underway, it's good to think about what the writing sample might be. It should be at least 1,500 words but needn't be much longer than that.

172   *Chapter 11*

If your book idea began with an article you wrote (as many do), the article itself can serve as your writing sample. This may mean you're already done with it and can check it off! If not, then pick a scene that introduces a key question—which means there is tension present—and end the scene before the tension is resolved. It's more intriguing to tell almost the whole story and leave the reader wanting more than to tell it all and that's that.

A way to approach this is to look back at chapter 5, on article writing, and apply those tips to your writing sample. If the work is fiction, pick a scene in medias res, in the middle of some action, and use the same trick—introduce tension and refuse to resolve it.

Day 12

Now it's time to write some of your writing sample. Don't expect it to be ace or even to be used in the final book. It might be. Just don't expect it. The point here is to break the ice, get the ball rolling, invent the analogy that involves neither ice nor balls—you want to start because blank pages can appear to us like Lovecraftian cliffs of ice or endless glaciers. So much whiteness that it's hard to imagine populating it all with, say, seventy thousand words. In fact, that whiteness is a little much for me, so I set my word processor to white text on a black background. Easier on the eyes and the audacity.

Don't feel pressured to write a whole scene, much less a full writing sample, in one go. The good news is that you get as much time and as many tries as you like to provide a writing sample that really sings. Remain willing to rewrite and delete some of your hard-won sentences. Even Michelangelo discarded his preparatory sketches and models countless times, showing only the finished product he was proudest of.

See what you can do. You may be surprised at what comes to you.

Chapter 12

12 Steps to Success

We've started with this theme of 12, so might as well keep it going, right? Congratulations on firing up your first 12 days of writing. This last chapter is a concise outline of what a 12-week plan could be, and then a 12-month plan that we imagine in two ways: writing a complete work of fiction in order to shop it, or writing and promoting a work of nonfiction with the 12-months beginning when the book is contracted.

YOUR FIRST BOOK: A 12-WEEK PLAN

The first two weeks were covered in the previous chapter (well, 12 days, but give yourself at least two days a week off). By this time hopefully you have a reading list, potential travel ideas if needed, a shifting and expanding mind map, a lite book proposal (for fiction or nonfiction), a draft of your writing sample, and a lot of ideas. That's a great foundation for your work and you should be proud of what you've already accomplished.

Before we continue, let's do that choose your own adventure exercise to determine, if you don't know already, whether you want a traditional publisher, hybrid, or self-publishing. If the answer is self-publishing, you don't need a proposal or sample at all. You should just look at self-publishing options (Ingram, Amazon KDP, and others) and consider which one best suits you. For traditional or hybrid publishing, you'll need the proposal or sample, so you can follow the recommended schedule.

-(a) Do you want to get the book out as soon as possible? (b) Would you like it when you'd like it, choosing your own reasonable schedule and release date? Or (c) is there no rush at all?

174   *Chapter 12*

-(a, b) Do you want absolute control over your book's contents, layout, title, and cover? Or are you (c) flexible and happy to yield to expert veterans in publishing to lead the way?

-(a) Do you feel supremely confident in your writing and book concept? Or would you (b, c) benefit from, and be willing to incorporate, feedback from a seasoned editor?

-Are you willing to (a) take on the job of editor and promoter of your own book (or hire someone freelance to do it for you)? Or do you want to have help with this (b, c)?

-(a) Do you have your own audience of significant size (in the thousands), through social media or a newsletter or some interest group? Or do you (b, c) need promotional assistance from the pros?

-Is making money from the book important to you (a, c), or are you willing to invest some money of your own to get it all moving more quickly and according to your preferences (b)?

If your answers were mostly A, then self-publishing is for you. B answers indicate hybrid is a good option, while C is for traditional.

Week 3

If I had you in a semester-long course, I would assign you to read two books, both perfectly written in my opinion, one fiction and one trade nonfiction. The novel is *The Russia House* by John le Carré, the greatest of all spy novelists. And this is his best book. It is particularly masterful in its play of tension. It is constantly planting questions in the mind of the reader and delaying the answers. Some are answered within a few pages, others within a few chapters, some not till the end of the book. There's not a comma out of place. Writing perfection.

The other is *The Tiger* by Jon Vaillant. It's a true story of a man-eating Siberian tiger in the wilds of rural Russia, deep into the Asian part of the country. It alternates ABAB chapters on scientists and hunters seeking the dangerous tiger with chapters on Siberian tigers generally: their biology, cultural history, everything one could want to know. It reads like a thriller—*Jurassic Park* with tigers—but it's all true.

I'd recommend that you read these two books over the next weeks. This will be a masterclass for you if you read them with a deconstructionist view, asking yourself what the author is doing to you, the reader, while you read. It will provide inspiration and show you true mastery to which we all can aspire.

If you're writing fiction, just keep on writing. The process from here on out is more straightforward than it is for nonfiction, because you don't need the proposal. I suggested you make a lite one because it helps sift your ideas into place, but what you'll need in order to submit your work is (a) the first fifty or so pages or three chapters, and (b) a synopsis of the rest of the novel. Keep that in mind. As I mentioned, publishers will actually want you to have finished the entire manuscript but will only want to see the first fifty pages because that's all they'll read for starters anyway. Actually, all they'll read is the first chapter at most unless they love it, in which case they'll keep going. They are looking for a reason to stop reading. But life is short, so I don't see any problem with sending out your first fifty pages and synopsis even before you've finished the entire book. It takes agents and editors so achingly long to get back to you—we're talking weeks if you're lucky, and often months— that it's not cosmically fair to expect you to wait to have the whole thing written, and it's especially unfair to expect you to submit only to one person at a time. I suggest that you send in your first fifty and synopsis when you think they are ace, as good as you can make them. Then keep on writing while you wait . . . and wait . . . and wait for a reply. By the time they actually get back to you, you'll probably have finished the rest of the book!

So consider this your instruction throughout this first 12 weeks, fiction authors: Your goal is to write around fifty pages of material that you're really happy with, plus a synopsis of the rest of the novel. Your synopsis should be no longer than ten pages. It should divide the rest of the action roughly into chapters and explain the actions of the protagonists and important secondary characters. It's about plot: Who does what when and with whom? What is the effect? Keep in mind that we readers want to see your character change in some way, to grow emotionally, between page 1 and "The End." The synopsis should indicate how this happens and what the key plot points are. Two sentences describing any given character is plenty for a synopsis.

Now that you've got your assignment, I'll focus on what nonfiction authors should aim for over the next weeks.

Week 4

Nonfictioners, you'll need a writing sample too, so if that's not ready yet, this is the week to finish it. It's short enough (maximum 2,500 words, minimum 1,500, let's say) that it should be doable in the two weeks you've had to work on it following our plan.

Week 5

This week you should edit your writing sample and look to expand your lite proposal to a full one. It shouldn't be tough to do, since the material in the lite version is usable for the full one. Your goal should be to have the full proposal plus writing sample done by the end of week 7, because that's when

176   *Chapter 12*

you should start sending out your proposal to editors (or agents, if you're feeling saucy).

Week 6

We are our own worst editors and the worst judges of whether our creative output is objectively good. We tend to fall into two camps: Some of us think everything we do is great so why mess with it, while others think that nothing we do is any good so why bother? In reality, of course, both camps are wrong: What you do can indeed be very good, so you should bother, but not everything you do is great, so you should get external opinions.

Your writing project is in its sixth week, and you've produced enough material that it's a good idea to show it to several friends to ask for their opinions. Don't show it to your parents and probably not your spouse either. Too much of a dynamic there. Show it to someone who is enough of a friend that they're willing to tell you what needs work. If you're working on fiction or trade nonfiction, show it to someone who knows nothing about the subject. If it's an academic book, you can show it to someone within your field. When you ask for advice, at this point you're not asking for a "redline edit"—meaning, you don't expect them to fix things for you. You want a general gist and, most specifically, you want to know what could be better and what isn't clear. If a colleague does not really want to say anything negative, it sometimes helps to get the ball rolling by asking them to "list at least three specific things that could be better" in your proposal or writing sample. The phrase "could be better" encourages positive criticism (it's a very different phrasing from asking for three things "you didn't like" or that "were bad"), and asking for at least three pushes the reader to look proactively for weak points.

If you can, ask three different people, each separately (not in the same email thread). It's like the police questioning suspects. If all three are in the same "room," they're likely to want to agree on everything, even if they wouldn't if you asked them each one on one. Asking an odd number of people is good because the third can be a tiebreaker. I once had my agent submit a fiction manuscript to two publishers. One said, "I like it, but would rather see the supernatural element come to the fore, then show me the next draft," while the other said, "I like it, but I don't like the possibly supernatural parts. I'd read it again if you get rid of those." What are you supposed to do in this case? A third opinion can be a useful indicator.

Ask your colleagues now if you can send them some material in a week's time.

Keep on writing and editing. Don't go for quantity. The most you should be writing here is those fifty pages plus synopsis for fiction, or the full proposal plus a writing sample for nonfiction. Don't let yourself write more.

12 Steps to Success   177

These samples are the most important part of the book. The publisher's entire decision rests on them. They are more important than the entire manuscript, because they determine how committed a publisher will be to promoting the book. So, within these 12 weeks, polish and rewrite and polish again. Your target is to have material ready to send you colleagues, as informal editors and advisers, by the end of week 7.

Week 7

This week is for the final preparations before sending material to your three hopefully enthusiastic colleagues. If you have trouble finding someone, you can always hire an editor. You can find them freelance—I do occasional editing or ghostwriting projects via Reedsy, and that's a good place to find industry pros who can help you. It won't cost much to hire someone to help with a sample that is less than sixty pages for fiction and probably less than twenty for nonfiction. It's worth getting professional assistance since so much potential is riding on these initial samples you'll be sending out. But with budget in mind, turning to helpful colleagues is a perfectly good way forward.

At the end of this week, send your material to these external readers. Give them two weeks to get back to you. It's good to give a deadline because otherwise even well-meaning people tend to put things off.

Week 8

Give yourself a week off from writing. Your brain has been like a race car engine (right?), so it can use some time to cool down.

But that doesn't mean you're off the hook. This is the week to research where you're going to submit your book. First, consider whether you really, truly must have an agent. I'm not trying to discourage you from seeking one, just to mentally prepare you for it being a long process without necessarily finding satisfaction even if you get one. Still, agents are a necessary middleman to access the big trade presses. Let's choose our own adventure and play the "Do I Need an Agent?" game. Circle your answer to the following questions.

-Do I (a) have plenty of time—a year or more—to devote to trying to find an agent, much less a publisher, or (b) would I like to get this book out sooner rather than later?
-Is my primary goal (a) making as much money as possible from my book and maximizing readership, or (b) getting my book out there with a good publisher and we'll see how it goes, hoping for the best?

178   *Chapter 12*

-Do I (a) feel certain that my book is a potential bestseller in terms of topic (don't worry about the writing style), or (b) am I unsure about the market size or pretty sure it has a narrower target audience?

-Am I ready to (a) rewrite my proposal or sample many more times before it is submitted to a publisher, or (b) would I rather just get it out there and hope for the best, perhaps rewriting if I don't make headway with the initial dozen submissions?

If you answered mostly A, you should try for an agent. If mostly B, trying for an agent is a waste of time and you should aim straight for submitting to publishers.

Spend some time searching for agencies or publishers. Identify which might be candidates for your book, based on what they list as their interests. Specify which agent or acquisitions editor seems like the best choice to submit to. If you have any leads or ins. take advantage of them. For instance, if a friend has an agent already and can put in a good word, or if a colleague has published a book and can recommend an editor, that's always helpful.

I'd suggest that you make a list of at least a dozen names and specific email addresses (to a named person, not to info@ or submissions@) to begin with. When the time comes, you'll submit to all of them at once.

Week 9

Craft your cover letter to agents or publishers, as described in part 1. Now you've got a specific project you're submitting, and you can use the short description of your book from the lite proposal as your initial pitch in the cover letter. You'll want to have all of this lined up and ready to go for when you are ready to submit.

I'd also recommend gathering a second dozen or so names and emails for a second round of submission. You want to have these on hand so that each time you get a no you can immediately spin it into three potential yeses by sending out three more submissions in the same sitting. That means you spend no time feeling sorry for yourself or angry at these foolish editors and agents who don't see your genius, but instead you turn each no into new hope, a fresh chance for new people to see your genius. Best to avoid grumpily googling for new people to submit to in the face of one or more "no thank yous." Prepare your mise en place for submission ahead of time, and expect that you'll need several rounds. How many rounds? I usually tell new writers to try at least two dozen submissions before you even think about adjusting your approach or setting this book project aside and turning to a new one. Some fun facts: Stephen King's *Carrie* was rejected thirty times before it went on to launch his career and sell more than a million copies. Dr. Seuss suffered through twenty-seven rejections. *Harry Potter and the Sorcerer's Stone* was rejected twelve times before J. K. Rowling found a publisher, and that publisher gave her an advance of only GBP 1,500 and told her to look for a teaching job because she was unlikely to make a living writing children's books. More than half a billion copies later . . . You get my point. Expect much rejection. Welcome the shock if you get a publisher more quickly than Stephen King.

At the end of this week, follow up with your external readers. I like to send a friendly reminder email the day after the deadline you gave them, just a quick check-in to see if they've had a chance to read your material. They will probably think, "Oh no, oops, I totally forgot about that, I'll go do it right now," which is also OK—they meant well.

Week 10

Hopefully those external readers will have provided you with useful notes. Consider which you agree with and apply them. You might not agree with all of them, and that's OK. You asked for opinions, and this is all very subjective. But if there is any consensus among your readers, it's a fair bet that they are right, or at least that they represent the majority of potential future readers out there. This is the week to apply the edits, finish your proposal and writing sample, and prepare to send it all out next week. That was fast, wasn't it?

The part you might still be working on is your novel synopsis or nonfiction chapter summaries. This should be your goal this week too. Get the material down and ready to send out. It needn't be perfect and it needn't be exactly what your final book will be.

Below is your checklist at this point.

For fiction:

-fiftyish-page sample with as strong a first page, and first chapter, as you can possibly write and with a cliff-hanger ending that leaves the reader aching for more
-synopsis of the rest of your novel, no longer than ten pages (and two to three pages is fine)
-cover letter template to agent or editor
-list of two dozen agents or editors with their direct emails, ready to submit

For nonfiction:

-writing sample (1,500–2,500 words long)
-full book proposal (with reader suggestions integrated)
-cover letter template for agent or editor

180 *Chapter 12*

-list of two dozen agents or editors with their direct emails, ready to submit

Week 11

At the start of this week, send out your first dozen submissions. Set reminders in your calendar to follow up on all submissions once every two weeks until you get a reply. It's good to keep a running list of where you submitted and when, as enough time can pass over the lifetime of a submission process that you may forget—I know I do.

Once you've sent the submissions, give yourself a short break. But I believe it's best to keep motoring along, assuming (this is positive thinking or manifestation) that it's only a matter of time before you get a yes for your book, so you may as well maintain your momentum and keep writing.

Week 12

By now, three months in, you probably have found your writing groove. Whatever your schedule in terms of when you fit writing in, you can also probably guess how much writing you can do in a session reasonably. Again, the analogy to working out is apt. The more you do it, and the more regularly, the easier it is and the less inertia you face. So keep up the rhythm. Set yourself a daily quota, probably in terms of words written. Over my years interviewing famous writers for a weekly column called How I Write that ran in *The Daily Beast* I learned that most of the writers I spoke to hammer out 1,000 words a day. That's their target to feel that it's been a day well spent. That seems like a great target if you're already a pro. Since books tend to be around 75,000 words or so on average, that means that you'd have a full draft in seventy-five days of writing. Add in a month or so of research and planning ahead of time, and your full draft could be a matter of "just" four months. Don't pressure yourself—that's a pace for seasoned professionals. We're giving ourselves as much time as we need (I've got six months planned in our 12-month program). But the point is to pick something you can reasonably achieve regularly, whether that's 250 words in a day or 2,500, put your head down, and make it happen while you await those agents and editors.

PUBLISHING SUCCESS: A 12-MONTH PLAN

We're 12 weeks in and the ball is very much rolling. Well done! Your proposal or novel is out with agents or publishers. You've written a good chunk. What next? Let's look at how a 12-month plan might look.

12 Steps to Success 181

We've covered the first three months already. Everyone's pace will vary—this is tough to predict—so you may need a lot of time or very little to find a publisher for your book. You may also decide to self-publish or go with a hybrid solution. Hopefully the questionnaire earlier in this chapter was helpful in determining which is for you. Self-publishing requires none of the proposals or samples. You can just get to it, contacting Ingram (the one I most often recommend) or starting the process yourself via Amazon KDP (my second choice for self-publishing). Hybrid options will still require a proposal, but publishers will be quicker in their response and most likely to say yes, whereas traditional publishing will be slow and looking for reasons to say no.

Month 4

We're scheduling optimistically for the sake of this plan. Let's say that you've got a contract offer in month 4. You're delighted. Congratulations! You sign and we're off.

Make yourself a schedule for actual writing and do your best to stick to it. See how much you can get done in the next four months. You can take as much time as you need, but in my experience giving yourself longer means you'll take longer but the end result won't necessarily be better.

If you're self-publishing, you can start here with planning your promotion and the details about what you'll need to do to get your book ready for release. For hybrid and traditional, your publisher will walk you through the necessary steps.

The steps will include the following:

-Work with an editor to make the book as good as it can be.
-Clear any image rights if you plan to include images that you did not create yourself.
-When the manuscript is all done, have it proofread (ideally by a professional).
-Don't forget acknowledgments, a bibliography, citations (if needed), and an index.
-Design a cover.
-Design the interior (typesetting).
-Make a book landing page (and possibly social media pages).
-Make a marketing plan.
-Reach out to potential interest groups to let them know that your book is in the works and perhaps they'd like to be involved in some way. This could mean appearing in the book if that is relevant (for example, a book on dragon boat racing might benefit from including the president of a national dragon boat racing federation), or preordering a batch of copies, or inviting

182   *Chapter 12*

you to appear at an event. This is largely promotional but can also be beneficial in terms of content.

Months 5–9

Finish writing the book. That may seem obvious, or the book may be done earlier, or it might take you longer than this to finish. But this is the business end of the work of a writer. There's so much preparation with proposals and whatnot that it's easy to overlook the real work, which is writing the book. Keep your rhythm going. Maintain an ongoing calendar, updating it to be realistic. At this point you are your own taskmaster. Don't stress yourself out. Your first book should be fun and a positive experience to create. If you've opted for my preferred method of checking off scenes, case studies, or chapters from your mind map, let that also guide you as to what you still need to do and roughly how long you'll need to do it.

If you get writer's block, take some time off. Do anything but write or think about your book. Something especially helpful is to do boringish exercise without any distractions like music, company, or podcasts. Jog with nothing but your thoughts to accompany you. Hike or stroll in the woods. Lift weights. The silence will be filled by your brain with inspiration.

Month 10

Let's assume that your book is done. Awesome sauce! If you're working with a publisher, they'll lead you through a schedule of their design (if it's a traditional approach) or mostly your design (if it's hybrid).

This is the period when the finishing touches are added to the book as an object: the cover, interior design, marketing plan. Once the design is determined and the book is laid out, your last step will be to do a final proofing and finish the index, searching through the laid-out PDF to note on which page(s) each word or name in your index falls. There's software that can do this, or you can hire someone to make it for you, but in practice most authors prepare their own.

When you get the final PDF, it's your last chance to make changes before the book goes to print. At this point you can only make changes that do not require altering the pagination. If the pagination must be altered, the typesetter has to do most or sometimes all of the book again, because every page change bumps other text onto other pages and it creates a mess. Typesetting doesn't flow like a Word document; rather, each page has to be built separately, usually using Adobe InDesign, as if each page were a single still image with text on it. So stick to punctuation or replacing a word here or there. No major surgery at this point.

12 Steps to Success 183

This is also a time for prepromotion. There are some publications, like *Library Journal*, *Publisher's Weekly*, and *Kirkus Reviews*, that like to have review copies of books several months before the book actually comes out. That's one of the reasons why publishing houses have timelines that seem far longer than anyone would actually need to bring a book to print. It's good to get these early-bird reviews advance copies to maximize the chance that you'll be featured in them.

Prepromotions can be good especially if you've got followers or some potential large-quantity orders in the works. Let's say you're in touch with a company that's up for making your book its holiday gift to all staff. It's great if you can coordinate this ahead of time, even before the book is out. As many presales as possible are to your advantage. If you can get more than 1,500 presales in the UK for nonfiction, for instance, there's a good chance your book will make the *Sunday Times* bestseller list. Just be aware that presales on Amazon only "count" toward bestseller status if no more than ten books are purchased at a time. So if you have a really friendly company with, say, one thousand employees, and the CEO is up for giving your book as the holiday gift, ask her kindly to please order ten copies at a time one hundred times to ensure that each one counts toward bestsellerness. (Presumably this CEO is your aunt if she's being this helpful to you.)

Your own friends and family will want to support you, particularly if this is your first book (I've long given up on expecting any of my friends or family to buy my books), but they will need reminders. Give them a heads-up and ask them to preorder, then send a reminder a month before release day . . . and a week before release day . . . and on release day.

If you've got the budget for it, you might also want to work with an independent publicist or promotion company. Publicists are very expensive with no guarantee that you'll earn back what they cost, but if you can afford it (I've never been able to but like the idea), they'll certainly get you and your book more attention than if your publisher is promoting it alone. Promotional companies can be a cheaper option. I've worked with Pubvendo and admired how transparent they were. They organize coordinated, highly targeted social media ads to promote your book and meet with you every two weeks to keep you up-to-date on the success rate (in terms of click-throughs to their ads). This is all stuff that you could do yourself, but it may be a better use of your time to outsource. You'll have to decide for yourself.

Month 11

Your book is going to print and the ebook edition is ready for action. Follow up on presale promotions. Pitch yourself to blogs and podcasts—those you can usually get yourself on alone, given that the bigger venues (high-end

184 *Chapter 12*

podcasts, magazines, newspapers) won't respond to individual author queries and will either come to you or need to be approached by a publicist or agent. But blogs and podcasts are hugely helpful, as many have dedicated audiences who are likely to take up a recommendation. This is the sort of preparatory guerrilla marketing you can do yourself if you're willing to put in the time.

Month 12

Revel in the release of your book (or its impending release)! It's a gorgeous moment, one to savor. You can do what I did with my first book: I asked my future wife to pour the box of books on me as I lay on the bed (they were hardcovers—I'm not sure I'd recommend this). Do something suitably distinctive.

IF YOU NEED ASSISTANCE

You can write your own book and find a publisher and earn money from writing. This book is just a collection of tips and behind-the-scenes glimpses to help you along the way, but you did all the hard work.

If, however, you'd like help with any of the process—the proposal, finding a publisher, editing your text, or ghostwriting a story you'd like to tell but that you don't feel you can write yourself—turning to a professional editor is always an option. You can go through a reliable marketplace like Reedsy, or you can even contact me through my website, noahcharney.com. Working with professional editors and ghostwriters isn't cheap—if there's a cheap one they likely aren't very good or will do a superficial job. For a full book, expect to pay in the low five figures. But then 100 percent of all profits are yours—that's the deal with editors and ghostwriters: They are paid a flat fee for services in most cases, not a percentage of future profits, and their role is invisible unless you want to announce it. And it may well be a good approach financially, considering the time you save in working with someone else to do some, the lion's share, or all of the actual writing, resulting in an optimal product (since working with an editor is always going to be a good thing for the book) and allowing you to earn in your day job while your book is being edited or even written.

In the end, you'll decide what feels best for you. Some people want to have a book of their own invention come out but don't necessarily want to write all of it (or even any of it). Some people find the act of writing pleasurable and wouldn't dream of subcontracting any of it out, but even they would benefit from a professional editor. An editor can be freelance or provided by your publisher. Whatever approach you choose, there are few more satisfying things one can do then produce one's own book.

Go ahead, then. Ask a family member to dump the first box of them on you. Just watch out if they're hardcover.

Notes

CHAPTER 1

1. https://www.vox.com/culture/2017/3/2/14779892/barack-michelle-obama-65-million-book-deal-penguin-random-house.

2. https://www.forbes.com/sites/quora/2014/05/28/what-is-the-percentage-of-books-published-on-which-publishers-actually-lose-money/.

CHAPTER 3

1. The novelist is Helen Oyeyemi and this was her first book, *The Icarus Girl*. The story I told is from what she'd told me when we were both students at the University of Cambridge. The partial version is cited in many of her origin story interviews, including https://www.npr.org/2014/03/07/282065410/the-professionally-haunted-life-of-helen-oyeyemi.

Index

12-day plan, 35, 165–72

act, 119, 122
advance payments, 3, 7–9, 12–15, 22–24, 37, 39, 51, 55, 60, 145, 152, 179
agent, 3–5, 8–19
AI, 33, 58, 76, 87, 93–95
Amazon, 21, 33, 67, 144, 146, 148–51, 156–57, 173, 181, 183
audience, 6, 25, 110–11, 129, 145–48, 152–53, 155, 169

bibliography, 36, 38, 56–57, 65, 69, 101, 131, 168–69, 181
blurb, 52, 67

character, 115–20, 124, 127–31, 165–66, 168–69
clarity, 103–5, 107–8, 110–12
complexity, 110
contracts, 10–12, 14, 56–71
cover, 20–24, 27, 39, 67–68, 174, 181–82
cover letter, 15–19, 51–52, 86–87, 178–79
creative writing, 4, 33

distribution, 21, 23, 143

editing, 24, 176–77
editor, 4–7, 11, 14, 17–23, 26, 29–31, 36–37, 42, 52–58, 61–64, 68, 73–74, 76–81, 85–88, 143, 174, 177–81, 184
efficiency, 5, 162
essay, 79, 100–108, 113, 136, 151

fiction, 3–5, 8, 14, 16–17, 25, 30, 41, 52, 109–10, 112–16, 127–30, 140–41, 143–44, 160, 166–70, 172–77, 179
flow, 64, 69, 182
focus, 30, 32, 161, 170
freelancing, 23, 76–77, 79, 174, 177, 184
full manuscript, 4, 7–8, 14, 20–21, 24, 36, 38, 56–60, 63, 67, 70, 181

goals, 122–25

hook, 5, 43, 48–49, 74–75, 97–98, 101, 113–14, 133

index, 36, 69–71, 181–82

language, 3, 10, 13, 34, 40–41, 56, 62, 64, 69, 84, 88–89, 102, 121, 128–29
logistics, 4, 21, 32, 34, 165

188 *Index*

marketing, 21, 23, 33, 37–38, 49, 55, 68, 74, 143, 145–48, 151, 181–82, 184
metrics, 148

nonfiction, 5–11, 27, 29, 33, 41–50, 160, 166–70, 173–77, 179, 183

openings, 32, 43, 48–49, 52, 95–101, 109, 133–41
outlining, 5, 103, 160

pitch, 6–7, 17–18, 30–36, 53–56, 73–81, 85–87, 178, 183–84
platform, 21–22, 24, 144–48
plot, 33, 41, 112–18, 122–25, 141, 175
portfolio, 4, 39
process, 19, 25–26, 40–41, 52, 54, 61–67, 69–70, 122, 130, 153, 172, 174, 177, 180–81, 184
progress, 61, 115, 163
proposal, 3–9, 13–19, 24–26, 29–32, 36–37, 39–43, 48–55, 61, 73, 112, 143, 169–84
publicity, 21, 23, 80, 143, 151–57
publisher, 6–10, 12–14, 18–26, 35–41, 52–69, 108, 143–46, 152, 154–55, 173, 177–84
publishing, 3, 5–15, 19–26, 37, 53–62, 65, 143–45, 151–52, 156, 166, 173–74, 181–83

research, 25, 30, 33–36, 54, 65, 73, 93–95, 127, 147, 160, 166–69, 177, 180

reviews, 12, 33, 37, 53–54, 87, 149
rights, 10–14, 20, 38–41, 56–59, 65–66, 69, 181
royalties, 13, 19, 22, 37, 55, 59, 145

samples, 7, 15–16, 29, 35–43, 49, 52, 78, 133, 143, 171–79
scene, 115, 117, 168, 172
scheduling, 14, 34, 173, 180–82
social media, 16, 38, 86, 144–46, 166, 174, 181, 183
story, 17, 51–52, 58, 63, 77, 81–82, 97, 101, 106–7, 109–22, 131, 138, 140–41, 165–66, 168, 172
strategy, 33, 101, 124, 146
structure, 18, 20, 100–101, 112, 115, 119, 122
style, 33, 38, 44, 49, 61–62, 64, 79, 86, 93–94, 103–8, 129, 134, 139, 148, 169, 178
summary, 5, 30, 37–38, 40–41

tension, 99–100, 112, 133, 172, 174
timeline, 60–61, 143
tone, 36, 129
tracking, 148

voice, 79, 110, 117, 129

website, 10, 26, 36–39, 42, 67, 87, 124, 146, 149–50
workspace, 162
writer's block, 182

About the Author

Noah Charney, PhD, is the internationally best-selling author of more than twenty books, translated into fourteen languages, including *The Collector of Lives: Giorgio Vasari and the Invention of Art*, which was nominated for the 2017 Pulitzer Prize in Biography, and *Museum of Lost Art*, which was the finalist for the 2018 Digital Book World Award. He is a professor of art history specializing in art crime, and he has taught writing for the University of Ljubljana, American University of Rome, and the Guardian Masterclasses in London. He has written often for major magazines and newspapers, including *The Guardian* and *The Washington Post*, and writes for the TED platform. He is also a TV and radio presenter, with programs for the BBC and the Great Courses, and he is an award-winning podcast host. Working behind the scenes, he has coached, edited, and ghostwritten for numerous other writers. This is his eighth book and counting with Rowman & Littlefield. He lives in Slovenia with his wife and children and their hairless dog, Hubert van Eyck. Learn more at www.noahcharney.com.